QUEST
FOR
STATUS

QUEST FOR STATUS

CHINESE AND RUSSIAN

FOREIGN POLICY

DEBORAH WELCH LARSON
AND ALEXEI SHEVCHENKO

Yale UNIVERSITY PRESS
New Haven and London

Yale University Press books may be purchased in quantity for educational, business, or
promotional use. For information, please e-mail sales.press@yale.edu (U.S. office)
or sales@yaleup.co.uk (U.K. office).

Set in Sabon type by Newgen North America.
Printed in the United States of America.

Library of Congress Control Number: 2018948575
ISBN 978-0-300-23604-0 (hardcover : alk. paper)

A catalogue record for this book is available from the British Library.

This paper meets the requirements of ANSI/NISO Z39.48-1992 (Permanence of Paper).

10 9 8 7 6 5 4 3 2 1

To our parents

Contents

Preface

Beginning in 2008–9, despite the end of the Cold War, both China and Russia adopted more assertive and sometimes aggressive stances on the international stage. China showed a sense of entitlement regarding control of its coastal waters and islands and reefs in the South China Sea, raising the risk of conflict with the United States as well as with other states in the region. Russia invaded Georgia in 2008 and established two protectorates. In 2014, Russia seized Crimea and helped to instigate an insurgency in southeastern Ukraine. Russia then used its military power to bolster Syrian President Bashar al-Assad against the interests of the West. While taking bold, assertive actions that surprise and antagonize potential partners, China and Russia tend to overreact to purely symbolic slights such as meetings with the Tibetan Dalai Lama or US references to Russia as merely a regional power.

China and Russia pose major challenges for American foreign policy. Misunderstanding the source of puzzling Chinese and Russian behavior, using outdated categories and theories, could result in heightened tensions, miscalculation, and even war. But avoiding war is not enough. Cooperation from China and Russia is essential for dealing with global challenges such as nuclear proliferation, climate change, financial stability, cyberterrorism, and failed states.

China and Russia are highly sensitive about recognition for their prerogatives and status, as repeatedly demonstrated throughout their history. In this book, we seek to answer three questions. First, how important was international status to Chinese and Russian elites in comparison to other objectives such as wealth and power? Second, what were their strategies for enhancing their state's international standing and why? Third, how effective was their preferred strategy in influencing other states' perceptions?

This book is the first to use social psychological theory to explain why China and Russia have pursued great power status. We base our analysis on Social Identity Theory (SIT), an established, well-developed research program that has not received a full-length treatment in international relations. Using SIT, we develop a typology of strategies that states may use to improve their status: *social mobility* (emulation of more advanced powers to be admitted to elite clubs), *social competition* (striving to match or surpass the dominant state in its area of superiority), or *social creativity* (seeking preeminence in a new area). Thus, we go beyond saying that status matters to discuss how status concerns affect a state's orientation to the international order—whether a state seeks to integrate into, change, or reorient the status hierarchy.

China and Russia have shared historical experiences that have contributed to their identities as great powers. Both were agricultural empires that experienced cataclysmic communist revolutions, and both remain outside the Western community of states after the end of the Cold War. Despite these similarities, there have been few comparisons of their foreign policies, and none that have analyzed their quest for great power status over history.

Our book is unusual in that it covers over 500 years. We review major turning points in Chinese and Russian foreign policy to uncover recurring patterns, contrasting the SIT interpretation with alternative explanations such as security and ideology. The book acquaints the reader with pivotal events in Chinese and Russian foreign policy, starting from the Middle Ages, including Ivan the Terrible, China's conquest of Xinjiang, Peter the Great's war against Sweden, and the Opium Wars in China. The Cold War chapter covers Soviet Russia's drive for acceptance, the Nazi-Soviet Pact, the breakdown of the Grand Alliance, and the rise and demise of the Sino-Soviet alliance. The chapter on Deng Xiaoping and Gorbachev compares the reforms of these two leaders.

The final chapter explains how the foreign policy paths of China and Russia have diverged since the end of the Cold War and highlights the challenges their policies pose to other world leaders.

We add support for our arguments by quoting public and private statements by Chinese and Russian leaders that reveal their desire for recognition and respect. We make inferences about the motivations behind Chinese and Russian foreign policy by considering alternative explanations for any given situation.

With this background, the reader should be able to view Chinese and Russian actions from a longer perspective and to understand better their sometimes hostile behavior toward the Western countries. A better understanding of status and identity offers insights into current Chinese and Russian foreign policy, which should be of interest to specialists, students, and foreign policy practitioners.

While states' quest for status may lead to costly and wasteful actions, the desire for enhanced recognition can also motivate more constructive behavior, such as diplomatic initiatives or institution building. It is the goal of this book to determine how to encourage these beneficial responses to the desire for greatness.

Acknowledgments

We owe our collaboration on this book as well as other publications to Richard Rosecrance, who organized a project at UCLA that was funded by the Carnegie Foundation on bringing states into the "club." We are grateful to our editor, Jaya Aninda Chatterjee, for encouraging us to write this book when it was just a few ideas on paper, and for providing helpful guidance and support throughout the process. We thank several anonymous reviewers at Yale University Press for their careful reading of the manuscript, corrections on issues of fact, and insightful suggestions based on substantial knowledge and expertise. For helpful comments and encouragement, we thank Andrei Tsygankov, Kimberly Marten, Sean Lynn-Jones, Yong Deng, Anne Clunan, Xiaoyu Pu, T. V. Paul, Bill Wohlforth, and Robert Legvold. Regina Heller, Reinhard Wolf, and Tuomas Forsberg offered warm hospitality in Hamburg and Helsinki as well as a stimulating workshop with a good group of people in which to develop our ideas on Russia. David Sherman Larson proofread all the chapters. Deborah would like to thank her parents, Lin and Jeanette Welch, to whom she dedicates this book. Unfortunately, her father, who asked about the book many times, was not able to read it. Alexei thanks his parents, Valentin and Ludmila, and dedicates the book to them.

Parts of the first and fifth chapters were published in Deborah Welch Larson and Alexei Shevchenko, "Status Seekers: Chinese and Russian Responses to U.S. Primacy," *International Security* 34:4 (Spring 2010), 63–95, © 2010 by the President and Fellows of Harvard College and the Massachusetts Institute of Technology, reprinted here by permission of MIT Press. Also appearing in the fifth chapter are excerpts from Deborah Welch Larson and Alexei Shevchenko, "Russia Says No: Power, Status, and Emotions in Foreign Policy," *Communist and Post-Communist Studies* 47, nos. 3–4 (2014), 269–79, reprinted with permission from Elsevier. We are grateful to both MIT Press and Elsevier for permission to use this material.

QUEST
FOR
STATUS

1 Status and Identity

IN HIS 1999 Millennium Message to the Russian people, acting president Vladimir Putin declared, "Russia was and will remain a great power." Putin is the most recent in a long line of rulers who have strained national resources to achieve or maintain Russia's standing as a great power, through military buildups, territorial expansion, buying off foreign rulers, and fighting numerous wars. China, too, has maintained an "unshakeable identity of greatness," beginning with Imperial China's self-image as the Middle Kingdom, "all under heaven." Although China's self-image as a great power was eventually shattered by imperialist intrusions and unequal treaties, after the 1949 communist revolution the People's Republic of China (PRC) sought to restore China's former centrality by promoting international revolution and providing a model of modernization that emphasized justice and equality. Having adopted capitalist economic principles beginning with Deng Xiaoping's 1978 "reform and opening policy," the Chinese are now even more determined to restore China's previous standing at the top of the hierarchical order, a goal viewed as "national rejuvenation" and a "restoration of fairness."[1]

Why do China and Russia identify themselves as great powers? Do concerns about status influence their foreign policies and if so, then in what ways? How have China and Russia sought to influence others' perceptions of their international standing? A classic tradition in international relations has discussed the rise and fall of great powers, their interactions, the impact of wars on their relative status, and the consequences for world order.[2] What has been overlooked is how a state's quest for international status shapes its foreign policy—including acquisition of arms, allies, participation in institutions, conflict initiation, and cooperation with other major powers.[3]

For insights into how status concerns and social identity shape Chinese and Russian foreign policy, we draw on social identity theory (SIT). SIT argues that social groups strive to achieve a positively distinctive identity.[4] When a group's identity is threatened, it may pursue one of several identity management strategies: social mobility, social competition, or social creativity. The choice of strategy depends on the permeability of elite clubs and the legitimacy and stability of the status hierarchy. Social mobility emulates the values and practices of the higher-status group with the goal of gaining admission into elite clubs. Social competition tries to equal or surpass the dominant group in the area on which its claims to superior status rest. Finally, social creativity reframes a negative attribute as positive or stresses achievement in a different domain.[5] Applied to international relations, SIT suggests that states may improve their status by joining elite clubs, trying to best the dominant states, or achieving preeminence outside the arena of geopolitical competition.

Using SIT as a framework, we address several questions in this book. First, how important were status considerations in shaping Chinese and Russian foreign policy? Second, why did China and Russia choose a particular strategy in a given context for improving their state's international standing? Third, how effective were their chosen strategies as measured by the perceptions and beliefs of the leading states?

We begin by discussing the basic propositions of SIT, explaining why groups are motivated to achieve positive distinctiveness. We then conceptualize and elaborate a typology of three strategies by which states may improve their relative status. This theoretical framework will be used in subsequent chapters to explain patterns in Chinese and Russian/Soviet foreign policies.

IDENTITY, STATUS, AND POWER

According to Henri Tajfel, the founder of SIT, a social identity is "that part of an individual's self-concept which derives from his knowledge of his membership of a social group (or groups) together with the value and emotional significance attached to that membership." In other words, people derive part of their identity from membership in social groups—nation, ethnicity, religion, political party, gender, or occupation.[6] Because their membership reflects back on them, people want their group to have a positively distinctive identity—to be not only better but different.[7] The innate human desire for one's group to be superior was exemplified in the famous minimal group studies of Tajfel and his colleagues, who found that members of artificial groups created on the basis of arbitrary criteria such as preference for the art of Kandinsky versus Klee showed in-group bias.[8]

Social identities are established relative to other groups and evaluated through social comparisons. People compare their group's attributes to a reference group, one that is similar but slightly higher. The propensity for upward comparison is found in the choice of reference groups in international relations, where Russians compare their country to the United States, the Chinese evaluate the PRC relative to other advanced societies, and Indians are obsessed with China.[9]

Groups that are generally believed to be superior on valued dimensions have higher status. Status is similar to prestige, with the additional connotation of rank order in a hierarchy. Just as a group's status depends on traits valued by society, so a state's international stature depends on its ranking on prized attributes, such as military power, economic development, cultural achievements, diplomatic skill, and technological innovation.[10] People prefer to belong to higher-status groups, and they are reluctant to be identified with lower-status ones. Having higher status increases collective self-esteem and pride. In the contemporary world, many people identify with their country and take pride in its achievements and victories.[11] Having a distinctive identity is also important to group members.

Status is hierarchical, such that higher-status group members are apt to treat lower-status members disrespectfully and inattentively. The same principle often applies to relations between states, whereby higher-ranking states expect deference from lower-ranking states. Status is a positional good, meaning that normally one group's status can improve only if another's declines.[12] SIT introduces an important modification to this prevailing zero-sum conception of status by pointing out that groups can be evaluated on multiple traits, so that comparisons among them need not be directly competitive. The use of multidimensional comparisons underlies social creativity, as is discussed below.

According to neorealism, status is based largely on military power, preferably demonstrated through victory over a major power in war. The English school has pointed out, however, that having the recognized status of great power with "certain special rights and duties" has always required approval from the other major powers and other states in the international community. Superior military capability does not necessarily confer status, acceptance, or respect. During the Cold War, the Soviet Union tried to win global status through military competition and geopolitical expansion, but the United States was reluctant to recognize the Soviet Union as an equal.[13] Status-seeking actions can be largely symbolic, aimed at influencing others' perceptions, as distinct from the search for raw material power. For example, hosting the Olympics or World Cup has become an indicator of rising power status, as illustrated by Russian President Vladimir Putin's remark that being awarded the 2014 Winter Olympics was a "judgment of our country," and Brazilian President Luiz Inácio Lula da Silva's tearful exclamation that Rio de Janeiro's selection meant that Brazil had gone from being a second-class to a first-class country and was now beginning to "receive the respect we deserve."[14]

The great powers have been recognized as an elite club. The 1815 Concert of Europe formalized the special responsibilities and prerogatives of the great powers. During World War II, there was the trio of US President Franklin D. Roosevelt, British Prime Minister Winston Churchill, and Soviet General Secretary Joseph Stalin, famously represented in the photo from the Yalta conference. Since the end of the Cold War, there has been the Group of Seven (G7), or for a time, when Russia was allowed to participate, the G8. As these examples illustrate, elite clubs may be formalized with regular meetings, as in the G7, or may be more informal groupings based on widespread consensus about the identity of the leading powers. Fear of being ostracized by other members of the club, leading to loss of status, can be an important motive for cooperation.[15]

International organizations are often hierarchical in their structure and therefore embody the status hierarchy. The United Nations (UN) Security Council was built on the premise of great power management of the international order, and the five permanent members reflect the distribution of power at the end of World War II. In 2004, Germany, Brazil, India, and Japan launched campaigns to become permanent members in recognition of their enhanced status. Smaller states expend great effort and financial resources to win election to one of the nonpermanent positions on the Security Council, even though those members cannot block decisions made by the permanent members. International financial institutions such as the International Monetary Fund (IMF) and World Bank are also hierarchical in their rights and functioning, as exemplified by the weighted voting structure.[16] Consequently, international institutions are arenas in which states often contend for status.

Indirect evidence of concern for status is provided by a state's reaction to perceived disrespect or humiliation, with a disproportionate response showing that deep emotional issues of self-esteem are involved. Humiliation results from being put in a lower position by a more powerful actor.[17] Displays of anger are often intended to restore status or dignity, as in the violent and emotional protests among Chinese youth following the May 1999 accidental US bombing of the Chinese embassy in Belgrade.[18]

Threats to a distinctive positive identity may come from a variety of sources: derogation from the outgroup, inferiority on a dimension that is important to the group's identity, defeat or humiliation by the outgroup, or failure in an important task. Inferiority is likely to stimulate efforts to remedy the situation through an identity management strategy designed to establish a more favorable image.[19]

IN SEARCH OF STATUS: IDENTITY
MANAGEMENT STRATEGIES

A group that wants to improve its standing may try to move into a higher-status group, compete with the dominant group, or achieve preeminence in a different area. The choice of one strategy over another depends on the group's beliefs about the permeability of the elite group as well as the security (stability and/or legitimacy) of the status hierarchy. States may likewise pursue varying strategies for attaining status, depending on both the openness of elite clubs and the similarity of their values with those of the established powers.

Social Mobility

If the boundaries of higher-status groups are permeable, a lower-status group may conform to the values, norms, and practices of an elite group to gain acceptance, thereby pursuing a strategy of social mobility. Just as individuals imitate the social norms and lifestyle of the upper class to be accepted into social clubs, so aspiring states may adopt the political, economic, and social norms of the dominant powers to be admitted to more prestigious institutions or clubs.[20]

The aim of social mobility is acceptance into a higher stratum of society. For example, Meiji Japan assimilated not only Western technology but also its culture and practices in order to be recognized by the West as a great power. In 1871, the Meiji elite sent the Iwakura mission to Europe and the United States to learn about the domestic institutions of the more advanced states. To bring Japan up to the level of a "first-rank country (*ittō-koku*)," the Meiji reformers adopted Western bureaucracy, education, banking, accounting methods, postal services, legal codes, dress, and even table manners. "What we must do," said the foreign minister Inoyue Kaoru in 1887, "is to transform our empire and our people, make the empire like the countries of Europe and our people like the peoples of Europe." The goal was to "join the West," to be admitted to an elite club of rich and powerful states. By adopting Western civilizational standards, the Meiji reformers also hoped to avoid being subjugated by foreign imperialists, as China and India had been.[21]

Social mobility has been the strategy pursued by states in two waves of democratization since World War II. After the end of the postwar occupation, West Germany and Japan sought admission to the "civilized states" by renouncing offensive military force and accepting liberal democracy. West Germany chose to transcend its nationalist identity through European integration, whereas Japan pursued membership in the IMF, the General Agreement on Tariffs and Trade (GATT), and the Organization for Economic Cooperation and Development. With the end of the Cold War, Eastern and Central European states have adopted liberal democratic reforms and capitalism to be admitted into the North Atlantic Treaty Organization (NATO) and the European Union (EU), organizations that symbolize identity as part of the West, and thus confer higher status. After being admitted to elite clubs, states continue to try to enhance their status, but they do so within the context of the club rules. Poland, for example, aspires to be one of the top tier members of the EU and is engaged in regular dialogue with France and Germany as part of a "Weimar Triangle," a club that may have greater status with the departure of Britain from the EU.[22]

From the standpoint of an aspiring great power, a major drawback of a social mobility strategy is that it implies the humiliating role of pupil vs. teacher. Imitation may also go against the need to maintain a distinctive identity.[23]

Indicators of a social mobility strategy include a state's emulation of the institutions, values, or norms of the dominant states. The state's leaders may adopt the explicit goal of joining a more elite organization or club as proof of higher status.

Social Competition

If elite group boundaries are impermeable to new members, and the status hierarchy is insecure, a lower-status group may strive for equal or superior status through social competition. The status hierarchy is insecure when it is perceived by the lower-status group to be *illegitimate* (unfair or unjust) and/or *unstable* (susceptible to change). The pecking order is unstable if the lower-status group can conceive of alternatives to the status quo. As Tajfel observed, "a combination of illegitimacy and instability would become a powerful incitement for attempts to change the status quo." For example, Marxism-Leninism held that the prevailing international order was based on imperialist exploitation of poorer countries and that it would be replaced by a community of socialist proletarians.[24]

An example of the relationship between the illegitimacy of the social order and adoption of a social competition strategy is Japan's turn to "racially justified regional hegemony" as a policy goal in the 1930s, after the Meiji-era social mobility strategy of emulating the values and institutions of Western powers failed to win recognition for Japan as an equal great power. Although Japan had adopted Western "civilization," observed international law, and defeated China and Russia in successive wars, its overseas immigrants were subject to discriminatory legislation and its diplomatic representatives were treated as part of a lower tier at the Versailles Peace Conference—suggesting that the great power club was closed to an Asian power such as Japan. The humiliating rejection by the Versailles conference of Japan's proposal for a "racial equality" clause in the League of Nations Covenant helped to increase support among the Japanese elite for the army's solution of fighting to secure Japan's rightful position.[25] In 1946, Japanese Emperor Hirohito recalled that "if we ask the reason for this war," it was that "the racial equality proposal demanded by Japan was not accepted" by the leading powers. Although Japan had won greater respect, the status hierarchy was still implicitly based on race until after World War II.[26] Whereas under the Meiji leadership the goal of Japanese foreign policy was to emulate the Western powers, and the Japanese sought to expand their influence in East Asia through economic imperialism and cooperation with the great powers, after 1931 the new consensus among Japanese journalists, politicians, and military officials was that Japan's racial superiority entitled it to dominance in East Asia, a position that could be achieved through force and anti-Westernism.[27]

Although not the target of racial discrimination, Germany was also a late developer and would-be imperialist. In the late nineteenth century, as Germany advanced in population and economic might, many Germans believed that it was unfair that the world's colonies and spheres of influence had been divided up before Germany's rise. In his famous "hammer or anvil" speech before the Reichstag in December 1899, then German Foreign Minister Bernhard von Bülow declared that "We cannot allow any foreign power, any foreign Jupiter to tell us: 'What can be done? The world is already partitioned.'"[28]

Overseas colonies were no longer a mark of great power status after World War II, as the possession of nuclear weapons became the key to membership in the great power club. But just as Germany perceived that valuable territories had already been colonized by the established powers in the late nineteenth century, so India as it aspired to great power status found that the nuclear option was closed off by the existing nuclear powers, who sought to prevent the further spread of nuclear weapons. India persistently contested the validity of the norms underlying the nuclear nonproliferation regime, with its arbitrary distinction between nuclear and nonnuclear states based solely on whether they had nuclear weapons when the 1967 Nuclear Nonproliferation Treaty was signed. Having viewed itself as a great power, after a decade of rapid economic growth due to liberalization, and with the accession of a more nationalist government, India felt sufficiently confident to challenge the existing major power order with its 1998 nuclear tests; the tests conveyed the message that "the present status hierarchy in the international system was no longer acceptable and needed to be modified by accommodating India." In general, "oppositional nationalists," feeling that they are entitled to equal or superior status, have been more likely to seek to acquire nuclear weapons.[29]

The status hierarchy is potentially unstable when the relative power of the leading and lower-ranking states is in transition. Rising powers may perceive that the prevailing order is capable of being changed, and feel that they should occupy a higher position. In the case of Wilhelmine Germany and 1930s Japan, both rapidly growing countries, the elites believed that they were entitled to first-class status as global powers.[30]

Social competition aims to equal or surpass the dominant group on the value dimension by which its superior status is measured.[31] In international relations, where status is in large part based on economic and military power, social competition often entails traditional geopolitical rivalry, such as competition over client states or arms racing. Wilhelmine Germany competed with Britain in the size of its battleship fleet and sought to acquire overseas colonies to attain its "place in the sun." State Secretary of the Navy Admiral Alfred von Tirpitz advised Kaiser Wilhelm II that "there are four World Powers: Russia, England, America, and Germany" and that it was a "life or death matter" for Germany to catch up in naval power in the areas where it was behind. While Germany may have required a larger navy to protect its expanding overseas commerce and merchant marine, it did not need a fleet of battleships in the North Sea directed against Britain. Rather than being guided by strategic logic, Germany's aims on that front were largely intangible and amorphous—*Gleichberechtigung* (equal entitlement) and *Seegeltung* (naval influence). The Anglo-German naval race served no strategic purpose for Germany—a power that could only be defeated on land and that lacked unimpeded access to the open sea (Britain could blockade the German navy from its bases in Scotland)— but merely consumed resources that should have gone to the army.

Worse, the naval program was the principal factor in shaping Britain's perception of Germany as an enemy and its decision to align with Russia and France, which resulted in Germany's encirclement.[32] Similarly, in 1935–36 Soviet leader Joseph Stalin ordered the construction of a large oceangoing navy, including large battleships, believing that possession of a great fleet was essential for the Soviet Union to be a global great power.[33]

Whether or not social competition leads to war depends on the criteria for status in a particular era and on the area of a state's comparative advantage. In the European balance of power system, admission to the great power club required defeating another great power in war. Status seeking that takes the form of territorial conquest or power projection may threaten the security of other states, arousing a defensive reaction that causes conflict to spiral. This occurred in the mid-1970s, when Soviet leader Leonid Brezhnev's military intervention in Africa, chosen as a relatively cheap and risk-free way to compete with the United States, sparked reciprocal moves and undermined détente. Once each side distrusts the other, war may occur in response to perceived threats to security or status, even if the two states have no conflicting material interests.[34]

When overtaking the system leader is unlikely, social competition may also be manifested in spoiler behavior, as in Russia's opposition in the 1990s to US intervention in the Balkans and Iraq, as well as its efforts since 2005 to eliminate the US military presence in Central Asia, despite its own interest in US defeat of the Taliban in Afghanistan. As Richard Pipes writes, "When the Kremlin says 'no' to Western initiatives, Russians feel that they are indeed a world power." Lower-status groups, especially those experiencing a threat to their self-esteem, feel a malicious pleasure or schadenfreude when a more prestigious outgroup is defeated by circumstances or by actions of a third party.[35] Both obstructing positive action and trying to outdo the system leader are manifestations of social competition, aimed at defeating the leader in an area visible to others.

According to SIT, social competition is pursued when elite groups are not permeable and the status hierarchy is perceived to be insecure (illegitimate or unstable). Evidence for impermeability would be the unwillingness to admit or even consider a particular state for membership in elite clubs. Related evidence would be the established powers' unwillingness to consult with the state on issues affecting its interests or their rejection of its claims for a voice. References by lower-status states to exploitation, unfairness, and "double standards" indicate perceived illegitimacy. Statements by their national elites referring to prospective changes in the balance of power, or the rise of new powers and the decline of old ones, are indicators that the status hierarchy is unstable. Social competition can be manifested in arms races, rivalry over spheres of influence, military demonstrations aimed at one-upmanship, or military intervention against a smaller power, so long as the purpose is to influence others' perceptions rather than to attain security or power. Social competition does not necessarily lead to war, because it is based on rivalry over position rather than the distribution of material resources.

Social Creativity

When elite groups are impermeable and the status hierarchy appears to be stable and/or legitimate, groups may seek prestige in a different area, pursuing social creativity. The pecking order is stable when change in the prevailing status hierarchy appears to be unlikely and legitimate when the lower-status group accepts that the criteria for social status are applied fairly.[36] Social creativity could entail either (1) reevaluating the meaning of a negative characteristic; or (2) identifying a new dimension on which the lower-status group is superior. A supposedly negative characteristic is reevaluated as positive in the African-American 1960s slogan "Black is beautiful." An example from international politics is China's recent reinterpretation of Confucianism—which Mao had earlier tried to eradicate as "feudal"—as part of Beijing's "soft power." The second tactic, identifying a different dimension for measuring status, is exemplified by the Eurasianist strand of Russian intellectual thought, which celebrates Russia's collectivism, spiritualism, traditionalism, and Orthodox Christianity in contrast to the West's spiritually impoverished individualism and materialism.[37]

States may also seek status on a dimension other than geopolitical power, such as promoting international norms or a particular model for economic development. At the height of the Cold War, Indian Prime Minister Jawaharlal Nehru, Yugoslav leader Joseph Tito, and Egyptian President Gamal Abdel Nasser achieved preeminence as leaders of the non-aligned movement, which advocated neutrality, decolonization, and non-use of force. Nehru soon learned from the humiliating defeat by China in 1962 that India needed a minimum level of military capability to act as a great power. India has also justified its pursuit of great power status with reference to its ancient civilization, in particular, its contribution to world religions through Buddhism and Hinduism. Similarly, Mikhail Gorbachev tried to achieve greatness for the Soviet Union as the moral and political leader of a new international order shaped by principles of the New Thinking, such as mutual security, nonoffensive defense, and the Common European Home.[38]

Social creativity is also associated with enhancing a state's "soft power" through diplomatic mediation and assuming a prominent role in international organizations. For example, Brazil joined with Turkey in promoting a possible solution to Iran's nuclear program not out of any particular interest in Iran, but because "Brazil wants to be recognized" as a "global diplomatic player," according to Rubens Ricupero, a former Brazilian diplomat and UN official.[39]

Unlike social competition, social creativity does not try to change the hierarchy of status in the international system. For example, French President Charles de Gaulle pursued a social creativity strategy of emphasizing France's *grandeur* and independence from the United States, but he did not challenge the bipolar order. In contrast, the principal goal of Adolf Hitler's social competition strategy was world domination under a "Great German Empire." The promotion of new racist criteria for international prestige was secondary.[40]

For a social creativity strategy to succeed, the dominant group must accept that the lower-status group's proposed criteria for status are valid and worthwhile, as well as accepting the group's positive standing on those attributes. Status cannot be attained unilaterally; it can only be conferred by others. The rise of a new enemy or the desire to maintain a balance of power can be an important incentive for a dominant state to recognize the status of a rising power. This was the case for Richard Nixon's accommodation of China in 1972, and for George W. Bush's tacit acceptance of India's status as a nuclear power when he agreed to a framework for establishing full civil nuclear cooperation in 2005.[41]

Although status is positional, two social groups may be able to attain positive status at the same time, so long as there are multiple criteria.

With more than one way to attain status, each of two groups may be superior to others, but in different areas. State A can claim to be better on dimension X while acknowledging that State B is stronger on dimension Y. Groups may acknowledge others' achievements, showing social cooperation. For example, in a study of national stereotypes among adolescents from six Central and East European countries, participants perceived the higher-status Western European countries to be more competent, but viewed their own countries as more "moral." Social cooperation is likewise evident in US-EU relations, where Europeans take pride in their generous social welfare benefits, cosmopolitanism, and social safety nets, while the United States emphasizes its military power, global reach, and international competitiveness.[42]

If the higher-status group refuses to acknowledge the other's social creativity efforts, the lower-status group will respond with anger and hostility and possibly take offensive action to restore its status and dignity.[43] A dominant group will be more likely to respond favorably to a lower-status group's efforts at enhancing its position if it has similar values and its own status is regarded as legitimate and secure.[44]

Social creativity will be preferred when a state perceives that the existing hierarchy is legitimate and/or stable. Indicators that the status hierarchy is legitimate would be general consensus on the norms of the system, as indicated by lack of concerted pressure for a new world order. Observable indicators of stability include acceptance of prevailing power relationships and the acknowledged identity of the leading powers in international institutions.

Indicators that a state is pursuing social creativity include advocacy of new international norms, regimes, institutions, or developmental models. While a social mobility strategy is aimed at acceptance into the elite group, the essence of social creativity is the attempt to stake out a distinctive position, emphasizing the state's unique values or contributions. Often social creativity is accompanied by high-profile diplomacy, with a charismatic leader, such as de Gaulle, Nehru, or Gorbachev, taking a prominent role on the world stage.

The individual strategies of social mobility, social competition, and social creativity are ideal types, and elements of all three may be found in a particular country's foreign policy. Nevertheless, these identity management strategies have different goals and tactics, so that selection of a particular identity management strategy alters the state's entire foreign policy. Social mobility entails emulating the values and practices of the established powers to attain integration into elite clubs. Social competition tries to supplant the dominant power on the geopolitical dimensions of status. Social creativity seeks a favorable position on a different value dimension, highlighting the state's uniqueness and differences from the dominant powers. The choice of strategy depends on the state's perceptions of the permeability of elite clubs and the legitimacy and stability of the status hierarchy, factors that can be influenced by the behavior of the dominant powers.

Within a society, different groups may have differing perceptions of these variables, so that domestic politics—a change in leadership, ruling coalition, or regime—may precipitate the adoption of a new identity management strategy.

METHODOLOGY AND CASE SELECTION

In what follows we apply SIT concepts and propositions to major developments in Chinese and Russian foreign policy. We use process-tracing and incorporate other variables as necessary to explain outcomes.[45] Because SIT has not been extensively applied to international relations, in the case studies we also elaborate the theoretical concepts, a form of theory development, which means that we cannot also use these same cases to test the theory we have elaborated. This study attempts to determine if more systematic testing of SIT might be worthwhile.[46]

We have chosen to examine China and Russia because their emphasis throughout history on acquiring and maintaining great power status has yielded a good deal of evidence in the form of statements and actions that are relevant to status concerns. Both China and Russia have a sense of exceptionalism, a hierarchical view of the world, and an obsession with how they are viewed and treated by other major powers. If status and identity have any influence on a state's foreign policy, then we should find evidence in the cases of China and Russia. These are extreme value cases, well suited for finding indicators of both independent and dependent variables and for assessing their relationships.[47] But at the same time, differences between China and Russia in their positioning in the international order, geopolitical attributes, and historical trajectories allow us to assess the relative impact of particular variables, such as the permeability of elite clubs or the legitimacy and stability of the international hierarchy.

We have used statements by social and political leaders—whether in public speeches, publications, or private comments—as evidence for status concerns. These statements may demonstrate the desire for greatness or equality, or fears about loss of prestige and so on. Excessive concern for protocol, titles, and precedence is also an indicator that the elite is motivated by the desire for prestige or great power status. Displays of emotion such as anger, overreaction to slights, and hypersensitivity may indicate deep-rooted status insecurity.

The desire for status can be a means to some other goal. The deference that status brings from smaller states could be used to attain specific strategic goals such as increased security, wealth, or military standing. SIT, however, views status as intrinsically satisfying, engendering collective self-esteem and pride. An indication of a fundamental desire for status could be the acquisition of costly, highly visible weapons such as large battleships and aircraft that have little strategic purpose. Another indication of intrinsic status motivation could be the expenditure of resources to conquer territory with low economic or strategic value. Competition for superiority in nonmaterial domains, such as protocol, leadership in international organizations, Olympic medals, or Nobel prizes is also an indicator of intrinsic status motives.[48]

In order to evaluate the effectiveness of various identity management strategies, we need to assess how China and Russia were perceived by other major powers. We have chosen the behavior of other states as evidence. In the eighteenth century, great power status was manifested in diplomatic representation, acting as a treaty guarantor, and interdynastic marriages. In the nineteenth century, the great powers' status was indicated by invitations to international conferences and consultation on global or regional issues of concern. In the 1920s and 1930s, signs of higher status included attendance at major international conferences, membership in the League Council, and participation in bilateral treaties with major powers. In the contemporary era, status is indicated by leadership positions in international organizations, the hosting of major international sports events such as the Olympics, membership in elite clubs such as the Group of 7 or the Group of 20, participation in working groups to handle challenging international issues such as the nuclear programs of Iran and North Korea, and invitations to summit meetings and formal state visits.[49]

The pursuit of status is usually combined with other objectives, such as power and security. There is also the question of whether status is derived from identity relations or from observance of norms, as a constructivist perspective would predict. Since foreign policy is rarely motivated by only one factor, it is important to consider alternative explanations.

SIT PREDICTIONS VS. ALTERNATIVE EXPLANATIONS

Based on the previous discussion of SIT, we may now develop general theoretical expectations for major changes in Chinese and Russian foreign policy and compare them with alternative explanations—explanations based on neorealism, ideology, or constructivism. Specific predictions derived from the historical context follow at the beginning of each chapter.

How would each approach explain major patterns in Chinese and Russian foreign policies? SIT suggests that elites evaluate their state's achievements and qualities in comparison to a reference group of similar but higher-status states, and that perceived inferiority would create an identity threat that would lead to remedial action. From the mid-sixteenth century, Russia was confronted with more technologically and economically advanced states to the West, a condition that would promote status insecurity and adoption of an identity management strategy. Russia's exclusion from the European great club and the perception that Russia was treated unfairly would encourage adoption of a social competition strategy. In contrast, Imperial China was satisfied with its identity as the Middle Kingdom, receiving tribute from smaller neighboring states, until humiliating military defeats by supposedly barbaric imperialist powers, beginning with the 1839–42 and 1856–60 Opium Wars, brought about a major identity crisis. As large, continental, multiethnic states with their own distinctive civilizations and traditions, both China and Russia would be reluctant to pursue a social mobility strategy of emulating the values of the higher-status states. Instead, Communist revolutions would encourage the USSR and China to compete with the Western states to prove the superiority of the communist model of development. In addition to its social competition with the West, for China the reference state was the Soviet Union, which would eventually generate tension over the asymmetry in the relationship. According to SIT, after the Cold War ended, given the futility of competing with the only remaining superpower, the United States, China and Russia should have been drawn toward some variant of social creativity, finding new areas outside of traditional geopolitical competition in which to seek preeminence. Whether the two powers would persist in social creativity would depend on the receptivity of the higher-status states to the new status dimensions and their recognition of China and Russia as major powers.

Neorealism would expect China and Russia to give priority to security and power over nonmaterial factors such as status. As a state without natural geographic borders, Russia would expand until it confronted a more powerful state or natural barrier. Russia would also balance against potential threats through alliances with other powerful states. Initially, Imperial China would be concerned about invasion by various steppe peoples to the north and northwest. It was only in the mid-nineteenth century that China faced a threat from the south and east, its maritime frontier.[50] Neorealism would predict that China would use force against the nomadic peoples when it felt powerful, but otherwise resort to realpolitik methods such as playing the barbarians off against each other, or giving titles and emoluments to Inner Asian rulers in return for their maintaining order, or exchanging security on the border for trading privileges. When faced with threats from Great Britain and other seafaring powers, China should have tried to ally with other Western states against the threat and to acquire a navy.[51] Whereas neorealism predicts that a state's ambitions and assertiveness will be correlated with increases in its military capabilities, SIT suggests that a rising power's aggressiveness depends on the permeability of elite clubs and beliefs about the legitimacy and stability of the status hierarchy.

Ideology, defined as a "set of beliefs about the proper order of society and how it can be achieved," can potentially shape foreign policy by coloring the interpretation of reality and providing the set of feasible policy alternatives. Ideology was also a powerful tool in the hands of such leaders as Stalin and Mao for mobilizing popular energies toward economic development and national greatness.[52] Although ideology is associated with the Cold War and Marxism-Leninism, the concept can also be applied to premodern belief systems about political order. In the traditional Chinese world order, there was only one civilization, China, the "Middle Kingdom," surrounded by concentric circles of peoples evaluated by the degree to which they had accepted Chinese culture; Western peoples were considered to be "barbarians." Russian imperial ideology was succinctly expressed in the famous slogan "orthodoxy, autocracy, and nationality," which was formulated in the 1830s under Tsar Nicholas I. In the late nineteenth century, Panslavism, which included the belief that all Slavs were destined to be led by Russia, was influential in Russian elite circles. In the twentieth century, Marxism-Leninism became the dominant ideology, envisioning a world of class struggle, war, and communist revolutions.[53] SIT would incorporate ideology in the context of its use for differentiating a state from others and establishing a positive identity.

Constructivists view status as socially constructed by the interaction of states. Status hierarchies evolve in the context of what states value. Constructivists view leaders as socialized by discourse and practice; the direction of influence is from society to individual. Constructivism would predict that China's and Russia's identities would respond flexibly to interactions with other states, as well as to influences from domestic discourse.[54] Constructivism predicts that as Russia entered into the European diplomatic system in the eighteenth century, Russian elites would be socialized to adopt the prevailing norms of territorial expansion and power politics. After China's abrupt, coerced entry into the Western-dominated international system, it would also eventually accept international law and state sovereignty. The subsequent shifts in Russia's and China's identities after they adopted Marxist-Leninist ideologies would have an immense impact on how they interacted with other states.

While also stressing the importance of identity, SIT gives more importance to human agency in shaping identities—for example, by the choice of social mobility, social competition, or social creativity. In a major difference from the dominant constructivist approaches, SIT is a theory of "group freedom," in which lower-status groups have a variety of means to improve their image and sense of self-worth—by reframing a negative characteristic as positive, by finding a new dimension of comparison, or by challenging the position of the dominant group. In short, given effective leadership, groups can decide to whom they should be compared and over what dimensions. Groups can also engage in collective efforts to improve their status.[55] Like other social groups, states do not necessarily accept the identity and status imputed to them by others, and they may seek to improve their standing.

As some prominent constructivists admit, because of its view of identities and preferences as mutually constituted and unstable, and because of its refusal to make assumptions about the "content or substance of identities and their relevance," constructivism has not provided a clear explanation for why identities change or why one identity is chosen over the other. Recent constructivist work has tried to remedy this problem by incorporating domestic discourse and practices, but why a particular discourse becomes dominant remains unclear.[56] SIT provides predictions about how social-structural factors, such as the permeability of elite groups and the stability and legitimacy of the status hierarchy, affect a state's choice of identity management strategy. In short, SIT can better explain why states choose to adopt social mobility, social competition, or social creativity as strategies for enhancing their status, choices that have wide-ranging implications for foreign policy.

In sum, neorealism predicts that Chinese and Russian foreign policy would be predominantly oriented toward security and acquiring the necessary power to defend state sovereignty. An ideological interpretation implies that Chinese and Russian leaders would adopt foreign policies consistent with their belief systems. Constructivism suggests that Chinese and Russian foreign policy would be shaped by their identities and by socialization by other states. SIT predicts that states' foreign policies will change in response to threats to positive identity, and that the choice of a strategy for status enhancement will be shaped by perceptions of the openness of elite clubs and the perceived legitimacy and stability of the status hierarchy. Specifically, when elite clubs are permeable, states will choose social mobility. When elite clubs are impermeable, and the status hierarchy is perceived as unstable or illegitimate, states will adopt social competition. Finally, when the higher-status clubs are closed, but status distinctions are viewed as stable and legitimate, states will pursue social creativity to achieve higher standing and recognition from others.

The book is organized around case studies that demonstrate how the quest by elites for a positive identity shaped major developments in the foreign policies of China and Russia in different historical eras—imperial, communist, reform communist, and post–Cold War.

In chapter 2 we contrast Imperial China's satisfaction with its identity as the Middle Kingdom ruling over tributary states with Russia's insecurity over its relative economic backwardness and exclusion from the European great power club. Beginning with Peter the Great, Russian rulers sought to supplant first Sweden and Poland, then the Ottoman Empire, as members of the great power club. In the mid-nineteenth century, both China and Russia suffered threats to their international standing. China's defeats by the barbarian powers in the 1839–42 and 1856–60 Opium Wars gave rise to an identity crisis. The "self-strengtheners" pursued selective modernization, seeking to blend Western technology with Chinese culture, but did not carry out a coherent, nationwide strategy, largely due to inconsistent support from the Imperial Court. After the industrial revolution, Russia also declined in relative power and status, as revealed by its 1856 defeat in the Crimean War. A succession of Russian diplomatic defeats by Germany and Austria over the Balkans, culminating with the military disaster of World War I, further undermined the legitimacy of the tsarist regime. For the Chinese intelligentsia, the decision by the Western powers at the Versailles conference to give Germany's concessions in China to Japan sparked radicalization and the birth of the Chinese communist movement.

Chapter 3 argues that both the Soviet Union and the PRC pursued social competition with the Western states while at the same time seeking recognition from the states they were trying to subvert. Stalin sought to increase the power and prestige of the Soviet state through coerced industrialization, and Khrushchev made an effort to "catch up and surpass" the West in economic production. The PRC sought to improve its status by allying with the Soviet Union, but the Chinese chafed under their status as "younger brothers" to their senior ally, and eventually Mao challenged the Soviets for leadership of the international communist movement. In the 1970s China took advantage of the US need to balance Soviet military power by putting aside communist ideology to become a tacit ally of the United States, part of a "strategic triangle."

Chapter 4 interprets the reforms by Deng Xiaoping and Mikhail Gorbachev in the context of their efforts to find alternative means to great power status—through social creativity. Deng launched the "reform and opening" policy, developing the economic foundation for China to play a great power role while exercising unparalleled diplomatic flexibility in dealing with some of China's most difficult territorial and sovereignty disputes. Gorbachev abandoned Russia's usual military methods for achieving great power status in favor of promoting a new, idealistic philosophy for a more peaceful and harmonious world—the "New Thinking." While Gorbachev's ideas enjoyed remarkable success internationally, the failure of his domestic reforms, along with the rise of nationalism, contributed to the breakup of the Soviet Union and an end to the Soviet Union's status as an innovator of new principles for world order.

Chapter 5 analyzes the varying responses of China and Russia to the collapse of communism and the breakup of the Soviet Union—the most serious threats to Chinese and Russian identities and status since the First World War. Frustrated with lack of recognition and respect by the United States and other Western powers, both China and Russia briefly pursued policies of social competition, but learned that efforts to compete with the United States were embarrassingly futile. China and Russia then adopted social creativity strategies for acquiring prestige—China as a responsible world power, and Russia as a partner with the United States in the War on Terror. China's "peaceful rise" strategy was welcomed by the United States, whereas Putin's cooperation after 9/11 was not reciprocated. Russia began to assert its right to a *droit de regard* in neighboring areas and to advocate a multipolar order, culminating in the 2014 takeover of Crimea and destabilizing of Ukraine. The Chinese briefly displayed hubris over the 2008 financial crisis but have since returned to social creativity, albeit with elements of competition on territorial issues with China's neighbors.

The concluding chapter summarizes SIT-based findings and suggests some general policy implications. Throughout history, China and Russia have sought acknowledgment of their great power status through a variety of means, including diplomatic cooperation. Why their strategies for achieving recognition have varied is the subject of this book.

2 Imperial Identities
Glory and Humiliation

IN HER FAMOUS 1767 instruction to the Legislative Commission, an ambitious effort to provide Russia with a unified legal code, Catherine II (1762–96), "the Great," proudly proclaimed Russia to be a European power—a bold statement of Catherine's intent to have Russia be a major player among the higher-status European states. The document, authored by Catherine, borrowed liberally from Montesquieu's *Spirit of the Laws* and the writings of Marquis di Beccaria on criminal punishment. Showing a flair for self-irony, Catherine, the most Western-oriented of the Russian rulers, commented to Frederick the Great that in her use of the most modern theories of government, she had acted like the raven in La Fontaine's fable, which adorned itself with the feathers of a peacock. Although the Legislative Commission was aborted, the instruction was translated into Latin, French, and German and distributed abroad to influence European opinions about Russia. Russia had adopted the West as its reference group—its baseline for comparison, aspiration level, and target for membership.[1]

In contrast, Imperial China was self-sufficient, basking in its own glory and superior culture. The attitude of the Qing dynasty toward Europe is illustrated by the encounter of the Qianlong emperor in 1793 with a diplomatic mission from Great Britain, Europe's preeminent commercial and naval power, requesting better facilities for trade. In his reply to King George III, "one of the most humiliating communications in the annals of British diplomacy," Qianlong made clear his contempt for the British effort to impress him with their manufactured products: "strange and costly objects do not interest me." While commending King George's "respectful humility" in dispatching a tribute mission and his "humble desire to partake of the benefits of our civilization," the emperor questioned the very ability of the British to "acquire the rudiments" of Chinese civilization.[2]

Imperial China for centuries was the Middle Kingdom, "all under heaven," accepting tribute from vassal states as acknowledgement of its superior culture and exalted status, whereas Russia strived to be considered part of the European great power system. Russia's position on the periphery of Europe, its relatively backward economy, and Western perceptions of its outsider status led Russian elites to adopt a social competition strategy to force their way into the European great power club. China, in contrast, tried to maintain the status quo of its exalted position as the only state, until humiliating defeats by Britain and France in the mid-nineteenth century inspired Confucian elites to try selective modernization, attempting to preserve China's cultural traditions while adopting the military technology of the Westerners in order to surpass them in the long run.

Neorealists argue that Russia, as a state without natural, geographic borders on a large, exposed plain, was driven to expand in order to survive in an environment of powerful rivals. Russia could also be expected to align with weaker powers against stronger states and to mobilize its domestic resources while emulating the military innovations of the most powerful states in the neighborhood. In contrast, Chinese rulers were concerned about preventing raids and attacks from nomadic peoples to the north and northwest, and later with potential invasions from the eastern coast.[3] Neorealism would predict that the Chinese would use force against the nomadic peoples when the dynasty was militarily strong and would play the tribes off against each other to divide their foes. When threatened by the maritime powers, China should have built its own navy, adopted the military innovations of the Westerners, and sought an alliance with the weaker "barbarians" against more powerful foes.

While neorealists stress security and material interests, other scholars emphasize ideology as a driver of foreign policy. As mentioned above,

China's outlook on foreign relations was influenced by the "Middle Kingdom" worldview, including the assumption of the superiority of China's civilization and rejection of equal inter-state relations. Ideational sources of legitimacy for Russian foreign policy have been diverse, ranging from protector of Orthodox Christianity, to Moscow as the "Third Rome," to Panslavism.[4]

Constructivists would predict that both China and Russia would define their identities relative to the Western "other." How they were treated by the other would also affect their self-concept. Chinese and Russian elites would be socialized by their interactions with foreign representatives into adopting the norms and practices of the Western diplomatic system. Domestic discourse about the state system could also be an important source of identity.

SIT would lead us to expect Chinese and Russian elites to seek a distinctive identity and to be concerned with external recognition of their superior status. National elites in both states would assess their country's qualities and achievements relative to a reference state. Recognition of inferiority on important dimensions would have a devastating impact on collective self-esteem and morale. Humiliating military defeats, by making inferiority visible to others, would be even more damaging to morale and self-image. SIT would expect Chinese and Russian elites to adopt technological innovations when necessary to remain competitive, but to eschew the "social mobility" strategy of assimilating Western political and cultural institutions because doing so would require giving up their distinctive identities.

We begin by discussing the heritage of Kievan Rus (882–1240), the rise of Muscovy (1362–1533), and Ivan IV's expansion to the east (1582–84). We follow this narrative of early Russian history with a parallel treatment of China's conquest of Inner Asia by Qing rulers (1683–1760), thereby establishing the dominance of the dynasty. The Qing clashed with Russian settlers in the Far East, but succeeded in negotiating two border agreements with Russia that helped to establish the boundaries of the two empires. We then provide an extensive discussion of Peter the Great's defeat of Sweden in the Great Northern War, which was supported by comprehensive social, economic, military, and administrative reforms throughout society, designed to bring Russia up to European standards and attain acceptance as a European great power. Catherine the Great completed Peter's mission through stunning military victories over the formidable Ottoman Empire. While Russia was rising, China turned inward, as witnessed by the Qianlong emperor's rebuff of an envoy from Great Britain and his overtures to open trade. Both China and Russia experienced challenges to their status due to military defeats by foreign powers, as represented by the Opium Wars and the Crimean War. China adopted some Western technology but tried to preserve Chinese moral philosophy, whereas Russia tried to retrench but expanded into Central Asia to achieve cheap victories over the British and fought the Turks over the Balkans. Both China and Russia responded strongly to humiliating defeats by Japan, but through different strategies. Whereas China sought more radical Westernizing reforms, Russia continued its social competition strategy, competing with foreign powers for influence in Manchuria and Korea, a strategy that resulted in the Russo-Japanese war, devastating defeat, and domestic revolution. The concluding section of this chapter finds commonalities in the increasing attraction of intellectual elites in both Russia and China to radical anti-Western ideologies, in the context of their countries' economic backwardness and humiliation by foreign powers.

KIEVAN RUS, THE MONGOLS, AND THE RISE OF MUSCOVY

After the destruction of Kievan Rus during the Mongol invasion (1237–40), the small rural settlement of Moscow became Muscovy, as successive princes regained Russian lands through conquest and alliance. Ivan IV established Muscovy's identity as a Eurasian empire through expansion to the East, and sought recognition from Western kings as "tsar."

The Rus princes are generally considered to be descendants of Scandinavians, the Varangians (Norsemen) who traveled across the Baltic in 980 to seize the throne of Kiev for Prince Vladimir I, part of the Riurikid dynasty. In 988, Vladimir converted to Eastern Orthodox Christianity imported from Byzantium and adopted Orthodoxy as the official religion of the Slavic tribes of Kievan Rus—a major event in the development of the Russian identity. Christianity helped Vladimir to unify the eastern Slavs into an integrated political unit and provided an ideology that legitimized his rule.[5]

Kievan Rus became a federation of more or less independent principalities, with the grand prince as the leading political ruler. Kievan Rus experienced a Golden Age under Iaroslav the Wise (1019–54) with flourishing cities, a flowering of religious fervor, and construction of impressive stone churches.[6]

But Kievan Rus was already internally divided by disputes over succession when the Mongols, led by Batu, the grandson of Genghis (Chinggis) Khan, engaged in a devastating invasion of Rus lands from 1237 to 1240, ushering in more than two hundred years of Mongol suzerainty as part of the Kipchak Khanate, or Golden Horde as it is usually known. The Mongols did not occupy Rus, but they did insist on tribute from the Riurikid princes and the right to approve candidates for rule, including the grand prince. Eventually, over the following century, Kievan Rus fragmented. The southwestern lands were absorbed by Poland and Lithuania, while the northeastern principalities remained under the suzerainty of the Golden Horde. The focus of Rus therefore shifted from Kiev to the northeast, and to the principality of Vladimir, where the grand prince ruled.[7]

By the second quarter of the fourteenth century, however, the princes of Moscow, the Daniilovichi branch (named after Daniil, the son of Alexander Nevsky), had become the Golden Horde's preferred candidates for grand prince, largely because the Moscow princes were more efficient and reliable in delivering tribute. Moscow was also advantaged by its strategic location near the headwaters of four major rivers—the Oka, the Volga, the Don, and the Dnieper.[8]

In the mid-fourteenth century, the weakening of the Golden Horde created a power vacuum and led to vigorous competition among its factions, successor khanates, Poland, Lithuania, and Moscow. Vasily II (1425–62) and his son Ivan III (1462–1505), "the Great," pursued a policy of steady territorial expansion, a process that has become known as the "gathering of Russian lands." Most notably, Ivan subjugated Novgorod, an important independent trading center that had competed with Moscow and was under the suzerainty of Lithuania. Ivan's military conquests, and in particular the acquisition of lands that had earlier been part of Kievan Rus, strengthened Muscovy's claim to be the rightful successor to Kiev. As an indication of Muscovy's improved status, Ivan negotiated with a variety of polities, including the Holy Roman Empire, the Vatican, Moldova, Lithuania, Livonia, and Sweden.[9]

The fall of the Byzantine Empire to Turkey in 1453 was a major shock, and left Muscovy as the last independent center of Orthodoxy. Ivan's 1472 marriage to Sophia Paleologue, the niece of the last Byzantine emperor, inspired him to appropriate the legacy of the Byzantines. He started using the title "tsar," which could mean either *basileus* (the Greek word for emperor used by the Byzantine rulers) or khan. However, in relations with Western countries, which did not recognize the term "tsar," he was referred to instead as the grand prince of Moscow and Vladimir. In 1499, Ivan added the Byzantine two-headed eagle to his court seal.[10]

Ivan IV (1533–84), "the Terrible," was the first grand prince to be crowned as tsar in 1547, in a ceremony that made use of Byzantine symbols, rituals, and regalia, implying that Muscovite rulers were the heirs to Byzantium.[11] In 1552, after several previous attempts, Ivan set out to conquer Kazan, one of the successor states to the Golden Horde, largely as revenge for 250 years of having to pay tribute to the Mongols. Kazan fell to Russian troops, and in 1556, Ivan also conquered and annexed the khanate of Astrakhan. Kazan was located on an important Volga trading route to the Caspian Sea and the markets of Iran, and possession of the two khanates gave Ivan control of the Volga. Ivan IV added "Tsar of Kazan and Astrakhan" to his titles as further justification of his claim to the position.[12]

The defeat of Kazan opened the way for Ivan to expand further eastward. Ivan authorized private entrepreneurs, and in particular the Stroganov family, to settle on the other side of the Urals in Siberia in pursuit of salt and furs. After the defeat of the Siber Khan by a Cossack regiment in the employ of the Stroganovs, Ivan sent soldiers to establish forts along the rivers. By 1639, Cossacks and soldiers had reached the Pacific Ocean. Thus Russian expansion into Siberia was not planned, but occurred piecemeal as a result of private enterprise, Cossack adventurism, state initiative, and military consolidation.[13]

Ivan fatefully decided to focus next on westward expansion, against Livonia, which was weak, internally divided, and ruled by the declining Livonian Order of Knights. Now that Muscovy was fighting more advanced opponents from the West, Ivan would need to import arms and military supplies. Acquisition of Livonia would give Ivan access to major ports on the Baltic coast, so that Muscovite trade would not be dependent on Livonian merchant middlemen who could cut off passage of goods or impose tolls. Even before the Volga conquests were consolidated, Ivan launched a surprise attack against Livonia in 1558, capturing the important port of Narva, followed by Dorpat and other cities. Moscow's rapid and devastating victories aroused the greed of other states in the region; the conflict eventually drew in Poland-Lithuania, Sweden, and Denmark in competition to acquire parts of Livonia.[14]

As Livonia was being divided up, Ivan extended the war to Lithuania. In 1563, Muscovite forces captured Polotsk, a key city and communications center that was formerly part of Kievan Rus and therefore a prized objective. Ivan then halted the offensive, allowing his foes to regroup. In 1569, Ivan's victories motivated Lithuania and Poland, already part of a dynastic union, to unite in a commonwealth against him. When Ivan renewed his offensive in Livonia in 1577, he suffered defeats even before Polish King Stephen Bathory, a highly effective military leader, entered the war against Moscow in 1579. Bathory recaptured Polotsk, along with other towns in northern Russia, shattering Ivan's confidence. In September 1581, Sweden retook Narva and other ports on the Gulf of Finland, depriving Ivan of his hopes for direct access to the Baltic.[15]

Finally admitting that the war was lost, in 1581 Ivan requested the services of a representative from the Vatican, Antonio Possevino, in mediating a truce with Poland-Lithuania. In January 1582, a ten-year truce was signed with Poland-Lithuania, followed a year later by a truce with Sweden. Ivan had lost his conquests in Livonia (and his hopes for direct trade with Europe) and Polotsk. He controlled only a small bit of coastline at the mouth of the Neva.[16]

During the negotiations, Possevino refused to recognize Ivan's title of "tsar" or "emperor" on the basis of his conquest of Kazan and Astrakhan. These were "Tatar principalities," which did not make Ivan equal to European kings. Ivan was so determined to have his title recognized that he was even willing to give up fortified towns to achieve his goal. As a compromise, Ivan was given the title of tsar in the Russian text but not the Polish one. This was humiliating, since as a relative latecomer to power politics, Moscow was highly sensitive to considerations of status and prestige, insisting on recognition of its equality. Kings were ranked in status, with hereditary stature and length of dynasty among the bases for precedence, and it was by no means clear where Muscovy stood. Titles and the form of address between monarchs, use of the term "brother," were important bargaining chips in negotiations and major issues of diplomatic contention. Previously, Ivan had engaged in a highly vituperative and insulting correspondence with the kings of Denmark, Sweden, and Poland because he considered their position as elective monarchs to be beneath his and hence claimed that the prevailing status hierarchy was illegitimate. In a 1573 reply to King John III of Sweden, Ivan rudely characterized the king's previous letter as the "barking of dogs." "You write your name before ours, but our brothers are the emperor of Rome and other great rulers," Ivan complained, "and you cannot call them brother for the land of Sweden is below them in honor." Ivan was referring to the legend that the Riurikid princes were descended from the Roman Emperor Augustus' nonexistent brother Prus, a story that he also used in a 1581 letter to the king of Poland, Stephen Bathory, who tartly replied that Ivan should not tell tall tales.[17]

Ivan IV directed Russian foreign policy toward the Baltic and Eastern Europe, away from the steppes. The expansion to Siberia made Russia a Eurasian empire. However, by the end of Ivan's reign, Russia's military forces were exhausted from conflicts with Poland, Sweden, and the Crimean Tatars; landholders as well as peasants fled to the steppe to escape the heavy burden of taxation and the regime of terror carried out by Ivan's special forces (the 1565–72 *oprichnina,* which evicted landowners, plundered the countryside, and demoralized the Russian people); and an increasing number of nobles ignored requests for their military service. Ivan's accidental killing of his son ultimately led to the extinction of the Riurikid dynasty and a period of civil war and foreign intervention, known as the Time of Troubles, which lasted from 1598 until 1613, when the Romanov dynasty gained power.[18]

Russian status concerns were evident, but Muscovy was not recognized by the other European states as a major player. The great power club was not yet open to Russia.

THE QING DYNASTY'S CONQUEST OF INNER ASIA

The Manchus conquered Ming China in 1644, establishing their own dynasty, the Qing (1644–1911), and then continued their conquest in the seventeenth and eighteenth centuries until they had doubled the extent of Chinese territory. The Qing dynasty derived from part of the

Jürchen peoples of northeast China, descendants of the former Jin dynasty, which had been overthrown by the Mongols. Between 1683 and 1760, the Qing conquered Xinjiang, Mongolia, Tibet, Kokonor, the southwest provinces, and Taiwan, extending China's borders roughly to where they are today (with the exception of 1.5 million square kilometers lost to the Russians in the three "unequal treaties" of Aigun [1858], Peking [1860], and Tarbagatai [1864]).[19]

The Jürchen tribes were united in a confederation by Nurhaci (1559–1626), a highly effective political leader. Nurhaci created a new, superior form of military organization, the banner system, which divided his army into permanent residential units with their families. The banner soldiers were renowned for their prowess as mounted archers.[20]

Nurhaci's son Hong Taiji (1592–1643) set up a shadow government modeled on that of Ming China (including a Grand Secretariat, six ministries, and so on), and recruited Chinese bureaucrats and generals as advisers. In 1636, Hong Taiji gave his people a new name, *Manju* or "Manchu" and proclaimed the Qing dynasty, a direct challenge to the Ming. After he died, his brother, Dorgon, became regent for the successor, Hong Taiji's ninth son. When a rebel military commander occupied Beijing, and a Ming general offered to allow Manchu troops to enter through the strategic Shanhaiguan pass in return for their collaboration against the usurper, Dorgon seized the opportunity. In 1644, the Manchus conquered the capital city, Beijing.[21]

The Manchus retained China's governing system—a multilevel bureaucracy staffed by officials who were selected by a highly elaborate and rigorous examination system based on knowledge of the Confucian classics. Manchu rulers studied Confucianism and adopted its rituals for the court. At the same time, however, the Manchus strove to maintain their distinctive identity, in a manner consistent with SIT. For example, they prohibited intermarriage with Han Chinese, forbade foot binding for Manchu women, maintained residential segregation, and retained separate religious rituals based on shamanism and Buddhism. The Qing also stressed martial values to prevent the Manchus from becoming "soft" and flaccid, traits that were supposedly responsible for the Ming dynasty's decline.[22]

In contrast to preceding imperial dynasties, the Qing dynasty was conceived of as a universal, multinational empire. After consolidating his authority and defeating rebellious Ming generals in the south, the second Qing emperor, Kangxi (r. 1661–1722), set about firming up China's borders to the north. The Russians had established forts in the Amur River valley, where the Cossacks had migrated, attracted by (false) rumors of a fertile river valley with abundant grain supplies. Kangxi feared that Russia might ally with a steppe empire, the Zunghar Mongols, who were led by the charismatic Galdan, which would allow them to take control of northern Mongolia and endanger the Manchu position in southern Mongolia. Kangxi ordered the destruction of the Russian fort of Albazin on the Amur River in 1685 and, after it was secretly rebuilt by local Russian officials, again in 1686, but he offered the Russians the possibility of an agreement in return for their neutrality toward China's conflict with the Zunghar Mongols.[23]

Despite differences in diplomatic systems, the representatives of Muscovy and the Qing empires who met at Nerchinsk in eastern Siberia in August 1689 successfully accommodated their mutual status concerns. Negotiations were conducted on a basis of strict equality: the site of the talks was at the frontier rather than in Beijing so that the Russians would not have to kowtow to the emperor; the language used in negotiations was Latin (Jesuit missionaries to the Qing provided translations); and open tents were placed side-by-side to avoid the issue of who should visit the other first. The Treaty of Nerchinsk established the border between Siberia and Manchuria. Russians were required to give up the Amur valley, but in return were granted the right to send merchant caravans to Beijing. The Chinese and Russians subsequently extended their border agreement to Siberia and Mongolia with the 1727 Kyakhta Treaty, which allowed Russians to send a trade caravan to Beijing every three years, and to trade at two border posts, establishing a profitable exchange of furs for Chinese silks and tea.[24]

A year after the Nerchinsk treaty, the Kangxi emperor led a military campaign against Galdan, the khan of Zungharia, which extended over western Mongolia, Turkestan, and Tibet. The emperor's military expedition into the steppes was strongly opposed by Confucian court officials, who were concerned about the high economic costs of provisioning a large army on the steppes and the risk of political instability in the emperor's absence. Nevertheless, Kangxi undertook four campaigns from 1690 to 1697, over distances greater than Napoleon's invasion of Russia and over even harsher terrain. During Kanxi's final campaign, Galdan was already defeated, leading only a small band of loyalists who were foraging for supplies. Because the Mongols were Buddhist and the Zunghars derived legitimacy from their ties to the Dalai Lama of Tibet, the Kangxi occupied Tibet in 1720, inaugurating China's dominance of the kingdom.[25]

Kangxi's mission to destroy Zungharia was completed by his grandson, the Qianlong emperor (r. 1736–95), who took advantage of a succession crisis to carry out a genocidal military campaign from 1754 to 1756, which culminated with the annihilation of Zunghar elites by 1760. Qianlong then moved into the areas south and west of Zungharia, extending Qing domination into eastern Turkestan or Central Asia. He renamed the territory Xinjiang or "New Frontier," suggesting an imperial mission, and annexed it into the Chinese empire in 1768. Qianlong now presided over the largest Chinese empire in history, but he bequeathed to his successors continuing ethnic-nationalist unrest.[26]

Qianlong carried out the conquest for his personal glory and prestige, as well as for the reputation of his dynasty. He called himself the "Old Man of Ten Perfect Victories," referring to his most celebrated military campaigns, although he had not led Manchu troops or accompanied them into battle.[27] He composed over 1,500 poems, commissioned official military histories, set up large stone tablets commemorating his victories all over the realm, and commissioned paintings of key military events from the Jesuit court painters. He ordered copper engravings of sixteen battle scenes from top-flight artists in France, which were duplicated many times, with copies making their way to Europe and the United States to inspire awe not just among the residents of his empire but also selected foreigners.[28]

Qianlong's annexation of Inner Asia was a departure from previous Ming policy. The Manchus could have secured the border from raids by applying their standard frontier policy of offering trade, titles, and marriage alliances to the tribal leaders. Leading Han Chinese Confucian literati criticized Qianlong's campaigns as wasteful imperial arrogance. Even after the court induced soldiers and civilian settlers to farm the area, mined silver deposits, and encouraged the creation of horse farms, Xinjiang was a net drain on the treasury, the costs of providing security and administering the territory always being much greater than the economic benefits. Qianlong's campaigns are estimated to have cost 150 million taels. Zuo Zongtang's campaigns in the northwest from 1866 to 1874 to extinguish rebellions there are estimated to have cost

36 million taels, while his subsequent efforts in Xinjiang, from 1874 to 1881, cost 52.5 million taels.[29]

Their disregard for costs and concern for publicity suggest that Kangxi's and Qianlong's imperial expansion was motivated at least in part by the desire for enhanced status—for their personal reputations and for the dynasty, as well as for China. After establishing control over the southeast, Kangxi was determined to expand the Manchu domain to the northwest. Qianlong was driven to fulfill and surpass the legacy of Kangxi. There was nothing inevitable about the Qing dynasty's expansion into territory populated by Tibetans and Uighurs.[30]

THE PETRINE REVOLUTION AND EUROPEAN GREAT POWER STATUS

Peter I (1682–1725), "the Great," carried out foreign policies that elevated Russia into the ranks of European great powers within a generation. Despite his efforts to penetrate the European great power club, Peter was pursuing social competition rather than social mobility. He aimed to depose Sweden as the leading Baltic power by defeating the Swedes in war, their area of superiority. While he adopted Western technology, Peter shied away from Western political institutions and norms, instead preserving traditional elements of the Russian political and economic systems, which were part of Russia's distinctive identity.

After assuming the reins of power from his sister, Peter attacked the Turkish fort of Azov partly to fulfill Russia's alliance obligations to Poland, Venice, and Austria but also to increase his own personal prestige. When the siege failed because of the Turks' ability to resupply from the sea, Peter built a fleet of galleys and succeeded in capturing the fort the following year, giving an early indication of his resilience and motivation.[31]

Peter's Grand Embassy to Europe from March 1697 to August 1698 was undertaken to recruit allies for war against Turkey, but also so that he could learn more about European technology, science, and military practices, which he had been introduced to by his visits to the German Quarter in Moscow, established by his father Tsar Alexei (r. 1645–76) for foreign mercenaries, engineers, physicians, and craftsmen. Peter sought to find out directly about a wide variety of technical subjects, including mathematical navigation, ship design, artillery, surgery, dentistry, and coinage. Impressed by European magnificence, might, and wealth, Peter resolved that in order for Russia to be as strong as the great powers, he must borrow these essentials as quickly as possible. Peter recruited over a thousand shipwrights, sailors, officers, navigators, architects, mathematicians, and other specialists for service in Russia, while at the same time making arrangements for Russians to study abroad.[32]

While Peter was unable to recruit any allies for a war with the Ottoman Empire, he began to conceive of an alternative plan for war against Sweden, to regain Ingria and Karelia on the Gulf of Finland so that Russia could trade directly with Europe. To Peter, Sweden's denial of Russian access to the Baltic hampered not only Russia's trade but also its development as a European power: the Swedes "in order to deprive us of the desire to see have put a heavy curtain in front of our mental eyes and cut off our connections with the whole world." Hence Sweden's hegemonic position was illegitimate. The Baltic provinces would provide Russia with an educated populace and economic resources for modernization, while defeating Sweden would remove the leading rival for power in the northeast. Nothing mattered more to Peter than respect for himself and for Russia. According to Vice-Chancellor Peter Shafirov, Peter wanted to be treated as a gentleman who had driven barbarism out of the Russian nation, but the Swedes continued to treat him as if he were a barbarian himself. One of the justifications for war, in Peter's mind, was Sweden's failure to give satisfaction for an insult to the tsar's honor: a Riga governor had asked the tsar, who was trying to sketch the city's fortifications, to move along. Peter became so obsessed over his mistreatment that in a 1709 rescript to the Ukrainian people this insult to his honor was listed along with Sweden's occupation of Russian territory as a reason for war.[33] Peter's long struggle with the Swedes over the Baltic "was as much concerned with status and standing in the eyes of the world as it was about land."[34] When the Russian siege against Riga began in 1709, Peter threw the first grenade, rejoicing that "[t]he Lord God has enabled us to see the beginning of our revenge on this accursed place."[35]

The war against Sweden, therefore, was not a defensive war. Sweden was very much a satisfied power, not seeking further conquest. In 1699, Peter joined a coalition against Sweden put together by Christian V of Denmark and Augustus II of Poland, in which Russia was very much the junior partner, in part out of opportunism, because the new king of Sweden was only seventeen and inexperienced. After announcing a thirty-year truce with Turkey in 1700, Peter declared war on Sweden. Peter and his allies had anticipated a short conflict (the war would last twenty years), but his Polish and Danish allies failed him: Augustus failed to take Riga, and Denmark was defeated before Peter even entered the war.[36]

Having entered the war before his military reforms were completed, Peter suffered a devastating defeat at Narva, as 40,000 Russian troops were routed in a surprise attack by 9,000 Swedish troops led by King Charles XII, who, despite his young age, proved to be a charismatic leader and military genius.[37]

While the Swedish king decided to give priority to defeating Poland and turning it into a Swedish satellite, Peter captured important forts in the Baltic provinces. Given respite from having to engage Charles's forces, Peter built a standing army, centralized the command and created a general staff, developed the domestic arms industry, altered the army's composition in favor of more European-style "new formation" regiments, and hired foreign officers to drill and train the soldiers. In 1703, near the mouth of the Neva, Peter began to build a new city, St. Petersburg, the future capital of Russia (1712–13), later called Russia's "window on Europe."[38]

Whereas the army reforms continued the pattern set by his predecessors, Peter's creation of a navy was a radical departure from the past. It has been estimated that 1,260 seagoing vessels were built during the Petrine era, for service on the White Sea, the Sea of Azov, the Baltic, and the Caspian. To keep the fleet operating, Peter established the St. Petersburg naval academy, staffed by British instructors, the first institution of higher technical education in Russia.[39]

In 1708, Charles embarked on the invasion of Russia that Peter had long anticipated. Charles had planned to conduct a blitzkrieg and have his troops live off the land, but Peter countered with a scorched earth policy, destroying or hiding all supplies that might replenish Swedish stores. When Charles turned south toward the Ukraine for provisions, his supply train, at some distance from Sweden's main army, was destroyed by Russian forces at the end of September. By the time Charles attacked Poltava on July 8, 1709, Peter and his forces were already well entrenched. While Charles was handicapped by numerical inferiority, fatigued soldiers, and a shortage of artillery, credit should be given to excellent Russian generalship and ingenious fortifications, which diverted Swedish troops directly into the line of Russian fire, creating a "killing field." Swedish forces were decisively defeated within a few hours.[40]

The battle at Poltava changed the balance of power and the European status hierarchy. Although the war was essentially won, Peter used his navy to bring the Northern War to a decisive conclusion, with a naval victory over Sweden at Hangö (1714) and raids by Russian galleys on the Swedish coast. After Charles was killed by a stray bullet, Peter was able to conclude the 1721 Treaty of Nystadt, which gave Russia control of the Baltic coastline from Vyborg to Riga—Estonia, Livonia, Ingria, Kexholm, and most of Karelia. Russia returned most of Finland to Sweden.[41]

Russia's victory in the Northern War made it a European great power. The Swedish Empire could not recover from the loss of its rich Baltic provinces, and began a long trajectory of decline. Russia's other leading rival, Poland, had been laid waste by Charles's forces, its trade, credit, and towns destroyed. To celebrate the victory over Sweden, the Russian Senate, in the Act of October 1721, conferred on Peter the titles of "Emperor," "Great," and "Father of the Fatherland" because he had "brought the all-Russian realm into such a strong and prosperous condition and his subject people into such glory before the whole world." According to Chancellor Gavriil Golovkin, Peter had led his subjects "from the darkness of ignorance onto the stage of glory of the entire world, promoted, so to speak, from nonbeing into being, and included in the society of political peoples."[42]

Peter's assumption of the title of emperor was unprecedented, showing that with the Peace of Nystadt he now believed that he had sufficient military power. In Christian Europe, there was only one western empire, the Holy Roman Empire. In Peter's era, the modern conception of an empire as a large territorial domain in which a state rules over a number of other states or subordinate units had not yet come into existence. After Poltava, Peter had unsuccessfully tried to get the Holy Roman emperor to recognize his new rank of Majesty and title of emperor, since "tsar" had no meaning in the table of precedence in Europe. As discussed previously, in Russian, the title of tsar could mean either khan or basileus. Peter adopted the Latin term, imperator, rather than the Greek basileus, for emperor in both Russia and Europe, as part of his "prestige policy" of being admitted to the concert of European powers. The northern protestant powers (Prussia, Sweden, Denmark, the Dutch Republic), who did not accept the jurisdiction of the Holy Roman Empire, readily accepted Peter's title of emperor. But rulers of the other major powers were more reluctant, because the title of emperor would outrank their position as kings. Britain and Austria did not recognize the title until 1742, and France agreed to accept it only in 1745. The Austrian Habsburgs staunchly resisted recognizing the Russian tsar as emperor because it might set a precedent and in any case would diminish their own status.[43]

The costs of attaining great power status were substantial: Peter was at war for twenty-eight years. The army and navy consumed half of the budget when he ascended to the throne in 1682; as early as 1701, it was three-fourths, and even at the end of his reign, it was still two-thirds of the budget.[44]

Peter also reformed Russia's social mores, dress, architecture, imagery, education, and industry to bring them more in line with Europe. Peter himself hacked off the beards of leading members of the Russian nobility, and required that the nobility wear Western dress—topcoats, waistcoats, and breeches for men, full skirts and fitted bodices for women—"for the glory and comeliness of the state and the military profession." But there were limits to Peter's Westernization policies, which did not extend to political institutions and norms, showing that he was concerned with social competition, not social mobility. Peter was primarily interested in technology—in mathematics, engineering, navigation, naval architecture, metallurgy, mining, manufacturing. He borrowed from the West in order to make Russia an equal with the other nations of Europe.[45] In his recruitment of serfs for the army and his requirement that the nobility serve the state, Peter was "working *with* the grain of Muscovite society, perpetuating and even intensifying its archaic features."[46]

The sweeping changes brought about by Peter exemplify the recurring pattern in Russia of "great reforms" or "revolution" "from above" —comprehensive efforts to modernize Russia quickly. The desire for speed in conjunction with the scale of the envisioned changes and resistance meant that Peter sometimes resorted to coercion. The Russian poet Maximilian Voloshin (1877–1932) famously labeled Peter the Great "the first Bolshevik."[47]

Peter had regarded Russia's low position in the international hierarchy of states as unjust, hence his drive toward social competition. In his published justification for the war against Sweden, Peter complained that "not only the Swedes, but also other and remote peoples, always felt jealousy and hatred toward the Russian people, and attempted to keep the latter in the earlier ignorance, especially in the military and naval arts. . . . the Lord God [made Russia] so famous, that those, who, it seems, were the fear of all Europe, were defeated by us. And I can say, that no one is so feared as we are. For which one should thank God."[48]

Much later, in jottings that he made for a ceremony commemorating Nystadt in 1724, along with his pride in Russian military achievements Peter showed continuing bitterness at what he regarded as efforts by Europe to exclude Russia. He recalled that all other nations "maintain the policy of keeping a balance of forces with their neighbor and were especially reluctant to admit us to the light of reason in all matters and especially military affairs, but they did not succeed in this."[49]

Peter did greatly elevate Russia's international standing, making it for the first time an indispensable player in Europe. As an indication of Russia's increased international importance, by 1725 Russia had stationed twelve permanent diplomatic missions in Europe, in contrast to one when Peter acceded to power. In 1726, a year after Peter's death, Russia entered into an important alliance with Austria. Whereas previously members of the Russian ruling dynasty had not been considered for interdynastic marriages, Peter married his daughter and nieces to German princes. Peter's triumph, however, was incomplete. His defeat of Sweden, a power not at the top of Europe's status hierarchy, had increased Russia's status in north and eastern Europe, but did not persuade Britain, France, or Austria that Russia was an equal.[50]

CATHERINE THE GREAT

Peter's goal of attaining status as a European great power was more fully achieved under Catherine II (1762–96), "the Great." Catherine gained an outlet on the Black Sea and recovered Ukrainian and Belorussian lands that had formerly been part of Kievan Russia. By pitting rivals against each other, presiding over a huge territorial expansion, and proving to be a master of ruthless realpolitik, Catherine made Russia a major player in European power politics. She also enhanced Russia's image by her professed interest in European Enlightenment political thought and culture, although she did not apply those ideas to Russia's domestic political system.[51]

Catherine, a minor Prussian princess before she married the heir to the Russian throne in 1745, was anxious to gain European respect as Russia's ruler—among other reasons because she was a usurper who had come to power as a result of a coup against her husband, Peter III. Since the reign of Peter the Great, a growing number of states had begun to recognize Russia as an empire. Diplomatic protocol was important because Russia's newfound status as a great power would not be on a firm footing unless the other states recognized Russia's claims. As Catherine's foreign minister Nikita Panin observed, "Etiquette strictly regulates forms of correspondence between states precisely because it serves as a measure of the mutual respect for each other's strength." Catherine placed a new emphasis on diplomatic ceremonial, which had been relatively informal and unpretentious under her predecessors, since most courts sent representatives of a lower rank than ambassadors to St. Petersburg. Early on, Catherine insisted that all foreign ambassadors kiss her hand when formally presented, a requirement that Vienna initially resisted. To show that Russia was a member of the Western international system, she insisted that negotiations be conducted in French, the language of international diplomacy. Determined to have her imperial title recognized, when the French reopened the issue in 1762 by neglecting to include the word "imperial" in a new French envoy's credentials, Catherine engaged in a bitter quarrel with France, during which relations were reduced to the level of chargé d'affaires, until 1772 when the French accepted Russian claims.[52]

In an attempt to be recognized as the most enlightened monarch in Europe, the great "Semiramis of the North" (legendary goddess and queen of Babylon), Catherine corresponded with a large number of French philosophes, including Voltaire and Diderot. At one point when the publication of the great enterprise of the *Encyclopédie*, a compendium of the world's historical and scientific knowledge, was halted by Parisian authorities, Catherine invited Diderot and the publishers to relocate to St. Petersburg at her expense. After Diderot had died, however, Catherine privately admitted that she listened to his ideas mainly out of curiosity; adopting his "fantastic theories" would have upended her empire.[53]

In writing her elegant letters, Catherine was concerned not only with her own personal prestige, however, but also that of Russia, of whose "vastness and complexity" she often reminded her correspondents. Trying to impress Voltaire with the level of affluence of her subjects, the empress went as far as to claim that Russian taxes were so low that every peasant in Russia could have chicken "whenever he wanted," unless he "preferred turkey."[54] Catherine (who spoke Russian with a rather heavy German accent until her final days) praised "the richness and conciseness of our language," the ostensible reason for Russian being so hard to translate. "My soldiers," boasted the empress in 1769, "go to war against the Turks as they would go to a wedding." Of all the nations in Europe, Russia alone enjoyed the glory of the victory over "the barbarians." "Our nation," asserted Catherine a year later, "has, in general, the happiest disposition in the world: there is nothing easier than to give them a state for goodness and reasonableness."[55] Her propaganda was designed to enhance Russia's international stature.

Catherine was soon confronted with her first foreign policy crisis, when Polish King Augustus III was on his deathbed in 1763. Since Peter the Great, Russian tsars had tried to secure the election of a pro-Russian king in Poland and ensure preservation of the "Polish liberties"—election of the king, the notorious *liberum veto* whereby any member of the Polish Diet could veto legislation, and the right of the nobles to form "confederations" for any purpose whatsoever, including overthrowing the king—all of which had made Poland a failed state. Having Poland as a Russian satellite was a considerable strategic asset in that it provided protection along Russia's long, exposed Western frontier and also served as a land route for Russian intervention in Central Europe. Concerned that France, Austria, or Turkey might intervene militarily to place their own candidate on the Polish throne, in April 1764 Catherine signed a treaty of alliance with Frederick II of Prussia, with a secret provision that both would cooperate to preserve Poland as a weak state. In August 1764, Catherine secured the election of her former favorite, Stanislas Poniatowski, as king of Poland, with the assistance of Russian troops.[56]

Having triumphed relatively easily, Catherine overreached by taking up the cause of the "dissidents," non-Catholic Christians, in Poland. In 1768, assisted by 10,000 Russian troops, Catherine's diplomatic representative Nikolai Repnin forced the Polish Diet to enact a law guaranteeing equal rights for religious dissidents. In addition, the Polish Diet was required to sign a treaty with Russia whereby the empress guaranteed the Polish constitution, confirming its vassal status. Polish resentment over Russian bullying erupted in the formation of the Confederation of Bar, which conducted guerrilla warfare against Russian troops, widening into a civil war that lasted four years.[57]

Already alarmed by the presence of Russian troops in Poland in violation of previous treaties and their expansion into the border regions, and egged on by France, Turkey declared war on Russia in 1768 when Russian Cossacks pursuing Polish rebels crossed the border into Turkish territory and burned a village. Although war with the Ottoman Empire came as a surprise to Catherine, she sought to take advantage of Russian victories to gain freedom of navigation on the Black Sea. In 1770, the Russian General P. A. Rumiantsev advanced into the Danubian principalities of Moldavia and Wallachia. In 1771, Russian forces seized the Crimean Peninsula. Even more striking, with British help, a Russian fleet sailed from the Baltic through the English Channel to the Mediterranean, subsequently defeating the Ottoman navy at the Bay of Chesme, a battle that ranks with Poltava in its impact on perceptions of Russia's international standing, because it symbolized Russia's arrival as a global naval power.[58]

The extent of Russia's military conquests and Catherine's expanding war aims alarmed both Prussia and Austria. Austria was strongly opposed to Russia's predominance in the Danubian principalities, which would extend Russian influence up to the Habsburg borders. Frederick, who had longstanding territorial objectives in Poland to unite separated Prussian territories, pressed Catherine to give up Moldavia and Wallachia in return for Polish Livonia, and to allow Austria to gain part of Poland to preserve a balance of power. In the first 1772 partition of Poland, Russia obtained Belorussian and Latvian Lithuania to the Dvina and Dnieper Rivers; Austria received Galicia; and Prussia took Polish Prussia (except Gdansk and Torun).[59]

The 1774 treaty of Kuchuk Kainardji, which concluded the first Russo-Turkish War, was a stunning victory for Russia. Russia gained control of the Black Sea coast between the Bug and Dnieper Rivers as well as major ports. Russia gained the right of commercial navigation in Turkish waters, including both the Danube and the Black Sea. The Crimean khanate was given independence from Turkish suzerainty. Russia was granted authority to build an Orthodox church in Constantinople and the right to make representations on behalf of the Orthodox Christians. The rights given to Russia to guarantee the privileges of the Danubian principalities and the religious freedoms of Orthodox Christians would later be construed as a pretext for intervention in the internal affairs of the Ottoman Empire.[60]

Victories over the Ottoman Empire increased Catherine's appetite for territory and status. About this time, Catherine, along with her favorite Gregory Potemkin, conceived the ambitious "Greek project," which entailed pushing the Turks out of Europe, establishing a kingdom of Wallachia and Moldavia, and if possible, restoring the Orthodox Byzantine Empire under the rule of her grandson, who was conveniently named Constantine. For expansion to the south, she would need the cooperation of Austria, which had common borders with the Ottoman Empire, rather than of Prussia. Russia and Austria shared an interest in driving the Ottoman Empire out of the Ukraine and the Danubian Valley.[61]

But negotiations with the Emperor Joseph II were complicated by Russia's status concerns. As head of the Holy Roman Empire, Joseph had the prerogative of signing the alliance treaty first, but Catherine proposed an "alternative," whereby they would take turns signing first on separate copies. Joseph was reluctant to agree because of the risk that it might set a precedent for other states. In the end, the alliance took the form of secret, parallel letters. The alliance was not revealed until Catherine decided to annex Crimea in 1783, which risked provoking Turkey.[62]

Catherine had not originally intended to annex the Crimean khanate, but decided to do so after futile efforts to install a pro-Russian khan who could maintain order while also serving Russia's interests. When Catherine hesitated, Potemkin launched an impassioned argument: "There is no power in Europe that has not participated in the carving-up of Asia, Africa, America. Believe me, that doing this will win you immortal glory greater than any other Russian Sovereign ever. This glory will force its way to an even greater one: with the Crimea, dominance over the Black Sea will be achieved." Although it was a rich and fertile land, Crimea was a drain on the Russian treasury for four decades, because the Muslim Crimean Tatars emigrated by the thousands to Turkey, leaving their lands fallow and reducing tax revenue.[63] In this case, as in other instances in Russian history, expansion proved to be a net loss to the treasury.

Catherine appointed Potemkin governor of the newly acquired lands, New Russia. Within a remarkably short period of time, he founded cities, established industries, and built the naval bases Sevastopol and Kherson. He also began to construct a sizable Black Sea fleet of warships, which aroused the concerns of the Ottoman Empire.[64]

Unreconciled to the loss of Crimea as a vassal state and concerned about Russian expansion, Turkey found a pretext to declare war on Russia in 1787, inaugurating an extended period of conflict during which Russia also had to deal with civil unrest in Poland and an inconclusive war with Sweden, which hoped to regain lands lost to Peter the Great. Catherine concluded a peace treaty with Sweden in 1790 by promising not to interfere in Swedish politics, while Russian generals achieved major victories on land and sea, forcing the Turks to sue for peace. The second Russo-Turkish War was concluded in the Treaty of Jassy (January 9, 1792), which gave Russia the strategic fortress of Ochakov, the strip of the Black Sea coast between the Bug and the Dniester Rivers, and Ottoman recognition of the annexation of Crimea. Annexation of Crimea made it possible for Russia to become a Black Sea naval power, while control of the coast allowed for development of additional ports such as Odessa. Russia now had direct access to the Balkans.[65]

In the meantime, having learned from the first partition, the Poles formed a confederation to reform their dysfunctional system, eliminating the notorious *liberum veto* and the elective monarchy in the May 3, 1791, constitution. While involved in war with Turkey, Catherine could do little but fume over the personal attacks leveled against her in the Polish Diet. The new Polish constitution was a major blow to Russia's prestige. After the Turkish war was concluded, however, Catherine was free to deal with Poland. She supported an anti-reform Polish confederation and sent in Russian troops. But this time Prussia would have to be compensated to prevent the Prussians from taking advantage of Russia's military involvement in Poland. In the second 1793 partition of Poland with Prussia, Russia acquired more of Lithuania, to add to what it had received in the first partition, and most of western Ukraine.

A valiant but doomed nationalist uprising in Poland in 1794 provoked Catherine to intervene militarily. As in Crimea, without a pliable local ruler to maintain order, and given the risk of recurring rebellions that would require Russian military action, it was too costly for Russia to maintain Poland's nominal independence. This time Russia and Austria colluded in dividing up the country, and imposed the solution on Prussia in 1795, the third and final partition, which eliminated the state of Poland from the map. Russia acquired the rest of Lithuania and the Ukraine as well as the Duchy of Courland.[66]

Catherine had acquired large swathes of territory and additional population, but the long-term geopolitical consequences of the Polish partitions were mixed. The Poles had a strong sense of nationalism and would launch repeated uprisings against Russian rule. Moreover, Russia had lost a buffer state, retaining only a portion of Poland, and her territory now bordered powerful rivals Austria and Prussia.[67]

By the end of the eighteenth century, under Catherine, Russia was a major player in European politics, courted by both Prussia and Austria. Its former rivals Sweden, Poland, and Turkey were weak and defeated. Russia controlled trade from the Baltic to the Black Sea. Other states respected Russian military power, which had inflicted humiliating defeats on the Ottoman Empire. While military glory came at the cost of Catherine's initial aspirations for domestic reform and liberalization, the cultural and economic gap between Russia and the West had narrowed.[68]

THE QING EMPIRE AND GREAT BRITAIN

While Russia was fully engaged in European politics, a far cry from the isolated Muscovy, the Manchu court became more insular, attempting to block intrusions from the maritime imperial powers. China was satisfied with its relative status and saw no need to adopt an identity management strategy. The Qianlong emperor was the longest-serving ruler in Chinese history, exercising power for 63 years, from 1736 to 1799. During the Qianlong era, the empire reached the apex of its economic prosperity and renown, but there were signs of decay and decline, especially near the end.[69]

Qianlong's most important achievement was the conquest of Xinjiang. In contrast to Peter the Great, who imposed numerous taxes to

pay for his wars while using the state to promote economic development, Qianlong allowed the revenue-enhancing tax reforms of his pre-
decessor Yongzheng (1723–35) to fall into abeyance, adhering to the
traditional Confucian belief that the wealth of the empire was fixed
and that the state should not take away resources from the people.
Also in contrast to his father Yongzheng, who had tried to homogenize
differences in status and ethnicity, Qianlong stressed the distinctiveness of the Manchus from the other ethnic groups. Qianlong viewed
himself as the ruler of a universalistic, multiethnic empire. He was also
reluctant to make bold decisions on his own. Partly because so many
festering problems were ignored, toward the end of his rule the country
was repeatedly torn apart by several large-scale rebellions, an uprising
led by a millenarian Buddhist Wang Lun in 1774, attempts by the Tri-
ads on Taiwan in the 1780s to establish a new dynasty, two revolts of
Muslim communities in Gansu in the 1780s, and the extended White
Lotus rebellion from 1796 to 1805. The revolts were symptomatic of
the decline of Qing domestic institutions, incompetence of the military,
and corruption in the bureaucracy.[70]

The 1793 encounter of the Qianlong emperor with the British envoy
Lord Macartney set off a contest over the relative status of their two
empires, symbolized by a dispute over ceremonies and titles. Constructivism suggests that the dispute over ritual represented two alternative
and mutually exclusive views of the meaning of sovereignty and the
construction of power relations.[71] In contrast, SIT explains the encounter as an effort by each state to preserve its status and self-esteem in the
face of a challenge by the other.

Among the rituals preserved by the Qing was the "Sinocentric" tribute system of foreign relations. The Middle Kingdom had no foreign
ministry because in the Chinese view, there was only one civilization—
all other peoples were barbarians. The Sinocentric world order was
underpinned by the tribute system of foreign relations, designed to in-
stitutionalize the status superiority of the Chinese emperor—known
as the Son of Heaven, mediator between heaven and earth—over all
other lords. Submission to the authority of the emperor and observance
of imperial rituals were the essence of Sinocentric culture. Trade with
China, actively pursued by China's neighbors, was viewed by the imperial elite "not as ordinary economic exchange" but as a "tribute" to
China's superiority.[72]

Tributary states to the south of China—Vietnam, Siam, Laos, Burma, Cambodia, Liqiu (Ryuku, modern Okinawa)—were expected to make periodic missions to Beijing, where after exchanging the prescribed gifts with the emperor and using submissive rhetoric, members of the mission would be allowed to conduct additional trade with Chinese merchants. Before meeting with the emperor, an emissary would have to perform the *kowtow*, which entailed kneeling three times, each time accompanied by full prostration with the forehead touching the floor— an acknowledgement of his place in the Sinocentric order. Appropriately, relations with tributary states were conducted by the Ministry of Rites.[73]

For relations with non-tributary states, the Manchus created the *Lifan Yuan*, known in Chinese as the Court of Colonial Affairs and in Manchu as the Ministry for Ruling the Outer Provinces, which dealt with areas of the empire outside China proper and was staffed by Manchus. The Qing followed the tribute system with representatives from the maritime states but behaved more pragmatically in relations with the Mongols and the Russians, showing that they could use ceremonial instrumentally, rather than being socialized by it into a new identity as constructivism would predict.[74]

China's relationship with the British was different. The British envoy to China was Lord Viscount Macartney, an able diplomat who had formerly been ambassador to the court of Catherine the Great in St. Petersburg, chief secretary to Ireland, and British colonial officer in the British Caribbean and Madras. To encourage Chinese interest in trade with Britain, Macartney brought numerous gifts for the emperor, including barometers, astronomical instruments, pocket globes, Parker lenses, and an expensive glass planetarium, along with other examples of high-quality British manufactures. Accompanying Macartney were scholars, physicians, painters, musicians, technicians, interpreters, scientists, and a watchmaker, to increase Chinese "respect for the country of which such men are natives."[75]

Misunderstandings plagued the British expedition. The Chinese characterized the mission as the British paying tribute to the emperor, and accordingly, expected Macartney to kowtow, an action that was forbidden by the British government because of its implication that the British king was a vassal of the Chinese emperor. To show that the British king and the Chinese emperor were equal, Macartney offered to carry out the same act of obeisance as a Chinese official of equivalent rank performed before a portrait of King George III—kneeling on one knee—but the Chinese insisted that there was no lord equal in status to the Chinese emperor.[76]

More than differences in subjective construction of sovereignty and power relations was at stake—rituals symbolized relative status. For the Chinese to follow Western diplomatic practices would have implied that Britain was equal in status to the Middle Kingdom. "We must impose our will on these Englishmen," the emperor declared, "demonstrating to them the effectiveness of our system and the superiority of our civilization."[77]

Qianlong finally conceded that Macartney could follow English court customs, which entailed kneeling on one knee before the emperor. However, the ceremony was conducted in a large tent, at the imperial summer estate in Chengde (Jehol), away from Beijing and the imperial bureaucracy. Official records did not record any departure from the tribute ritual.[78]

Macartney's success in avoiding kowtowing was a pyrrhic victory, because Qing officials refused to discuss the British trade requests. To the great disappointment of the British, Qianlong displayed no interest in the British telescope, planetarium, or other scientific instruments, having his own collection of European clocks, watches, music boxes, and automatons that had been given to him by the Jesuits. In the communication mentioned in the introduction to this chapter, Qianlong summarily dismissed British requests for additional ports for trading, a warehouse, or a permanent diplomatic mission in Beijing.[79]

Both China and Britain had a low opinion of the other's relative status, with the Chinese viewing the British as uncultured barbarians while the British marveled at the stagnant Chinese economy.[80]

RUSSIA AS ARBITER OF EUROPE

With the allied victory over Napoleon, Russia's status reached its zenith, a standing not equaled again until the end of World War II. As a member of the Concert of Europe and the Holy Alliance, the elite great power clubs, Russia followed a moderate, conservative foreign policy designed to preserve its position. On the domestic front, however, post-1812 triumphalism led to the growing complacency of the

Russian government, which ultimately cost Russia dearly in wasted opportunities for meaningful modernization and reforms, a squandering of possibility that would have damaging consequences for Russia's status vis-à-vis the West. By the mid-nineteenth century Russia's identity as a great European power was threatened by its increasing backwardness. Within Russia, the growing chasm between Western Europe's liberalization and Russian autocracy stimulated the famous debate over Russia's identity between Slavophiles and Westernizers, between social creativity and social mobility strategies.

In June 1812, Napoleon had embarked on an invasion of Russia with from 450,000 to 600,000 troops, eventually staggering out with only 30,000 to 50,000 men. Tsar Alexander I (1801–25) insisted upon pursuing Napoleon westward, reversing his conquests and creating a new international order. Alexander triumphantly marched into Paris at the head of the allied troops on March 31, 1814.[81]

Viewed as the liberator of Europe, Alexander played a leading role at the Congress of Vienna from 1814 to 1815. Russia was now the greatest land power in Europe, with some 800,000 troops, whereas Britain was the leading sea power. After some squabbles among the victors and Napoleon's abortive comeback in March 1815, ending in his defeat by the Duke of Wellington at Waterloo, Alexander obtained his wish for a redrawn kingdom of Poland, with himself as king. With the addition of Finland (acquired from Sweden in 1809) and Bessarabia (acquired from the Ottoman Empire in 1812), Russia had attained its furthest expansion to the West and a secure western frontier.[82]

Both Alexander and his successor Nicholas I (1825–55) viewed the Congress of Vienna settlement as legitimate and satisfactory to Russia. The renewal of the Quadruple Alliance (Britain, Russia, Austria, and Prussia) in November 1815, which evolved into the Congress system when France was added in 1818, solidified Russia's status as one of the leading powers of Europe. The Congress system or Concert of Europe was in charge of maintaining the peace through periodic consultations in the event of crises, and lasted until the 1878 Congress at Berlin. There was also the Holy Alliance of Russia, Prussia, and Austria, which cooperated to suppress revolution in Europe.[83]

Despite Tsar Alexander's pretensions to be Europe's savior, his post-1815 foreign policy was remarkably conservative and cooperative—especially in comparison with Russia's eighteenth-century expansion—

largely because the Russian ruler was pleased to be part of the Congress and did not wish to risk expulsion by the other major powers, an example of how state ambitions can be tempered through membership in high-status clubs.[84]

In contrast to Alexander I, who had been tutored on Enlightenment thought, his younger brother Nicholas I was brought up during the era of reaction and witnessed the threat of the 1825 uprising of the Decembrists—noble officers from the Napoleonic wars who advocated Russia's conversion to European-style constitutionalism and refused to accept the tsar's designated successor. Nicholas was therefore determined to stamp out any possible spark of revolution and was averse to serious institutional reforms. After 1825, instead of pursuing a coherent strategy for upholding and enhancing its prestige, Russia increasingly stagnated both internally and externally.[85]

Nicholas's conservatism was embodied in the prevailing ideology of Official Nationality (Orthodoxy, autocracy, and nationality) proclaimed by the minister of education Sergei Uvarov in 1833, which guided Russian foreign as well as domestic policy. For the supporters of Nicholas, "nationality" (*narodnost'*) referred to the unique qualities of the Russian people and Russia's special place in history. Whereas Catherine the Great had proclaimed Russia to be a European power, Nicholas stressed Russia's distinctiveness.[86]

Convinced that the survival of Russian autocracy depended upon preserving foreign regimes, Nicholas used Russian troops repeatedly to suppress revolutionary uprisings—in Poland in 1830–31, in the Danubian principalities of Moldavia and Wallachia in June 1848, and in the Hungarian revolt against the Austrian Habsburg crown in 1848–49. Whereas Alexander I had been praised as the liberator of Europe, Nicholas I was detested for being its "gendarme."[87]

Despite the best efforts of Nicholas to repress independent thought, the 1840s and 1850s were an era of intense intellectual ferment and discussion among the intellectual elite regarding Russia's identity and relationship to the West. The debacle of the Decembrists uprising, followed by repression and rejection of the constitutionalist option by Nicholas, raised serious doubts among some Russian intellectuals about Russia's ability to follow the European example. In his *Philosophical Letter*, published in 1836, Peter Chaadaev shocked Russian intellectuals by arguing (in French) that Russia had no history, no culture. Russia had given "nothing to the world" and "bestowed not a single idea upon the fund of human ideas." The purpose of Russia's very existence was "to serve as a terrible lesson to mankind."[88]

The famous debate between Slavophiles and Westernizers was in part a reaction to Chaadaev's contention that Russia had no past, present, or future. The Slavophiles, a group of landholders and gentlemen-intellectuals, constructed an identity of Russia as superior to other nations in some respects and having a unique historical mission. For Slavophiles, Russia was a messianic mother figure destined to progress along its unique developmental path to an even higher level of development than Europe had achieved. The West may have been richer and more dynamic, according to the Slavophiles, but its individualism, secularism, and materialism were inferior to the Russian sense of community, spirituality, and mutual obligation. Russian Orthodoxy provided *sobornost'*, an association of love, freedom, and truth, as exemplified by the peasant commune, in contrast to Western rationalism, legalism, and compulsion—principles that had been imported into Russia by Peter the Great.[89] Thus, the Slavophiles identified new dimensions on which to demonstrate superiority, a tactic of social creativity.

The Westernizers read the same books as the Slavophiles and moved in the same social circles but evaluated Western and Russian traits completely differently. For the Westernizers of the nineteenth century (or "Europeans" and "Cosmopolitans" as they were frequently called at the time), Russia was a child, destined to copy and learn from the enlightened Western way of life. Whereas the Slavophiles exemplified social creativity, the Westernizers favored social mobility as a strategy for enhancing Russia's international status. Far from being just a geographic destination, Europe was also "a region of the mind" where Westernizers chose to live, a "spiritual source of their civilization," both an ideal and an idea vital for defining the meaning of Russia. Westernizers approved of the reforms of Peter the Great, but argued that Russia needed to go even further down that path. Although internally divided between radicals and moderates, the Westernizers tended to be relatively optimistic about Russia's future, expecting that Russia would eventually emerge as the most advanced European civilization by borrowing from Europe, exploiting its own youthful energy and freedom from the burden of historical institutions to lead the way.[90]

Nicholas believed that Russia was not part of the new liberal Europe, and tried to wall off the country from such seditious ideas through censorship and restrictions on travel. In 1853–54, the growing ideological rift with Western Europe, along with Russian and French status concerns, helped to escalate an otherwise trivial Russo-French diplomatic dispute over the rights of Catholic and Orthodox Christians in the Holy Places of Palestine into a full-blown Russian "war with Europe." In response to Napoleon III of France's demand that Catholics assume custodianship over the Holy Places of Palestine, at the expense of Orthodox Christians, Nicholas issued an ultimatum to the Ottoman sultan demanding the right to protect Orthodox Christians in the Ottoman Empire, and sent in Russian troops to occupy the Danubian principalities to coerce Turkey to cooperate. Confident of British and French support, Turkey declared war on Russia in 1853.[91]

Unwilling to allow Turkey to be defeated by Russia again, Britain and France intervened, their decision based largely on the misperception that the conservative Nicholas was scheming to gain control of the Ottoman Empire. In fact Nicholas preferred to preserve Turkey as a weak state under Russian influence, and if the empire were to disintegrate, to carry out an orderly partition with other great powers. The only location at which France and Britain could reach Russian power was the Black Sea coast—the Crimean Peninsula, where the maritime powers could bring their naval superiority to bear.[92]

After a hard-fought yearlong siege by Britain, France, and Turkey against Sevastopol, the leading Russian base on the Black Sea, involving nearly 100,000 Russian casualties, the Russian commander surrendered in September 1855. The recently installed Tsar Alexander II (1855–81) had to deal with the difficult issue of getting Russia out of the Crimean War. The Treaty of Paris (1856) greatly undermined Russia's prestige by demilitarizing the Black Sea coast, prohibiting a Russian fleet in the Black Sea, depriving Russia of southern Bessarabia and control over the mouth of the Danube, and ending the tsar's historic claims to protect Christians in the Ottoman Empire.[93]

The Crimean War revealed an embarrassing gap between Russia's claims to great power status and the backwardness of an empire that had not yet experienced the industrial revolution. Russia's network of railroads had not been extended to the south, and communications between the populated center of the country and the Black Sea were poor. To Russia's embarrassment, the French and British could more easily supply their troops in Crimea by sea than the Russians could in their own country. The rifles of the Russian troops were not as accurate at a distance as those of the British and French. Russian ships were so inferior that they were kept in port the entire time rather than risk a battle with the Anglo-French alliance.[94] Russia could not continue playing a great power role with inferior logistics, communications, and weaponry, which ultimately reflected the weakness and backwardness of the Russian economy and society.

CHINA'S HUMILIATION AND "SELF-STRENGTHENING"

Like Russia after the Crimean War, China also experienced traumatic defeats and loss of status as a result of the Opium Wars (1839–42, 1856–60). The Qing dynasty adopted some Western diplomatic practices while trying to preserve the tribute system, but was unable to halt the slide in China's position.

Just as the Crimean War awakened Russia to its technological backwardness, the triumph of Western military technology in the Opium Wars, and the Qing dynasty's rapid and humiliating loss of control over major components of foreign and domestic policy, were a shock to Chinese complacency over its superior status. Initially, the Qing responded to the defeat with selective modernization, or "self-strengthening," designed to improve China's ability to compete with Western countries while preserving China's traditions. To protect China's self-esteem against the shame of inferiority, the self-strengtheners used social creativity tactics that stressed the superiority of Chinese culture and civilization over that of the barbarians.

The 1839–42 Opium War with Britain was provoked by the actions of imperial commissioner Lin Zexu, who confiscated and destroyed British opium that was stored in China for sale, refusing demands for financial compensation. In order to pay for imports of tea, the British had begun to ship opium from India to China, where as many as one-tenth of the population became addicted, including some in the military and the Confucian literati. So much opium was being purchased that silver was being drained from the Chinese economy, arousing the outrage of the Daoguang emperor (1821–50), who appointed Lin to eliminate the trade. In retaliation for the destruction of British shipments of opium, the British government sent a fleet of warships to attack Shanghai and other coastal ports. The British ships easily over-powered the Chinese junks and proceeded to sail up the Yangtze.[95]

The central issue leading to war, however, was not opium, but Brit-ain's free trade ideology, derived from Adam Smith, and China's refusal to allow unrestricted commercial intercourse. The British achieved some of their goals in the 1842 Treaty of Nanjing, which opened up five ports to trade and residence for the British, inaugurating the "treaty port" system. The Chinese ceded the island of Hong Kong. China had to pay $21 million in compensation and reparation—an immense sum. The treaty also included a most-favored-nation clause granting Brit-ain any concessions subsequently made to any other foreign power. A subsequent treaty with the United States provided that Americans committing crimes in China could only be tried and punished by US officials, according to the laws of the United States—extraterritoriality. The Treaty of Nanjing with Britain and the extraterritoriality agree-ment with the United States were the first of the famous "unequal treaties."[96]

China's humiliation in the Opium War was witnessed by Wei Yuan (1794–1857), a failed candidate for the highest national examination for the bureaucracy and adviser to provincial governments. In 1826, Wei had reintroduced the term "wealth and power" (*fuqiang*, an abbre-viation of *fuguo qiangbing*, "enrich the state and strengthen military power") borrowed from a rival to Confucianism, the Legalist school, in an anthology on statecraft that he co-edited. The anthology drew on the earlier practical statecraft strand of Confucianism in propos-ing practical competence, rather than moral self-cultivation or classical scholasticism, as the goal of Confucian scholar-officials. "From ancient times, there have been wealth and power that were exercised apart from the Kingly Way (moral purposes of the Confucian regime), but never the Kingly Way exercised apart from wealth and power," Wei Yuan wrote. The need for China to acquire "wealth and power" would serve as a stimulus to reformers in China in the latter half of the nine-teenth century.[97]

The shock of military defeat by the barbarians caused Wei to ap-ply practical statecraft to foreign affairs. In the same month as the Treaty of Nanjing, Wei appealed to the Chinese elite's feelings of shame and humiliation over the diminished prestige of the empire, hoping that these emotions would serve as catalysts for reform. In *Records of the Conquest*, he wrote a lengthy historical account of the glory of the early Qing empire and the expansionist foreign policy of the Kangxi emperor, showing that the Chinese had not always been victims of foreign conquest. He also introduced a theme that would recur repeatedly, even in modern China—humiliation as a motivation for reforms to restore China's greatness. In the preface, quoting from an ancient Confucian classical text, Wei wrote: "Humiliation stimulates effort; when the country is humiliated, its spirit will be aroused." In his prescient 1843 geopolitical analysis of Western power and its threat to China, *Illustrated Treatise on Sea Powers*, Wei emphasized the need to master the barbarians' "superior techniques" (warships, firearms, and military training) "in order to control them." Wei died in obscurity, but his ideas would influence later generations of Chinese determined to raise China's position by increasing its wealth and power.[98]

Before that, China would undergo even worse humiliations. Dissatisfied with Chinese compliance with the treaty port system, in late 1856 the British used the Chinese boarding of a ship supposedly under British registry, the *Arrow*, as a pretext to launch the second Opium War, or Arrow War. When no apology was forthcoming, British gunboats repeatedly shelled the city of Canton. In 1858, Lord Elgin, accompanied by a French task force, sailed north, took the Dagu forts, and occupied Tianjin, only one hundred miles from the capital Beijing, threatening the Qing representatives. The 1858 Treaty of Tianjin provided for ten additional treaty ports and free access for foreigners to the interior of China. Opium was implicitly legalized. Most galling to the Xianfeng emperor (1850–61) was the provision for permanent diplomatic residence of foreigners in Beijing, because it challenged a major precept of the tribute system. Qing officials tried to persuade the British diplomatic representative to take a back route to Beijing, which would be less conspicuous and less humiliating for the Chinese. When the British nevertheless tried to force their way up a different river to Beijing, despite spikes and other obstacles, Chinese forts on both shores fired on the British ships, sinking four of them. The British diplomatic party sent to prepare the way for Elgin's formal exchange of ratification instruments in Beijing was taken hostage, along with other British and French representatives. When the hostages were later released, nineteen had been killed and some tortured. Enraged, Lord Elgin led a military expedition into Beijing, and to teach the Chinese a lesson, burned and looted the emperor's exquisite summer palace, destroying priceless artworks—a deliberate effort to hurt the emperor's "pride as well as his feelings." Anglo-French forces occupied Beijing. The 1860 Beijing Convention reiterated the Chinese obligation to observe the Treaty of Tianjin, and added Tianjin itself as a treaty port, along with an increased indemnity.[99]

Demoralized and in despair over the presence of foreign troops in Beijing, the emperor fled to Jehol (Chengde), where he died a year later. The new emperor was a boy of five, who died at the age of nineteen before he could exercise personal power. Effective power was shared among the emperor's uncle Prince Gong, who had been forced to remain behind in the capital; the empress dowager and regent Cixi; and outstanding provincial officials Zeng Guofan, Li Hongzhang, and Zuo Zongtang, who had risen to prominence fighting the domestic Taiping, Nian, and Muslim rebels respectively. The Taiping Uprising (1850–64) had culminated with the occupation of Nanjing and the Yangzi region for eleven years by a regime headed by a village schoolteacher claiming to be the younger brother of Jesus Christ; the Nian rebels (1851–68) had conducted mobile guerrilla attacks in the southern part of north China; and two Muslim revolts (1855–73) had erupted in northwestern and southwestern China. The Qing tried dispatching banner troops and enlisting Western mercenaries, but the most effective means of restoring their authority was to delegate responsibility for raising an army and fighting the rebels to eminent members of the Confucian scholar gentry. While devolution of power staved off the imminent collapse of the Qing empire, the decentralization of financial resources and military power to regional authorities would later impede efforts to mobilize popular support for a reformed Confucian regime.[100]

Reflecting the sharing of power among the regent Cixi, the court, and provincial officials, the reign name chosen for the young emperor, "Tongzhi," meant "joint rule." As early as 1869, the literati began referring to the Tongzhi reign (1862–74) as a "restoration," a traditional Chinese term used to describe reforms undertaken to save a declining dynasty under pressure from natural disaster or domestic rebellion.[101]

The basic rationale for reform came from Feng Guifen (1809–74), an intellectual heir to Wei Yuan and one of the most prominent Chinese political thinkers in the second half of the nineteenth century. In

1860 Feng wrote several essays outlining a series of reforms, which he presented to Zeng Guofan a year later. Like Wei, Feng was motivated by humiliation and shame over the imperial decay. "Once one feels a sense of shame, nothing is better than self-strengthening" (*ziqiang*), he wrote.[102] Why were Western countries "small and yet strong," while China was "large and yet weak?" asked Feng. To catch up with the West, argued Feng, the Chinese should "self-strengthen"—that is, learn foreign languages, mathematics, and science. "What we then have to learn from the barbarians is only the one thing, solid ships and effective guns." Shipyards and arsenals should be established in selected ports, with foreign experts hired to teach the Chinese how to manufacture such products. Since "the intelligence and wisdom of the Chinese are necessarily superior to those of the various barbarians," Feng believed, China would eventually surpass them—revealing his preference for social competition.[103] Status concerns were central in Feng Guifen's passionate advocacy of the indigenous production of Western-style weapons: "only thus can we play a leading role on the globe; and only thus shall we restore our original strength, and redeem ourselves from former humiliations."[104]

Wei's and Feng's statements highlight the role of social comparison and feelings of inferiority in the self-strengthening efforts at rejuvenation of the empire. "I feel deeply ashamed that the Chinese weapons are far inferior to those of foreign countries," wrote Li Hongzhang (1823–1901), a leading self-strengthener and later China's principal diplomat for thirty years, to his former patron Zeng Guofan in 1863. "Every day I warn and instruct my officers to be humble-minded, to bear the humiliation, to learn one or two secret methods from the Westerners in the hope that we may increase our knowledge." "The greatest shame in the world is the shame of being inferior to others," repeated Prince Gong and his reformist colleagues.[105]

Feng became a leading adviser to Li Hongzhang, who implemented many of his ideas, including the establishment of the modern Jiangnan arsenal in Nanjing in 1865, along with a language school and translation bureau, and another arsenal and shipyard in Fuzhou in Fujian province. Another of Feng's innovations, a school to train Chinese in English and French so that they could serve as interpreters, was set up in Beijing, later followed by schools for the study of foreign languages and science in Shanghai, Canton, and Fuzhou. Later, the Beijing school was expanded into a college with the addition of such subjects as mathematics, chemistry, geology, mechanics, and international law, despite opposition from well-connected conservatives who argued that China had no need of "barbarians as teachers" to instruct them in "trifling arts."[106]

In 1861, a rudimentary foreign office, the *Zongli Yamen*, was established, later evolving into an effective bureaucratic advocate for reform. The Zongli Yamen was originally supposed to be temporary, until the foreign crises had passed, and was located in a run-down building, the former Department of Iron Coins, to show that it was inferior in status to other government bureaus, thereby preserving the distinction between China and other countries. Despite the seedy setting, Prince Gong, the emperor's uncle and close adviser to the empress dowager Cixi, was placed in charge. At the same time, the Chinese preserved the old tributary system for countries in East Asia, receiving tributary missions from states that continued to accept China's "rule by prestige" despite its imperial decline, again demonstrating the instrumental use of ceremonial and practice to enact different identities.[107]

The treaty port system continued the traditional divide between the coastal areas of China and the interior provinces in their openness to foreign influences. The pattern of Chinese responses to the Western challenge can be categorized as an interplay between the recommendations of those residing in the more outward-looking "littoral" areas of China (favoring commerce) and the resistance of representatives from the Chinese "hinterland," associated with cultural conservatism and radical nativism. China's first major modernization project, the reforms of the Tongzhi Restoration and the "self-strengthening" movement, which spanned the period from the early 1860s to China's defeat in the Sino-Japanese war of 1894–95, can be viewed as an effort to carve out a third way between these two traditions, incorporating both the innovation of the littoral tradition and the respect for tradition of the hinterland, thus providing some form of "indigenous validation."[108]

The very idea of "self-strengthening," including advocacy of learning from the West, was predicated on retaining traditional Confucian culture and values, which Feng Guifen and other prominent self-strengtheners never questioned or doubted. The self-strengthening movement was an attempt to overcome Chinese inequality vis-à-vis the West by making changes within the framework of the Confucian order.[109] The reformers were not pursuing a social mobility strategy, but used social creativity to rationalize reforms necessary to restore China's competitiveness. In contrast to Meiji-era Japan, in China from 1860 to 1870, Westernization and modernity were not accepted political and cultural goals. The superior position that the Western countries had adopted was seen as illegitimate in light of China's superior civilization and morality. "Would not the best of all possible stratagems be to retain the social relationships and the illustrious moral principles of China as the foundation, and to reinforce them with the techniques that the various countries [of the West] have used to attain wealth and power?" argued Feng.[110]

In 1898, just as the successors to self-strengtheners were preparing for even bolder reforms aimed at fundamentals of the Chinese tradition, Zhang Zhidong, a well-known provincial governor and reformer, coined the famous slogan "Chinese learning as the essence, Western learning for practical use" (Zhongxue weiti, xixue weiyong, usually abbreviated as ti-yong).[111] Ti-yong was a plea for advocates of Westernization and traditionalists to cooperate and compromise to help China achieve power and wealth.[112]

Consistent with neorealism, a majority of Chinese officials favored using Western military technology and weapons to ward off the foreign threat.[113] While neorealism can explain the self-strengtheners' focus on acquiring military defenses, SIT can account for the reformer's choice of selective modernization rather than wholesale Westernization because of the need to maintain a distinctive identity.

Li Hongzhang and his supporters took the first steps toward technological and infrastructural modernization, including the establishment of telegraphs, railroads, and a new type of "government supervised, merchant managed" (guandu shangban) public-private enterprise—an alliance between commercial wealth and state power—to promote the development of trade and to restore China's economic sovereignty by getting "a share of the foreigners' profits." This strategy was exemplified by the China Merchants Steamship Navigation Company (founded in 1872), which was designed to allow China to take control of its coastal shipping.[114]

Self-strengthening achieved notable results, allowing the Qing empire to make "a remarkable comeback" in the 1870s and 1880s. What was lacking was centralized, energetic leadership. After the premature death of the Tongzhi emperor in 1875, to retain power, the empress dowager Cixi appointed her three-year-old nephew, Guangxu, as emperor. The imperial court, including Cixi, while supporting self-strengthening initiatives in some provinces, failed to build on successful local experiments to initiate a Meiji Japan–style systematic, coordinated, national reform drive to catch up with the West, which meant that the self-strengthening movement amounted to little more than a "patchwork" of isolated provincial reform efforts. After the remarkable Confucian scholar-officials died, many of the reforms fell victim to the ignorance, prejudice, and conservatism of the imperial elite and the Confucian literati.[115]

Self-strengthening was vigorously opposed by proponents of an ultraconservative, xenophobic "muscular Confucianism," a current of thought known as "pure discussion" (qingyi), which had an extraordinarily belligerent attitude toward the Western barbarians. Whereas the self-strengtheners showed social creativity in acknowledging that the West had some noteworthy achievements, the pure discussion group engaged in social competition. These Confucian literati and lower-level officials, who presented their ideas in poems, essays, and songs, were proponents of a "purer" Confucianism and were dismissive of Western technology and science. As one committed qingyi proponent put it, "the superiority of China over foreign lands lies not in reliance on equipment but in the steadfastness of the minds of the people." The pure discussion group opposed any derogation from China's status as the center of the world order. They tried to bully and intimidate officials who favored adopting Western technical innovations and practices such as diplomatic representation.[116]

In 1884–85 an even more extreme manifestation of the qingyi, the so-called Purist Party (Qingliu Dang), pushed Cixi into war with France over control of Vietnam and yet another predictable Chinese defeat. The French had taken over southern Vietnam, a Chinese tributary state, and were establishing a military presence in the north as well. Although both Prince Gong and Li Hongzhang warned that China was not yet ready to fight a Western power, scholar-officials bombarded the court with memorials attacking those who were brave enough to speak out against war with France. The results were as disastrous as Li had predicted—in an engagement lasting little over an hour the French navy destroyed eleven of China's best warships and the prized naval shipyard at Fuzhou, dismantling twenty years of reform and casting doubt on the self-strengthening movement. In another setback for the self-strengthening cause, empress Cixi became preoccupied with building a new summer palace, an extraordinarily expensive "escapist fantasy," including a man-made lake and a marble boat, which diverted imperial funds from real modernization projects. The project was completed in 1894, the same year that China became involved in yet another losing war over Korea.[117]

China had attempted to hold on to its tributary state, Korea, against Japanese penetration by applying some of the techniques of Western imperialists. Korea paid tribute to Qing China but also maintained good relations with its neighbor Japan. After the Meiji Restoration in 1868, Japan adopted modernization policies and sought to extend its "civilizing" influence to Korea. In 1882, China dispatched 3,000 troops in response to a Korean soldiers' mutiny that was followed by a coup—the first time that the Chinese had intervened militarily in Korea in over two hundred years. Two years later, the Chinese used their troops again to quash an even bloodier succession dispute between pro-Chinese and pro-Japanese factions in the Korean court. But the Japanese deeply resented the Chinese interventions and in 1894, in response to a Korean domestic rebellion, Japan declared war on China.[118]

A decade after China's humiliating loss to France, its unexpected and hence even more traumatic defeat in the war against Japan dealt the last blow to the self-strengthening movement. Many Chinese officials wrongly believed that after nearly two decades of self-strengthening China would be in a position to vanquish the Japanese. Adding insult to injury, Japan had previously emulated Chinese civilization (including borrowing Wei Yuan's rendition of the Legalist principle of "rich country, strong army" as the rallying cry of Meiji reforms) and was traditionally considered by the Chinese to be inferior, a nation comprising "dwarf people."[119] "Affairs in my country have been so confined by tradition that I could not accomplish what I desired. . . . I am ashamed of having excessive wishes and lacking the power to fulfill them," confessed Li Hongzhang during the signing of the devastating 1895 Treaty of Shimonoseki, which made Korea in effect a Japanese protectorate; ceded Taiwan, the Pescadores, and the Liaodong Peninsula to Japan; opened up four additional treaty ports; and provided Japan an indemnity of 230 million silver taels, which were used to pay for Japan's industrialization.[120] In 1895, Kang Youwei, an intellectual and leader of the 1898 Hundred Days' Reform in China, characterized the war as China's "greatest humiliation in more than two hundred years since the advent of the Qing Dynasty."[121]

RUSSIA'S GREAT POWER ILLUSIONS

Russia's foreign policy after the Crimean War was originally intended to provide a breathing spell in which Russia could focus on domestic reforms and modernization. But Russia was continually drawn into military conflicts by the lure of open borders and the temptation to repair Russia's great power standing through military victories.

In the wake of the damage inflicted by the Crimean War, Alexander II embarked on another era of top-down reforms, similar to those of Peter the Great, to restore Russia's status as a European power. During the "era of Great Reforms" from 1856 to 1874, Alexander abolished serfdom, created an independent judiciary with criminal trial by jury, established elected local councils, opened up higher education, and relaxed censorship.[122]

To provide a favorable environment for domestic reforms, Foreign Minister Alexander Gorchakov favored a policy of geopolitical retrenchment (or, as it was termed at the time, *recueillement*, literally "self-contemplation"). While this policy made perfect sense, retrenchment had to counter the Russian aspirations for great power status that informed the regime's understanding of "dignity" and "honor."[123] While the foreign and finance ministries advocated rebuilding Russia's prestige through reform and diplomacy, officials in the Asiatic department of the foreign ministry, the war ministry, and field commanders strongly urged an aggressive policy in Central Asia to restore Russia's great power status through force of arms and to obtain revenge against Great Britain for the Crimean War defeat. From the cooperative policy pursued by Alexander and Nicholas in the Concert of Europe, Russia shifted to a course of social competition with Great Britain, pursued in Central and South Asia, known as the Great Game.[124]

Advocates of expansion argued that Central Asia was an area where Russia could achieve cheap victories over inferior opponents while showing up the British, who were too far away to block Russian expansion. Local Russian military commanders pressed their authority to the limit for glory and honor, confronting the government in St. Petersburg with a fait accompli. When Russian commanders were sent to close a gap in the line of steppe fortifications, Gorchakov tried to reassure Britain and other European states by sending out a circular comparing Russian actions with those of the British in India, the French in North Africa, and the United States in America, all of whom had been "irresistibly forced, less by ambition than by imperious necessity, into this onward movement where the greatest difficulty is to know where to stop." These powers had all been driven by the need for security to subjugate "half savage, nomad populations, possessing no fixed social organization." Now that Russia's frontier was near the settled agricultural and commercial populations of Khokand, Gorchakov promised, Russia would halt. But his words were soon contradicted by the actions of Colonel M. G. Chernyaev, who conquered Tashkent, undermining the credibility of future Russian reassurances.[125]

On Chernyaev's dispatch Alexander II wrote: "A glorious affair." Others were less charitable in their reaction, questioning the economic and geopolitical logic behind Chernyaev's conquest. As the perplexed Russian Minister of the Interior P. A. Valuev noted in his diary, "General Chernyaev has taken Tashkent and nobody knows why. . . . There is something erotic in everything that happens on the distant frontiers of the Empire."[126] Continuing the pattern, in 1868 the extremely vain and intensely ambitious Adjutant General Konstantin Kaufman conquered Samarkand, an ancient city from which the Mongols had invaded Russia, and later the khanate Bokhara. Five years later, after a well-planned, swiftly executed campaign, he subdued the khanate of Khiva, and in 1876, he added Khokand to the tsar's new Central Asian empire.[127]

While supporters claimed that extending Russia's borders into the khanates would enhance security by establishing more defensible borders and providing control over trade routes, the foreign affairs and finance ministries regarded the expansion as unnecessarily extravagant and noted that it would require additional troops to subdue a hostile population. Russia already had substantial territory. Development of Central Asia would have required vast sums that could be better spent protecting Russian interests in Europe and domestic affairs. Far more important than raw materials or trade in driving the Russian advance were "considerations of power and prestige."[128]

In contrast to the concerns of the war ministry and Asiatic department, the most important priority for Gorchakov was to end the humiliating provisions of the 1856 Treaty of Paris, an objective that he achieved in 1870 when he took advantage of the defeat of France by Prussia to repudiate the provisions demilitarizing the Black Sea. The British reacted strongly to Russia's unilateral action, but were unable to recruit support for anything more than an international conference.[129]

Despite Gorchakov's diplomatic victories, the policy of retrenchment was even more strongly challenged by developments in the Balkans that affected Russia's prestige and honor, abetted by grassroots activism in favor of Panslavism, a more radical and anti-Western offshoot of Slavophilism. Russian Panslavism is generally considered to have begun with the 1858 formation of the Moscow Slavic Benevolent Committee to encourage Slav religious and cultural activities under Ottoman rule and to educate Slavs in Russia. Slavic committees were subsequently formed in St. Petersburg and other Russian cities, with support from elements of the military, journalists, officials, and the court. The Panslavs called for liberation of Orthodox Slavs from foreign rule, their formation into independent states, and the federation of those states under Russian leadership. Although Panslavism was not a coherent body of thought, the desire of some proponents to undermine the Habsburg and Ottoman Empires and to establish the superiority of Slavs over Germans is an illustration of the strategy of social competition.[130]

Panslav ideas were given an outlet for expression in the Balkan crisis set off by an agrarian revolt in the Ottoman domains of Bosnia and Herzegovina in 1875, followed by an uprising in Bulgaria. In June 1876, against the advice of Tsar Alexander II, the independent states Serbia and Montenegro joined the war with their fellow Slavs against the Ottoman Empire. Compelled partly by pressure from Panslavs—and even more, by the desire for international prestige—Russia was drawn into fighting Turkey in 1877–78, in a war that was not wanted by Tsar Alexander II, Gorchakov, or Minister of War Dimitri Milyutin. Set against the very prudent reasons for avoiding war—that Russia's military reforms had not been completed and its finances were in dire straits—were Russia's historic claims to be protector of the southern Slavs and the potential damage to Russia's "honor and dignity" if it did nothing. Inside Russia, Slavic committees raised money and recruited volunteers for Serbia.[131]

Even without pressure from the Panslavs, however, Alexander probably would have intervened in the Balkans given Russia's identity as an imperial power with historic interests in the area, a status that would not allow him to stand by while Serbia and Montenegro were decisively defeated. Accordingly, Alexander was maneuvered by Russian officials into issuing an ultimatum to Turkey in order to save Serbia, and to mount a partial Russian mobilization, which made war inevitable.[132]

At the front, temporarily deluded by Panslav sentiment and hubris over Russian military victories (Russian troops were approaching Constantinople), Alexander II allowed Russian diplomat Nicholas Ignatiev to secure concessions in the 1878 Treaty of San Stefano between Russia and the Ottoman Empire that were bound to upset Britain and Austria—in particular, the creation of Greater Bulgaria, which extended from the Black Sea to the Aegean and would presumably be a Russian client. War Minister Milyutin counseled that Russia was in no position to fight both Britain and Austria. St. Petersburg was humiliated when major provisions of the Treaty of San Stefano were reversed by the Western powers at the Congress of Berlin (1878) and Bulgaria was divided into three territories. Austria-Hungary was given the territory of Bosnia-Herzegovina to administer, although it had not fired a shot. Although Russia achieved an autonomous Bulgaria, recovery of southern Bessarabia, and territory in Asia Minor, in light of the unrealistic expectations aroused by the Panslavs, the public perceived the treaty as a defeat.[133]

Public outrage over the outcome of the Congress of Berlin further diminished the authority of the tsar, who had already disappointed many intellectuals by failing to approve a constitution or representative institutions for Russia. A terrorist campaign and repeated attempts culminated in the assassination of Alexander II in 1881, the first Romanov to be killed not in a palace coup, but by a commoner. His successor, Alexander III (1881–94), convinced that reform had contributed to instability, presided over a period of reaction.[134]

Although Russia had lost the Crimean War largely because of its economic backwardness, Russian foreign policy was not influenced by economic interests in either Central Asia or the Balkans. Both Russia's economy and that of the Balkan nations relied on selling agricultural products and raw materials in return for industrial machinery and finished products, and were therefore competitive rather than complementary.[135]

Russia's great power illusions diverted resources from the domestic reforms necessary to maintain that status, as was apparent to many officials in the foreign office and finance ministry at the time. As Gorchakov commented bitterly in 1876, "we are a great, powerless country." He continued, "One can always dress up finely but one needs to know that one is dressing up."[136]

CHINA'S FAILED "GREAT REFORMS FROM ABOVE"

Even the Qing was not immune to fears of a permanent loss of status, fears that led to the rejection of the self-strengthening ethos in favor of more sweeping reforms, but also to illusions about China's ability to fight more advanced nations. Just as Russia underwent reforms in reaction to its defeat in the Crimean War, so China enacted "great reforms from above" (albeit temporary ones) after the shock of its loss in the 1894–95 Sino-Japanese War. The failure of the reform movement would set the stage for "totalistic iconoclasm," a rejection of Chinese culture and institutions for their presumed responsibility for blocking China's modernization.[137]

After hearing the terms of the Treaty of Shimonoseki with Japan, Kang Youwei (1858–1927), a brilliant scholar from a distinguished family, who was in Beijing to sit for the highest examination level, the *jinshi*, worked with his student, Liang Qichao (1873–1929), to gain the support of 1,200 examination candidates, "the best and the brightest" of the Confucian scholars, for a joint memorial to the throne advocating fundamental reforms.[138]

Kang continued to send reform memorials, which eventually reached the Guangxu emperor, who wanted to assert his independence from his aunt, the regent Cixi, and take action on behalf of his country. He appointed Kang Youwei to a special position in the Zongli Yamen and other radical reformers to positions in the Grand Council. In the 1898 Hundred Days reforms, the emperor issued a remarkable series of decrees, revamping the examination system, promoting tea and silk for exports, mandating use of Western training techniques for the armed forces, rebuilding the Chinese navy, and eliminating sinecure positions. But the reforms, which at least in the cultural and educational spheres promised to go significantly beyond earlier self-strengthening efforts, were abruptly revoked by the emperor's aunt, the empress dowager Cixi, who, fearing a plot against her by the reformers, placed the emperor under house arrest. Six reformers were summarily executed; Kang and Liang Qichao escaped by fleeing the country into exile.[139]

The 1898 Reform Movement was an ambitious effort to emulate not just technological and scientific aspects of Western "new learning," but also Western ideas, institutions, and policies, proposing profound changes in education and even adoption of Western political institutions and practices, a product of the littoral Westernizing trend. The intellectuals who inspired the movement advocated abandoning the traditional Sinocentric worldview and implementing radical reforms so that China would no longer be what Liang Qichao, a prominent journalist and philosopher, famously labeled the "sick man of Asia," and would catch up with the Western world in "wealth and power."[140]

Like the proponents of self-strengthening, some members of the 1898 Reform Movement were motivated by an acute feeling of shame over China's decline, underscored by the humiliation of the 1895 military defeat by Japan. Revealingly, one of the societies founded by Liang Qichao in Beijing to promote reformist ideas was named the Sense of Shame Study Society.[141]

Despite disillusionment with the self-strengthening ti-yong formula, some of the key reformers, such as Kang Youwei, were still operating implicitly within the framework of selective modernization. Kang hoped to preserve the best of the Chinese cultural legacy by radically reinterpreting Confucianism in order to make it compatible with far-reaching institutional reform and the fundamentals of Western industrial society.[142] Kang's optimism about the possibility of redeeming Chinese tradition notwithstanding, most of the reformers of the late 1890s—despite their deep roots in the traditional culture and emotional attachment to it—no longer shared such confidence in China's fundamental values, but distanced themselves from the core principle of the self-strengthening paradigm. The West was increasingly viewed "as the source not only of instrumental and secondary but also of essential and central values."[143]

Because of their progressive distancing from Chinese tradition, the reformers of the late 1890s shared a less secure, less confident, and more conflicted identity, an important break from their predecessors' identity security based on pride in the Chinese cultural heritage. While purportedly based in gradualism, Kang Youwei's reform proposals amounted to sweeping "great reforms from above" modeled on those of Peter the Great and Meiji Japan. As Kang assured the young Guangxu emperor during their first meeting in June 1898, "After three years of reform China could stand on her own. From then on China would daily make progress and outstrip all the other countries in terms of wealth and power."[144]

Virulent anti-Western nationalism and xenophobia fueled the violence of the Boxer rebellion of 1900, which targeted Chinese Christians, foreign missionaries, and ultimately foreign diplomats, and "removed the last vestiges of international respectability" from the Qing's court, making China a pariah state. Cixi's eventual decision to side with the Boxers, who besieged the Foreign Legation Quarter in Beijing, resulted in the occupation of Beijing by a military expedition of eight nations, which forced the empress dowager and her nephew the emperor to flee to Xi'an. The September 1901 Boxer Protocol resolved the conflict, but at the cost of massive reparations (450 million silver taels) which the Qing government was forced to pay over the next four decades, secured by Western control of the Chinese government's principal sources of revenue.[145]

With xenophobic attitudes toward the West discredited, the empress dowager felt obliged to announce a sweeping reform program. Replicating many of the Hundred Days proposals, Cixi's New Policy (*xinzheng*) reforms called for modernization of the military, legal, and educational systems and for the drafting of a state constitution.[146] Imperial commitment to the large-scale coordinated reform effort thus belatedly materialized, some forty years behind that of Japan. By that time, however, the authority and legitimacy of China's Manchu rulers had already been fatally shattered in the eyes of the majority of ethnic Han Chinese.

RUSSIA'S EXPANSION TO THE EAST

Russia responded to its decline in Europe with an adventurist policy in the Far East, resulting in defeat by Japan and domestic revolution. Russia then returned to its historic mission of leading the Balkans and its perennial effort to gain control of the Turkish Straits, but this time it was confronted with a united German-Austrian front, setting the stage for defeat on the battlefield and radicalization at home.

Nicholas II's (1894–1917) pursuit of glory and influence in Asia, based in part on a messianic vision of Russian national grandeur and the desire for international status, led to a disastrous war with Japan (1904–5), a national humiliation that led to further decline of the Tsarist regime's domestic legitimacy.[147]

Russia's expansion to the Far East was encouraged by Finance Minister Sergei Witte (1892–1903), who was also the dominant influence on foreign policy. Witte considered it his mission to "overcome as quickly as possible the lag resulting from 200 years of economic sleep in Imperial Russia." A former railroad executive, Witte took responsibility for overseeing construction of the Trans-Siberian railway, which would link Moscow to Vladivostok, a project of major strategic and economic significance, begun in 1891. By developing the resources of Siberia, Witte aimed to make Russia a "mother country" equal in status to the European powers, rather than a colony of Europe, a mere source of raw materials and market for the products of more developed countries.[148]

Witte favored "peaceful penetration" of China by such means as railroad networks, roads, and loans, believing that territorial annexation was anachronistic and that indirect rule was the wave of the future. Although he favored different means, Witte was no less concerned with raising Russia's international status than those who advocated military expansion, and no less a proponent of social competition with the Western powers, particularly Britain.[149]

Alarmed by Japan's victory over China in the 1894–95 Sino-Japanese War and the risk that Japan posed to Russian interests in Manchuria, Russia joined with Germany and France to force Japan to give the Liaodong Peninsula back to China. Witte helped to negotiate a loan to China to pay for the indemnity to Japan. The Russo-Chinese Bank was set up to finance Russia's commercial penetration into China. In 1896, Witte signed a secret defensive alliance with Li Hongzhang against Japanese aggression, and in return received permission to extend the Trans-Siberian railroad through Manchuria, shortening the distance to Vladivostok by 450 miles and creating what would be called the Chinese Eastern Railway.[150]

A year later, when Germany seized a naval base at Kiaochow (Jiaozhou) in 1897, setting off a frenzy of land-grabbing among the European countries, Russian forces occupied Port Arthur (Lüshun)—a move opposed by Witte because it was in flagrant contradiction of the alliance with China. Nicholas had long coveted a warm-water port in Asia. Russia negotiated a twenty-five-year lease on the Liaodong Peninsula, with the right to build a naval base at Port Arthur and a commercial port nearby at Dalny (Dairen); and permission to construct a branch of the Chinese Eastern Railway southward to Port Arthur, the South Manchurian Railway.[151]

When the anti-foreign 1900 Boxer rebellion in China resulted in attacks on the Chinese Eastern Railway as well as a large part of the South Manchurian Railway, Russia sent in 170,000 troops, ostensibly to reestablish order and protect property, but then refused to withdraw them even after a March 1902 agreement with China on a phased withdrawal over eighteen months, demanding extensive concessions from China that would preserve Russia's privileged position in Manchuria. China's firm opposition to these demands was supported by Japan, whose ambitions were threatened by Russia's expansion into Manchuria.[152]

In 1903, Japan offered to recognize Russia's railroad interests in northern Manchuria in return for acknowledgement of Japanese predominance in Korea, but certain elements of the Russian elite were unwilling to relinquish Russia's rights in Korea or to allow any non-Russian foreign presence in Manchuria, even though a deal would have been in Russia's interests. In 1903 Witte, who had accumulated many enemies, was asked by the tsar to resign. Nicholas then gave control of Russian policy in the Pacific to Admiral Evgeny Alekseev, named viceroy of the East, a decision that was viewed by the Japanese as provocative, given the admiral's expansionist proclivities.[153]

Nicholas II scoffed at the idea that Japan might go to war, deriding the Japanese as "monkeys" and their army as "infantile," and believed that there would be no war unless he wanted it. A surprise Japanese attack on the Russian fleet at Port Arthur in February 1904 was the first of many Russian defeats in major battles. The most humiliating defeat occurred after the Baltic fleet had sailed halfway around the world to the Far East, where despite having superior numbers, it was defeated by the Japanese navy at the Straits of Tsushima. Both Russia and Japan had fought to a state of mutual exhaustion. But although Japan could not defeat the Russian army, which had reinforcements en route, the tsar accepted a US offer of mediation because he feared that Russian troops might be needed to quell the threat of revolutionary activity within Russia. The August 1905 Treaty of Portsmouth required Russia to give up most of its gains from a decade of reckless expansion—the lease of the Liaodong Peninsula, along with Port Arthur and Dalny, and the South Manchurian Railway. Korea was declared to be independent, but was tacitly recognized as being within the Japanese sphere of influence.[154]

The loss to the Japanese undermined the authority of the tsar, which was based in large part on maintaining Russia's great power status and on military victories. Under threat of a general strike by the Russian people and the risk of widespread bloodshed, in October of 1905 Nicholas was persuaded by Witte, who had been recalled to negotiate the treaty with Japan, to agree to a constitutional monarchy, with civil liberties and an elected legislature (the Duma).[155] Russia's territorial expansion in Asia was thus a sign of weakness, not strength, the consequence of "a compensatory psychological need to at least *appear* to be a great national power."[156]

RUSSIA'S HISTORIC MISSION

Despite the devastating loss of prestige resulting from the defeat by Japan, the Russian military, diplomatic corps, and tsar had not given up the goal of maintaining Russia's great power status and fulfilling Russia's "historic mission" of gaining control over the Turkish Straits and increasing influence over the Balkans. Russia elites believed that Austrian and German domination of the Balkans and the Near East, areas of the historic Russian interest, was illegitimate.

Partly to restore morale, Russian Foreign Minister Alexander Izvolsky (1906–10) aspired to achieve a diplomatic victory on the issue of the Turkish Straits. In 1908, Izvolsky made a secret attempt to trade international recognition of Russia's right to send warships through the Straits in return for recognizing Austria's annexation of Bosnia and Herzegovina (two provinces liberated by Russia in the 1877–78 war with Turkey). His plan backfired when Austrian Foreign Minister Alois von Aehrenthal unilaterally annexed the provinces, conveniently forgetting Izvolsky's conditions. The Russian public was outraged at the sacrifice of Slav lands to Austria in the Bosnian annexation. Izvolsky

refused to recognize the annexation unless it was ratified by the signa-
tories of the Congress of Berlin and unless Serbia was compensated—
conditions that neither Germany nor Austria would accept. When in
late February 1909 Austria threatened to invade Serbia, and Germany
issued an ultimatum to Izvolsky that the Russians compel Belgrade to
accept the annexation, the Russian foreign minister had no choice but
to back down. At a Council of Ministers meeting, the Russian war
minister warned that Russia lacked sufficient soldiers, artillery, and for-
tresses to oppose an alliance of Austria and Germany. Russian public
opinion regarded the Bosnian crisis as an abject humiliation, a "diplomatic Tsushima" in the words of the Russian press, alluding to the
earlier devastating Japanese defeat of the Russian Baltic fleet.[157]

This humiliation of Russian officials reinforced the belief that Russia would have to rebuild its military in order to avoid being bullied
in the future. From 1910 to 1914, Russia undertook a major rearmament program, including construction of a sizable Baltic fleet, with
dreadnoughts, although Russia was a land power, as was its principal
opponent, Germany. The fleet program owed much to the personal efforts of Nicholas II and Izvolsky, who believed that Russia's status as a
great power and its ability to influence the settlement of global issues
required a strong navy. In the opinion of the tsar, a naval fleet must be
created to correspond with the "dignity and glory of Russia" for upon
it would depend "both our external security and our international position." In that era, as illustrated by the Anglo-German naval race, all
major powers believed that they had to maintain a blue-water navy.[158]

To curb Austrian ambitions in the Balkans, Russia encouraged an
alliance between Bulgaria and Serbia, later joined by Greece and Mace-
donia, which led to the Balkan Wars (October 1912–August 1913) and
the doubling of Serbian territory, at the expense of Turkey, which was
driven off the European continent. Under the threat of Austrian military intervention against Serbia, Russia nevertheless had to restrain
Serbia from seizing all the territory it had conquered.[159]

In July 1914, fresh memories of the 1909 humiliation and the Austrian ultimatum during the Balkan Wars, now evoked by the Austrian
threat to take action against Serbia, fueled Russia's decision to support
Serbia's opposition to the humiliating Austrian demands.[160] At a critical July 24 meeting, after receipt of the Austrian ultimatum to Serbia,
Foreign Minister Sergei Sazonov observed that since 1905, Russia's

military weakness had forced it "always to give way when faced with Germany's arrogant demands" and "to conduct negotiations in a tone unsuitable for one of the great powers." Such concessions and weakness had only increased the Germans' aggressiveness. Having made sacrifices to liberate the Balkan countries, if Russia backed down now and "failed to fulfill its historic mission," it would henceforth have to take "second place among the powers." The finance minister Peter Bark conceded that war would place strains on Russian financial and economic stability, but "since the honor, dignity, and authority of Russia were at stake," he saw no reason to dissent from the majority view.[161]

In 1914, Russia went to war, driven by fear of rising German power, the desire to preserve the balance of power, interest in maintaining a dominant position over the Balkans and the Straits, and the need to preserve its great power identity.[162]

DEFEAT, BACKWARDNESS, AND LENINISM

By the beginning of the twentieth century, both China and Russia were facing complex internal crises as well as declining international standing. Russian radicals used social creativity to posit that economic backwardness would help bring about socialist revolution. The Bolshevik revolution then inspired Chinese radicals to embrace Marxism-Leninism as the most efficacious way to restore national dignity while throwing off the imperialist yoke, allowing them to improve China's international standing without having to imitate Western political and social values.

As discussed above, creative reframing of Russian backwardness informed both Slavophiles' and Westernizers' thinking about Russia's international role. A combination of Westernism and Slavophilism led the Russian peasant socialism of Alexander Herzen and Mikhail Bakunin with its messianic overtones, based on the belief that Russian "backwardness" vis-à-vis the West actually contained a bold promise of "young Russia," unburdened by historical traditions, with its proto-socialist peasant communes, charting the path to the socialist future ahead of Europe, whose revolutionary potential was spent.[163]

A creative synthesis of this Russian populist brand of socialism and Marxism helped to account for the eventual success of Leninism over competing ideologies. Marxism, an ideology that envisioned the proletariat rising up to take power, was poorly suited to an industrially backward country with an underdeveloped working class. The program of Georgy Plekhanov, the leader of the Russian Marxist school of thought, would postpone socialist revolution until Russia had experienced a bourgeois stage of development, imposing an almost intolerable period of inactivity on the Russian radical intelligentsia. Russian populists, on the other hand, maintained that Marxist theory did not apply to Russia, whose village communes would allow it to bypass the stage of bourgeois capitalism and proceed directly to building socialism. Despite its historical materialism, Marxism also contained elements that exalted human will and revolutionary activity, features that became increasingly attractive to the radical wing of the Russian intelligentsia. Marxism on Russian soil was thus ripe for reinterpretation as a doctrine of deliverance, of the messianic mission of the proletariat and the possibility of a miraculous regeneration of society.[164]

The leaders of the Russian revolution, Trotsky and Lenin, successfully adopted this interpretation and allowed revolutionary will to overcome the "armchair interpretation of Marxism." Trotsky's theory of permanent revolution rested on the argument that the working classes of the relatively backward societies were more revolutionary than the proletariat in the developed Western countries, and were thus capable of serving as a creative force for transforming the "bourgeois democratic" revolution into a socialist one. Leninism provided an ultimate "magic" shortcut—a theory and organization ("party of a new type") that would allow Russia to skip the stage of capitalist development and to become the catalyst for a world socialist revolution. In a sweeping act of social creativity, the Bolsheviks pronounced the industrial backwardness of Russia and the rudimentary character of its capitalism to be not liabilities but great assets for the social revolution. Leninism also radically redefined the status of the revolutionary intellectuals, freeing them from their role as mere mouthpieces for the interests of the proletariat (as they were in the Marxist system of thought) and transforming them, through the concept of the "party of a new type," into the incarnation of the will of history.[165] The special role of intellectuals in leading the masses to revolution would be appealing to China's intelligentsia as well.

Despite the technological superiority of the Western countries, China rejected social mobility—wholesale Westernization and repudiation of

China's distinctive identity—but also rejected a return to the preservation of traditional Chinese culture. Leninism, with its emphasis on ex-
altation of human will and leadership by professional revolutionaries,
was attractive to many Chinese intellectuals. The Bolshevik revolution
became a model for how to modernize quickly, restore national dignity,
and strengthen the state without adopting Western values—indeed, in
the future for competing with the West for international standing.

The Chinese revolution, which overthrew the Qing in 1911, led to a
political vacuum at the heart of the Chinese state, with rival warlords
seeking to fill it. Disappointed with the results of the revolution, alienated from what was left of the Chinese state, and liberated from the
bonds of tradition, the radical intellectuals who formed the New Culture movement (1915–27) saw the solution to China's backwardness in
"totalistic iconoclasm," an attack on the Chinese "national character"
(*guomin xing*) and wholesale rejection of the remnants of Chinese traditional social and cultural values, which they viewed as fundamentally oppressive and responsible for China's poverty and inequality. The
goal of their proposed "Chinese Enlightenment" project was "a radical transvaluation of values," including replacement of traditional culture by its antidote, the Western values of "science and democracy."[166]
Wholesale Westernizers, they launched a fierce attack against syncre-
tists who continued to subscribe to the goal of "a synthesis of the best
of China and the West."[167]

In their repudiation of traditional values and culture and in their preference for social mobility, the intellectuals of the New Culture movement resembled the radical Westernizers in Russia. Much like Russia's
Chaadaev a century before, Lu Xun, the literary giant of the movement,
despaired over the "slave mentality" of the Chinese people and insisted
that contemporary Chinese problems were rooted in the "man-eating"
traditional values of Chinese society. Another prominent Westernizer,
Hu Shi, rejected the very notion of the "spirituality" of the Chinese
civilization, argued that selective modernization was impossible, and
blamed Chinese backwardness on the inability of the Chinese leaders
to embrace "complete Westernization." Chen Duxiu, one of the most
radical iconoclasts of the New Culture movement, the founder of the
path-breaking *New Youth* journal, the future "commander-in-chief" of
the May Fourth movement, and one of the founders of the Chinese
Communist Party, disparaged Chinese traditional culture as "rotten

and decayed," warranting large-scale "destruction before construction." Chen favorably contrasted Western competitiveness with Eastern tranquility and inertia, Western individualism with Eastern familism, Western rule of law and utilitarianism with Eastern devotion to conventions and emotions.[168]

At the other end of the identity spectrum, the nativist reaction against attempts at Western-based modernization from the late 1890s to the emergence of the New Culture movement was epitomized by neotraditional intellectual currents of the early twentieth century and the 1920–30s such as the National Essence movement, "national character" discourse, and attempts to restore Confucianism as a modern Chinese belief system. Similar to the Slavophiles in Russia, the neotraditionalists rejected Western individualism, materialism, and utilitarianism, and defined Chinese spiritual values as their superior antitheses. Responding to the iconoclasm of the New Culture movement, Liang Shuming, a prominent leader of cultural conservatism and a seminal neo-Confucianist, while admitting that China had to imitate the West in order to survive, advocated universalization of the Confucian spiritual heritage and using "the Chinese way" to rectify Western civilization.[169]

Despite the cultural radicalism of the New Culture movement, its dominant themes were liberalism, democracy, "pluralistic skepticism," individualism, gradualism, and experimentalism—a corollary to the scientific, facts-based approach to reality. Following John Dewey's brand of liberalism, China's wholesale Westernizers such as Hu Shi, a professor of philosophy and literary scholar, embraced cosmopolitanism and intended to reconstruct Chinese civilization by adopting a gradualist and particularist liberal strategy, focusing on solutions to specific and concrete problems rather than on grand theoretical panaceas.[170] Despite their differences with liberals like Hu Shi, many of the Chinese nativists and conservatives also shared a commitment to stability, gradualism, and compromise as the key principles of social change.[171]

The gradualist, evolutionary approach to China's development, however, would be soon overwhelmed by "messianic historicism" and a "chiliastic" understanding of societal progress. Compared to their Russian counterparts, in the context of a collapse of traditional values, China's Westernizing intellectuals were far less comfortable in the world of Western ideas, and experienced a much more acute crisis of identity, a crisis of meaning, and a sense of disorientation, which often translated into the need for a sense of national dignity and an inclination toward "totalistic" ideologies that could provide an all-encompassing solution to China's social and political problems.[172]

The May Fourth movement, named after the May 4, 1919, student protests against the Treaty of Versailles, grew into a general opposition to Western democracy. The protests, which spread to numerous Chinese cities, were set off by the Western democracies' transfer of German rights in the Shandong province to Japan instead of returning control over the territory to China, a cynical violation of Wilsonian principles of self-determination and open diplomacy. Disregard for China's territorial integrity was perceived by the Chinese as an ultimate humiliation, permanently destroying the radical Westernizers' faith that a liberal and progressive West would tutor China in principles of "democracy and science." As Li Dazhao wrote at the time, "The shame of having lost our independent nature is a thousand times deeper than the shame of losing territory." Galvanized by the West's betrayal of Chinese interests, most participants in the May Fourth movement abandoned their emotional and intellectual reliance on the West and placed their faith in China's ability to define its own future, free from Western influence. As a result of Versailles, some prominent Chinese radicals turned to Leninism.[173]

In the context of an assault on traditional authority and disillusionment with the West, Marxism—especially Leninism with its theory of imperialism—resonated powerfully with the complex "love-hate" attitudes of non-Western societies like China toward the West. As Mao Zedong would remark in 1949, Chinese patriots found it increasingly difficult to accept the West in its dual role of teacher and oppressor. For young Chinese intellectuals, socialism, the highest—but as yet unrealized—form of Western democracy, was a way "to reject both the traditions of the Chinese past and the Western domination of the present."[174]

The appeal of Marxism-Leninism to China's increasingly radical intellectuals also bore some striking similarities to its attractiveness to the Russian intelligentsia. Marxism-Leninism offered both the imminent promise of national redemption and a dramatic role for intellectuals in leading and organizing the masses toward this goal. The first Chinese interpreter of Marxist theory, Li Dazhao, the head librarian at Peking

University, saw in a Leninist voluntaristic interpretation of Marxism and the revolutionism of Bolshevism an opportunity for China to emerge as not just a follower of advanced countries but a vital player on the stage of international history. In rejecting the belief that all the problems of mankind would be solved in the West and by the West, Leninism differed sharply both from the liberal theory that Li Dazhao had earlier embraced and from Western Marxism.[175]

If Russia, as Li believed, was uniquely qualified by its geographic position to bring together Western and Eastern civilizations, this was a mission to which China could make a distinctive contribution. Li believed that backwardness was an advantage—that the backwardness of nations like China and Russia held the promise of youth and progress, whereas the more advanced West was on the way to decline and decay. In an article comparing the French and Russian revolutions, Li argued that France and England had reached a period of maturity and could not advance any further. Germany, at the height of its influence, would soon decline. Russian civilization had returned to barbarism and stagnation as a result of the Mongol invasions, which had isolated Russia from the Renaissance and other trends in European civilization. But precisely because of this isolation and backwardness, in Russia there was "surplus energy" for development. Following this logic, it is easy to imagine the amount of such "surplus energy" in even more underdeveloped China. Along the lines of Trotsky's theory of "permanent revolution," Chinese backwardness was thus reframed as an advantage in moving toward the socialist utopia, a tactic that exemplified social creativity. The Leninist vision of history thus would place China in the vanguard of a historic movement, which would advance beyond the West.[176]

The conversion of the other co-founder of the Chinese Communist Party, Chen Duxiu, initially also an adherent to Western democratic thought, followed his disillusionment with the liberal program proposed by social philosopher John Dewey, which offered no prospect of immediate and dramatic results. While Chen had earlier believed that Marxist ideas could not be implemented in "retarded" China, by 1920 he was convinced that Marxism-Leninism and its scientific social engineering promised a solution to the problems of Chinese society and the Chinese state—socialist modernization. Chen embraced the belief that China could progress rapidly from one historical stage to another, bypassing capitalism.[177]

Similar to other Chinese radicals, Mao Zedong was motivated by a visceral antagonism to the foreign threat and an intense desire to restore China's international greatness. Mao Zedong's early writings are similar to those of the Russian populists in stressing the advantages of backwardness not just in avoiding the mistakes of forerunners, but also in providing a reservoir of energy and moral purity. In 1919, he wrote that while the Chinese people had been oppressed for a long time, once reformed, they would advance to a new "golden age," for "the more profound the oppression, the greater its resistance." Much later in his career, in an early 1957 speech, Mao argued that China's poverty and "illiteracy" were superior to the wealth of the West because they provided the motivation for revolution. A year later, in the midst of the Great Leap Forward's millenarianism, Mao developed "the advantages of backwardness" idea further, turning it into a classic voluntarist statement of revolutionary creativity. China was "both poor and blank," "like a sheet of white paper." With its supposed lack of historical (Western) traditions, China would be more receptive to socialism: "Blank paper is best for writing on."[178]

The parallels between Maoism and Russian populism cannot be explained by diffusion of ideas (for there is no evidence that Mao read Herzen or Nikolai Chernyshevsky) but rather by the shared need to find another source of self-esteem and pride, by changing the valence of fundamental attributes from negative to positive.[179]

Leninism was thus amenable to a fusion with the radical nativism of the hinterland tradition, a blend that would inform much in the thought of the leaders of the Chinese Communist Party such as Li Dazhao and Mao Zedong, and lead to a period of status competition not only with the West but ultimately with the Soviet Union.[180] For both China and the Soviet Union, the higher standing of the West was illegitimate because it rested on imperialism, and unstable because it would be overthrown by communist revolutions.

CONCLUSIONS

The deep longing of elites in both Russia and China for respect and international status after their encounters with the West—a longing distinct from the desire for material wealth and power—is well explained by SIT. Peter the Great was motivated just as much by the desire for recognition as by the quest for material power, as indicated by his insistence that the Russian nobility adopt Western dress, hold European-type salons, and adopt European manners. The Qing dynasty was determined to preserve the rituals of the tribute system, which placed Imperial China above the rest of the world, even at the expense of reality.

The elite great power clubs were initially closed to both China and Russia. China was isolated from the European international system by choice until the middle of the nineteenth century. Russia was not part of the European great power club until after the military victories of Peter the Great. Nursing personal slights, Peter embarked on a policy of social competition against Sweden, the dominant Baltic power, to force the Western countries to accept Russia as a great power. Nevertheless, the major European powers would not recognize the Russian ruler as emperor, the title adopted by Peter, until Catherine the Great compelled them to do so as a condition for doing business. Catherine also pursued social competition with the Ottoman Empire, and used alliances first with Prussia and then with Austria to gain diplomatic support for Russia's territorial expansion at the expense of Poland and Turkey.

After Russia was accepted as an equal in the 1815 Concert of Europe, Alexander I and Nicholas I pursued a cooperative policy in order to retain their good standing in the great power club. Defeat in the Crimean War and the subsequent humiliation of the Treaty of Paris caused Russia to return once again to a strategy of social competition, reflected in the Great Game with Britain and competition with Austria over the Balkans.

As represented by the self-strengthening movement (early 1860s–1895), after imperialist intrusions on their independence, Chinese reformers tried to overcome their sense of shame and to gain recognition from the European powers as an equal by adopting Western military technology to control the barbarians. But their efforts failed, as evidenced by their military defeats by both France and Japan. After the 1911 revolution, Chinese elites were divided between Westernizers and nativists over how best to restore China's international standing and defeat the imperialists. The decision by the Western powers at the 1919 Paris Peace Conference to award Germany's Shandong concessions to Japan stimulated the May Fourth movement and undermined the support for Western science and democracy as the solution to China's

problems. This decision proved that the elite clubs were truly impermeable to China, despite the overthrow of the Qing dynasty and subsequent reforms, and caused many patriotic Chinese elites to move toward "totalistic iconoclasm."

Neorealism provides at best an incomplete explanation of the territorial expansion of both China and Russia. Some imperial expansion may have been motivated by the desire to gain additional security
through creation of buffer zones and stable borders, but geostrategic
and economic interests related to the status of a great power may have
been more important. The expansion of the Qing into Xinjiang and Tibet was largely motivated by the desire for dynastic glory. When Peter
initiated the Northern War, Sweden was a satisfied power with no desire to add to its imperial burdens. Poland was already a failed state
when Catherine meddled in its internal affairs. The Crimean Tatars
were likewise no threat to Russian borders when she decided to annex
Crimea. Russia achieved its most secure borders after 1815, but still
fought the Crimean War to defend Russia's right to protect Orthodox
Christians in the Ottoman Empire. Russia's subsequent expansion into
the khanates of Central Asia, which overextended Russian military and
economic resources, is inexplicable in terms of economic or strategic
interests, other than the desire to gain an advantage over Britain. Apart
from the coalition against Napoleonic France, Russia aligned with other
countries not to counterbalance superior power or to deter attack, but
to guard against potential resistance to its territorial conquests.

Likewise the resistance of the Chinese imperial court to adoption
of Western science and technology is difficult to explain by neorealist
theory, given the extreme threat that the West posed to Chinese security. China's presumption of its innate cultural superiority to the West
encouraged Confucian elites to resist Western technology; accepting
Western science and education would have been an admission that Chinese morals and philosophy were lacking.

Ideology influenced both Chinese and Russian foreign policy to some
degree—for China, the view of China as the "Middle Kingdom" and
the beliefs underlying the tributary system; for Russia, the belief in Russia's sacred mission to lead Orthodox Christians and later fellow Slavs.
Ideology could help to legitimize expansion. The Qing ideology of universal empire supported the conquest of Xinjiang and Tibet. Russian
Panslavism created a favorable context for the 1877–78 Russo-Turkish

War and for World War I. Russia's foreign policy was also influenced by conservative ideology in the first part of the nineteenth century, when Nicholas I tried to preserve autocracy in Poland and Hungary against the threat of revolution. The content of Russia's ideology varied—its identity as a great power did not.

Contrary to the tenets of constructivism, Chinese and Russian elites were not socialized by diplomatic rituals and practices. Constructivism gives insufficient weight to the role of human agency in determining Chinese and Russian foreign policy. The Chinese were capable of using the ideas of the tribute system instrumentally, applying them to smaller Asian states but treating Russia as an equal power. Similarly, even after the Opium Wars supposedly forced the Qing to accept sovereign equality, China attempted to preserve the tribute system for Asia—fighting wars to preserve its suzerainty over Korea and Vietnam—while accepting international law and diplomatic representation for its relations with Western powers. Russian tsars played an important role in selecting from alternative identity discourses—portraying Russia as a European power rather than a Eurasian one.

Russia gave secondary importance to economic considerations in its foreign policy. In the eighteenth century, Russia sought to assure access to the Baltic and the Black Seas through control of their coastlines, but its objectives were mercantilist, to strengthen the power of the state, rather than to benefit private enterprise. In the nineteenth century, Russia fought the Crimean War and the 1877–78 War with Turkey, which required heavy borrowing and nearly bankrupted the state.

The development of China and Russia reached similar ideological ends despite the disparity in their beginnings—China as the Middle Kingdom and Russia as the barbaric kingdom. The first Marxist-inspired revolutions occurred in empires accustomed to glory and grandeur that had suffered humiliating military defeats, confronted problems with backwardness, and whose elites had a complex love-hate relationship with the West.

3   The Communist Contest for Status

AS HENRY KISSINGER observed, "it has always been one of the paradoxes of Bolshevik behavior that their leaders have yearned to be treated as equals by the people they consider doomed." While continuing to embrace an ideology meant to supplant that of the West, Soviet leaders waged a ceaseless struggle to achieve political-diplomatic equality vis-à-vis the West. During the Cold War, Soviet officials wanted recognition of their political equality (especially with the United States), greatly valuing even symbolic indicators that would validate the USSR's arrival as "the other superpower" on the world stage, thus injecting a significant element of theatricality (sometimes dramatic but also frequently comical) into the competition. The Chinese Communists sought recognition as a great power by not only the Western countries but also the Soviet Union, as confirmation that the Chinese Communist Party (CCP) had improved the country's international position. Concerning the Sino-Soviet split, Deng Xiaoping later acknowledged, "The real problem was the inequality. The Chinese people felt humiliated."[1]

The drive by Soviet and Chinese elites to restore and preserve their states' previous status as great powers could not be viewed as fulfilled without recognition by the leading states, but both states were shunned and ostracized by the leading capitalist states after their communist revolutions, and they were never accepted as bona fide members of the elite clubs, but merely tolerated. That Communist elites in both the Union of Soviet Socialist Republics (USSR) and the People's Republic of China (PRC) attached importance to great power status, quite apart from security and power, is strong evidence in favor of SIT, showing the resilience of national identity and its perseverance despite the vicissitudes of power trends and external circumstances. Marxist-Leninist ideology would not seek the respect of imperialist states, which were expected at best to be hostile to socialist regimes, and at worst to intervene to seek their destruction.

In this chapter, we argue that the impermeability of elite clubs and the perception that the capitalist order was not only illegitimate but doomed to fail encouraged both the USSR and the PRC to pursue social competition. When the status hierarchy was stable, the Soviet Union and China used social creativity to improve their prestige by means other than geopolitical competition, for example, through Zhou Enlai's Bandung spirit and Khrushchev's "peaceful coexistence" policies.

SIT would expect the elites of the Soviet Union and China to be conscious of their states' relative standing in the world and to seek to restore their former status as great powers. At the outset, this would entail recreating the former imperial boundaries, which had receded due to foreign intervention and nationalist secession. Unfavorable comparisons with the West should have elicited soul-searching and reevaluation of policy. While neorealism would also predict that states would emulate the practices of the leading powers, SIT emphasizes both states' need for a distinctive identity. One of the attractions of Marxism-Leninism to the Russian and Chinese intelligentsia was that it offered a different path to modernization, in which each state could preserve its exceptionalism without undergoing wholesale Westernization.[2] Both states would be expected to seek indicators of their improved international standing in the world, such as diplomatic recognition, bilateral negotiations, and invitations to international conferences (especially summit meetings). SIT would predict tensions in the Sino-Soviet alliance over their relative positions, because the Soviets would expect to play the superior role as the first socialist state and leader of the communist movement, while the Chinese would resent being placed in an inferior position.

Neorealism would expect both countries to give priority to security and protecting the state. Once it became apparent to the Bolsheviks that world revolution was not imminent, the focus of Soviet foreign policy would be on defending the state rather than on promoting world revolution. Since the United States threatened China's security through its support for the Chinese Nationalists (Guomindang), Beijing could be expected to seek an ally in the Soviet Union. Out of the need for security in an anarchic world, the Soviet Union and the PRC would compete for military power with rivals and form an alliance against the most threatening states—regardless of ideology.[3]

An interpretation from the standpoint of ideology would highlight how Soviet and Chinese leaders viewed the world through the lens of Marxism-Leninism, using concepts such as class struggle, proletarian internationalism, and imperialism. Relations between imperialist and socialist states would be viewed as zero-sum games, with opportunities for cooperation strictly limited to particular issues and times. Ideology creates policy predispositions and suggests general directions for policy; on occasion, it may sway policy decisions.[4]

Constructivism implies that Marxist-Leninist ideology, as the predominant discourse, would affect how the world was perceived and set standards of appropriate conduct. As Soviet and Chinese officials took their cues from the Other, how the West treated the two communist states would also play a major role in shaping their self-images and their relationship to the outside world. Political elites in the Soviet Union and China would define their own identities relative to the Other—similar in some ways but also distinct.[5]

We first draw attention to the Soviet Union's quest for recognition by the Western powers in the 1920s and for Western cooperation against Hitler in the 1930s, a quest that was only imperfectly achieved. We then discuss the rise of the Soviet Union to superpower status after World War II, when Stalin's opportunistic expansion provoked a backlash in the form of the US containment policy. When the Chinese Communists took power they aligned with the Soviet Union to enhance their global status as well as attain economic assistance and military protection. After the end of the Korean War and the death of Stalin, intense social competition by the communist powers with the United States gave way to a period of East-West thaw and promotion of the norms of coexistence, as the Soviet Union and the PRC engaged in social creativity. This interlude broke down in 1957 due to the Soviets' launch of Sputnik and its missile tests, which contributed to Soviet and Chinese beliefs that the status hierarchy was unstable, and was succeeded by another period of social competition in the form of rivalry for global prestige and the allegiance of the newly developing states of the Third World that had been established in the wake of decolonization. The Soviet Union's achievement of strategic parity provided incentives for the Nixon administration to accommodate the status aspirations of the USSR in the détente period. As added insurance against the possibility of Soviet adventurism, the United States sought a rapprochement with China, initiating a policy of strategic cooperation with the Chinese. China therefore achieved enhanced international status as part of a strategic triangle with the United States and the Soviet Union. Soviet perceptions that the status hierarchy was in flux due to the US defeat in Vietnam encouraged the Soviets to contest US dominance in Africa, thus putting an end to détente, and with it Soviet aspirations for recognition by the United States as a diplomatic and political equal.

THE SOVIET DRIVE FOR RECOGNITION

Soviet Russia persisted in its efforts to gain recognition from the leading Western states but was ostracized and excluded from the major power clubs. The Soviet Union was too weak to pursue a social competition strategy; diplomacy and propaganda were insufficient to challenge the dominant European powers Britain and France. Beginning in 1929, the Soviet Union embarked on rapid industrialization in part to create the material basis for a return to great power status.

Initially Lenin and Lev Trotsky had believed that the October 1917 revolution would spark a chain reaction of socialist revolutions in Europe, ensuring the survival of the infant Bolshevik state while making conventional international relations unnecessary. As Trotsky, the newly appointed People's Commissar for Foreign Affairs, advised the Foreign Office, "I will issue some revolutionary proclamations to the peoples and then close up the joint."[6] But it soon became apparent that the new regime would have to use diplomacy in order to survive.

Not only did the allied powers (France, the United States, Britain, and Japan) refuse to recognize the Bolshevik regime, but they sent their troops to occupy parts of Russia, while offering aid to the anti-Bolshevik White forces in the Russian civil war. The Bolsheviks, however, enjoyed the advantage of interior lines of communication, while the allied forces were war-weary and lacked a coherent strategy. In November 1919, British Prime Minister David Lloyd George admitted that the military intervention had failed, and two months later he persuaded the allied supreme council to lift the blockade against Soviet Russia.[7]

As a last-gasp effort to dismantle the Bolshevik state, Polish troops under Marshal Joseph Pilsudski invaded Ukraine in April 1920, but the Red Army recaptured the territory and advanced to the outskirts of Warsaw, where it was repulsed, leading to the armistice negotiated between Soviet Russia and Poland in October 1920.[8]

Besides defeating the anti-Bolshevik troops in the civil war, the Soviets managed to restore most of Imperial Russia's territories, laying the basis for an eventual return to great power status. As the British withdrew from the South Caucasus, Soviet forces swiftly moved into the independent republics of Armenia, Azerbaijan, and Georgia. In April 1920, Soviet forces captured the oil fields of Baku in Azerbaijan. Armenia was the next, falling to a coup, followed by invasion by the Red Army. In February 1921, Lenin authorized the takeover of Georgia.[9] The Soviets also restored their borders in Central Asia, occupying the former tsarist protectorates, Khiva and Bukhara, which were overrun by the Red Army in 1920 and turned into Soviet republics.[10]

After securing the borders, Lenin sought to obtain foreign loans and trade to acquire the industrial machinery and technology needed to rebuild Russia after seven years of war and civil war. Soviet officials placed the highest priority on obtaining a trade agreement with Great Britain, the most powerful state in Europe, as a precedent for relations with other states. Negotiations began in May 1920, and, after an interruption due to the Soviet-Polish war, concluded in the Anglo-Soviet trade treaty in March 1921, which afforded de facto recognition of Soviet Russia. Formal diplomatic recognition of the Soviet regime by Persia, Afghanistan, and Turkey aroused British fears of communist subversion in southwest Asia, and motivated them to conclude a trade agreement with the new Bolshevik regime.[11]

The increased emphasis on diplomacy and trade was related to changes in Soviet domestic policy. In March 1921, Lenin announced the New Economic Policy (NEP), an admitted (but temporary) retreat from war communism, in response to growing protests from some of the regime's former supporters, including a rebellion of the sailors at the Kronstadt naval base, and armed resistance to government grain requisitions from the peasants in the Volga, a central grain-growing region. The NEP allowed for small-scale industry, retail trade, and a market in agricultural commodities.[12]

The NEP increased the respectability of the Soviet regime in Britain, where some observers believed that Lenin had come to his senses, making possible Soviet Russia's invitation to the Genoa conference. In October 1921, Chicherin had sent a note to the Supreme Allied Council (Great Britain, France, Italy, the United States, and Japan) offering to repay loans that the tsarist government had contracted before 1914 in return for credits and recognition of the Soviet regime, and proposing an international conference to discuss the issues. Chicherin, who had replaced Trotsky in 1918, had served in the tsarist foreign service as an archivist, where he had specialized in the records of the Crimean War and had written a biography of Alexander M. Gorchakov.[13]

A favorable response from Lloyd George, who was worried about prospects for European recovery without Russia and Germany, eventually resulted in the April–May 1922 Genoa Conference, attended by representatives of thirty-four states, which marked Soviet Russia's debut on the world stage. The Soviet regime's newfound desire to be treated with respect as a legitimate state, as well as its "social insecurity" generated by Western ostracism, were displayed by Soviet diplomats at the conference, the first international forum to which Soviet representatives were invited. Soviet delegates changed their revolutionary uniforms to top hats, silk gloves, and cutaways and behaved "exactly as diplomats were expected to behave," becoming "sticklers for diplomatic etiquette."[14]

While the Genoa Conference was a frustrating experience due to the diplomatic stalemate over tsarist debts and Soviet compensation for foreign owners of nationalized property, on the outskirts of the conference German and Soviet representatives reached agreement on the Rapallo treaty, which entailed mutual diplomatic recognition and renunciation of financial claims on both sides. The treaty was a major step forward in the Soviet Union's desire to be treated as a normal state, and a bombshell to the other Western countries.[15]

The Soviets finally achieved full diplomatic recognition (although only at the level of chargé d'affaires) by Britain in February 1924, followed by their recognition by the Radical government in France in late

October 1924.[16] In 1927, however, the Soviet Union suffered a series of humiliations and blows to its reputation and status. These blows were in large part a backlash to Soviet efforts to spread communism to other countries. In 1920, a representative of the Soviet Comintern (Communist International, 1919–43) helped to organize the Chinese Communist Party. As part of its "united anti-imperialist front" policy, the Comintern directed that the Chinese Communists join the Chinese Nationalist Party (Guomindang) as a "bloc within." In December 1926 and January 1927, Soviet advisers in China mobilized anti-British sentiment by organizing rallies in Shanghai, threatening British economic interests. The British sought to counter Soviet policy by encouraging anti-Communists within the Guomindang. In April 1927, with the permission of the foreign diplomatic corps, Chinese metropolitan police raided the Soviet embassy in Beijing in search of subversive material, arresting twenty-two Russians and making off with seven truckloads of papers. The same month, the leader of the rightist faction of the Guomindang, Chiang Kai-shek, who had received substantial military and economic assistance from the Soviet Union, massacred his Communist allies in Shanghai. The British were also suspicious of Soviet subversive activities in Britain, where Soviet labor unions gave financial assistance to striking British coal miners in a 1926 general strike. In May, on the pretext of searching for a missing War Office document, British police invaded the premises of the Anglo-Russian Cooperation Society (Arcos) and Soviet trade delegation in London, although the latter was in theory protected by diplomatic immunity, and seized many documents. Despite the failure of the raids to find incriminating evidence, Britain broke off diplomatic relations with the Soviet Union, a significant blow to Soviet prestige and self-esteem. In June, the Soviet political representative to Poland, Peter Voikov, was assassinated by a White Russian émigré—an act that many Russians blamed on the British as a provocation. In October, the Soviet political representative to France, Christian Rakovsky, was declared persona non grata for having signed a Trotskyite declaration in Moscow.[17] All these events, occurring in different countries around the world, were setbacks to Soviet international status, showing that the major powers would not tolerate the Soviet Union's dual policy of seeking to subvert the very states that they engaged in trade and political relations with.

A full-blown war scare ensued in the Soviet press, with Machiavel-
lian intentions imputed to Britain, which was supposedly trying to organize an anti-Soviet bloc. The foreign shocks coincided with a domestic economic crisis: in November 1927, amidst the war scare, the
peasants were hoarding grain rather than sell to the state at low, pre-
set prices. Stalin proposed forceful measures to requisition grain from
the peasants, coerced agricultural collectivization, and jump-started
rapid industrialization to overcome Russian backwardness. The first
Five Year Plan (1929–33) called for forced collectivization, emphasis
on heavy industry, a "furious" pace of industrialization, and proactive
state terror—a "Great Leap Forward" strategy.[18] As Stalin famously
argued in 1931, "The history of Old Russia consisted, among other
things, in continual beatings for her backwardness. She was beaten
by the Mongolian khans. Beaten by the Swedish feudals. Beaten by
the Polish-Lithuanian nobles. Beaten by the Anglo-French capitalists.
Beaten by all of them—for backwardness. For military backwardness,
cultural backwardness, governmental backwardness, industrial backwardness, agricultural backwardness. . . . We have lagged behind the
advanced countries by fifty to a hundred years. We must cover that
distance in ten years. Either we'll do it or they will crush us."[19]

As Stalin's speech suggests, he had concluded that the Soviet Union
would have to build up its industrial and military power in order to be
respected by the more advanced Western states. Britain reestablished
formal diplomatic relations with the Soviet Union in 1929, including
exchange of ambassadors, followed by the United States in 1933.[20]

During the 1920s, the Soviet Union sought desperately to obtain recognition from the Western powers, particularly Britain, and break out
of its diplomatic isolation. A social mobility strategy was precluded by
the Bolsheviks' efforts to overthrow the established international order.
Contrary to constructivism, the Soviet Union resisted pressures to conform to international norms and to accept the world order at the price
of diplomatic isolation. While the Rapallo agreement might be viewed
as an example of balancing or realpolitik, it was not an alliance. Germany wanted to maintain good ties with both the Soviet Union and the
Western states. The Soviet Union was too weak to act as a great power:
it had a weak agrarian economy, and the Red Army was not capable
of fighting a major European army. The Soviet Union was not even

recognized by most European states until 1929, and the major power clubs were closed to the regime.[21]

THE SEARCH FOR COLLECTIVE SECURITY

In the 1930s, the Soviet Union adopted a more traditional foreign policy, joining the League of Nations and forming nonaggression pacts with other states to curb Hitler, while touting Russia's great power status to legitimize its policies with the Soviet people.

From 1934 to 1939, the Soviet Union tried to cooperate with the Western states against Hitler largely for security reasons. But the major power clubs were not permeable to the Soviet Union, the Western countries were unwilling to give firm security guarantees, and its efforts to establish cooperation received a humiliating rebuff.

In reaction to Hitler's accession to power, in December 1933, the Soviet Politburo formally approved a secret resolution in favor of collective security and alliances with Western countries against Germany. The policy of collective security would be carried out by People's Commissar of Foreign Affairs Litvinov, an Anglophile who distrusted Germany and believed that peace was indivisible because a war between any two countries would inevitably draw in European powers.[22] Litvinov argued that Germany and Japan were the leading threats to peace. In his view, the Soviet Union should enter into a web of agreements with Western states, such as nonaggression pacts, disarmament agreements, regional security pacts, and a reinvigorated League of Nations.[23] At the same time, Stalin hedged against the failure to obtain such cooperation by allowing Vyacheslav Molotov, head of Sovnarkom (Council of People's Commissars), to maintain contact with Germany.[24]

An important indicator of the shift in policy was the Soviet Union's joining of the League of Nations in September 1934, and obtaining a permanent seat on the Council, after years of denouncing the organization as imperialist. A year later, as part of the Soviet collective security policy, the Soviet Union signed a mutual defense pact with France, which was a major boon to Soviet prestige but not to security, given the French failure to implement a military agreement.[25]

Stalin also began to revive Russian nationalism, using history books and rhetoric to evoke popular pride in Imperial Russia's history as a great power, despite the tsars' exploitation of the Russian people. The implication was that the Soviet Union was continuing on this path toward greatness and empire, but would go even further.[26]

At the end of 1935, Stalin decided to build a large ocean-going navy, despite the fact that the Soviet Union was a land power. Stalin insisted on large battle cruisers with heavy guns as an intrinsic element of what it meant to be a great power. His grandiose plans for ship-building were wholly fantastic, because the Soviet Union did not have industrial equipment that could construct guns and boilers of such dimensions.[27]

The "great power" mentality of Stalin and his coterie was displayed at a private celebration with the party hierarchy of the twentieth anniversary of the Bolshevik revolution in November 1937, where Stalin gave a toast: "The Russians tsars did much that was bad. They robbed and enslaved the people. . . . But they did one thing that was good—they amassed an enormous state, all the way to Kamchatka. We have inherited that state."[28]

While the Soviet Union had returned to great power circles in 1934 with its membership in the League of Nations, and its military power had earned respect, Stalin's 1937–38 purges of military officers and diplomats damaged whatever status the regime had gained. With the Soviets preoccupied with internal affairs, British Prime Minister Neville Chamberlain was able to negotiate with Hitler without consulting with the Soviet Union. The Soviet Union was not invited to the Munich conference in September 1938, where Hitler received the Sudetenland, although the Soviets had signed a mutual assistance pact with Czechoslovakia. Once again the Soviet Union was treated as a pariah, beyond the bounds of civilization, a rejection reminiscent of the 1920s.[29]

After Hitler revealed his duplicity and aggressiveness by occupying the rest of Czechoslovakia in March 1939, Litvinov proposed a set of comprehensive security guarantees to Britain and France, but received no response for several weeks. While the British were deliberating their reply to the Soviet initiative, on May 3, Litvinov was replaced by Molotov, who had no diplomatic experience, an indication of Stalin's growing impatience with the West as well as his desire to take personal control of the negotiations. Finally, on May 8, the British responded by suggesting that the Soviet Union make a unilateral declaration that it would come to the assistance of Britain and France if they decided to fight Hitler and if they desired such Soviet assistance—an offer regarded by the Soviets as humiliating. The Soviets got the impression that the British were unwilling to "place their signature side by side" with that of representatives of the Soviet Union.[30]

In response to Molotov's demands for a military as well as political agreement, the British and French sent a low-level delegation by slow merchant ship (airplanes being supposedly unavailable) to Moscow. The delegation did not arrive until August 11, 1939. As negotiations between Molotov and British and French representatives dragged, Berlin sought an invitation for German foreign minister Joachim von Ribbentrop to visit Moscow. Impatient to invade Poland, Hitler wanted to negotiate a nonaggression pact with Stalin, to eliminate the possibility of having to fight a two-front war against the Soviet Union and Britain. At Stalin's invitation, Ribbentrop arrived on August 23, and an agreement was signed that same day. In addition to the nonaggression pact, Stalin and Ribbentrop agreed upon a secret protocol that divided Eastern Europe into Russian and German spheres of influence, with the Soviet sphere including eastern Poland, Latvia, Estonia, Bessarabia, and Finland.[31] Stalin later confided to Georgy Dimitrov, the head of the Comintern: "We would rather have reached agreement with the so-called democratic countries, so we conducted negotiations. But the English and French wanted to use us as field hands and without paying us anything!"[32] Summing up Stalin's comment, from 1933 to 1939, the Soviet Union sought cooperation with the West and collective security despite only mixed success and repeated humiliation, but was largely distrusted and ostracized by Britain and France until after the Nazi invasion.[33]

ORIGINS OF THE BIPOLAR STATUS RIVALRY

Although the USSR was recognized by the West as an equal great power during World War II, between 1945 and 1947 the Grand Alliance (United States, Great Britain, and the Soviet Union) against Hitler fractured into a bipolar US-Soviet rivalry over geopolitical influence. Stalin wanted to continue Big Three cooperation after the war, but disagreement over escalating Soviet geopolitical objectives culminated in the emergence of US-Soviet rivalry.

The end of World War II left the Soviet Union as the only great power in Europe, with an army unrivaled by any other in the world except for that of the United States. Great Britain, the former bastion of world order, was declining rapidly and France was a great power in name only.

Soviet plans for the postwar period envisioned a great power concert composed of Britain, the United States, and the Soviet Union as proposed in Franklin D. Roosevelt's idea of the "Four Policemen" (which included China). The Four Policemen were later incorporated into the United Nations (UN) Security Council, where the permanent members were each given a veto, reflecting Roosevelt's desire to accommodate the status aspirations of the Soviet Union while recognizing the special responsibility of the great powers for maintaining peace. An intangible factor promoting cooperation was Stalin's desire to preserve the wartime partnership with Franklin D. Roosevelt and Winston Churchill, a relationship that must have been especially prized after the West's ostracism in the 1920s. The Big Three were a kind of private club, with its own jokes and camaraderie. Here, at least, was Stalin's reference group—men whose respect he valued. For the first time, the Soviet Union was treated as an equal great power, able to participate in world councils to draw the lines of the postwar settlement.[34]

Stalin's postwar objectives were in part derived from geopolitics and his reading of Russian history. He often used tsarist borders as a benchmark for evaluation of Soviet territorial acquisitions. He insisted on recovering territories that had been lost after the Russian revolution—the Baltic States, parts of Finland, eastern Poland, and Bessarabia (Moldavia). But he also wanted to go beyond the tsars by creating a set of client states in Eastern Europe and the Balkans. Stalin pursued the long-standing tsarist goal of control over the Turkish Straits. In Asia, he was determined to reestablish Russian influence in Xinjiang, Outer Mongolia, Manchuria, and Korea, despite the conflicts that this would create with both the Chinese Nationalists and the Chinese Communists.[35]

At the 1945 Potsdam Conference (July 17 to August 2), Stalin requested not only a sphere of influence in Eastern Europe, but also a share of the German navy, participation in the trusteeship system for former Italian colonies, and bases on the Turkish Straits. Having long believed that a great power must have a big fleet, Stalin planned to enlarge the Soviet navy after the war, an objective that would require a share of the Italian and German navies and port facilities. As for the Straits, Stalin explained to Truman: "For a great power such as Russia the question of the Straits has great significance." If a base on the Straits was unacceptable to the United States, "then give me some other base where the Russian fleet would be able to carry out repairs and re-equip and where, together with its allies, it would be able to defend Russia's rights."[36] It is noteworthy that Stalin referred to "Russia" and to its entitlement by virtue of being a "great power" as justification for a base on the Straits, rather than stressing security from an invasion from the South, which would arguably have been more persuasive to the American president.

While the Americans and the British were not willing to grant Soviet demands in the Mediterranean, the Soviets did secure their principal aims in Eastern Europe, through recognition of the Soviet-made Polish government and a new border that granted eastern Prussia to the Soviet Union. Molotov was also pleased that the procedures for drawing up the peace treaties for southeastern Europe (excluding Italy) would give the Soviet Union a dominant role. He confided to Georgy Dimitrov, the former head of the Communist International, that the decisions "in effect recognized [the Balkans] as a [Soviet] sphere of influence," apparently seeing no need to camouflage great power geopolitical categories with proletarian ideology.[37]

But this confidence in the Soviet Union's newfound status as an equal great power was upset by the explosion of an atomic bomb at Hiroshima on August 6, 1945, and another at Nagasaki three days later. The atomic bomb meant that Japan was likely to surrender before the Soviet Union could reap the benefits of intervening on the side of the United States, as promised by Roosevelt at the Yalta Conference. Stalin hurried to declare war, sending troops into Manchuria, Mongolia, North Korea, South Sakhalin, and the Kurile Islands. On August 16, Stalin renewed his request to occupy the northern half of the Japanese island, Hokkaido, the second-largest island, which would allow the Soviets to dominate the Sea of Okhotsk. Stalin's justification was that the Russian public would be incensed if the Soviets did not get a share of the occupation in view of Japan's occupation of Siberia during the civil war. Bolstered by the US atomic monopoly, however, Truman refused. "I and my colleagues did not expect such an answer," Stalin complained bitterly.[38]

Determined not to be intimidated by US efforts to exploit its atomic monopoly, at Stalin's direction, Molotov took hard-line positions on all issues at the London conference of foreign ministers in September 1945. He demanded a trusteeship over the former Italian colony Tripolitania (western Libya) so that the Soviet Union could have port facilities in the Mediterranean, a proposal that was transparently aimed at undermining the British Empire.[39]

When Secretary of State James Byrnes proposed a treaty demilitarizing Germany for twenty to twenty-five years, Molotov was at first inclined to consider the idea, but Stalin regarded the proposal as a deceptive device to distract attention from the Far East where the United States was posing as Japan's friend, to undermine the basis for Soviet alliances with Eastern Europe, and to enable the United States to play a role in European affairs equal to that of the USSR, and in conjunction with Britain, to control the fate of Europe. His reaction suggests that Stalin already viewed the United States as a rival.[40]

In another effort to gain a Soviet foothold in Japan, Molotov requested the establishment of an Allied Control Council for Japan (including Britain, the United States, China, and the Soviet Union) similar to the one for Germany, but Byrnes refused even to discuss the issue. Stalin, in an angry letter to Molotov, deemed the US response the "height of impudence" from the British and Americans "who call themselves our Allies," but who lacked a "minimal sense of respect" for the Soviet Union.[41]

Stalin ultimately broke up the conference over a procedural issue—that China and France should not be allowed to take part in discussions concerning peace treaties for the former German satellites. In Stalin's view, this was another violation of the principle that the Big Three would shape the postwar order, and was an attempt to take away the Soviet Union's hard-fought gains.[42]

When Ambassador to Moscow Averell Harriman carried a private message from Truman to Stalin at his vacation home on the Black Sea to address the procedural issue, Stalin's first indignant reaction was that "the Japanese question is not touched upon here." He complained that the Soviet Union was not being informed or consulted about the occupation of Japan. The USSR was being treated as an "American satellite in the Pacific." Perhaps it would be better for the Soviet Union to withdraw from Japan rather than remain "as a piece of furniture." Stalin ultimately accepted a face-saving solution, establishment of a purely advisory Allied Council for Japan on which the Soviet Union would be represented.[43]

In February 1946, Foreign Minister Molotov proclaimed an important change in the Soviet perception of its international position: "The USSR now stands in the ranks of the most authoritative of world powers. Now it is impossible to resolve the important issues of international relations without the participation of the Soviet Union or without heeding the voice of our motherland."[44]

A recurring theme in Soviet complaints during the postwar conferences was that Britain and the United States were preventing the Soviet Union from achieving the gains to which it was entitled by virtue of its status as a great power and a major victor in the Second World War.[45] "There is no corner of the world in which the USA cannot be seen," Molotov complained to Secretary of State Byrnes in May 1946. "The US has air bases everywhere: in Ireland, Greece, Italy, Turkey, China, Indonesia and other places and an even greater number of air and naval bases in the Pacific Ocean."[46] For Stalin, who regularly compared his territorial gains to the tsars' geopolitical reach, not to receive the same *droit de regard* and privileges as the United States was a significant humiliation.[47]

Stalin sponsored the creation of an Azeri secessionist state in northern Iran in December 1945, and then demanded an oil concession from the Iranian government as the price for withdrawing Soviet troops from northern Iran after the March 1946 deadline for their withdrawal previously negotiated with Britain. In August 1946, Stalin demanded bases on the Turkish Straits and conducted military exercises near Turkey.[48]

The US invitation to Eastern European countries to participate in the Marshall Plan to aid European recovery was the final blow for Stalin, because of the risk that the Soviet security zone in Eastern Europe would be undermined by American dollars, a domain where the Soviet Union was unable to compete. From then on, although the United States did not pose a direct threat to Soviet security, as Germany and Japan had in the 1930s, the Soviet Union embarked on a campaign of social competition against a richer and more powerful Western state. The Soviet Union added to traditional geopolitical rivalry the ideological conviction that communism would inevitably overcome the bankrupt capitalist world, based on an assumption of the inherent instability and illegitimacy of the prevailing international status hierarchy.[49]

A ONE-SIDED ALLIANCE

After defeating the Guomindang in the Chinese Civil War, Mao immediately decided to align with the Soviet Union but quickly discovered that China's dependence on Moscow was reminiscent of previous humiliations by imperialist powers. The Chinese Communists sought to improve their standing through emulation of the Soviet Union, but found themselves involved in an unequal relationship. The Chinese Communists did not want to give up their independence and dignity, but partly due to the disparity in the two states' power and level of economic development, the partnership between the Soviet Union and the PRC was inherently unequal, resulting in tensions over relative status in the Sino-Soviet alliance from the beginning.[50]

While the Soviet Union played a major role in the founding of the Chinese Communist Party in 1921, Moscow and the Comintern soon showed a patronizing attitude toward the CCP leadership, going so far as outright *diktat* (command). Mao and his colleagues blamed Moscow's advice for the CCP's near annihilation by the Guomindang in 1927. From 1932 to 1934, Mao suffered numerous humiliations at the hands of the "28 Bolsheviks" (Chinese students who had studied in Moscow) sent by the Comintern to establish Stalinist control over the leadership of the CCP. The slogan "Sinification of Marxism" (including "heretical" advocacy of the peasant road to the Chinese Revolution), put forward by Mao Zedong in 1938 and later enshrined in the CCP constitution, reflected China's urge to reaffirm national dignity in the face of pressure to slavishly follow the Soviet model. As Mao emphasized, there was "no such thing as abstract Marxism, but only concrete Marxism" applied to the "concrete conditions prevailing in China, and not Marxism abstractly used."[51] Nevertheless, the PRC had little choice but to ally with the Soviet Union because the new regime needed Soviet economic assistance and security guarantees.

After the establishment of the People's Republic of China (PRC) in 1949, the CCP leadership tried to restore the country's international prestige, which "had dwindled to almost nothing" during the post-1911 warlord era and the last years of Chiang Kai-shek's rule. Despite the Republic of China's formal membership in the Big Four (characterized by Churchill as an "absolute farce"), Chiang Kai-shek had never been accepted as an equal by Roosevelt, Stalin, or Churchill. Roosevelt did his best to grant China great power status by including it as a permanent member of the UN Security Council, as a potential counterweight to Russia in Asia and to appeal to US public opinion. But even FDR recognized that China's great power status was merely potential. Echoing China's 1919 Versailles humiliation, at the February 1945 Yalta Conference, the Big Three approved concessions to Stalin that infringed on Chinese sovereignty and territorial integrity without bothering to consult their Chinese ally. In return for entering the war against Japan within three months after Germany's surrender and for recognizing the Chinese Nationalists as the government of China, the Soviet Union would regain territory lost as a result of the earlier defeat by Japan, such as South Sakhalin and the Kurile Islands; lease the strategically important naval base of Port Arthur (Lüshun) and enjoy the use of the internationalized Manchurian port of Dalian; and have a "predominant interest" in Chinese railways in Manchuria.[52] These concessions were formalized in the August 1945 Sino-Soviet treaty of friendship and alliance, concluded under pressure of the Soviet occupation of Manchuria, which made only minor accommodations to Chiang Kai-shek. Stalin sold out his Chinese Communist allies in order to get geostrategic benefits from Chiang Kai-shek and to maintain great power cooperation. The Chinese Communists, who were not informed about the treaty until later, regarded it as a betrayal.[53]

With the establishment of the PRC, the Chinese Communists were determined to eradicate all vestiges of imperialism such as foreign concessions, spheres of influence, and unequal treaties. Their opposition to imperialism, however, did not extend to the Muslims, Mongols, or Tibetans, because of the "association of national greatness with the integrity of inherited territorial limits." As Mao triumphantly stated, "Ours will no longer be a nation subject to insult and humiliation. We have stood up." At the first meeting of the PRC Foreign Ministry in November 1949, Zhou Enlai declared the century of humiliation to be over, excoriating previous Chinese rulers who had "kneeled down to the ground to conduct China's diplomacy." In reality, Mao's "lean to one side" policy placed China in the role of a junior partner to the Soviet Union, continually threatening its status and integrity. Mao's relationship with Stalin resembled at best that of a shy student and domineering, stern teacher. Mao may have felt a sense of obligation to Stalin, who had been instrumental in helping him defeat rivals for leadership of the CCP in the mid-1930s, and had provided the Chinese Communists with generous financial support. Yet Stalin privately mocked Mao as a "caveman Marxist" and even more chillingly compared him to a radish ("red on the outside," "white on the inside").[54]

While the New China wanted to delay establishing diplomatic relations with the Western countries, fearing subversion by internal enemies colluding with foreign powers ("clean the house before entertaining guests"), Mao was eager to obtain recognition from the Soviet Union, the world's first socialist state. In addition, Mao desperately needed Soviet assistance for the construction of socialism, security against the threat of US intervention, and technology for modernization. It was to attain these objectives, as well as to remove the stain of the 1945 Soviet alliance with Chiang Kai-shek, that Mao sought and obtained an invitation to visit Moscow. In a telling indicator of Mao's inferior position in this relationship, at his first meeting with the Soviet leader on December 16, 1949, Stalin refused Mao's request to negotiate a new treaty to replace the treaty with the Guomindang. A stalemate of two weeks ensued. On Stalin's seventieth birthday, December 21, Mao was seated in a place of honor near Stalin's right. This was no favor to Mao, but was rather an attempt by Stalin to associate himself with Mao's status as the leader of the world's second communist power, who had just achieved a stunning victory. A December 24 meeting that Mao had requested with Stalin did not even bring up the issue of a treaty but instead discussed the communist parties of Japan, India, and Vietnam. Mao decided to sulk in Stalin's dacha, declining Russian invitations to sightsee. According to Mao's recollection, Stalin would not even return his phone calls. Finally, on January 2, Stalin relented and agreed to negotiate agreements on a range of issues, enabling Mao to invite Chinese Premier Zhou Enlai to Moscow.[55]

In a report to the Chinese leadership, Mao argued that the Sino-Soviet treaty would enhance the status of the PRC: "it will press the capitalist countries to play by the rules that we ourselves will set, it will be favorable for the unconditional recognition of China by various countries, [it will lead to] the cancellation of the old treaties and the conclusion of new ones, and it also will deter the capitalist countries from reckless undertakings."[56]

But not unlike the imperialist powers that had imposed "unequal treaties" on Qing China, Stalin used China's dependence to extract multiple economic and geopolitical concessions, such as recognition of Outer Mongolia's sovereignty and, in a separate secret protocol (no less humiliating), the Soviet right to transport troops across Chinese territory by rail. Another secret protocol prohibited parties from "third countries" from residence or commercial activity in Xinjiang or Manchuria. Later Mao would accuse Stalin of treating Xinjiang and Manchuria as "half-colonies." The most important concession made to the Chinese by Stalin in the February 14, 1950, Treaty of Friendship, Alliance and Mutual Assistance, was that the Soviets would withdraw from Port Arthur and the Chinese Changchun Railroad (CCR, formerly the Chinese Eastern Railway) after a peace treaty with Japan was signed, but in any case, no later than 1952.[57] The entire experience left a bad taste for Mao, who felt that Stalin had treated him as an inferior "younger brother."[58]

In general, in their treatment of the PRC the representatives of the Soviet Union, from top leaders to lower level advisers and diplomats, seemed to be utterly "oblivious to a heritage of empire in Russian history," while the legacy of the Russian imperialist past and "great-power chauvinism" (as well as fears of Soviet "great power hegemony") were integral to the Chinese perceptions of Moscow's actions and attitudes.[59]

The Sino-Soviet alliance was severely tested in the Korean War, which began when North Korean forces invaded South Korea on June 25, 1950. To Stalin's surprise, US air, naval, and ground forces under the auspices of the UN Security Council intervened to save South Korea. After General Douglas MacArthur's daring Inchon landing on September 15 turned the tide of the war and forced North Korean troops into a disorganized retreat, Stalin urgently requested that Mao send in Chinese forces.[60]

On October 8, Mao issued an order to establish the Chinese People's Volunteer Army in support of North Korea and notified Kim Il-sung of the Chinese decision. Mao gave the final order on October 13, fearing that inaction would allow the enemy "to press to the Yalu border, and the arrogance of reactionaries at home and abroad to grow." Ultimately, Mao decided to intervene in part for security reasons—to prevent US troops from establishing a base on China's borders that could encourage internal resistance—but also because of his desire to advance the cause of revolution, boost China's national pride, and elevate its international standing.[61]

China's success in forcing US troops to retreat across the 38th parallel did enhance Mao's prestige both in the international communist movement and in the United States. For the first time in 150 years, China had stood up to a powerful imperialist nation and had not lost the war. China would force the United States and other powers to accept China's great power status through a social competition strategy to defeat the US in its area of supremacy—military power.[62]

The Sino-Soviet alliance may be explained by neorealism as a balancing response to the threat posed by the United States to the two weaker powers, the Soviet Union and China. Adding to security as justification for alignment was their ideological similarity. However, given these compelling reasons for partnership, it is difficult to understand Stalin's effort to impose humiliating demands that violated the territorial integrity and sovereignty of the PRC, Mao's enduring resentment at his reception in Moscow, or the beginning of tensions in the Sino-Soviet alliance despite their shared enmity toward the United States—behaviors that reveal the kinds of status concerns that are integral to SIT. As the Korean War demonstrated, China was also competing with the United States to demonstrate its moral superiority and commitment to social justice, a strategy of social competition.

BANDUNG DISCOURSE

In the early 1950s, the position of the Western countries at the top of the status hierarchy appeared to be relatively secure. After the Korean War, China elevated its prestige through creative and flexible diplomacy aimed at transcending the bipolar rivalry, using social creativity to position itself as a diplomatic leader favoring peaceful coexistence and an end to colonialism. China advocated new international norms, distinct from those of the Cold War.

Chinese foreign minister Zhou Enlai's skillful and creative diplomacy —positioning China as a "new yet responsible member" of the world community," tempering ideological rhetoric, and cultivating warm relations based on the principles of "peaceful coexistence" with key developing nations (such as India and Indonesia)—rapidly enhanced China's international prestige during the early 1950s. The Chinese leadership placed great importance on a successful outcome of the Geneva Conference on Indochina and Korea (April–July 1954), China's first

participation in an international conference, because it would overcome the US-sponsored exclusion of the PRC and establish its status
as a major power. Contributing to the desire to attend the conference
were practical considerations relating to the need for a peaceful environment in which to focus on reconstruction and economic development after the Korean War.[63]

Before leaving for Geneva, Zhou told his aides, "China is a major
power and [we] go to Geneva to attend formally an international
conference, thus getting on the international stage." Zhou emerged as
one of the stars of the conference, mediating an agreement ending the
French-Indochina conflict, despite US attempts to ostracize him. Zhou
held out his hand to US Secretary of State John Foster Dulles, and when
the latter rudely refused to shake the Chinese foreign minister's hand,
shrugged, delighting his audience and turning what could have been a
major humiliation into a minor triumph.[64]

During a recess in the conference, Zhou visited India and Burma,
where first with Indian Prime Minister Jawaharlal Nehru and then
with Burmese Prime Minister U Nu, he announced agreement on the
Five Principles of Peaceful Coexistence: mutual respect for territorial
sovereignty, nonaggression, nonintervention in internal affairs, equality
and mutual benefit, and peaceful coexistence—the norms that would
comprise the "Bandung Discourse." That the principles were initiated
by China and were distinct from Western liberal norms enhanced the
PRC's status in a new area, apart from geopolitical competition, and
consistent with social creativity, that of promoting equal relations between states. Determined to achieve an agreement, Zhou skillfully maneuvered among British and French delegates, and persuaded Ho Chi
Minh to accept the division of Vietnam at the seventeenth parallel and
the neutralization of Laos and Cambodia. As a senior Chinese diplomat commented, China's presence at Geneva "established the PRC's
unchallengeable position as one of the Five Powers while, at the same
time, greatly expanding its influences in politics, diplomacy, economic
affairs, and culture."[65]

Even more impressive was Zhou's performance at the 1955 Bandung
conference of twenty-nine Asian, African, and Middle Eastern countries, where he announced that the Asian and African countries, despite
differences in ideologies and social systems, shared the experience of

colonialism. In private meetings, Zhou reassured other countries that China would not try to export revolution.[66]

Another indicator of China's growing desire for status was the inception in the mid-1950s of an aid program to developing countries, beginning with neighboring countries in Asia and later extending to Africa. Aid was not limited to states with revolutionary potential, but included nationalist regimes as well. China stressed light industry and agricultural projects, and offered aid on generous terms with no strings.[67]

Further enhancing China's influence in the developing world was the conscious effort made by Chinese leaders to avoid "great power chauvinism." Mao spoke of a PRC that would "stand tall and proud, but not arrogant," that would be "strong and powerful, but loved, not feared by weaker and poorer nations in the world." "Should China ever get cocky in the future, should China ever be infected by the deadly disease of great power chauvinism, everyone in the world must criticize China, denounce China," admonished Mao two decades before Deng Xiaoping's 1974 solemn pledge to this effect in the United Nations. Reacting to the 1956 Polish and Hungarian crises, China persuaded the Soviet Union to issue a formal declaration pledging more equal relations among socialist countries, in line with the Five Principles of Peaceful Coexistence.[68]

For a brief period, China pursued social creativity through the flexible diplomacy and norm entrepreneurship of Zhou Enlai, an identity management strategy authorized by Mao. Mao had hoped that diplomatic contacts with the United States would lead to recognition and resolution of the Taiwan issue, but the United States was intransigent.[69] While China achieved increased status, the US-dominated great power club was closed to China. By the late 1950s, non-ideological pragmatism in Chinese foreign policy and creative efforts to enhance China's appeal to the Third World would be jettisoned in favor of Mao's increasingly radical approach to international affairs.

SOVIET PEACEFUL COEXISTENCE
AND SUMMIT MEETINGS

After Stalin's death in March 1953, his successors briefly carried out an innovative and flexible foreign policy that improved the Soviet

Union's image and global reputation—an interlude of social creativity. Soviet leaders were reacting to Stalin's senseless belligerence and insistence on ideological conformity from allies, which had provoked a backlash from the West in the form of containment.[70] The Soviet leadership wanted to be recognized by the Western countries as a member of the great power club, as symbolized by participation in a summit meeting.

The Soviet Union captured the world's attention with a series of unilateral concessions and cooperative initiatives designed to meet President Dwight David Eisenhower's conditions for a summit meeting as expressed in his April 1953 Chance for Peace speech. Soviet diplomats helped to mediate the Korean armistice in July 1953. In September 1953, the Soviets withdrew their demands for territory from Turkey. The Soviet Union signed the Austrian State Treaty on May 15, 1955, withdrawing Soviet troops from the country. [71]

First Secretary of the Communist Party Khrushchev would accompany the mediocre Nikolai Bulganin, then chairman of the Council of Ministers, to the summit meeting at Geneva. Khrushchev, for all his pride about his peasant origins, hubris about economic "catching up and overtaking" the United States, and bluster (which overall was harmful to Soviet status), displayed acute status anxiety and an almost pathetic desire for personal acceptance by the West. As Fursenko and Naftali observe, Khrushchev "thought of the Soviet Union much as he thought of himself." He wanted "Moscow to be viewed as the equal of the West, yet he was well aware of the Soviet Union's weakness relative to the United States."[72]

Khrushchev revealed his status insecurity on numerous occasions when he made diplomatic forays into the West. On the eve of his first major diplomatic initiative with the West, negotiations with the Austrian leadership that led to the May 1955 Austrian State Treaty, Khrushchev confessed that he felt as if he were an illiterate country bumpkin preparing to visit Europe for the first time.[73] Before the July 1955 Geneva summit meeting (British Prime Minister Anthony Eden, President Eisenhower, French Premier Edgar Faure, and Premier Bulganin), Khrushchev was "morbidly suspicious" that he would not be granted the respect befitting a head of state because as head of the Communist Party he lacked a formal governmental title. When Khrushchev arrived at the summit he felt humiliated that the Soviet delegation plane looked like "an insect," compared to the airliners that transported the Western leaders.[74]

Khrushchev famously compensated for his insecurity by boorishness and bluffing. Assistant Secretary of State Livingston T. Merchant was struck by his "extraordinary" table manners and his habit of interrupting conversations with boasting about Soviet achievements (including such dubious ones as "crossing zebras with cows"). While Harold Macmillan was shocked by Khrushchev's vulgarity, he at the same time pitied the poor Russians who so obviously wanted "to be liked—even loved." The Geneva summit deadlocked over the issue of German unification. Nevertheless, what was most important for the Soviet representatives was that they had met with Western leaders and had been treated as equals.[75]

When Khrushchev toured Great Britain in April 1956 in the company of the elegant prime minister Anthony Eden, he was obsessively concerned with his attire, with not making a fool of himself, and with making a good impression on his hosts, yet he could not resist boasting about Soviet missiles that "could easily reach your island and quite a bit farther."[76]

In October 1955, Khrushchev led a Soviet delegation on a two-month tour of India, Burma, and Afghanistan to great fanfare and publicity. The Soviet Union adopted a new foreign policy of greater tolerance for nonalignment and increased outreach to the Third World, an area that Stalin had ignored. Henceforth, generous foreign aid to developing countries would be a major instrument of Soviet foreign policy, even to states that had nationalist governments. Moscow announced that it would finance the construction of a large steel complex in Bhilai, India. An important arms deal was negotiated with Egyptian President Gamal Abdel Nasser, with subsidies, in an attempt to woo him away from the United States. The ideological justification for a change in policy toward the Third World was provided at the 20th Communist Party Congress of the Soviet Union in 1956, where in addition to announcing his support for "peaceful coexistence," Khrushchev referred to the Third World as a "zone of peace," which could adopt a noncapitalist path of development that would allow for future movement toward socialism.[77]

Despite Soviet success in moving toward a less confrontational policy, after Khrushchev defeated his political opponents in an internal power struggle in 1957, Soviet foreign policy returned to aggressive competition, largely due to the perception that the forces of history were moving in the Soviet direction and that the status hierarchy was unstable.

CATCH UP AND SURPASS

Under Khrushchev, the Soviet Union made more ambitious efforts to catch up with and surpass the United States in agricultural production, influence over the Third World, nuclear weapons, even space exploration. The United States was the benchmark against which Khrushchev measured Soviet achievements—the leading capitalist power and rival for influence and prestige.[78] Khrushchev's status seeking took the form of geopolitical, economic, and scientific-technological competition with the United States.

Beginning in 1957, Khrushchev offered substantial aid and technical assistance to Guinea, Ghana, and Mali as part of the wave of decolonization, although they had noncommunist rulers, not so much to promote communization as to show the superiority of the Soviet model of development. But Soviet aid did not have much impact on the local economies because spending was focused on large-scale "prestige" projects such as stadiums, presidential palaces, and airports.[79] The Soviets had little to show for their financial investment in the form of trade or raw materials, and their prestige suffered when friendly leaders were overthrown in right-wing coups—as happened, for example, in Ghana and Mali in 1966 and 1968, respectively.[80]

After the Soviet Union launched Sputnik in October 1957, Khrushchev was euphoric about beating the United States in technological competition and radically changing the balance of power in the superpower rivalry. Suddenly a country that could not feed its own people was ahead in science and technology. In an interview with *New York Times* columnist James Reston, Khrushchev boasted: "It must be realized that the Soviet Union is no longer a peasant country." As he warned Averell Harriman, "Don't think the Soviet Union still wears bast shoes as it did when the tsar sold Alaska to you."[81]

Gratified by the international reaction to Sputnik, Khrushchev became infatuated with ballistic missiles as a shortcut to equalizing the military balance with the United States, one that would force the United States to lose its arrogance and to treat the Soviet Union with respect as a global power. Although the Soviets had not yet produced any operational missiles, Khrushchev made outrageous boasts about Soviet missile capabilities, a deception that he was able to carry out for some time because the United States did not yet have adequate aerial surveillance capabilities.[82] In early 1958, for example, he boasted that the Soviet Union would turn out missiles "like sausages on an assembly line."[83]

In a December 1958 meeting with Senator Hubert Humphrey, Khrushchev bragged about the range of Soviet missiles, promising "to spare" the senator's native city Minneapolis when "the rockets fly." Humphrey described Khrushchev as an insecure man dealing with a powerful bully who had to "pretend that he is secure," but who demonstrated "his insecurity by overstatement." British diplomats accompanying Prime Minister Macmillan on his visit to Moscow in early 1959 observed that Khrushchev displayed "an inferiority complex that still goes very deep" and that he was "[e]xtremely sensitive to any imaginary slight."[84]

The desire for the Soviet Union to be recognized as a major player in international politics contributed to Khrushchev's eagerness for détente with Eisenhower. "Who would have thought that capitalists would invite me, a worker? Look what we have achieved in these years!" exclaimed Khrushchev when he learned about Eisenhower's July 1959 invitation to visit the United States. According to Soviet UN official Arkady Shevchenko, Khrushchev viewed the invitation as an implicit admission that "the USSR was an equal with whom solutions to international problems must be sought"; a visit would "bring him and the Soviet Union prestige."[85]

Preparing for the visit, he was obsessed with the idea that the capitalists would try to humiliate him, a fear that led him to study diplomatic protocol because being denied the proper level of recognition "would have inflicted moral damage." In a telling example of his anxiety as well as ignorance about the United States, the Soviet leader was concerned about Eisenhower's decision to hold talks at Camp David, fearing that this was "a place they put people they don't trust," "where they put people in some sort of quarantine," the equivalent of Prinkipo Island near Istanbul where the Soviet delegation had been invited to meet with Western representatives in 1919, a symbol of profound diplomatic humiliation in the Soviet leader's eyes, since it was the place where "stray dogs were sent to die."[86]

Khrushchev decided to fly nonstop to the United States to make a better impression on the West, even though the only plane that had sufficient fuel capacity had experienced technical problems, causing the KGB to worry that it would crash en route. After the plane landed, it was too tall for the American motorized stairs, so that Khrushchev and his party had to climb down the emergency ladder in a rather undignified fashion. Despite this ignominious beginning, Khrushchev recalled that he felt immensely proud that the greatest capitalist power in the world, a country that had regarded Russia as unworthy or infected with some kind of plague, gave him a twenty-one-gun salute, the honors of a head of government.[87] A validation of his personal status translated into a great honor for his country.

Khrushchev was determined "not to be amazed by the grandeur of America, not to appear as an envious provincial" according to his son-in-law Aleksei Adzhubei, but instead he touted Soviet achievements, criticized decadent American popular culture (Khrushchev was supposedly offended at being invited to observe the filming of a dance number from the Twentieth Century Fox musical *Can Can*), and flaunted his humble origins before American economic elites and Hollywood celebrities.[88] He became enraged and "almost violent" when Eisenhower innocently asked whether Khrushchev was also bothered by telephone calls when he was taking a vacation, interpreting the question as implying that the Soviet Union lacked adequate telephone connections. The Soviet leader insisted that when he went swimming, telephones were even installed on the beach.[89]

The collapse of Khrushchev's relationship with Eisenhower was precipitated by the Soviet leader's desire to get back at the Americans for years of humiliating overflights of Soviet territory by U-2 spy planes. When the Soviets shot down a U-2 spy plane less than two weeks before the May 1960 Paris summit, Khrushchev decided not to disclose that the Soviets had both the plane and the pilot, to trap the United States into issuing a false cover story that he could then expose. He assumed that Eisenhower was not responsible for the surveillance mission, that it was the work of the CIA and the US military. When Eisenhower finally admitted that he had authorized the flight because spying was a "distasteful but vital necessity," Khrushchev treated this as a personal insult, a "betrayal" that "struck him in his very heart."[90] As Khrushchev told the journalists prior to his departure to the Paris summit, "I am a human being and I have human feelings. I had hopes and they were betrayed."[91] Eisenhower had called Khrushchev his "friend" at Camp David and even taught him the English word. Now, as Khrushchev complained to Prime Minister Macmillan in Paris, "his *friend* (bitterly repeated again and again), his friend Eisenhower had betrayed him."[92]

Knowing that this would almost certainly wreck the summit, Khrushchev nevertheless demanded that Eisenhower apologize for the incident to salvage Soviet prestige. As he told Macmillan at the summit, "The Soviet Union is not Cuba, not Guatemala, not Panama, not Iceland." But apologize Eisenhower would not do. Both Eisenhower and Khrushchev allowed considerations of personal prestige to outweigh their countries' national interests, as neither would swallow his pride to save possible diplomatic agreements on Berlin and a test ban, causing these issues to be continued over to the Kennedy administration.[93]

Khrushchev's boorishness would peak during the infamous October 1961 "shoe-banging" episode in the United Nations, an incident that left an indelible imprint on his image and prestige both abroad and at home. In a telling illustration of both Khrushchev's desire to impress the Western audience with his sophistication and his profound ignorance about Western diplomatic procedures and norms of civility, Khrushchev's bizarre behavior was probably a calculated gesture, "the sort that Khrushchev recollected from the prerevolutionary Russian duma and assumed still occurred in Western legislatures." As a delighted Khrushchev explained to embarrassed members of the Soviet delegation, "It was such fun! The UN is a sort of a parliament, you know, where the minority has to make itself heard one way or another."[94]

After Yuri Gagarin's 1961 pioneering space flight, the first to put a human being into space, Khrushchev proudly celebrated that "once-illiterate" and "barbaric" Russia, which the West had believed would "never become a great power," had trumped the United States in space competition. Khrushchev's exuberance carried over into domestic policy. The 1961 Program of the Soviet Communist Party solemnly promised to surpass the United States in per capita production by 1970 and usher the Soviet Union into communism by 1981.[95]

The competition between the Soviet Union and the United States extended beyond the traditional geopolitical rivalry or arms racing to include science and technology, agricultural production, and space exploration. The USSR was not just balancing US military power but competing for global status. While Khrushchev was exulting in his space triumphs, however, he was being openly challenged for supremacy within the international communist movement. Khrushchev's insecurity and eagerness to please (balanced by belligerence) were duly exploited by Mao.

THE SINO-SOVIET SPLIT: COMPETITION FOR PRIMACY

China's junior partner status in the Sino-Soviet alliance had long bothered Mao and his associates. Recurring tensions brought about by Soviet insensitivity, China's insistence on being treated as an "equal" partner, and Mao's attempts to use ideology to distinguish China from the Soviet Union all contributed to the Sino-Soviet split.

Chinese leaders resented being placed in a position of inferiority to the Soviet Union and were humiliated by what they perceived as its arrogance and imperial habits. In one telling example of the Soviets' exceptional insensitivity to China's status in the alliance, the Soviet ambassador to the PRC Pavel Yudin complained in early 1955 to the Chinese foreign minister Zhou Enlai about the absence of a monument to General Makarov, the imperial conqueror of the Russian Far East, in Lüshun (Port Arthur)—a port central to tsarist Russia's claim to control Northeast China.[96]

Mao wanted to establish China's identity separate from the Soviet Union and to achieve a global position of leadership in the international communist movement. While Mao could tolerate being subordinate to Stalin, one of the original Russian revolutionaries and the architect of the Soviet Union's victory over Hitler, he had no respect for Khrushchev, whom he regarded as immature and superficial. Khrushchev also contributed to the breakup through his obliviousness to China's status concerns, over-eagerness to please, and angry reaction to perceived slights.

There was seemingly nothing that Khrushchev could do that would satisfy Mao. Khrushchev's efforts to accommodate Mao by offering economic and political concessions backfired by causing the Chinese leader to lose respect. In 1954, Khrushchev made the mistake of visiting Mao first, which the Chinese leader construed as an indication of inferior status. Khrushchev offered Mao a long-term foreign currency loan equal to 520 million rubles and technical assistance for the construction of 141 industrial enterprises. He renounced the special privileges that Stalin had extorted from Mao, agreeing to withdraw from the naval base at Port Arthur (Lüshun), to give up special privileges in Manchuria and Xinjiang, and to dissolve the joint Sino-Soviet stock companies. Nevertheless, Mao, who respected strength above all, perceived Khrushchev as a fool and mistook his benevolence for a sign of weakness. After returning to Moscow, Khrushchev offered more benefits. He decided to help the Chinese industrialize by providing at no cost 1,400 technical blueprints of major industrial enterprises and more than 24,000 scientific-technical documents. Soviet advisers continued helping the Chinese extensively with their first Five Year Plan (1953–57), which turned out to be a great success.[97]

But instead of being grateful, Mao patronized Khrushchev. Mao criticized Khrushchev's 1956 "secret speech" denouncing Stalin, made without consulting China in advance, as "great power chauvinism." Mao later claimed that while Stalin had made some "serious mistakes" (particularly when dealing with the Chinese Revolution), overall his record was positive—revealing that Mao had arrogated to himself the authority to determine what was revisionist.[98] Thus, tensions between China and the Soviet Union emerged even before Mao's progressive radicalization culminated in an open challenge in November 1957.

Khrushchev and Mao began a game of Marxist-Leninist one-upmanship. In May 1957, when Khrushchev announced the goal of surpassing American agricultural production, Mao responded by promising to surpass the United States on every economic dimension within fifty years. When at the November 1957 celebration of the fortieth anniversary of the October revolution, Khrushchev upped the ante by proclaiming the goal of overtaking the United States economically within fifteen years, the CCP chairman in an impromptu speech boasted that China would surpass Great Britain in steel and heavy industrial production within the same period. This speech marked the origin of the "Great Leap Forward" idea, designed to liberate Chinese creativity from the shackles of Soviet economic orthodoxy and bring China to communism ahead of the Soviet Union, enabling Mao to eclipse Khrushchev as the supreme leader of the communist world. Mao viewed the Soviets' launch of Sputnik and its missile tests as proof of the superiority of the communist system over the capitalist one, thus justifying his own efforts to advance to communism quickly. At the November 1957 meeting, he proclaimed the coming victory of socialist forces in the global competition with capitalism ("the East wind was prevailing over the West wind"), challenging the Soviet idea of "peaceful coexistence" with the West. Destroying the fruits of the previous investment in the Chinese image as a "responsible" power, Mao proceeded to make a chillingly cavalier prediction about a socialist victory in a nuclear war: "If the worst came to the worst and half of mankind died, the other half would remain while imperialism would be razed to the ground and the whole world would become socialist."[99]

Although Mao referred to catching up with Great Britain, his real target was the Soviet Union.[100] As early as 1956, in his seminal article on "ten relationships," Mao suggested that "China is as much a socialist country as the Soviet Union, so I wonder if it is possible for us to get greater, quicker, better, and more economical results in building socialism." At the Eighth National Congress of the CCP in May 1958, Mao observed that as a latecomer, China could build socialism faster than the Soviet Union.[101]

Contributing to Mao's foreign policy radicalization was his belief that elite clubs were closed to China. In June 1958, Mao told the Chinese Politburo in a session devoted to foreign policy that he had reconsidered his earlier decision to enter into diplomatic contacts with the United States via the Chinese-American ambassadorial talks. "The Americans were not necessarily willing to deal with us." Nevertheless, it was an "advantage to be at an impasse with the United States."[102]

A month later, Mao launched the Great Leap Forward at home, a millenarian effort to reach the communist utopia before the Soviet Union through gigantic peasant communes, and to industrialize China within a few years by such means as backyard steel furnaces. The first commune in Henan was called the "Sputnik Commune" and special agricultural plots with higher yield targets were known as "sputnik fields." Industrialization was essential to making China a great power and an equal partner in the Sino-Soviet alliance.[103] According to Mao, the Great Leap Forward was also intended to demonstrate that China could grow faster than the Soviet Union, based on its superior developmental model.[104] Mao's "storming" approach to development, his line of building socialism "greater, faster, better, and more economically," won out over the more moderate, gradualist, and realistic program advocated by Liu Shaoqi, Zhou Enlai, Chen Yun, Li Xiannian, and Bo Yibo.[105]

Mao's radicalization accompanied his growing rebellion against China's lower-status position in Sino-Soviet relations; confronting the Soviet Union on ideological issues was a means to establish China's independence and authority. In challenging Khrushchev and insisting on the CCP's authority to interpret Marxism, Mao aimed at achieving more than an equal position—he wanted ideological supremacy over the Soviets on Marxist-Leninist issues and leadership over the world's communist movement. "The competition over interpretation of Marxism-Leninism actually was a struggle for the leadership position in the international Communist movement."[106] The Soviets might have been more developed economically and militarily, but China could be more revolutionary. Increasingly charged ideological polemics with the USSR, culminating in the struggle against Soviet "revisionism," not only reflected Mao's revolutionary philosophy, but supported his claim to be the preeminent Marxist, thereby proclaiming his "unsurpassed greatness abroad."[107] In November 1962, at a work conference on foreign affairs, China's foreign minister Chen Yi declared that "only our Chairman Mao is able to develop Marxism-Leninism. The practice of the Chinese Revolution fully proves this. [The Soviet] revisionists could not match our Chairman." Chen went on to conclude that "the center of world revolution has moved to our country." As Khrushchev acknowledged later at the June 1963 meeting of the CPSU Central Committee Presidium, the Chinese side clearly wanted "to play the first fiddle."[108]

Mao's dissatisfaction with being the inferior partner was again revealed by his explosive reaction to Moscow's request for military cooperation. In 1958, Khrushchev proposed establishing a radio station on the Chinese coast to communicate with Soviet submarines in the Pacific and a "combined" submarine fleet. Mao viewed Khrushchev's sincere request for military cooperation between allies as a substitute for helping the Chinese build their own nuclear submarines and a serious infringement of Chinese sovereignty, reminiscent of the joint stock companies that Khrushchev himself had renounced. In his July 1958 meeting with the Soviet ambassador, some of Mao's accumulated resentment and grievances spilled out, including his perceived isolation during his 1950 visit to Moscow, the "arrogance" of Anastas Mikoyan (a confidant of Stalin who visited Mao in January 1949), and the refusal by Soviet advisers to listen to Chinese experience. Mao accused the Soviet leadership of viewing the Russians as first-class people but the Chinese as "among the inferior who are dumb and careless," comparing the Soviet-Chinese relationship to that "between father and son or between cat and mice."[109]

In response to Mao's belligerence, Khrushchev made a secret visit to Beijing at the end of July in a futile effort to smooth relations, but he was subjected to Chinese humiliation and condescension. When Khrushchev arrived at the airport, there was no red carpet or honor guard. Mao refused to listen to Khrushchev's explanation about why a "common fleet" was in both countries' strategic interests.[110]

The following day, Mao (always proud of his swimming abilities and obviously trying to show off his superior skills) deliberately attempted to humiliate the clumsy Soviet leader by unexpectedly proposing that they take a dip in the swimming pool. Khrushchev paddled around with a life belt, while Mao dove into the deep end and skillfully demonstrated several strokes. As Mao's physician, who was present at the scene, observed in his memoirs, Mao "was deliberately playing the role of the emperor, treating Khrushchev like a barbarian come to pay tribute." Mao further offended and angered his guest by bragging that China was entering communism before the Soviet Union, thanks to the Great Leap Forward achievements. Convinced that Khrushchev was using China as a "pawn" to improve Soviet relations with the United States, Mao decided not to inform the Soviet leader about his plans to shell islands in the Taiwan Strait several weeks later, thereby challenging Soviet leadership of the communist camp.[111]

Perceiving that China had nearly entangled the Soviet Union in nuclear war with the United States over a few islands, Khrushchev began to reconsider his 1957 agreement to provide the Chinese with a prototype nuclear weapon. On June 20, 1959, the Soviets informed the Chinese that due to the upcoming negotiations for a test ban with the United States, the Soviet Union could not supply the Chinese with nuclear weapons, which merely caused the Chinese to accelerate their nuclear program. As a symbol of Beijing's defiance, the first Chinese nuclear weapon was code-named "596" in reference to the year and month of Khrushchev's withdrawal of the earlier offer.[112]

The Sino-Soviet status competition was turbocharged by Mao's and Khrushchev's clash of personalities and their contest for personal prestige, which produced multiple displays of anger and attempts to insult and denigrate one another. During the Chinese visit to Moscow in November 1957, Khrushchev treated the delegation with far greater respect than Stalin had shown the Chinese in 1950, but Mao complained about Soviet snobbishness, using every opportunity to display disrespect for his hosts, rudely interrupting Khrushchev's prolonged dinner speech and walking out of a performance of Swan Lake. After Khrushchev's visit to the United States, during what was to be his last meeting with Mao, in October 1959, the Soviet leader offended the Chinese—already resentful at being second on the Soviet leader's itinerary—by requesting the release of five US prisoners held on suspicion of espionage. Adding to the Chinese leader's irritation, Mao had learned about Khrushchev's comment in Poland that the Chinese communes reflected the ideas of people who "do not properly understand what communism is or how it is to be built."[113] Khrushchev infuriated the Chinese further by blaming China for several armed border skirmishes with India, which grew out of a March 1959 rebellion in Tibet that led to the flight of the Dalai Lama to India, and was followed by increased Indian attention to Chinese incursions into Indian territory. The foreign minister Chen Yi accused Khrushchev of being an opportunistic "time-server" in collusion with the American imperialists.[114] Later, among the Soviet delegates in a room that he must have known was bugged, Khrushchev ridiculed his Chinese hosts by rhyming their names with Russian obscenities, referring to Mao as an "old galosh" (something that should be thrown out), an insult that he would repeat in February and May 1960 in the presence of Chinese representatives.[115] In May 1960, at the Romanian Communist Party Congress, Khrushchev labeled Mao "a Buddha who gets theory out of his nose." Challenged and mocked by Chinese Central Committee Party member Peng Zhen, Khrushchev impulsively decided to pull all Soviet advisers out of China immediately, precipitating the cancellation of 343 contracts and 257 scientific and technological cooperation projects, despite protests from Soviet officials in charge of the program that doing so would deprive the Soviet Union of information and leverage.[116]

When the Great Leap failed, Mao's offensive extended to criticism of Soviet foreign policy, especially Khrushchev's notion of a peaceful transition to communism and peaceful coexistence with capitalist countries. Mao, infuriated that he was not consulted during the Cuban Missile Crisis, accused Khrushchev of both "adventurism" for deploying the missiles and of "capitulationism" for withdrawing them. Mao clearly relished Khrushchev's humiliation and believed that such a major blow to Soviet prestige in the Third World would enable China (and its preeminent leader) to position itself as a genuine protector of developing countries and the leader of the world revolution. Khrushchev was concerned that Chinese propaganda could persuade Cuba, which was outraged by the Soviet decision to remove the missiles, to break openly with the Soviet Union, which would have been a "major loss to Soviet prestige, and for Khrushchev's self-perception as a great revolutionary leader."[117]

The Sino-Soviet status competition spilled over into border issues. When Khrushchev responded to Beijing's post–Cuban crisis criticisms by deriding Chinese accommodation of British and Portuguese colonialism in Hong Kong and Macao, the Chinese side listed all Sino-Russian treaties from the nineteenth century as unequal treaties, thereby raising the territorial issue with the Soviet Union. While the Sino-Soviet border issue was merely a symptom of the rift between the two countries, it was also at the root of the confrontation in the sense that it represented China's historic humiliation in the nineteenth century, when Russia had acquired large tracts of Chinese land. In 1964, after the Sino-Soviet rift grew significantly wider, in a conversation with the Soviet ambassador Stepan Chervonenko, Peng Zhen, a prominent member of the Politburo, compared the Soviet leadership to "gods" and "tsars," a revealing reference to Chinese memories of humiliation by the Russian Empire, suggesting that he was less disturbed by Soviet ideological "revisionism" than he was by Khrushchev's "great power arrogance."[118]

For the Soviet side, Chinese territorial claims brought back historic fears of invasions from the East. In September 1964, commenting on Mao's famous slogan about "the East wind prevailing over the West wind," Khrushchev compared the CCP chairman to Chinggis Khan. The revived specter of the "yellow peril" contributed to the Soviet leadership's abandonment of ideological differences as the explanation for conflict with China and their reversion to the image of China as an alien and culturally inferior civilization. For example, Khrushchev praised the late nineteenth-century Russian explorer Nikolai Przheval-sky's racist and derogatory writings about the Chinese (a "treacherous and cowardly set of thieves" that "only respect force"), as prescient, "like it was written today," recommending that his subordinates read where "he writes about the evil, hypocrisy, insidiousness [and] cunning of the Chinese." The negative Soviet image of China persisted after Khrushchev's removal from power. During the Cultural Revolution, at-tacks on Soviet diplomats in China increased skepticism about Chinese civility—Beijing's respect for international law, diplomatic protocol, and elementary norms of international behavior. In his 1973 conversa-tions with Nixon, Brezhnev referred to the Chinese as "not honorable," "spiteful," and "exceptionally sly and perfidious." Brezhnev even com-plained to Kissinger that the Chinese "are certainly beyond the capacity of a European mind to fathom."[119]

Arguably, the Sino-Soviet alliance served both states' interests. From the Chinese point of view, trade with the Soviet Union helped compen-sate for the Western economic embargo; the alliance and the Soviet Union's nuclear guarantee assured China's security; and Soviet techni-cal assistance played a critical role in China's modernization and eco-nomic development. For the Soviet Union, good relations with China bolstered Soviet bargaining power and influence in its rivalry with the United States. The Sino-Soviet split was manifested in the form of ideo-logical debates and polemics, but the source of these differences needs to be explicated.[120] A major factor in the breakup of the alliance was the relative imbalance in international power and status. While many alliances are unequal, the imbalance was intolerable to China, which historically had accepted tribute from smaller states rather than inter-acting with equal powers. The differences were even more difficult to reconcile because of the rivalry over leadership of the international communist movement, fought in the domain of principle, which did not allow for compromise.[121] For the Chinese, the illegitimacy of the status hierarchy in the world communist movement, and the prospect that it could be reversed by Mao, encouraged social competition with the Soviet Union.

Khrushchev was placed in an unenviable position because he had to compete with two rivals at the same time—with China for ideological supremacy and with the United States for military superiority. These two interests converged in Khrushchev's decision to put missiles in Cuba.

THE CUBAN MISSILE CRISIS

Khrushchev's attempt to claim nuclear parity with the United States using bluff and boasts was eventually exposed by the Kennedy administration, motivating him to provoke the most dangerous crisis of the Cold War.

At the June 1961 Vienna summit, President John F. Kennedy prematurely characterized Sino-Soviet forces and the forces of the United States and Western Europe "as being more or less in balance." Kennedy's "admission" was greatly valued by Khrushchev, who cited it in numerous speeches and his memoirs.[122] But to Khrushchev's disappointment, early acknowledgement of Soviet parity did not extend to the political and diplomatic spheres. In response to Kennedy's request for mutual restraint in Third World conflicts, Khrushchev objected that the United States seemed to want the USSR "to sit like a schoolboy with its hands on the desk." The Soviet Union could not accept being told, "don't poke your nose" in, especially since the United States had "spread its forces all over." He accused the United States of wanting to "humiliate the USSR," which could not be accepted. Khrushchev later protested to Ambassador Llewellyn Thompson that US policymakers frequently referred to various Cold War issues as matters of prestige, but "never seemed to take Soviet prestige into account."[123] At the Vienna summit, Khrushchev renewed his six-month deadline for an agreement on Berlin, threatening to sign a separate peace with East Germany that would end US rights of access to West Berlin.[124]

But in an October 17 speech, at the cost of substantial prestige, Khrushchev backed down from his ultimatum, on the grounds that negotiations on Berlin's status were under way. Despite this comedown, Kennedy was concerned that Khrushchev might still underestimate US resolve. Accordingly, in October Kennedy had Deputy Defense Secretary Roswell Gilpatric reveal that, based on satellite surveillance and the reports of a spy in the Soviet military intelligence service, the image of a "missile gap" in the Soviets' favor, cultivated by Khrushchev, was a myth. In another embarrassing development for Khrushchev, in February 1962, Secretary of Defense Robert McNamara informed the Senate Foreign Relations Committee that the United States had "clear military superiority for major nuclear conflict."[125]

Given the exposure of Khrushchev's bluffs and his failure to achieve any changes in West Berlin, the desire to redress the balance of power and to attain greater respect from the United States must have played a prominent role in Khrushchev's decision to put Soviet missiles in Cuba. Consistent with that interpretation, in conversation with the recently appointed Soviet ambassador to the United States Anatoly Dobrynin, Khrushchev characterized US efforts to attain nuclear superiority as "particularly arrogant" and suggested that it was high time that Washington's "long arms were cut shorter."[126]

In addition, the Soviet Union's most recent ideological triumph, the Cuban revolution, was in jeopardy. Soviet intelligence had picked up indications of the US program of covert operations in Cuba designed to subvert and overthrow the communist regime, despite the fiasco of the US invasion of the Bay of Pigs. Khrushchev recalled that "the fate of Cuba and the maintenance of Soviet prestige in that part of the world preoccupied me." Loss of Cuba "would gravely diminish our stature throughout the world, but especially in Latin America."[127]

For Khrushchev, putting Soviet missiles in Cuba increasingly emerged as a solution to all his difficulties. While strolling on the Black Sea with Soviet Defense Minister Marshal Rodion Malinovsky, the Soviet leader grew indignant when he was reminded that the United States had nuclear missile sites on the opposite shore in Turkey that were capable of destroying major centers in Russia and the Ukraine in six to seven minutes. Khrushchev suggested putting missiles in Cuba and complained of the Soviets' "double inequality" vis-à-vis the United States—inequality in the number of weapons and inequality in means of delivery. In spring 1962, Khrushchev decided to secretly install intermediate range ballistic missiles in Cuba that could reach US territory.[128] By "throwing a hedgehog down Uncle Sam's pants" in Cuba, Khrushchev hoped to restore Soviet prestige and psychological parity. He predicted to the Soviet ambassador to Cuba Alexander Alekseyev that "we will be able to talk to the Americans as equals" after the missiles were in place.[129]

Khrushchev repeatedly stated to US representatives that he intended to get a settlement of the Berlin problem after the US congressional elections in November 1962, perhaps planning to unveil the missiles during his scheduled visit to the United Nations. But the missiles were discovered before the installation was completed. In an October 27, 1962, letter to Kennedy, Khrushchev revealed his consternation at the US demand that he remove the missiles: "How then can recognition of our equal military capacities be reconciled with such unequal relations between our great states? This is irreconcilable."[130]

In part, Khrushchev was acting on the basis of security considerations, as predicted by neorealism; he was trying to restore the nuclear balance. However, status concerns and the desire to get back at the United States for perceived past humiliations contributed to his choice of means—a secret installation in Cuba that would embarrass Kennedy and put him in a difficult political position, while providing a shortcut to overcoming strategic inferiority.[131] Khrushchev's attempt to overcome the imbalance of power in one dramatic gesture might be attributed to his impatient and impulsive personality, as well as to the lack of checks on his personal authority within the Soviet decision-making system, but it could also be argued that the strains of acting as a superpower without having the necessary material base offered incentives for the use of quick fixes and risky gestures. Khrushchev's insecurity combined with his acute desire for great power status frequently led him to behave belligerently, alarming and threatening the United States and other Western powers, when he felt insulted or humiliated.

ORIGINS OF THE STRATEGIC TRIANGLE

Maoist radicalism in foreign policy culminated in Cultural Revolution diplomacy, with self-imposed isolation (during the 1969 border war with the Soviet Union, the PRC could rely only on Albania, North Korea, and Pakistan for support of its policies) and an increasingly dangerous "dual adversary policy" toward the Soviet Union and the United States.[132] What Beijing lost in international standing by the late 1960s, however, it eventually regained many times over in the perception of Washington in the course of rapidly improving relations beginning in the early 1970s. China achieved the height of its status in the twentieth century as part of the "strategic triangle" due to the policies of the Nixon administration. The PRC was able to compensate for inferior capabilities and improve its status through flexible diplomacy.

In 1969–70, fears of a Soviet attack motivated Mao to decide to seek better relations with the United States; the Soviet Union had over a million troops on the border with China. Whereas previous US administrations had ostracized the PRC or "Red China," President Richard Nixon favored opening relations with China to gain leverage over the Soviet Union and assistance in ending the war in Vietnam. The Nixon administration was motivated to accommodate China's status aspirations in order to preserve the balance of power, which was endangered by the improvements in Soviet strategic forces relative to those of the United States.[133] Status incentives for China factored into Nixon-Kissinger's blueprint for strategic rapprochement with Beijing and the "strategic triangle" diplomacy of the early 1970s. As Kissinger argued, preparing for his July 1971 secret visit to the PRC, a Sino-American summit would be "spectacular proof" of the Chinese goal to be recognized as a great power. Nixon's hand-written notes on dealing with Mao before his PRC visit even included "Treat him (as Emperor)," based on advice from Kissinger and US foreign and intelligence officials.[134]

While Mao probably would have sought some form of rapprochement with the United States in any case for security reasons, the immediate status benefits for the PRC facilitated further evolution of the Sino-American partnership. At the outset of his secret negotiations with Zhou Enlai, Kissinger alleviated the problem of Taiwan—a critical identity and prestige issue for Beijing—by endorsing Beijing's "no two Chinas; no one China, one Taiwan; no independent Taiwan" formula. Kissinger also promised diplomatic recognition of the PRC during Nixon's second term in office, thus implicitly accepting the outcome of the Chinese civil war as legitimate. After Nixon's 1971 announcement of his China trip, the UN General Assembly voted against the US-sponsored (but noticeably half-hearted) motion allowing Taiwan to keep its UN seat, making way for the PRC to assume the seat and for the humiliating expulsion of the Taiwanese delegation. Soon after, major American allies in Asia, including Japan, switched their diplomatic allegiance to Beijing from Taipei.[135]

The US reaction to the December 1971 India-Pakistan war illustrates the heightened attention to China's security and prestige. Rather than approaching the crisis as a regional development or treating it first and foremost as a humanitarian catastrophe, Nixon and Kissinger viewed it primarily in the context of the global Cold War competition for power and status with the Soviet Union. Nixon and Kissinger, who by that time had developed an intense dislike of India and its leader Indira Gandhi, believed that the Soviet Union was trying to humiliate China and secondarily the United States by pushing India to dismember Pakistan. But they were also preoccupied with the potential consequences of the Indian-sponsored secession of East Pakistan for China's standing in the region. Their concern was that China's attempt to support its ally Pakistan could provoke a Soviet intervention to defend India, in line with the August 1971 Indo-Soviet mutual security treaty. Kissinger expected China to intervene, and even encouraged China to mobilize its troops to threaten India, but the Chinese were evasive. According to Kissinger, "Nixon understood immediately that if the Soviet Union succeeded in humiliating China, all prospects for world equilibrium would disappear." Nixon and Kissinger sent a US naval task force led by the USS *Enterprise* toward the Bay of Bengal as a warning to India not to invade West Pakistan and if that failed, to deter the Soviet Union from moving against China.[136]

Kissinger's first impressions of the Chinese leaders during his secret visit were surprisingly flattering and full of favorable comparisons with the much better known Soviets. He reported to Nixon that the Chinese were pleasant to negotiate with since they were open about their key priorities, a refreshing change after the Soviets' pettiness and bluster. The usually skeptical Kissinger recalled that his chief interlocutor Zhou Enlai was "one of the two or three most impressive men" he had ever met, "a figure out of history." Zhou was "[u]rbane, infinitely patient, extraordinarily intelligent, subtle," navigating through diplomatic exchanges "with easy grace." Zhou's firmness during negotiations, he advised Nixon, was "not the kind of brutalizing toughness which we have come to expect from the Russians, but rather a hardness and consistency of purpose derived from fifty years of revolutionary experiences."[137]

During Nixon's 1972 trip to China, Kissinger was even more impressed by Mao, recalling that he had met "no one, with the possible exception of Charles de Gaulle (whom Nixon revered), who so distilled raw, concentrated willpower." Fascination with Mao's personality was shared by other members of the American delegation, who believed so strongly in the CCP chairman's mythical wisdom that they searched for (and usually discovered) "deeper meaning" in Mao's frequently scattered remarks. After his meeting with Mao during a subsequent trip to China in February 1973, Kissinger reported to Nixon that the CCP leader "radiates authority and wisdom" and that he was "even more impressed by the grandeur of the Chairman this time than last."[138]

President Nixon's 1972 visit to China was heavily laced with status-related symbolism. That the leader of the West came to see Mao seemed to confirm China's renewed centrality in international politics. Nixon's public handshake with Premier Zhou Enlai in Beijing airport was meant not just to atone for the insult inflicted by Dulles in Geneva eighteen years before. That this slight loomed large in the Chinese memory was confirmed by Chinese officials' bringing up the issue in the first few minutes of Kissinger's secret visit, asking him if he intended to shake Zhou's hand. More importantly, the handshake symbolized that the PRC was treated as an equal by a Cold War superpower. As Margaret Macmillan emphasizes in her description of Chinese behavior at the opening banquet honoring Nixon in Beijing, "It was about status, about fears of being snubbed as Dulles had once snubbed Zhou, and about losing or maintaining prestige in the eyes of the world or, equally important, in the eyes of the Chinese and the American peoples. It also carried echoes of the long and sometimes difficult relationship between the Chinese and foreigners."[139]

Nixon's visit confirmed the new US position on Taiwan and the PRC's status as the government of China. The Shanghai Communiqué signed by both sides at the end of Nixon's visit, despite deliberately ambiguous wording inserted by the American side, essentially accepted the "one China" principle insisted upon by Beijing. In his private communications with the Chinese leaders, Nixon reiterated Kissinger's earlier promises regarding Taiwan and diplomatic recognition. Another indication of the heightened status of the Chinese leadership and their developing "special relationship" with the United States was Kissinger's sharing during the meeting of intelligence data about the Soviet military and top secret information about US-Soviet negotiations on security matters. In his toast at the opening banquet in Beijing, Nixon spoke about the United States and China together solving global problems, neglecting to mention the Soviet Union, an omission that Brezhnev noticed and later complained about.[140]

During his conversations with Nixon and Kissinger, Zhou frequently referred to China's relative weakness and backwardness, emphasizing that China had no ambitions to become a superpower. Chinese modesty impressed Nixon, who wrote approvingly in his memoirs, "Unlike the Soviets, who ritually insisted that everything they had was the biggest and the best, the Chinese were almost obsessed with self-criticism and with seeking advice on how to improve themselves." But Nixon entirely missed the significance of Chinese leaders' diffidence. As Kissinger now observes in retrospect, the Chinese intended to pursue a different kind of great power status, one based not on power but on moral rectitude, similar to Confucius's. Zhou's self-deprecation was designed to establish the moral high ground for his country, positively distinguishing it from the "hegemonic" superpowers, the United States and the Soviet Union.[141]

Mao made this idea explicit in his "Three Worlds" concept, articulated by Vice Premier Deng Xiaoping in his April 1974 address to the UN General Assembly, castigating the behavior of both superpowers. The First World consisted of the two superpowers, the United States and the Soviet Union, who were seeking world hegemony, subjecting other countries to their "control, subversion, interference or aggression." The Second World included the developed countries, both East and West. The real power, however, lay with the Third World. Deng then touted the Chinese struggle against colonialism, imperialism, and hegemonism, and finished by solemnly promising that the PRC would never develop superpower ambitions, unlike the Soviet Union, the imperialist superpower, "which flaunts the label of socialism." While including some elements of international class struggle rhetoric, the "Three Worlds" concept also suggested that the Third World countries would have to confront the problem of economic development, creating ideological space for Deng's later policies.[142]

Deng's statement, which reflected Mao's ideas, also shifted China's policy focus from seeking world revolution to establishing better relations with "reactionary" states, partly because Mao recognized that prospects for revolution were not promising. Such ideological creativity and individual leadership are not predicted by constructivism. Mao acknowledged that the status hierarchy was stable—there were only two superpowers—but he was attempting to enhance China's position and to differentiate it from the US and the Soviet Union by inventing a new category of major power—not a superpower—but a leader of the Third World. For the Chinese, the terms "superpower" and "hegemony" both had negative connotations of bullying and power politics. While the Soviet Union pursued the traditional path to status through military power and global power projection capabilities, the Chinese would choose the "princely way" of leadership by moral example.[143]

DÉTENTE AND THE PROMISE OF US-SOVIET EQUALITY

From 1971 to 1973, the United States accepted both Soviet and PRC claims to be global players, ushering in a period of mutual cooperation. But the US defeat in the Vietnam War and increased Soviet military capabilities convinced some Soviet leaders that the Soviet Union had the right to act as a global power by intervening in the Third World. With the international status hierarchy perceived as unstable, the Soviet Union adopted more assertive policies, undermining the political basis for the fragile détente relationship with the United States.

American recognition of the Soviet Union's attainment of nuclear parity initially contributed to unprecedented cooperation. Having abandoned Khrushchev's "quick fix" solution to the problem of military competition with the West, the Brezhnev leadership concentrated on achieving a real military strategic balance with the United States. By the early 1970s, the Soviet effort was visible and impressive: this time, missiles were really coming out of Soviet factories "like sausages"; the Soviets had matched and in some respects even surpassed American nuclear deployments quantitatively while retaining their conventional force superiority. The Brezhnev leadership also acquired global power projection capabilities, including a blue-water navy, airlift and sealift capacity, and amphibious and airborne assault forces—military forces that were unrelated to defense of the homeland.[144]

As the détente of the 1970s evolved, Soviet leaders felt vindicated by US recognition of Soviet military parity and the shift in the world's "correlation of forces." As Foreign Minister Andrei Gromyko proudly put it in 1971, virtually replicating Molotov's 1946 statement, détente meant that "there was no issue facing the world community that could be settled without the participation of the Soviet Union."[145]

Public ideological triumphalism and portrayal of Soviet superiority notwithstanding, privately Soviet leaders continued to be far less confident about their status than their official rhetoric suggested. After all, despite periodic Soviet triumphs and intense efforts to make other countries believe in its economic and military might—Gorcha-kov's "dressing up" once again—the USSR remained by most accounts at best the "junior" superpower. Henry Kissinger recounts that on his first meeting with Soviet leader Leonid Brezhnev, "[h]e expressed his pleasure when in my brief opening remarks I stated the obvious: that we were approaching the summit in a spirit of equality and reciprocity. What a more secure leader might have regarded as cliché or condescension, he treated as a welcome sign of seriousness." While, according to Kissinger, Brezhnev "boasted of Soviet strength, one had the sense that he was not really sure of it. . . . [He] seemed to feel in his bones the vulnerability of his system." Whereas Khrushchev manifested his insecurity in boasting and bombast, Brezhnev channeled his lack of confidence into a drive for recognition through negotiation and co-operation. In a memorandum before the May 1972 summit, Kissinger advised Nixon that for Brezhnev a meeting with the president fulfilled a "deep seated personal need to be accepted as an equal," an observation that Nixon underlined.[146]

Tellingly, Brezhnev and his colleagues attached great importance to the Soviet-American Basic Principles Agreement (BPA) of 1972 because it contained rhetoric about equality as a basis for the US-Soviet dé-tente relationship. Brezhnev told Nixon that he regarded the BPA as the most important achievement of the May 1972 summit, more important than the SALT I agreements. According to Brezhnev's foreign policy assistant, the general secretary attached the most significance to the principle of equality as a basis for US-Soviet détente. Ambassador Do-brynin recalled that "the summit and its documents symbolized mutual recognition of parity between the Soviet Union and the United States as great powers." In May 1973, on his visit to the Politburo hunting lodge to prepare for the Soviet leader's visit to the United States in June, Kissinger began each session with the "mantra" that during his American trip, Brezhnev would be treated as an equal, whereupon the general secretary would rise from his seat, walk around the table, and embrace him.[147] During his trip to the United States, Brezhnev's con-cern that he appear equal to Nixon led to insistence on the installation of a telephone to Moscow and Washington at every location, including the San Clemente airport, although he never picked up the phones. Brezhnev proposed to reach a "gentleman's agreement" on the key is-sues discussed and proudly emphasized the special role played by both superpowers in international politics. "Are we to blame for being big? Are we to blame for being strong?" asked the Soviet leader. "Neither the United States nor the Soviet Union can turn themselves into a Luxembourg, where the entire army is made up of 78 policemen."[148]

Kissinger and Nixon, on the other hand, did not take the BPA agreement seriously, regarding it as harmless rhetoric. Dobrynin observed in retrospect that "the administration did not give away much by signing the document," which recognized Soviet equality only in the field of "mutual security and armaments."[149]

The United States was willing to accept Soviet nuclear parity but not political equality. Contrary to Soviet expectations, the United States did not believe that the Soviet Union by virtue of its strategic equality had the right to act as the United States did—to project power globally, station military forces close to the other superpower, acquire overseas bases, or support regime change in small and medium-size states. One reason for this refusal was that the United States conception of international status was significantly broader than the Soviet one, and included economic development and political influence as key constituents. As Kissinger explained, "For centuries it was axiomatic that increases in military power could be translated into almost immediate political advantage. It is now clear that new increments of strategic weapons do not automatically lead to either political or military gains."[150]

In contrast, Soviet leaders believed that détente signified recognition of Soviet-American equality and the increasing safety of the superpower rivalry in peripheral areas. According to Gorbachev's adviser Georgy Shakhnazarov, Yuri Andropov, chief of the Central Committee Department on Liaisons with Communist and Worker Parties in the sixties, commented, "We and the Americans hold each other at a distance based on mutual respect. . . . The struggle shifted to the areas where both sides can wage it without directly harming themselves."[151]

The Soviets were initially reluctant to intervene decisively in the 1974–75 Angolan civil war, which followed a left-wing coup in Portugal and subsequent Portuguese plans to withdraw from its colony, for fear of negative repercussions for US-Soviet relations. However, Cuban pressure and, decisively, the South African invasion of Angola impelled the Soviet Union to make a commitment, which included transporting 12,000 Cuban soldiers and heavy weapons to assist the MPLA (Popular Movement for the Liberation of Angola) in their struggle against US-backed factions FNLA (National Front for the Liberation of Angola) and UNITA (National Union for the Total Liberation of Angola)—the first such intervention by the Soviet Union. With Cuban advisers and Soviet equipment, the MPLA had defeated both the FNLA and UNITA by spring 1976. The Soviet leadership could take satisfaction in having supported its ally with troops and weapons, defeating the United States and its regional allies in an area 5,000 miles away from Moscow.[152]

The Soviet victory in Angola, along with the US loss of South Vietnam, contributed to a Soviet perception that the global "correlation of forces" was changing, with the world balance shifting in their direction. In other words, the international status hierarchy was unstable as well as illegitimate, conditions that were conducive for a social competition strategy. A new wave of social revolutions in the Third World created new opportunities for the Soviet Union to increase its power and prestige and to promote the Soviet developmental model.[153]

In the view of Odd Arne Westad, based on Russian documents, "the main foreign policy aim for Soviet involvement in Africa was to score a series of inexpensive victories in what was perceived as a global contest with Washington." Moscow's interpretation of détente as conferring an "equal right to meddle" in different corners of the world and the belief that Soviet military power ensured US interest in cooperation quickly clashed with Washington's continuing unwillingness to grant the Soviet Union political equality.[154]

Although initially reluctant to get involved in Ethiopia, the Soviet leadership was won over in 1976 by the promise that the radical military leader Major Mengistu Haile Mariam, who later took power in a coup, intended to pursue a Marxist-Leninist path of development modeled on that of the Soviet Union. Beginning in September 1977, in response to a Somali invasion, the Soviet government airlifted $1 billion in military equipment to Ethiopia in the largest Soviet-directed military intervention since the Korean War. A Soviet general directed military operations for the successful Ethiopian offensive to recover the Ogaden (Ethiopian territory claimed by Somalia), including over 11,600 Cuban troops and 6,000 Cuban advisers and technicians, supported by a thousand Soviet military personnel. Although the effort cost the Soviet Union its investment in Somalia, including a naval base, in the view of the Soviet leadership, through its intervention in the Horn of Africa the Soviet Union had demonstrated that it was a global power able to orchestrate political developments in far-off territories. By the end of 1978, however, while most officials in the Foreign Office and CPSU regarded the Ethiopian intervention as proof of the Soviet Union's new superpower position, some International Department and KGB experts were beginning to question whether the Soviet Union's new socialist allies—Iraq, South Yemen, Ethiopia—were genuinely progressive or were simply drains on the Soviet treasury.[155]

The 1979 Soviet intervention in Afghanistan was motivated by security fears as well as the desire to prevent loss of prestige. The Soviet leadership had been surprised by the April 1978 coup by a radical Marxist faction in Afghanistan, but felt obligated to support the feuding Afghan Communists despite their lack of political skills, which were reflected in extreme leftist reforms in the countryside that provoked an Islamist insurgency in March 1979. Although the Politburo initially ruled out sending Soviet troops to prop up the Afghan regime, a small group within the Soviet leadership engineered a winning coalition in December 1979, when an Islamic revolution in Iran, a failed KGB assassination attempt on the leader Hafizullah Amin, and surreptitious efforts by Amin to contact the United States made it appear likely that Afghanistan was in danger of becoming either a US base or a center of radical Islam on Soviet borders. While the Soviets did not anticipate that their intervention would cost them US-Soviet détente, relations with the Carter administration had already deteriorated so that seemingly there was little for the Soviets to lose.[156]

When the Carter administration charged that Soviet involvement in Africa and Afghanistan violated the rules of détente, Soviet leaders accused the United States of practicing double standards and denying to Moscow what Washington did on a routine basis. Détente broke down in part over disagreements as to whether the Soviets could emulate American behavior. According to Soviet Ambassador Dobrynin, in several meetings of the Soviet Politburo that he attended in 1977–78 in Moscow to discuss Soviet policy toward Angola, Ethiopia, and Somalia, there was no sense that the United States had legitimate concerns. The participants included Brezhnev, Defense Minister Dmitry Ustinov, Foreign Minister Gromyko, KGB head Yuri Andropov, the ideologist Mikhail Suslov, and the chief of the International Department of the Communist Party of the Soviet Union Boris Ponomarev. Dobrynin suspected that top generals supported by the Defense Ministry "privately played on Brezhnev's vanity on the theory that all this somehow demonstrated the Soviet Union was already a world power to be reckoned with." Ideology was then used to justify opportunistic Soviet intervention in African conflicts that the Soviet Union had not brought about. Their new status as a global superpower gave the Soviets the impression that they could send troops abroad without damaging détente with the United States. After all, did the United States consult with the Soviet Union before overthrowing a government in Chile?[157]

Soviet status aspirations gave the military an increasingly important voice in the formulation of foreign policy in the developing world. The deputy head of the International Department of the Central Committee Karen Brutents recalled: "In the second half and especially toward the end of the 1970s the weight of the military in the formation and conduct of our 'Third World' policy grew. The Soviet bid for a global presence, reinforced by the acquisition of strategic parity, facilitated by the possibilities of moving our forces great distances, by the construction and appearance on the open sea of 'the great fleet,' required the creation of strong points in various regions of the world."[158]

Status aggrandizement also fueled rapidly increasing Soviet defense expenditures. As the Soviet leadership's key adviser on relations with the United States Georgy Arbatov admitted, one possible reason for the Soviets' excessive appetite for military build-up was a "deeply rooted inferiority complex that constantly drove us to catch up with the United States in nuclear arms." The Soviet rulers armed themselves enthusiastically, "like binging drunks, without any apparent political need."[159]

Paradoxically, because its adventurism in Africa and overreaction in Afghanistan had alienated the West, the Soviet Union entered the 1980s with even lower political and diplomatic standing around the world than at the beginning of détente. Soviet influence in the post-Stalin era was limited to Cuba, Laos, Kampuchea, Ethiopia, Angola, Mozambique, Benin, Congo-Brazzaville, and parts of Yemen and of Afghanistan. While the Soviet post-1945 empire was territorially expansive, as Kenneth Jowitt once noted, Soviet leaders would very likely have traded all of this for the half of Austria they gave up in the mid-1950s. For a Soviet leader looking at Soviet achievements in the early 1980s, "it must have come as a depressing shock to realize that the expansion begun in the early 1920s with 'Third World' Outer Mongolia was repeating itself sixty years later with 'Third World' Afghanistan—and less successfully." The widespread feeling in the 1970s that the Soviet Union had finally "arrived" at a position of prominence in the international system was gradually giving way to awareness that expansion of Soviet military power and international presence did not necessarily translate into enhanced status. In addition, the lagging Soviet economy and increased military expenditures threatened to undermine what was left of Soviet great power status, bringing Moscow's international position humiliatingly close to what West German Chancellor Helmut Schmidt liked to describe as "Upper Volta with missiles."[160]

As the "New Cold War" unfolded, the Reagan administration not only denied the Soviet Union equality in political matters, but also accused the Kremlin of barbarism and incivility. Reagan labeled the Soviet Union an "evil empire" and in the wake of the accidental Soviet shooting down of the Korean Airline 007, accused it of having no regard for basic humanitarian values.[161] While Reagan's "full court press" by no means made Gorbachev's foreign policy revolution inevitable, the desire to repair damage done to Soviet status was an important motivation behind the New Thinking policies of the late 1980s.

CONCLUSIONS

Despite their Marxist-Leninist ideology, which depicted the capitalist world order as both illegitimate and doomed to fall, both the Soviet Union and the PRC wanted to be recognized as great powers by the very states they expected to succumb to revolution. The resilience of their great power identities is visible in the efforts of both the Bolsheviks and the Chinese Communists to restore the former imperial borders during their respective revolutions. Both states were initially isolated by the dominant power, the USSR by Great Britain and the PRC by the United States. But both communist powers held fast to the goal of attaining great power status, regardless of their relative military capabilities or rejection by the West.

The effects of Marxism-Leninism on the Soviets and of Maoism on the Chinese provides one explanatory framework to interpret events. But ideology is not sufficient to explain Soviet and Chinese actions. It was interpreted differently by various leaders, for example, to justify cooperation with capitalist powers, or support for nationalist leaders in the Third World. Some Soviet actions, such as Stalin's pursuit of geopolitical objectives at the postwar conferences (including demands for control of the Turkish Straits and concessions in Northeast Asia at the expense of China), had nothing to do with promoting communism. Brezhnev had to override his orthodox ideological opponents in the Politburo to pursue détente with the United States.[162]

As neorealism would predict, at times the Soviet Union and China gave priority to security over status—for example, in the 1930s when the Soviet Union sought cooperation with Britain and France against Hitler, and in the 1970s when the PRC sought to align with the United States against the USSR. That the Soviet Union and the United States would compete militarily in a bipolar world is also predicted by neorealism. But Soviet competition with the United States—in economic production, geopolitical influence, space, culture, and sports—far exceeded in scope and intensity what could be predicted from the bipolar distribution of power.

Contrary to constructivism, the Soviet Union's identity was not established through interactions with the capitalist countries. During the 1920s and 1930s, the Soviet Union was regarded with extreme distrust and hostility by the Western countries. The Soviet Union's self-image as a great power derived from its history and size. Similarly, China resisted efforts by the Soviet Union to cast it in the role of "little brother" in the international communist movement. Also inconsistent with constructivism is the role of individual agency in selecting from among available identities. In the Soviet Union, the transition from Stalin to Khrushchev led to a major change in ideological discourse about the Third World, from a "two camp" view of the world to a willingness to work with noncommunist leaders, a change that cannot be well accounted for by domestic variables or systemic interaction.

Neither neorealism nor constructivism can explain the strong desire by the Soviet Union and China to be recognized and admired by higher-status states as equal great powers. The need for recognition as a basis for self-esteem was manifested in the Soviets' acute status anxiety vis-à-vis Great Britain and the United States. Similarly, having initially allied with the Soviet Union to compensate for its relative weakness, China increasingly became dissatisfied with being a junior partner. China first sought equality with the Soviet Union and then superiority as leader of the world communist movement. Competition for relative status in the international communist movement, symbolized by Khrushchev's and Mao's petty score-keeping and one-upmanship, exacerbated and embittered ideological differences.

To explain the self-defeating aspects of Soviet and Chinese foreign policy, in conjunction with Marxist-Leninist ideology, we must consider China's and Russia's aspirations to restore their international greatness, which, given the perception of the international status hierarchy as unstable and illegitimate, led to social competition. Social competition can lead to non-rational, provocative, and costly policies that are ultimately counterproductive to the long-term security and economic interests of the state. Following World War II, Stalin's demands for an Italian colony, a share in the Japanese occupation, and a base on the Turkish Straits further alienated the Truman administration, which was already concerned about Soviet domination of Eastern Europe. Khrushchev gained international respect for Soviet space and scientific achievements, until his bluffs about Soviet missile capabilities were exposed and his efforts to achieve a strategic advantage in the Cuban Missile Crisis only led to an even more humiliating defeat. Under Brezhnev, the Soviet Union tried to achieve great power status through the traditional means of military power (real ICBMs and a blue-water navy) and acquisition of client states, but its intervention in the Third World alarmed and alienated the Western countries, resulting in its virtual isolation after the invasion of Afghanistan. Although the post–World War II Soviet Union was a powerful global player, feared by the West, its competitive policies ultimately backfired, failing to realize Soviet aspirations for respect and recognition.

On the other hand, the demonstrated futility of social competition laid the basis for a major shift in both states' foreign policies. The failure of Soviet geopolitical and military competition to secure the desired status position created conditions conducive for Mikhail Gorbachev's efforts to reorient Soviet foreign policy. Mao's revolutionary fervor and campaign against Soviet revisionism damaged China's standing in the international communist movement and frightened the West, but in doing so, it chastened the Chinese Communists and increased receptiveness to Deng Xiaoping's more pragmatic policies. We discuss the shift in both states' policies in chapter 4.

4 The Social Creativity of Deng and Gorbachev

ON A VISIT to Japan to sign the peace and friendship treaty in fall 1978, Deng Xiaoping—the first Chinese leader to visit Japan in two thousand years and the first to meet with the Japanese emperor—was profoundly impressed by the Japanese industrial, technological, and consumerist "miracle." "Now I know what modernization means," Deng sighed when during his visit to the Nissan Auto Company he learned that the company's annual output per worker was ninety-four times greater than that at China's best auto manufacturer. When one of his Japanese hosts observed that Japan had learned much of its culture from China before creatively adapting it, Deng readily acknowledged that now China was a student willing to learn from Japanese teachers. "We must admit our deficiencies. We are a backward country and we need to learn from Japan," he remarked at a press conference.[1] As China's paramount leader, Deng pursued social creativity in fashioning a pragmatic, non-ideological foreign policy conducive to "opening up" China to interactions with the West and integrating China into the global economy.

Similarly, when Mikhail S. Gorbachev became the Soviet leader in March 1985, he was well aware that the Soviet Union lagged behind the United States and other Western countries. In contrast to most communist party secretaries, he had traveled extensively in the West. When he had visited Italy, France, Belgium, Holland, and the Federal Republic of Germany in the 1970s, his faith in the superiority of the Soviet system was shaken. Gorbachev was most impressed that the people of Europe lived in better conditions and were better off than in the Soviet Union. "The question haunted me: why was the standard of living in our country lower than in other developed countries?"[2]

Both Deng and Gorbachev presided over creative foreign policies that enhanced their states' international standing by achieving preeminence in areas other than geopolitical power, in the process transforming their societies and relations with other states. Unlike Deng, who used foreign policy to compensate for China's weaknesses and to develop the foundation for redressing them in the long run, Gorbachev and his team pursued a version of social creativity that was firmly and stubbornly rooted in the historic pattern of Russian "shortcuts to greatness"—seeking great power status *despite* relative economic and technological backwardness vis-à-vis the West.[3]

Deng made his foreign policy serve economic reforms that increased the Chinese standard of living and elevated China's status to that of a global power. In stark contrast, Gorbachev's promotion of "universal human values," arms control, and nonuse of force increased Soviet prestige for only a brief period of time, and the failure of his domestic reforms culminated in the breakup of the Soviet Union, an astonishingly rapid loss of Russia's power and status. Soviet status aspirations and great power illusions go a long way toward explaining Gorbachev's failure to adopt a pragmatic neorealist foreign policy more suitable for Soviet developmental goals, as well as his reluctance to learn from China's successful foreign policy and domestic reform experience.

Neorealism suggests that China and the Soviet Union would retrench following their costly involvements in the Third World and reduce military spending while reinstituting their alliance against the United States, the leading power. Neorealism, however, would not expect both countries to deemphasize geopolitical and military goals in favor of seeking preeminence in new, "softer" areas.

Marxist-Leninist ideology might suggest that the Chinese and Soviet leadership would accommodate the West in an attempt to encourage contradictions among the capitalist powers, and give themselves a breathing spell while building up their power for renewed competition. Thus, in some respects, neorealism and Marxist-Leninist ideology make similar predictions about realpolitik and great power balancing.[4] Chinese and Soviet leaders might also be expected to conduct a peace offensive, similar to the rhetoric about disarmament in the 1920s from Chicherin and Litvinov.

SIT, on the other hand, suggests that given the failure of social competition, Chinese and Soviet leaders would be motivated to find new domains in which to be preeminent. China's radicalism and support for global revolution had alienated most of its former friends in the Third World while failing to achieve recognition for the PRC as the leading Communist power. Being closed off to the world economy had resulted in a diminution of China's status, making it even more backward. The Brezhnev strategy for attaining preeminent status through military power and Third World interventions had aroused the security concerns of Western states and alienated developing countries, while failing to win recognition for the Soviet Union as a political equal. Having reached the limits of mobility in the international system and having understood the futility of competition on Western terms, both Chinese and Soviet leaders could be expected to try a social creativity strategy.

Constructivists would expect China and the Soviet Union to be socialized to international norms as both states increased their interactions with the West. Between October 1970 and December 1972, China established full diplomatic relations with forty-three countries. The Soviet Union had opened up as well to exchanges with academics and foreign officials during the détente era. Constructivists would also attribute changes in Chinese and Soviet behavior to domestic discourse, such as the writings of international relations specialists in the Communist Party and academic institutes.[5]

Contrary to constructivist expectations of socialization, SIT would predict that China and Russia would not opt for a social mobility strategy, adopting Western norms and institutions in order to join the club, but would instead emphasize their cultural uniqueness, moral superiority, and originality.

We first lay out the premises of Deng's pragmatic reform and opening up policy, which was aimed at attaining great power status for China in the long run based on acquisition of wealth and power. We then contrast Deng's farsighted strategy with Gorbachev's adoption of the idealistic principles of the New Thinking, a focus on promoting new international norms that was motivated by his search for a domain in which the Soviet Union could achieve preeminence over the United States without having to catch up. We then compare the implementation of reform ideas in the foreign policies of Deng and Gorbachev. Deng's domestic reform policies contributed to pragmatism and cooperation in China's foreign policy toward the United States, Japan, and other advanced states, which overall enhanced China's status and reputation. In contrast, Gorbachev carried out the New Thinking by means of dramatic unilateral concessions intended to reshape the image of the Soviet Union in the West. Gorbachev and Deng reacted very differently to the unintended consequences of their reforms—the Tiananmen Square demonstrations in China and the collapse of the Soviet sphere of influence in Eastern Europe, which was followed by the breakup of the Soviet Union. Deng did not shy away from ruthless suppression of the protesters, while Gorbachev was constrained by the new self-image he had created for the Soviet Union as the moral leader of a new international order, in which force was no longer an instrument of foreign policy. In the concluding section, we propose that status considerations related to maintaining a sense of superiority over the Chinese help to explain why Gorbachev and the New Thinkers gave relatively little attention to the earlier economic reform experience in China.

DENG'S SELECTIVE MODERNIZATION AND REFORM IDEAS

Deng's foreign policy was creative in seeking a new status for China that was not based on promotion of global revolution or on military might but on economic production and diplomatic flexibility. To overcome China's backwardness and restore its status as a great power, Deng opened up the Chinese economy to the outside world, jettisoned ideology as a practical guide to policy, and pursued a pragmatic foreign policy designed to acquire technology from foreign states while creating a peaceful environment for China's economic development. China would maintain its unique identity through selective modernization—fusing communist rule with markets. China would achieve status over the long run through modernization and economic development, not military power and alliances, in effect through a strategy of social creativity.

China was falling further behind economically, unable to keep up with the newly industrializing states of Asia. The PRC was viewed with suspicion and hostility not only by its neighbors in Southeast Asia, many of whom had sizeable Chinese diaspora populations and distrusted China's past support for revolutionary movements, but also by its ideological brethren, the other Communist states, due to the Sino-Soviet split. Even after Nixon's opening to China, the country was still relatively isolated, with strictly limited contacts with the outside world and restricted trade.[6]

SIT suggests that failure of social competition, represented by a stable status hierarchy, is conducive to social creativity. After failed efforts to overturn the US-dominated order by supporting revolutionary movements in the Third World, Deng's supporters in the Chinese leadership had concluded that the international system was not going to change in the near future. Of the Asian Communist parties that Beijing had supported in the 1950s and 1960s—in Burma, Thailand, Malaysia, India, the Philippines, Vietnam, Laos, and Indonesia—only in Vietnam had the revolutionary movement succeeded, and despite China's substantial assistance, that country had become a Soviet client.[7] Henceforth, instead of being a revolutionary leader of the Third World, China would win admiration for its economic modernization and development—a different route to great power status, but one that worked for China.

At the historic Third Plenum of the Eleventh Party Congress in December 1978, Deng Xiaoping launched his "reform and opening up" policies, urging the Chinese to give priority to modernization and economic development over the class struggle. It was Deng's central insight that economic modernization was essential for China to recover its greatness and national dignity. "The role we play in international affairs is determined by the extent of our economic growth," Deng said in a major programmatic speech.[8]

Just as the Chinese quest for modernity as defined by the wealthiest and most advanced nations was historically inseparable from China's struggle for national and individual self-definition and status, for Deng the goal of economic prosperity was also linked to Chinese international prestige and influence. As he explained at the outset of his reforms, "By achieving the four modernizations, we mean shaking off China's poverty and backwardness, gradually improving the people's living standards, restoring a position for China in international affairs commensurate with its current status, and enabling China to contribute more to mankind." As a fourteen-year-old, Deng had participated in the May Fourth demonstrations against the Western powers' failure to return the Shandong province to China at the Versailles conference, his political awakening that was now associated with the national effort to undo the humiliations that China had suffered at the hands of the imperialist powers.[9]

While Deng did not have a blueprint for changing China—he acknowledged at the outset that his modus operandi was the well-known principle of "crossing the river by groping for the stones"—he did have a framework for developing policy. The Deng coalition sought to open up the economy to the outside world, supplement command planning with market principles, and offer market-based material incentives to peasants, workers, and local governments—all radical changes to the Stalinist/Maoist model of popular mobilization.

Implementation of Dengist reforms followed principles of incrementalism, experimentation, and gradualism, in contrast to Mao's "storming" approach to development, epitomized by the Great Leap Forward. Catching up to the West could not be accomplished overnight and would have to make use of US technology and assistance. The historic Third Plenum at which Deng consolidated his power and set the country on a course of reform described the task of modernization as a "New Long March."[10]

The idea of opening up to the outside world (*kaifang*) was one of the earliest and most consistent themes in the reform project. Rejecting the nationalist/communist tradition of blaming Chinese weakness on Western imperialism, Deng argued that an "open policy" was vital to break away from centuries of poverty, stagnation, backwardness, and ignorance caused by China's self-imposed isolationism. Whereas Mao had distrusted the West, Deng was prepared to downplay Chinese nationalism in his quest to enhance China's power and prestige, and to accept a foreign presence in China, as well as the political and social risks of the "opening up" policy, in order to obtain badly needed technology and investment.[11]

The "opening up" policy emulated the Japanese model of export-led industrialization centered around export processing zones, and directly replicated the Qing-era experience of allowing enclaves of Western influence in China's treaty ports by creating special economic zones

(SEZs) (built in close proximity to Hong Kong, Macao, and Taiwan) to take the lead in borrowing from the West and high-technology manufacturing. By the late 1980s, mushrooming SEZs, "development zones," and "open cities" transformed coastal China into a giant "development belt" linking the PRC to the global economy. Nevertheless, in another parallel to the nineteenth century, some CCP conservatives attacked the SEZs, comparing them to foreign concessions and colonies, and worried about potential loss of dignity. Some influential CCP "elders" never accepted the legitimacy of SEZs, which they viewed as hotbeds of bourgeois decadent influence and an affront to national sovereignty.[12]

Deng's "reform and opening up" policies were rooted in the sobering recognition that despite nearly thirty years of gargantuan social mobilization efforts, China lagged shamefully behind not only the West but also the newly industrialized countries in East Asia, including the tiny city states of Singapore and Hong Kong, as well as South Korea and Taiwan. Deng understood well that to start learning from the West, the Chinese had to be willing to swallow their pride. In contrast to Mao, who had delusions of grandeur for China, Deng was realistic in recognizing China's weaknesses and backwardness. "Backwardness must be recognized before it can be changed," he argued, a mantra reinforced by his traumatic personal experiences of the Great Leap Forward and Cultural Revolution. Exiled in Jiangxi province during the Cultural Revolution, Deng had witnessed the appallingly low living standards of ordinary Chinese citizens. At one point, when he offered to have his son fix radios as a way of filling the time, he was heartsick to learn that none of the workers' families could afford a radio—after twenty years of socialism.[13]

Acknowledging China's relative backwardness vis-à-vis developed Western and Asian societies was central to Deng's reforms, providing the motivation for intensive learning from foreign experiences. In the past, a major obstacle to adoption of foreign technology had been unwillingness to admit the inferiority implied by the act of borrowing from foreigners. Deng boldly admitted at the outset of the reform drive that the PRC was significantly lagging behind the West on most economic, technological, and scientific indicators. The only possible solution to the problem, he argued, was continuous learning from the Western experience. In 1978, Deng sent top members of the Chinese elite on fact-finding tours of Eastern Europe, Hong Kong, Japan, and

Western Europe, which played a role similar to the Iwakura Mission at the outset of the Japanese modernization drive in the 1870s.[14]

Nevertheless, the "opening up" policy did not represent socialization by the West. Instead of simply borrowing Western ideas and norms, the reformers questioned and creatively reinterpreted them to fit China's conditions. For example, the decision by the Deng faction to join the International Monetary Fund and World Bank in early 1979 was the product of the Chinese reform policies rather than the cause. Although contacts by Chinese intellectuals, academics, and officials with the West had increased dramatically since 1971, the interchanges were of limited duration. Unlike the Soviet Union, China did not have international relations specialists who had attended international conferences and discussed international issues with Westerners. Their counterparts in China had been sent to the countryside to shovel pig manure or work in factories during the Cultural Revolution.[15]

Deng's reform program represented a sharp break with Mao Zedong's ideological and isolationist "self-reliance" approach to Chinese economic development, emphasizing "emancipation of thinking," economic pragmatism (officially embodied in the slogan "seek truth from facts" and unofficially, and more famously, conveyed by Deng's claim that "it does not matter if the cat is white or black as long as it catches mice"), and showing respect for and learning from the achievements of the advanced Western economies.[16]

Dramatically downplaying communist ideology as an influence on Chinese international strategy allowed Deng to foster a new image for China as a status quo, constructive power. China's approach to regional conflicts and civil wars in the developing world increasingly emphasized conciliation instead of the struggle and revolution promoted previously. After Deng took power in 1978, Beijing ended its material support for foreign revolutionary movements, toned down its support for a New International Economic Order (a Marxist-flavored agenda for radical global economic reform on the developing countries' terms), and reduced ideologically based economic aid to developing countries, scaling back Maoist claims to leadership of the Third World.[17]

Was Deng Xiaoping, then, pursuing social mobility? Out of concern for political stability and order, Deng was firmly opposed to "wholesale westernization" or a "fifth modernization" (western-style democratizing reforms). As Deng argued, "China must modernize; it must absolutely not liberalize or take the capitalist road, as countries of the West have done." The idea of "socialism with Chinese characteristics," which emerged in 1984, represented China's distinctive identity as well as Deng's pragmatism in combining capitalist-style markets with some centralized planning.[18]

A century after the Qing dynasty's self-strengthening movement, Deng's faction in the leadership of the CCP presided over a similar but far more radical version of selective modernization. In a quest for the wealth and power perennially sought by China, Deng and his colleagues aspired to revitalize China and enhance its international prestige and influence through pragmatic adoption of foreign techniques to serve China.[19]

SOVIET "NEW THINKING" AND ITS ALTERNATIVES

Confronted by loss of Soviet status, Gorbachev would also choose an innovative path to great power status, but in contrast to Deng, the Soviet leader articulated a coherent set of ideas that supposedly justified the transformation in Soviet foreign policy. Similar to Deng, Gorbachev sought to create a new identity for the Soviet Union, divorced from its traditional emphasis on military power, based on promotion of idealistic international norms and principles. Between 1985 and 1991, the foundation of Soviet foreign policy changed from a Marxist-Leninist view of inevitable conflict between capitalism and socialism to an idealist vision of cooperation between states in solving global problems—the New Thinking. Gorbachev was not pressured to adopt this global vision, and in fact he did so against the advice of many of the foreign policy professionals within the Soviet Union and despite the availability of more practical alternatives.

In adopting the ideals of the New Thinking—including global interdependence, universal human values, the balance of interests, and freedom of choice—Gorbachev fundamentally altered Soviet foreign policy theory and practice. He accepted the dismantling of Soviet medium-range missiles in Europe and asymmetric reductions in Soviet conventional forces, withdrew support from other communist movements, and helped mediate an end to regional conflicts in the Third World. He applied the principle of freedom of choice to Eastern Europe, culminating in his decision to tolerate the fall of East European Communism and to acquiesce to reunification of Germany. The change in Soviet identity, in how the Soviet Union viewed itself in relation to the rest of the world and its mission in international politics, brought an abrupt end to the Cold War. The most striking aspect of the new Soviet identity was the determination of Gorbachev and his comrades to discard the traditional Soviet approach to foreign policy without substituting any moderate, reformed version of realism for it. What explains Gorbachev's introduction of such a "surprising element of idealism" into Soviet foreign policy?[20]

According to neorealists, the New Thinking was merely instrumental to policies required to redress Moscow's deteriorating geopolitical position and economic decline. The rate of Soviet economic growth had begun to decline in 1960 and dropped precipitously beginning in the mid-1970s, which meant that military expenditures consumed an increasing proportion of the gross national product (GNP). The burden of subsidizing Soviet allies in Eastern Europe and propping up unreliable Third World clients was increasing at a time when the Soviet economy could no longer support such expenditures without some strain. In short, the monetary costs of maintaining the foreign policy status quo—the arms race, regional conflicts in the developing world, and the Soviet sphere of influence in Eastern Europe—were too high.[21]

To improve economic productivity and use its resources more efficiently, the Soviet Union needed to become more fully integrated into the world economy, reduce defense spending, and acquire advanced technology from the West. By this logic, the New Thinking was merely a rationalization intended to legitimize retrenchment and accommodation in the eyes of domestic and foreign audiences. By establishing a more benign image for the Soviet Union, this approach could also make the United States and other Western countries more receptive to sharing technology and increasing trade.[22]

In contrast to the materialist perspective of neorealism, constructivism views the New Thinking as a philosophy of universal humanism that stressed international cooperation. Gorbachev's adoption of the New Thinking has been attributed to a variety of factors, including cognitive learning, policy entrepreneurship, transnational networks, and the influence of the Soviet "Westernizing" academic elite.[23] The ideas of the New Thinking constituted a new identity and new interests for the Soviet Union, an identity that ruled out arms racing and the use of military force.

While accepting the importance of the New Thinking, SIT provides an alternative explanation of its adoption. SIT suggests that a precipitous decline in the Soviet Union's international status in the post-détente period, combined with the succession of a new leader, Mikhail Gorbachev, created the conditions for rethinking the standard Soviet route to greatness based on social competition with the United States. As discussed in the previous chapter, by the mid-1980s the Soviet Union possessed most of the conventional elements of power—a sizeable nuclear arsenal, huge conventional forces, and a territorial empire in Eastern Europe—but still was not accepted as a diplomatic or political equal by the United States and other advanced Western industrial powers. Contrary to the Soviets' earlier euphoria about a change in the "correlation of forces," the Western-dominated status hierarchy was now secure. The Soviet invasion of Afghanistan had alienated both the Western countries and most of the Third World apart from clients such as Ethiopia, Vietnam, Angola, Mozambique, Libya, and Afghanistan—weak developing countries of doubtful loyalty. In a June 1982 speech at Westminster, US President Ronald Reagan predicted that "the march of freedom and democracy" would leave Marxism-Leninism on the "ash heap of history"—a major insult given the Soviets' claim to represent the vanguard of historical progressive forces.[24]

Bold and ambitious, Gorbachev took Soviet status very seriously. His furious reaction to Matthias Rust's May 1987 landing of a small plane on Red Square, bypassing the Soviets' supposedly impregnable air defense systems, is quite telling. "It is even worse than Chernobyl. It is an absolute disgrace!" he exclaimed.[25] As Martin Malia observes, "throughout his career, Gorbachev always insisted on his country's dignity as a great state." The realization that technological backwardness and lack of foreign policy resources were thwarting Soviet aspirations for international greatness was a powerful and deep-seated motivation for foreign policy reforms. In a December 1984 speech, Gorbachev declared that only intensive economic development would maintain the country's status and allow it to enter the new millennium "with dignity as a great and flourishing power."[26]

Since social competition for geopolitical power had proved not only costly but also ineffective in achieving Western acceptance, the new Soviet leader could be expected to try to achieve preeminence in a different way. One social creativity avenue open to status-disadvantaged states is to seek indirect, co-optive "soft power"—augmenting and exercising their influence through the attraction of their culture, values, norms, or ideals, rather than through military or economic power. This strategy would entail stressing the originality or moral superiority of Soviet foreign policy rather than simply trying to assimilate Western values. Social identity theory would also lead us to expect Gorbachev to play up his reforms before a global audience, and to reshape Soviet foreign policy in line with his rhetoric to attain Western acceptance of the new Soviet identity.

Perhaps the best evidence that Gorbachev was not compelled to adopt the New Thinking by geopolitical and economic pressures is that he considered and ultimately rejected alternative foreign policy ideas that would also have facilitated his domestic economic reforms.

At the time of his ascension to the post of the General Secretary, Gorbachev was presented with several alternative visions of Soviet international strategy.[27] There was also considerable support for a return to Soviet hard-line policies, despite unfavorable economic trends.

The first alternative, a "détente plus" strategy, favored reducing defense spending and overseas commitments somewhat until the Soviet Union had recovered its power, then resuming expansion.[28] Such a strategy could have enabled Gorbachev to carry out cautious domestic economic reforms without endangering the Soviet empire. A prudent conservative leader could have improved the Soviet economic situation substantially without making major changes in foreign policy priorities by cutting defense spending sharply—by 10–20 percent or even much more—and seeking an expansion of East-West trade and technical cooperation. Deep Soviet arms cuts need not have worsened the Soviet security position, because even a minimum number of nuclear weapons would have guaranteed the state's territorial integrity. Unilateral arms cuts quite possibly would have induced comparable cuts in Western spending, as actually happened under Gorbachev in 1989. Soviet withdrawal from the Third World could have been justified with a few doctrinal modifications, as had been done repeatedly and relatively painlessly in the history of the USSR. Adjusting Soviet foreign policy in accordance with a "détente plus" scenario was a genuinely popular idea among the Soviet elite. That Gorbachev's nomination was supported by Foreign Minister Andrei Gromyko, the ultimate gatekeeper of the Soviet post-Stalin foreign policy, suggests that the top Soviet leadership was not contemplating radical changes in Soviet foreign policy in early 1985.[29]

A second modified realpolitik vision of Soviet foreign policy criticized the traditional Soviet ideological approach to foreign policy as inefficient; it wasted valuable resources on weak Third World allies and provoked an unprecedented threat from the antagonized West. These critics advocated modifying Marxist-Leninist ideology to guide Soviet foreign policy in line with a realpolitik interpretation of Soviet/Russian interests. Realpolitikers proposed such actions as swift rapprochement with the PRC to play the "China card" against the United States (a realistic possibility, given the Chinese interest in gaining more leverage over Washington), playing Western Europe off against the United States, and withdrawal from Afghanistan.[30] The Soviets could also have radically shifted their policy toward Japan—the key technological giant in the Western bloc—and negotiated for significant technological and economic assistance and investments in exchange for conceding the Kurile Islands.[31]

Significant elements of realpolitik were visible in discussions during a May 31, 1983, Politburo meeting presided over by Yuri Andropov, who favored rapprochement with China and, in a major departure from the orthodoxy, suggested involving Japan in "more active cooperation with the Soviet Union in the economic sphere" through joint economic development of the disputed Kurile Islands. Strikingly, Gromyko, usually cautious and unyielding on territorial issues, was prepared to go even further, proposing as "a prestigious offer" returning to Japan two of the disputed territories (Habomai and Kunashir) and other "trivial islands," which, he acknowledged, "after all are small dots in the ocean and do not really have a great strategic importance."[32]

This proposal was still under consideration when in April 1985, Georgy Arbatov advised Gorbachev to surrender "two if not all four" islands to the Japanese. While Gorbachev wound up rejecting the realpolitik alternative, it influenced some of his early ideas, such as his grand vision for the implicitly anti-American "new strategic triangle" uniting the Soviet Union, India, and China under Soviet leadership—a project that quickly faded away due to the lack of interest from either Beijing or New Delhi.[33]

A third alternative differed from both "détente plus" and "realpolitik" options in projecting a much more hard-line course for the Soviet Union. Leaders of the Soviet military-industrial complex, some of the top leadership of the KGB, and the neo-Stalinist/Russian nationalist wing within the Communist Party of the Soviet Union favored increased defense expenditures with a focus on advanced military technologies (including a Soviet version of the "Star Wars" system) and an assertive neo-Stalinist anti-Western foreign policy.[34]

A fourth vision, the New Thinking, while accepting some of the "détente plus" and realpolitik criticisms of past Soviet foreign policy, advocated more far-reaching changes. The initial group of New Thinkers included Alexander Yakovlev, Georgy Shakhnazarov, Anatoly Chernyaev, Alexander Bovin, Evgeny Primakov, Vadim Zagladin, Alexei Arbatov, Oleg Bogomolov, Vyacheslav Dashichev, and other members of academic institutes (such as physicists Roald Sagdeev and Evgeny Velikhov), as well as the International Department of the Central Committee of the Communist Party of the Soviet Union.[35] Future New Thinkers no longer saw the West as a political-ideological or geostrategic adversary. While differing on many specific points, the New Thinkers rejected the inevitability of conflict between capitalism and socialism and the class-based model of international relations.[36] The New Thinking argued that because the world was complex and interdependent, states had to cooperate in solving global problems such as the growing gap between rich and poor nations, the threat of nuclear war, and ecological disasters. Universal values should have priority over class interests.[37]

In summary, Gorbachev was presented with at least four distinct programs for his foreign policy. The availability of the plausible alternatives discussed above suggests that geopolitical and economic factors alone were not powerful enough to establish an elite consensus on Soviet foreign policy. The idea that almost any Soviet leader selected in 1985 would have pursued policies similar to Gorbachev's—which is essentially the neorealist interpretation of the end of the Cold War—is therefore not persuasive. In fact, it is almost inconceivable that any of Gorbachev's serious rivals in 1985 would have replicated his most important foreign policy choices or conducted his liberalizing political domestic reforms.[38] We may now address the puzzle of why Gorbachev chose the New Thinking over more "realistic" and conventional alternatives.

THE SOVIET UNION AS MORAL VISIONARY LEADER

Gorbachev adopted the radical New Thinking out of concerns for Soviet status and identity. The cautious and incremental approach of both the realpolitik and "détente plus" strategies failed to offer any means of halting the erosion in the Soviet Union's relative power and prestige.[39] In striking contrast, however, the New Thinking promised not merely to manage the USSR's accelerating decline but to arrest and reverse it. In choosing this philosophy, therefore, Gorbachev's reformers were motivated not by the material pressures in favor of retrenchment but by the desire to be recognized as a great power and to be a member of the club.

The radical New Thinkers' intellectual breakthrough was the realization that to transform their country into a real great power, and not just a "one dimensional" one, they had to reject military might as the criterion for international influence in the contemporary world. The social creativity hypothesis suggests that Gorbachev and his advisers adopted the principles of the New Thinking to establish a new dimension on which the Soviet Union could excel in the world arena. They sought to develop a new positive international identity for the Soviet Union as the moral and political leader of a new cooperative international order.[40]

Moral visionary leadership thus became the new criterion for Soviet "greatness." As Foreign Minister Eduard Shevardnadze would state in April 1990: "The belief that we are a great country and that we should be respected for this is deeply ingrained in me, as in everyone. But great in what? Territory? Population? Quantity of arms? Or the people's troubles? The individual's lack of rights? In what do we, who have virtually the highest infant mortality rate on our planet, take pride? It is not easy to answer these questions: Who are you and what do you wish to be? *A country which is feared or a country which is respected? A country of power or a country of kindness?*"[41]

Historically, Russian rulers sought great power status despite their country's relative backwardness through military victories, territorial expansion, and when necessary, top-down reforms. The New Thinking offered a way to achieve truly prominent status in the international system and political equality vis-à-vis the West without first attaining a level of economic and technological development comparable to

that of the United States; it was a shortcut to greatness. As emphasized by Jacques Lévesque, while New Thinking principles ultimately
meant a break with Leninism, the foreign policy of Gorbachev and his
colleagues had distinctive Leninist overtones in its "Promethean and
messianic ambition to reshape the world order" based on discovery of
"new 'objective' processes and trends emerging in the world, which allowed for the construction of an entirely new international order more
advantageous to the USSR." Similarly, Andrei Grachev, an adviser to
Gorbachev and later foreign policy spokesperson, recalls that "while
retreating from old-fashioned communist dogmas and proclaiming a
new Soviet foreign policy free of ideology, Gorbachev and his supporters were *de facto* replacing one ideology with another" based on "'universal democratic values,' which curiously enough were supposed to
bring about the same result as the apparently discredited and failed
theory of world revolution: an assured and honorable place for the
Soviet Union in the vanguard of world history."[42]

Gorbachev's goals of reshaping the international order and placing
the Soviet Union at the forefront demonstrate that he was not trying
to assimilate into the international system by adopting Western values, as constructivist accounts would expect. To be sure, some New
Thinking ideas were derived from Western arms control experts and
scientists, through the Pugwash and Dartmouth movements. Others
can be traced to conferences and discussions sponsored by Western
European Social Democrats, such as the Palme Commission (named
after the Swedish Prime Minister Olof Palme). Gorbachev was familiar
with European Social Democratic works.[43] Nevertheless, Gorbachev
and the New Thinkers were not interested in social mobility, meeting Western conditions to join the club of "civilized" states. The New
Thinking strove to distinguish the new Soviet identity from the West,
a goal not sufficiently recognized by ideational accounts of the end of
the Cold War. As SIT leads us to expect, the goal of the New Thinkers
was not just to tear down the "iron curtain" and join the community of
advanced industrial nations. The New Thinkers saw themselves as edu-
cating the West to adopt new modes of international conduct.[44] They
were not only "norm takers" but norm entrepreneurs as well.

By the early 1980s, Soviet foreign policy thinkers realized that the Soviet Union was lagging behind the United States economically and militarily, but they were unwilling to give up great power status. Consistent

with SIT, Gorbachev and the other New Thinkers sought a new domain in which the Soviet Union could be superior—promoting new international norms and ideas. Gorbachev found the New Thinking more attractive than alternative foreign policy programs because it offered a new role for the Soviet Union as a norm entrepreneur, and a distinctive status as the author of principles underlying a new world order. Soviet New Thinkers thus found a way to reframe their country's innate characteristics as both positive and distinct from the West, developing an ideology that they hoped would reshape the world and assure Soviet recognition by the West. In contrast to such idealism, Deng Xiaoping chose to use diplomacy to foster an international environment favorable to China's economic development and modernization.

In the 1980s, both Deng and Gorbachev faced the task of implementing a new identity in foreign policy, translating ideas into actions. For both leaders, rapprochement with the United States was a priority, with Deng pursuing economic modernization and Gorbachev pursuing arms control agreements. Both tried to open up their societies to the West while preserving their countries' distinctive identities. But as will be seen, Deng's foreign policy was focused more on practical economic objectives, while Gorbachev ostensibly aimed at transformation of the world order.

DENG'S PRAGMATIC DIPLOMACY

While fostering China's future economic development, Deng used foreign policy to improve China's international standing. He initially aligned with the United States but, as with the previous Sino-Soviet alliance, found it humiliating to be the subordinate partner and moved instead toward rhetorical independence, which allowed China to stake out a distinctive position.

Deng had given priority to fostering better relations with the United States as the key to China's modernization. As a result, he was gratified by the long-awaited establishment of diplomatic relations with the United States in 1979, after years of uncertainty, a qualitative breakthrough in the "special relationship" between Washington and Beijing and an indication of China's international importance.[45]

Superpower competition eased the PRC's path to enhanced status. While President Jimmy Carter had initially downplayed relations with

China, placing emphasis instead on détente with the Soviet Union and arms control, the Soviets' 1978 intervention in Ethiopia and the April 1978 coup d'état in Afghanistan motivated the president to "play the China card" to induce the Soviet Union to behave more cooperatively, a strategy signaled by his decision to send the anti-Soviet national security adviser Zbigniew Brzezinski to China.[46]

Status incentives played a role in the US negotiations with China. During his May 1978 visit to Beijing, which jump-started the process of normalizing Sino-American relations, Brzezinski played to China's status aspirations, using every opportunity to emphasize the PRC's strategic importance to the United States, citing "China's central role in maintaining the world balance." In negotiations over normalization in December, Brzezinski, the consummate Cold War warrior, was careful to signal to the Chinese side that relations with Beijing took precedence over those with Moscow, making sure that the conclusion of an agreement on normalization and the announcement of Deng Xiaoping's visit to the United States occurred prior to scheduling the anticipated Soviet-American summit in January, which would finalize the Strategic Arms Limitation Talks (SALT) II agreement then under negotiation.[47]

In response to Brzezinski's implicit suggestion, Deng offered to come to Washington, DC, in January, thereby delaying the US-Soviet summit and infuriating the Soviets. While Secretary of State Cyrus Vance was in the Middle East, Brzezinski persuaded Carter to move up the date for announcement of the prospective establishment of Sino-American diplomatic relations to December 15, 1978, instead of January 1, which caused the Soviets to stall, making it impossible for Vance to conclude the SALT negotiations. Demonstrating US respect for Chinese priorities, the normalization of diplomatic relations communiqué acquiesced to the Chinese demand for the withdrawal of US troops from Taiwan and termination of the mutual defense treaty, yet did not contain an explicit Chinese commitment not to use force against Taiwan.[48]

As an indication of China's growing prestige and popularity in the West, *Time* magazine named Deng the 1978 "Man of the Year"—the first Chinese leader so recognized since Chiang Kai-shek. Deng Xiaoping's triumphal visit to the United States in January 1979, and the "generally masterful public relations campaign" accompanying the visit, significantly bolstered China's reputation in the eyes of the American public. A photo of Deng at a Texas rodeo, smiling in a ten-gallon hat, became the symbol of the visit, persuading the American public that he was not only good-natured, but "less like one of 'those Communists' and more like 'us.'"[49]

Deng's sense of urgency for his visit to the United States reflected not only an effort to outdo the Soviets, but also his desire to "teach Vietnam a lesson" through a Chinese invasion. Aware that an attack by China on Vietnam carried the risk of a Soviet military retaliation, Deng tried to convey the impression of tacit US support by launching the invasion shortly after the conclusion of his visit. Although China had provided billions of dollars of assistance to Hanoi in Vietnam's war with the United States, Vietnam had since become a Soviet client state, signing a virtual treaty of alliance with the Soviet Union in November 1978 that allowed the Soviets to use the former American naval bases at Da Nang and Cam Ranh Bay. In Deng's view, Vietnam was clumsily trying to become a regional rival with China while assisting the Soviet Union in its effort to encircle China with a ring of hostile alliances. Despite Chinese warnings, Vietnam invaded Cambodia on December 25 and replaced the pro-Chinese Pol Pot government with a friendlier regime.[50]

By invading Vietnam, the Chinese had also hoped to gain more equality and respect in their relationship with Washington by demonstrating their value as an ally, but instead of achieving the expected quick victory, China suffered more than thirty thousand casualties. Deng retaliated against the military for this loss of face by making significant cuts in the PLA budget and by downgrading military modernization to last place in the "four modernizations"—agriculture, industry, defense, and science and technology. Deng wanted China to be one of the world's foremost military powers in the long term, but he knew that the development of modern weapons required developing the civilian economy first and securing technological assistance from the West.[51]

Once the euphoria over normalization of the Sino-American relationship had ended, the Chinese complained about what they perceived as patronizing US behavior and failure to treat China on equal terms. In particular, Chinese leaders were offended by US reluctance to share advanced weapons technology despite repeated requests and, even worse, by the Reagan administration's continuing arms sales to Taiwan. Deng believed that US support made Taiwan's President Jiang Jingguo more intransigent in negotiations for reunification. Deng feared that the Sino-American relationship was becoming too one-sided, threatening (not unlike the earlier alliance with the Soviet Union) to relegate China to the perennial status of junior partner.[52] "The Chinese people . . . will never bow and scrape for help," Deng defiantly told a Hong Kong journalist in 1981. It was wrong to believe that "China is insignificant and that the US has no need for any help from China while China needs US help. Those holding this view feel that as long as the US is tough with the Soviet Union you can do what you feel about China and China will swallow it," Deng warned Vice President George H. W. Bush in May 1982. As Deng readily acknowledged, however, the "China angle" in the strategic triangle was not strong enough.[53]

Concern about China's subordinate status in the strategic triangle contributed to the adoption of an "independent foreign policy" in September 1982 at the Twelfth Communist Party Congress, where Chairman of the Communist Party (later called General Secretary under the new party constitution) Hu Yaobang declared that "China never attaches itself to any big power or group of powers, and never yields to pressure from any big power." A receding danger of armed confrontation with the Soviet Union, due to the assertive US reaction to the Soviet invasion of Afghanistan and the Soviets' diplomatic isolation in the Third World, encouraged China to pursue a policy of greater independence from the United States. Disregarding Mao's obsession with international conflict and worldwide class struggle, Deng Xiaoping declared on several occasions in the early 1980s that it should be possible to avoid war for an extended period.[54]

The policy of independence, declining to ally with any major power, was designed to give China the maximum possible freedom to maneuver, and thereby enhance China's international position. As Zhao Ziyang explained shortly after the policy was proclaimed, China would not be "equidistant" from the United States and the Soviet Union, but would evaluate the circumstances before taking a position. Chinese officials began to criticize both US hegemonism in Central America, the Middle East, and South Africa and that of the Soviet Union in Cambodia and Afghanistan, showing that China was independent from both superpowers. During his 1984 visit to the United States, Chinese Premier Zhao Ziyang went so far as to deny the very existence of "a strategic partnership" between the PRC and the United States. In an address to the Chinese military leadership in 1985, Deng declared that "in accordance with our independent foreign policy," China's improvement of relations with the Soviet Union and the United States "will enhance China's international status and enable us to have more influence in international affairs." Eight years later, Deng had not changed his position. "China is in itself a poor country, [so] why do people talk about China-US-USSR 'great triangle'? It's just because we act independently and keep the initiative in our own hands."[55]

At the same time, Deng was careful not to allow his denunciation of hegemonism to jeopardize China's developmental goals by offending Japan and the United States, whose support was critical for China's economic modernization. Despite their rhetoric, the Chinese also regarded the Soviet Union as a more serious threat to Chinese security than the United States.[56]

From 1982 to 1989, Deng's foreign policy displayed the most creativity. A good example was the idea of "one country, two systems" publicly articulated in 1982 as a proposed vehicle for future peaceful reunification with Taiwan and Hong Kong. The idea, which led to the Sino-British Joint Declaration on Hong Kong signed in 1984, was unprecedented in international diplomacy because it was based on coexistence of two different socio-economic systems under one state sovereignty, described by Prime Minister Margaret Thatcher as an "idea of genius." The Joint Declaration gave the British a transition period of thirteen years to prepare a "high degree of autonomy" for Hong Kong before it was transferred to the sovereignty of the PRC. Deng emphasized that the "one country, two systems" formula, the embodiment of the "peaceful coexistence" philosophy, would "serve as an example for other nations in settling the disputes history has bequeathed to them."[57] Chinese flexibility increased China's reputation for constructiveness and good will.

In a dramatic departure from orthodox Marxism-Leninism, in 1984, Deng proclaimed global North (developed countries) and global South (developing countries) economic interests to be compatible since the North wanted new markets and the South craved advanced technology. He also ascribed to China a special role in realizing the potential benefits of such interdependence, linking Chinese economic development to enhanced global prosperity and peace.[58]

As China became more integrated into the international system, Deng sought to develop a special role for China that would allow it to contribute to world peace, prosperity, and stability. In 1988, Deng revived the Five Principles of Peaceful Coexistence (initially formulated by Zhou Enlai and promulgated at the Bandung Conference of Asian and African nations), suggesting that the Five Principles could constitute the basis for a "new international political and economic order," one that would end the "politics of hegemony" and the "politics of contending blocs."[59] Thus, on a smaller scale than Gorbachev, Deng was also a norm entrepreneur.

At the end of the 1980s, China's international standing and influence greatly exceeded its economic and military capabilities, due in part to its impressive economic growth rate but also because the Chinese confidently articulated an alternative position on international issues and demonstrated diplomatic skill in encounters with foreign officials, as evidenced by the generally favorable impression of China among US officials in the Carter and Reagan administrations. The Carter administration extended most-favored-nation trading status to China, a concession that proved to be enormously important for China's economic development, while denying that benefit to the Soviet Union. The United States also removed export controls and sold advanced military-related hardware and technology to China. In part, US receptivity to China's status claims was based on balance of power considerations: China was a strategic partner against the Soviet Union.[60] Another motivation for status accommodation may have been the attraction of the China market and an abundant cheap labor supply, both in stark contrast with the stagnant Soviet economy. The American people supported closer relations with China because many were encouraged by Deng's reforms to believe that China's entry into the global economy would eventually lead to domestic liberalization. In SIT terms, Americans may have misperceived Deng's self-strengthening as part of a social mobility strategy.[61]

While Deng's initial tacit alignment with the United States against the Soviet threat is consistent with neorealism, his subsequent search for an independent foreign policy posture is outside the scope of that theory, which would predict that China would rely on the United States for security. Constructivism cannot explain Deng's concern for maintaining a distinctive Chinese identity, separate from the West as well as from the Soviet Union, or his efforts to articulate alternative norms of international relations such as the Five Principles of Peaceful Coexistence.

In line with SIT, Deng maintained China's traditional policy of seeking status through moral superiority.

THE SOVIET UNION AS NORM ENTREPRENEUR

To demonstrate his commitment to the New Thinking, Gorbachev made numerous arms control concessions and helped to resolve regional conflicts, while neglecting to reduce Soviet defense spending or to seek economic benefits such as trade and technology. He was still fixated on Europe and on the military-security sphere where Russia had traditionally enjoyed preeminence, an illustration of the resilience of Russia's traditional identity.

In adopting the ideas of the New Thinking, Gorbachev declared nothing less than his commitment to bridging "the gap between political practice and universal moral and ethical standards." In his report to the Twenty-Seventh Communist Party of the Soviet Union Congress in February 1986, he argued that "global problems affecting all humanity" required states to cooperate. An "interdependent and in many ways integral world" was emerging. Security, stressed Gorbachev, could only be obtained by political means and must be mutual. Disrupting the foundations of the Cold War realpolitik calculus, Gorbachev contrasted militarism and the balance of power with a "balance of interests," that is, voluntary agreement among states. Finally, Gorbachev advocated the establishment of a "comprehensive international security system" that would guarantee states' economic, political, and humanitarian as well as military needs.[62]

Since persuading others to accept the new Soviet identity required matching words with deeds, Gorbachev understood the imperative to implement the New Thinking principles in his own foreign policy. These norms were never meant to be just rhetorical window-dressing. On January 15, 1986, he proposed to eliminate nuclear weapons by the year 2000, as well as introducing other arms control measures. Disappointed at the US lack of response, at the special October 1986 Reykjavik summit he tried to persuade Reagan to agree to a 50 percent cut in strategic weapons, with no intermediate range missiles in Europe. No agreement was reached due to Reagan's unwillingness to accept Gorbachev's condition that research and testing of the Strategic Defense Initiative (a space-based missile defense system) be confined to the laboratory. Stymied on strategic weapons limitations, Gorbachev pressured the Soviet military to agree to onsite inspection and confidence-building measures in Europe, embodied in the October

1986 Stockholm agreement. Finally, Gorbachev delinked arms control measures from limits on strategic defenses in the December 1987 treaty to eliminate medium- and shorter-range missiles from Europe. "The New Thinking is the bridging of the gap between the word and the deed, and we embarked on practical deeds," Gorbachev wrote. "In all these issues the Soviet Union is a pioneer."[63]

Gorbachev also tried to strengthen the role of the United Nations (UN) and worked for cooperative solutions to regional conflicts. In October 1987, the Soviet government paid the UN $200 million in accumulated arrears for peacekeeping operations that the Soviets had declined to support since 1973. From 1988 to 1991 the Soviet leadership helped mediate political conflicts in Ethiopia, Angola, Namibia, Cambodia, Nicaragua, and El Salvador. The Soviets disengaged from occupation of Afghanistan, encouraged the Cubans to pull their military forces out of Ethiopia and Angola, urged the Vietnamese to withdraw from Cambodia, persuaded the Nicaraguans to agree to free elections even if it meant loss of power for the Sandinistas, and promoted a solution to the Salvadoran civil war.[64] Gorbachev's foreign policy went beyond the pragmatic elimination of costly commitments, as the Soviets could simply have withdrawn their troops and advisers from Afghanistan, Angola, and Mozambique.

Contrary to the neorealist argument about economic imperatives, Gorbachev's disarmament initiatives and conflict mediation did little to reduce the economic burden of Soviet foreign policy. Gorbachev did not reduce defense spending, despite its unusually high toll on the Soviet economy, until 1989.[65] Nuclear weapons—the focus of Gorbachev's arms control concessions in the first part of his tenure—were a relatively small component of the overall Soviet defense budget and, at least in the short term, dismantling existing weapons cost more than maintaining them. Nor did the Soviet Union dramatically reduce its costly foreign and military assistance programs to Third World clients such as Syria, Ethiopia, and Nicaragua until 1990.[66]

Compared to the impressive synergy between Deng Xiaoping's "reform and opening up" project and the Chinese reform-era realpolitik "practical statesmanship" in international affairs, Gorbachev's New Thinking diplomacy was surprisingly disconnected from his attempts to restructure the Soviet economy. While Gorbachev sometimes complained about discriminatory US trade policies, in making critical decisions that paved the road to the end of the Cold War, he did not bargain for economic quid pro quo such as technological assistance, trade concessions, or membership in economic institutions in return for arms control and other political concessions. Gorbachev's self-image as a world leader and his enormous sense of pride increased his reluctance to request economic cooperation and technological assistance from foreign countries. As Gorbachev warned former Japanese Prime Minister Yasuhiro Nakasone in July 1988, the Soviet Union could not be expected "to bow down" to get new technology. Gorbachev emphasized that it was wrong to think that the Soviet Union needed Japan more than the other way around.[67]

Gorbachev's preoccupation with grandiose global visions to the detriment of economic pragmatism and realpolitik cost his country dearly. For example, his search for sweeping global solutions for Asian security distracted Gorbachev from settling the more mundane territorial issue of the four Kurile Islands with Japan, squandering opportunities for Japanese financial and technological assistance in Soviet modernization and development of Siberia. Similarly, Gorbachev's concerns with the Soviet reputation in the Third World led him to continue to prop up North Korea, thus needlessly postponing diplomatic recognition of South Korea and wasting yet another chance for a successful economic partnership with an advanced capitalist economy. As a result, the Soviet Union never managed to tap into the Asian-Pacific economic dynamism and growing prosperity. Instead of becoming another California, Gorbachev's 1986 grand idea borrowed from Khrushchev, the Soviet Far East remained a laggard on the sidelines of the Asian miracle.[68]

In the New Thinking, the moral dimension was paramount and trumped economics. As observed by Leon Aron, Gorbachev and his team "first set out to right political and moral, not just economic wrongs." According to Gorbachev's key fellow New Thinker Anatoly Chernyaev, "before Gorbachev began to analyze and study concrete aspects of Soviet foreign policy, he had first created for himself a moral foundation on which any future political construction would be based." As some observers of Gorbachev's foreign policy recognized, the New Thinking was an ambitious project resting on incredibly idealistic premises. It was quite unprecedented for a great power that was "armed to the teeth" to be guided by such an idealistic view of the world, based on the chimera of universal reconciliation. In contrast to

Deng's pragmatic low-key diplomacy which served the needs of domestic modernization, through the New Thinking Gorbachev actively promoted a set of grand universal norms designed to reorient the international system from ideological rivalry and geopolitical competition to common human values and international cooperation, as a means of achieving preeminence for the Soviet Union in a new area, that of international norm entrepreneurship. Economic reforms lagged behind political changes. Shockingly, and in sharp contrast to the PRC, the Soviet Union "was no more part of the global economy at the end of the 1980s than it was at the beginning."[69]

When Gorbachev and his team were preparing for the most impressive display of the New Thinking before a world audience, his December 1988 address to the UN General Assembly, Gorbachev told his advisers that he wanted his speech to be a bold reply to Churchill's "Iron Curtain" speech at Fulton, Missouri, in March 1946. It "should be anti-Fulton—Fulton in reverse," he said, stressing the "process of demilitarization and humanization of our thinking." Gorbachev's UN address advocated overturning the principles that had ordered the world for at least four decades—deterrence, spheres of influence, and the balance of power. Gorbachev ruled out "force or the threat of force" as an instrument of foreign policy and called for freeing international relations from the influence of ideology. For the Soviet Union, he said, "freedom of choice is a universal principle to which there should be no exceptions."[70]

Gorbachev also announced that the Soviet Union would unilaterally cut its army by 500,000 and reduce its military forces in Eastern Europe by 50,000 troops and 5,000 tanks. Granted, Gorbachev recognized that *perestroika* (restructuring of the Soviet economy) could not succeed so long as the army consumed all of "the best scientific-technical forces, the best production funds, reliable supplies," but he was also concerned with the credibility of the New Thinking principles. If "we let the scope of our expenses be known," Gorbachev exclaimed at one point, "all our new thinking and our new foreign policy will go to hell." In short, Gorbachev's cuts were motivated by concerns for image and reputation as well as defense conversion, for he could have made the reductions without publicity. Summarizing his UN address to the Politburo, Gorbachev said, "We want and propose to build a new world, new relations."[71] The New Thinking offered the Soviet Union the promise of attaining a transcendent status as the creator of a new, more cooperative world order.

Our SIT-based interpretation contradicts the neorealist interpretation of the New Thinking as little more than a justification for Soviet retrenchment and defense cuts, as well as the rival constructivist view that the international relations philosophy represented Soviet socialization to Western values. Both of these interpretations ignore the messianism of the New Thinking and overlook the fact that alternative, more moderate policies would also have been consistent with domestic economic reforms.

Gorbachev's foreign policy was neither adaptive nor responsive to Soviet economic problems and was overly ambitious for a power in relative decline. In the words of a former Soviet economic official, "from the outset Gorbachev dreamed of the empire surging ahead, rather than merely surviving." It was also remarkably idealistic, aimed at ending the Cold War and positioning the Soviet Union as the moral leader of a new cooperative international order. The Soviet Union should never aspire to be the "same as everybody else" in order to enter the world community, Gorbachev's adviser Anatoly Chernyaev insisted at an April 1988 Politburo meeting, because then the Americans would ask, "excuse me, if you are the same as us, tell us—how many personal computers do you have, per capita? Oh, forty-eight times less than we do! Then say goodbye to the place of a superpower." "We are a powerhouse of modern world development of morality and justice," Chernyaev argued vehemently. "This is our strength."[72]

By the end of the 1980s, the Soviet New Thinkers' desire for positive recognition by the West seemed to be within reach, as Gorbachev's prestige eclipsed that of Deng and China. Foreign leaders would try to boost their own popularity by scheduling a meeting with the General Secretary, either in Moscow or in their own country.[73] Gorbachev's arms control concessions and appealing vision put the United States on the defensive. But Gorbachev's foreign policy would soon face acute challenges posed by the Eastern European allies' drifting away toward the West and by the severe economic crisis caused by his reforms. The Chinese leadership would likewise confront a political crisis brought about by the side effects of China's domestic reforms—corruption, inflation, and increasing inequality.

TIANANMEN AND CHINA'S STATUS DILEMMA

In April 1989, peaceful observances by students in honor of liberal former Politburo member Hu Yaobang, who had died unexpectedly, snowballed into a nationwide protest movement for democracy and freedom in China. Thousands of student protesters assembled in Tiananmen Square, the symbolic heart of the PRC.[74] To the shock and dismay of Chinese leaders, the spring 1989 Democracy Movement turned the Sino-Soviet normalization summit—Deng's expected diplomatic triumph and the potential beginning of a truly "independent foreign policy"—into a profound embarrassment for the regime.

Gorbachev's visit to China from May 15 to 18, 1989, was to be the symbol of full normalization of Sino-Soviet relations after three decades of animosity, proof that the Soviet Union was now willing to recognize China as a great power and to deal with it on the basis of genuine equality, and it was anticipated by the Chinese as a crowning achievement of diplomacy. Since Brezhnev had made public overtures to the Chinese in his March 1982 Tashkent speech, Chinese negotiators had insisted that the Soviet Union remove the "three obstacles"—the Soviet military presence on Sino-Soviet borders and in Mongolia, Vietnam's occupation of Cambodia, and the Soviet troops in Afghanistan.[75] Chinese officials had warned Soviet representatives that they were unwilling to return to the Soviet fold as a junior partner. In December 1985, Li Peng bluntly informed Gorbachev that China would not become the Soviet Union's "younger brother," insisting that Sino-Soviet relations must be equal. Being of a different generation, Gorbachev had no direct experience with the 1950s Sino-Soviet partnership, and he acknowledged to the Politburo that the Chinese had the "right to become a great power"—ideological heresy, but necessary for reconciliation with China.[76]

Plans for a triumphal ceremony were placed in jeopardy a few days before Gorbachev's arrival when some leaders of the student protests at Tiananmen Square began a hunger strike just as hundreds of foreign journalists and photographers were assembling in Beijing to record the historic Deng-Gorbachev summit. As Deng complained to his colleagues, "Tiananmen is the symbol of the People's Republic of China. The Square has to be in order when Gorbachev comes. We have to maintain our international image. What do we look like if the Square's a mess?" General Secretary Zhao Ziyang, who was sympathetic to the protesters, agreed that "to welcome Gorbachev in the right place and the right way involves the country's honor" and promised to make this clear to the students.[77] Desperate to end the strike before Gorbachev's visit, Zhao and other representatives visited the students to offer dialogue and request that the strikers end the hunger strike and withdraw from the Square before the Soviet leader's arrival, but most of the students defiantly resisted compromise. To Deng and many other top Chinese officials, the students' refusal was an insult, discrediting the moderates' strategy of trying to negotiate with the strikers.[78]

Humiliatingly, the meticulously planned welcoming ceremony for Gorbachev had to be moved at the last minute from Tiananmen Square to the old Beijing airport, without even a red carpet. The Chinese whisked Gorbachev from the airport to the Great Hall of the People at Tiananmen Square taking back roads and alleys so that he would not be seen by the students, for whom he was the symbol of democratic reforms, but they could not prevent the Soviet leader from witnessing the government's inability to uphold order in the capital.[79]

In his May 16 meeting with Gorbachev, Deng denied that ideological differences were the root of the Sino-Soviet split. "We were also wrong," he said. "The Soviet Union incorrectly perceived China's place in the world. . . . The essence of all problems was that we were unequal, that we were subjected to coercion and pressure." Gorbachev had informed his advisers in advance that he intended to treat Deng as a respected elder, deference that was "valued in the East." As prearranged, the meeting ended with a handshake rather than an embrace, a gesture that symbolized China's equality with the Soviet Union.[80]

The same day, the number of protesters in Beijing swelled to an estimated 1.2 million. The students defied the Chinese leadership's request that they vacate the square for the Gorbachev summit, and on May 17 Deng decided to bring in troops and declare martial law. "When the students chose Gorbachev's visit as the time for their hunger strike, they seriously disrupted the conduct of foreign affairs and sullied our national image," complained elder Bo Yibo, an adviser to Deng and former Politburo member. As Prime Minister Li Peng stressed to Beijing officials at the meeting where the imposition of martial law was announced, having to alter previous arrangements for Gorbachev's welcome "greatly damaged the image and prestige" of the PRC "in front of the international community." Even more disturbing for Chinese leaders, General Secretary Zhao Ziyang had conveyed the impression to Gorbachev that there was a deep rift within the leadership of the CCP on how to deal with the student demonstrations by saying that Deng was in charge of major political matters.[81]

At the June 2, 1989, meeting of the party Elders and a rump of the Standing Committee of the Politburo, a decision was made to use the military to clear Tiananmen Square. Deng stressed the priority of the PRC's sovereignty and angrily denied that the West had any right to judge Chinese domestic politics: "Look how many people around the world they've robbed of human rights! And look how many Chinese people they've hurt the human rights of since they invaded China during the Opium War!" Deng continued the theme several days after the Tiananmen crackdown: "We Chinese have self-confidence; inferiority complexes get you nowhere. For more than a century we were forced to feel inferior, but then, under the leadership of the Communist Party, we stood up."[82] For Deng, foreign criticism of China's human rights record was not just a threat to internal stability but also an insult to China's dignity and prestige.

Optimistic Western assessments of the trajectory of the PRC reforms had already been tempered by emerging concerns about the limits of political liberalization in China due to student protests in 1986–87, the dismissal of liberal General Secretary Hu Yaobang, and a campaign against "bourgeois liberalization." Gorbachev's acceptance of political pluralism in the Soviet Union and a worldwide wave of political liberalization (including neighboring South Korea and Taiwan) provided additional reasons to shine a spotlight on the Chinese human rights record.[83]

Powerful pro-democracy images generated by the intense global media coverage of the demonstrations in Beijing (such as the US Statue of Liberty–inspired "Goddess of Democracy" built by the students that stood on the square "eyeball-to-eyeball" with the iconic portrait of Mao) amplified Western public shock over China's use of military force against unarmed civilians and the deaths of hundreds if not thousands of protesters, and unleashed a storm of outrage directed at the Chinese leadership. Almost overnight, the Western public's image of China's "enlightened" rulers, committed to economic and political opening, was replaced by the image of the "butchers of Beijing," and even previously strong proponents of normal relations with Beijing predicted that China was fast becoming the "South Africa" of Asia. Members of the US Congress who had once observed that the human rights situation in post-Mao China was "better now than at any time since 1949," now depicted China as the "most repressive nation on earth." As a result, American popular attitudes toward the PRC shifted from 72 percent "favorable" in February 1989 to 59 percent "unfavorable" six months later.[84]

By late 1989, as "velvet revolutions" swept Eastern Europe and as Romanian dictator Ceausescu's attempt to adopt the "Chinese solution" to antigovernment demonstrations resulted in his overthrow and televised execution (Deng and his colleagues reportedly watched a recording in "stunned silence"), China was more isolated than at any other time since the Cultural Revolution.[85]

In the aftermath of the Tiananmen Square massacre, the Chinese leadership decided to wait out the crisis in relations with the United States, counting on Western outrage to subside over time, and to shame the United States by claiming unfair and humiliating treatment of China. During his July 1989 meeting with National Security Adviser Brent Scowcroft and Deputy Secretary of State Lawrence Eagleburger, Deng complained that Washington's sanctions had injured Chinese dignity.[86] Deng also evoked images from the Chinese "century of humiliation" at Western hands, saying that when seven Western countries imposed sanctions, he was reminded of the intervention by six of these countries in 1900 in response to the Boxer rebellion.[87]

Nevertheless, despite the Chinese leaders' fears that Western-sponsored "peaceful evolution" was designed to overthrow Chinese communism, they ultimately rejected conservative calls to reorient Chinese foreign policy toward confrontation with the West. Deng advised caution in Chinese foreign policy: "First, we should observe the situation coolly. Second, we should hold our ground. Third, we should act calmly. Don't be impatient; it is no good to be impatient. We should be calm, calm, and gain calm, and quietly immerse ourselves in practical work to accomplish something—something for China."[88]

In August 1991, when a Chinese official recommended issuing a statement of support for the anti-Gorbachev coup, Deng replied that China should "keep a low profile" (*taoguang yanghui*), "never take the lead" (*juebu dangtou*), and "try to accomplish something" (*yousuo zouwei*) in international affairs, the slogan that was to guide Chinese foreign policy in the early post-Deng era.[89] Overall, despite the immediate threat to China's positive identity, the strategy of social creativity, of achieving status through an independent foreign policy combined with long-term economic development, was still viable.

GORBACHEV AND THE SOVIET COLLAPSE

Ironically for Gorbachev and the other New Thinkers, Soviet success in projecting "soft power" internationally coincided with an acute crisis first within the Soviet sphere of influence in Eastern Europe and then within the Soviet domestic political system. Nevertheless, Gorbachev and his advisers remained faithful to the New Thinking.

As SIT would predict, with their efforts focused on winning over key Western power brokers and opinion makers, Gorbachev and the New Thinkers paid much less attention to traditional Soviet reference groups such as the Eastern European "fraternal" parties managing the Soviet sphere of influence. According to the testimony of Gorbachev's advisers, he was frustrated with the small-mindedness and conservatism of most Eastern European communist leaders such as Zhivkov, Ceausescu, and Honecker. They were too far beneath him to deserve consideration.[90] As the New Thinkers struggled to implement their understanding of true greatness on the world stage, they tended to perceive the Eastern European regimes not as prized possessions but as embarrassing reminders of Stalinism. The New Thinkers' lack of interest in Eastern European affairs is also evidenced by the lack of a coherent new policy for the region, apart from Gorbachev's strategy of "meticulous non-interference" in those countries' domestic affairs.[91]

Gorbachev's refusal to interfere in the internal affairs of Eastern European countries was not motivated by concern about the costs of maintaining the Soviet bloc, but by his belief in the principle of freedom of choice, which culminated in the Soviet decision not to prop up floundering communist regimes in the Warsaw Pact alliance.[92] Gorbachev did not originally anticipate or envision that Eastern European countries would abandon socialism; on the contrary, he was convinced that New Thinking and perestroika "would provide an inspiring example" for the Soviet socialist allies and strengthen Eastern European socialism. Nevertheless, he was prepared to accept loss of the Soviet security zone rather than undermine the New Thinkers' grand design for a cooperative world order.[93] The Soviet Union could have easily maintained its hegemony in Eastern Europe by means of the implied threat of intervention, made credible by the Soviet invasions of Hungary in 1956 and of Czechoslovakia in 1968. Eastern European leaders kept waiting for the Soviet Union to signal that it would send troops if necessary, but instead Gorbachev encouraged the reformers.[94] The New Thinkers' determination to avoid any display of Soviet military power—even symbolic—was nothing short of extraordinary. For former Soviet Foreign Minister Gromyko, the epitome of the Stalin-Brezhnev tradition, it was a mystery "why Gorbachev and his friends . . . cannot comprehend how to use force and pressure for defending their state interests."[95]

For the New Thinkers, Gromyko's "realist" calculus, based on coercion and the balance of power, was not only immoral, but "absurd" and inefficient as a means of attaining true superpower status. At one point Gorbachev labeled Gromyko's relentlessly assertive approach to diplomatic negotiations as "caveman-like." When Henry Kissinger rebuked Gorbachev for relying on "idealism" as his compass and founding his foreign policy on notions of "good and evil" to the detriment of European stability, Gorbachev refused to consider the possibility of a US-Soviet condominium over Europe. In a 1991 interview with *Izvestia*, Yakovlev said that he was "perplexed" by the "ultra-hardliners" who insisted that the country's prestige had been undermined by political changes in Eastern Europe. "A power's 'greatness,'" Yakovlev emphasized, "should be assessed by different criteria nowadays—by the criteria of morality, peaceableness, a desire to cooperate, and so forth."[96]

Even if Eastern Europe had lost its significance for Soviet security, East Germany might have been placed in a different category; its pro-Soviet regime was perhaps the most important strategic gain from the Soviets' hard-fought victory in World War II. Nevertheless, while he did not favor German reunification at first, once he had articulated the New Thinking, Gorbachev was constrained to apply its principles to his own foreign policy, which meant allowing the East Germans freedom of choice. To make an exception for Germany would have contravened his identity as a "norm entrepreneur" and undermined the Soviet Union's newly obtained status as a moral and political leader on the international stage. During a February 1990 meeting with West German Chancellor Helmet Kohl in Moscow, Gorbachev formally approved German reunification by acknowledging that "the Germans in the Federal Republic and in the GDR themselves have to know what road they want to take."[97]

Gorbachev's consent to Germany's membership in NATO was influenced by the US invocation of the freedom-of-choice principle. Initially, Gorbachev was "genuinely and adamantly opposed" to a unified Germany's joining the Atlantic alliance. During the US-Soviet summit of May–June 1990, Bush remarked that all nations had the right to choose their own alliances. He then asked Gorbachev whether Germany, too, had the right to decide for itself which alliance to join, forcing the Soviet leader to acknowledge that "the matter of alliance membership is, in accordance with the Helsinki Final Act, a matter for the Germans to decide."[98] Bush recalled that "the dismay in the Soviet team was palpable. [Marshal] Akhromeyev's eyes flashed angrily." His national security adviser Brent Scowcroft concurred that "I could scarcely believe what I was witnessing." It was obvious that Gorbachev "had created a firestorm in his delegation and faced bitter opposition."[99]

Social identity theory might help to explain why Gorbachev's drive for world recognition and acceptance seemingly took precedence over material considerations, as he agreed to German reunification and membership in NATO without gaining much tangible in return. After a meeting with Kohl in February 1990 at which Gorbachev acceded to German reunification, Horst Teltschik, Kohl's chief foreign policy adviser, commented in his diary, "Gorbachev does not commit himself to a specific solution; no demand of a price, and certainly no threat. What a meeting!" Despite the critical state of the Soviet economy, the Soviet leadership did not establish a firm quid pro quo between Soviet consent on the NATO issue and large-scale West German economic and financial aid.[100] This would have undercut the image Gorbachev was trying to establish as the creator of a new, more cooperative international order. According to Chernyaev, Gorbachev considered attaching stringent economic conditions to a unified Germany's NATO membership "undignified."[101] Not until the "end game" of German reunification did the Soviets request economic assistance to compensate for the loss of East

Germany, after the critical decisions had already been made, the Soviet economy had taken a nosedive, and Gorbachev's market-oriented economic advisers had argued that large-scale Western assistance was needed to save perestroika. Even after Gorbachev realized that the West was not really interested in setting up new post–Cold War pan-European security structures "from the Atlantic to the Urals" with his country as an equal partner, and that he had "fallen into a trap" (his angry description to Kohl in September 1990), the Soviet leader still made no attempt to play his remaining card, the presence of 300,000 Soviet troops in East Germany. When the critical Soviet economic crisis in 1990–91 finally impelled Gorbachev to ask for Western economic assistance, he sought to preserve Soviet dignity and prestige.[102]

Emboldened by his success and acceptance on the international stage, Gorbachev until the last moment was hoping to reverse Soviet domestic fortunes through economic reforms (perestroika) and democratization of the Soviet system. As one of Gorbachev's aides put it, "He [Gorbachev] had become so good at convincing the rest of the world of his ability to perform political miracles that perhaps he eventually believed it himself."[103] Nevertheless, Gorbachev's domestic reform strategy failed miserably, obliterating his hopes to transform the system (and state) from within.

In contrast to Deng's embrace of evolutionary, decentralized market-based reforms, which were based in large part on local experimentation, Gorbachev's initial approach to domestic reforms fell squarely within Russia's historical legacy of periodic "great reforms from above" designed to remedy previous failures and adapt to a changed international environment, a "shortcuts to greatness" approach to modernization.[104] Similar to his New Thinking in foreign policy, Gorbachev's "great reforms" were significantly influenced by the messianic ethos of romantic Leninism. Instead of gradually reforming the Soviet economy to allow more integration of market forces, in 1985–87, Gorbachev insisted on refining the traditional top-down Soviet planned developmental model and attempted to inspire the Soviet Communist Party with a new "heroic" task—a remarkably ambitious but also wildly unrealistic program of "acceleration" of socio-economic development.[105]

After the program of "acceleration" failed, due to the weakened mobilizational capacity of the Soviet regime, the search for economic solutions branched out in more radical directions. While Gorbachev and his colleagues ultimately (and belatedly) accepted the need to utilize market forces to enliven the Soviet economy and even tried to imitate some Chinese-style market measures, for the Soviets "the question of *how* to move to a market was never adequately resolved." In contrast to Deng, Gorbachev and his team did not provide economic and political incentives for party and state officials to embrace perestroika's relatively modest market reforms, with the result that the market-enabling measures tended to be ignored by Soviet bureaucrats or enacted with inadvertent consequences. In short, "bottom-up reforms worked in China; top-down reform failed in Russia."[106]

In contrast to Deng's reform strategy of tempering market mechanisms with Communist rule to preserve political stability, Gorbachev's dissatisfaction with the performance of the Soviet party-state bureaucracy (whom he accused of sabotaging his 1985–87 attempts to perfect the Soviet administrative-command system) ultimately led him to enact political and administrative reforms that eviscerated Soviet centralized control over both the economy and politics. Deng reportedly later called Gorbachev "an idiot" for deciding to implement political reforms in the Soviet Union prior to the economic ones, accurately predicting that Gorbachev "won't have the power to fix the economic problems and the people will remove him."[107]

The summer 1988 Nineteenth Party Congress endorsed multicandidate elections for the Soviet legislature and its complete restructuring, steps that signified the beginning of democratization of the Soviet political system. By summer of 1990, after empowerment of the new legislature, legalization of multiparty competition, and creation of the post of USSR president, the Communist party for all intents and purposes ceased to be a functioning political mechanism.[108]

Unfortunately for the fortunes of perestroika, as Gorbachev reduced the role of the party and branch ministries in economic management and decision-making, he lost control over the Soviet economy, sending it into a tailspin. By the end of Gorbachev's tenure in office, planning mechanisms had been weakened, but a market system was not yet in place, so the Soviet economy was a halfway house. The socialist system's inability to provide for basic human needs led to a loss of legitimacy, and the removal of restraints on freedom of speech encouraged protests and strikes.[109] An article in *Moskovskie novosti* by Alexander Kabakov titled "HUMILIATION" (in capital letters) complained that

"Queuing for everything—from sausages to razor blades—has become a necessary part of Soviet life." Then he tied the food shortages to the Soviet identity: "For the citizens of a country that built atomic power stations and space shuttles, queuing for a bar of soap is humiliation."[110]

On top of this, Gorbachev's decentralization and liberalization stimulated nationalist sentiments in the Soviet republics. The disintegrative forces that resulted were unexpectedly facilitated by the formal structure of the Soviet Union—a federation based on national territories existing within the purportedly unitary Soviet state.[111]

Independence movements within the USSR itself posed the crucial test of Gorbachev's adherence to the freedom of choice idea. Yet, even when faced with a nightmare of national dissolution and a backlash of conservative forces at home, the New Thinkers by and large managed to rule out resorting to force. As Shevardnadze explained to his American counterpart, James Baker, following the April 1989 unrest in Georgia, "If we were to use force then . . . it would be the end of any hope for the future, the end of everything we are trying to do, which is to create a new system based on humane values. . . . We cannot go back."[112]

While refusing to betray the ideals of the New Thinking, Gorbachev and his colleagues ultimately fell victim to the formidable challenges of "dual transitions"—simultaneous political liberalization and economic restructuring—becoming unable to enforce basic political and economic rules or to provide essential public goods. Successful application of a Chinese-style evolutionary reform program, a less cavalier attitude toward macro-economic controls, and, crucially, preservation of the clear lines of political authority in the Soviet system might have yielded dramatically different results. Gorbachev might also have chosen to adopt a pragmatic realist international strategy subordinated to the needs of Soviet modernization, following Deng's example.[113]

WHY GORBACHEV DID NOT LEARN FROM THE CHINESE

While both the PRC and the Soviet Union tried to reform the socialist system while adding market principles, and although Chinese reforms were enjoying remarkable success by the time Gorbachev came to power, Soviet reformers did not pay much attention to the Chinese experience. The Soviet identity as a great power and leader of the international communist movement inhibited any inclination to learn from lower-status China.

The Soviet leader was reluctant to admit that any aspect of the Chinese experience was relevant to the Soviet economy. His 1987 reform manifesto *Perestroika: New Thinking for Our Country and the World* devoted just one sentence to Chinese ideas about modernization. Given Gorbachev's "desperate search for perestroika and then a path to marketization, neglect of the Chinese experience seems scarcely comprehensible," writes Gilbert Rozman. China had accumulated "innumerable lessons for Gorbachev if he cared to look her way," argues Sergey Radchenko. Granted that the scope and complexity of the challenges confronting Gorbachev in modernizing the Soviet economy were unprecedented, "it is still remarkable to what extent he ignored, or even dismissed the Chinese reform experience."[114]

Neorealist theory would expect the Soviet Union to emulate or at least study any potential lessons to be gained from China, a rapidly growing socialist state with success in making a transition from a centrally planned economy to markets. One possible explanation for Gorbachev's failure to acknowledge the Chinese experience was the distorted information he received about Chinese reform dynamics from Soviet think tanks specializing in China. On the other hand, while influential advisers of Gorbachev such as Alexander Yakovlev openly confessed that they knew little about China, other more knowledgeable scholars and reformers favored emulating some aspects of the Chinese reforms.[115]

SIT suggests that Gorbachev's skeptical attitude toward the Chinese experience and his unwillingness to emulate Deng's domestic and foreign policy reforms can be better explained by Soviet superpower status concerns and related cultural biases, including "traditionally dismissive" stereotyping that inhibited learning from lower-status Asian powers. If Deng Xiaoping's maxim that "backwardness must be recognized before it can be changed" is correct, then Gorbachev's unwillingness to borrow from the Chinese experience stemmed from his reluctance to admit that the Soviet Union was increasingly losing economic dynamism and attractiveness as a developmental model in comparison not only to advanced Western countries but also to its rapidly developing Asian neighbor and, more recently, sworn Cold War rival. The Soviet elite and public found it hard to believe that any East Asian country

—not even Japan, let alone China—could be superior to the Soviet Union in any respect. While Gorbachev put an end to the Soviet tradition of treating China as a "little brother" and recognized it as a legitimate great power, Soviet exceptionalism, sense of superiority, and great power mentality still affected the Sino-Soviet relationship.[116]

States measure themselves against a reference group that is equal or higher in status, not a lower one. If Gorbachev was willing to learn from abroad, it would be from the advanced Western economies, the Soviets' key reference group, not from a developing country such as China.[117]

The superior status of the Soviet Union within the socialist camp also inhibited emulation of Beijing. Since the Chinese rebellion against the Soviet developmental model under Mao had resulted in spectacular debacles such as the Great Leap Forward, Soviet elites were predisposed to look at China with derision, assuming that Chinese economic problems would persist even as China was discovering a successful reform path. As noted by a Soviet China-watcher, competition with Beijing over the correct definition of Marxism-Leninism produced a "China syndrome," encouraging Soviet policymakers to "glorify" the Soviet "social mechanism" rather than try to repair it.[118] Not surprisingly, Gorbachev's private comments on the Chinese reform experience frequently focused on their deficiencies and limitations compared to the "wisdom" and "promise" of the Soviet approach to reform. For example, he believed that the Chinese agricultural reforms, despite their remarkable success, would eventually face difficulties due to China's lack of technology and intensive methods (which the Soviet Union, of course, possessed). Gorbachev also somehow convinced himself that the abundance of consumer goods in China was not a genuine success since nobody in China could afford to buy them. In another telling example, at one point Gorbachev falsely accused the Chinese SEZs—almost universally considered to be one of the most dazzling achievements of Deng's "opening up" policy—of producing "uncompetitive" products, forcing the Chinese to repay the loans with their gold reserves. In sum, Gorbachev systematically underestimated China's achievements and overestimated Soviet economic prospects.[119]

Finally, and perhaps most importantly, under the influence of the New Thinking, Gorbachev insisted on positioning the Soviet Union (and himself personally) as a messianic trailblazer and tutor, if not a prophet, entirely convinced that his domestic reforms would have universal transformational implications for the entire world. Compared to the reforms in other socialist countries (including, first and foremost China), the Soviet perestroika naturally had "decisive significance" because the Soviet Union was "one of the greatest powers or superpowers of the modern day, upon which depends the fate of the world more than on anyone else," argued Gorbachev's adviser Shakhnazarov in August 1987. Perestroika is a "universal lever capable of transforming not only Soviet reality but also the world situation in general," proclaimed Gorbachev in his *Perestroika* bestseller. As he explained to one of his advisers in response to being designated "man of the decade" by *Time* magazine, "The scale of our design is global. Look, we've turned our country upside down. Europe will never be the way it was. And the world will not return to the past. . . . Once again it's turned out that our new revolution is not only national, Russian, but global. At least we've managed to launch the beginning of world perestroika."[120]

Rather than becoming an attentive student of Chinese reforms, Gorbachev expected China to learn from perestroika. After he embraced political liberalization in the USSR, Gorbachev became an ardent proponent of rapid simultaneous political and economic transformation and a vocal critic of the Chinese "partial" reform model for not delivering the sweeping changes his passionate "almost evangelical" reformism demanded. Deng's temporary return to austerity measures in 1988–89 convinced Gorbachev that the Soviet Union was ahead of China in both political reform and marketization.[121] Such a dismissive attitude toward the Chinese experience was validated for Gorbachev by the shock of the Tiananmen crisis, which he personally witnessed. As Gorbachev declared to his team on the first day of his May 1989 visit to Beijing, "We saw today where [the Chinese] road leads. I do not want Red Square to look like Tiananmen Square." In the aftermath of the Tiananmen crackdown, liberal Soviet supporters of perestroika increasingly viewed China as a negative (and failing) alternative to more advanced Western economic and political models.[122]

In sum, the Soviet self-image as a superpower and the leader of the international communist movement, together with Moscow's continuing fixation on the West as a status reference group, inhibited Gorbachev and his team from studying Chinese reforms and foreign policy and adapting them to Soviet conditions.

CONCLUSIONS

Consistent with SIT, both Deng and Gorbachev opted for social creativity—seeking preeminence in areas other than geopolitical power. China under Deng pursued prestige through an independent foreign policy, pragmatism, and diplomatic flexibility rather than military power or revolutionary success. While neorealist theory would predict that China would downplay its revolutionary aspirations in order to align with the United States against the Soviet Union, the theory does not anticipate Deng's efforts to establish an independent foreign policy identity for China, nor his creativity in devising solutions to the problems of Hong Kong and Taiwan, such as "one country, two systems." Revival of the Five Principles of Peaceful Coexistence would assist China's efforts to establish a new post–Cold War international order while highlighting the PRC's unique contributions to world peace and stability.[123]

The Soviet Union under Gorbachev sought a new domain in which to compete with the United States—promoting new international norms and ideas. Gorbachev found the New Thinking more attractive than alternative foreign policy programs, because it offered a new role for the Soviet Union as a norm entrepreneur and a distinctive status as the author of principles underlying a new world order. Gorbachev advocated universal human values such as nonuse of force, a comprehensive international security system, and mutual security. Gorbachev did make arms control concessions to the West, but he did so as part of his effort to educate the rest of the world on new international norms that would replace the Cold War.

Conventional neorealist interpretations of Gorbachev's New Thinking as little more than a rationalization for Soviet retrenchment fail to account for the surprising idealism of New Thinking, its lack of suitability for alleviating Soviet domestic economic problems, and its ambition and scope in light of Soviet economic decline. Far more consistent with neorealist prescriptions would be a modified version of the Brezhnev détente policy or balancing between the United States, Asia, and Western Europe. Despite the Soviet need for Western technology and investment, in contrast to Deng, Gorbachev gave relatively little attention to integrating the Soviet Union into the global economy. Gorbachev's decision to give up the Soviet sphere of influence in Eastern Europe because it contradicted the principles of New Thinking is a stunning example of how status concerns may outweigh material interests, behavior that neorealism cannot explain. To be sure, subsidies to Eastern Europe were a drain on the Soviet economy, but Gorbachev could have chosen to encourage reformist communists, instead of allowing the region to join the West.[124]

Constructivism is well attuned to the importance of changing discourse, such as Deng's "reform and opening up" or Gorbachev's New Thinking. The question is why both leaders adopted new foreign policy rhetoric. Constructivism does not give adequate weight to the efforts of both leaders to forge a distinctive foreign policy and to enhance their state's international standing, which enhanced the appeal of these ideas. The ideas of the New Thinking were abstract and idealistic—they had to be translated into concrete policies, subject to interaction with other states. Gorbachev used the ideas of the New Thinking instrumentally to advance his foreign policy and domestic agendas.

Gorbachev viewed himself as a Leninist, restoring basic socialist values, although he came to project onto Lenin his own worldview. Nevertheless, the New Thinking's view of an interdependent, interconnected global world in which there were universal interests contradicted the traditional Marxist-Leninist view of international relations as a class struggle in which there were two opposing camps. Gorbachev did not display much interest in promoting the spread of communism in the Third World. As evidenced by his discussions with Brzezinski and Lee Kuan Yew, Deng viewed regional conflicts and relations between states from a geopolitical perspective, as opposed to a Marxist-Leninist-Maoist ideology.[125]

When the Cold War ended, the new identity that Gorbachev had constructed for the Soviet Union could not be sustained. The moment of the Soviet Union's triumph as a multi-dimensional superpower was sweet, but extremely short-lived. Gorbachev's political liberalization, in conjunction with elimination of centralized economic controls, resulted in the catastrophic collapse of the Soviet economy and the breakup of the Soviet Union, destroying the remaining façade of superpower status. For Gorbachev's successors, the problem of establishing Russia's status vis-à-vis the West would quickly return with a vengeance. In contrast, the identity that Deng had created for China as an industrious, capable, fast-growing but pragmatic power endured for his successors to modify and build on as the country became stronger and more capable of acting independently.

5 Status and Identity after the Cold War

CHINA NEEDS a distinctive foreign policy suitable for a "major country," declared President Xi Jinping in an authoritative foreign policy pronouncement at the Foreign Affairs Work Conference (FAWC) in December 2014—the first such conference since 2006—to an audience of Politburo members, military officers, diplomats, and hundreds of other Chinese officials. Xi's language implied that he was abandoning Deng Xiaoping's admonition from the days of the Soviet collapse to "take a low profile" (*"taoguang yanghui"*). "The growing trend toward a multipolar world will not change," he declared confidently, implying that America's dominance was coming to an end. Xi's foreign policy address culminated a period of high-profile diplomacy, including hosting the annual meeting of the Asia-Pacific Economic Cooperation (APEC) forum, participation in a Group of 20 summit in Brisbane, Australia, and visits to Australia, New Zealand, and Fiji. Nearly a quarter century after the Tiananmen crisis, the end of the Cold War, and the collapse of the Soviet Union, with the PRC poised to overtake the United States as the world's largest economy, a "discourse of greatness," or *shengshi huayu*, was emerging, as evidenced by the popularity of Xi's concept of the "Chinese dream."[1]

The contrast with Russia's international standing was striking. Just as China, a rising global power, was increasing its engagement in international diplomacy, Russia experienced the biggest chill in its relations with America and Europe since the Cold War. The May 9, 2015, Victory Day parade in Red Square—the largest military parade ever staged in Red Square, with 16,000 soldiers marching, more than 140 aircraft streaming overhead, and three updated intercontinental ballistic missiles, showcasing the achievements of Russia's military modernization—provided a stark symbol of the decline in Moscow's new international standing. Of the sixty-eight world leaders invited, only twenty-seven attended. Western leaders—collectively boycotting the celebrations in protest against Russia's involvement in the Ukraine crisis—were represented by their ambassadors. At President Vladimir Putin's right was the guest of honor President Xi Jinping of China. Presidents of Egypt, South Africa, Cuba, and Venezuela also attended.

A month earlier, Putin had claimed in a television documentary that after the Communist Party's fall from power, even he, a seasoned foreign intelligence officer, had harbored "illusions" about the prospects of establishing good relations with the West. However, such illusions had been shattered by the West's refusal to recognize Russia's interests and treat it with respect.[2]

What accounts for the diverging foreign policies of the former Communist powers since the end of the Cold War? Russia's and China's central status predicament—their exclusion from the liberal democratic "core" of great powers, rooted in history and intensified by Communist revolutions and Cold War politics—was exacerbated by the end of the Cold War. Both experienced major threats to their identities as great powers. Beijing's crackdown on protesters at Tiananmen Square placed China on "the wrong side of history" in the eyes of the West, while Russia's continuing political and economic instability fueled doubts about the country's ability to make a successful transition to liberal democracy. Yet in both countries the leadership held fast to the goal of recovering great power standing.

For neorealism, the changing distribution of power after the end of the Cold War—with Russia losing one-third of its territory, half of its population, and much of its military might, and China growing at an average rate of 10 percent per year—should have prompted significant changes in both the Russian and Chinese grand strategies. In the immediate aftermath of the Cold War, neorealists would predict that the two powers would accommodate or bandwagon with the United States because of its economic and military primacy. As China increased its military and economic power, neorealists would expect the PRC's ambitions to grow and to be translated into efforts to achieve dominance over the United States in East Asia. A resurgent Russia would try to reassert control over states of the former Soviet Union or at least try to prevent them from being absorbed into a rival alliance or sphere of influence.[3]

Constructivism would anticipate changes in China's and Russia's identity as both states were more intensively exposed to liberal norms and rules through diplomatic interaction in the context of new understandings of international status. Interaction with other states and diplomatic practice would help to determine which identity discourse emerged as dominant within China and Russia.[4] With the end of the Cold War and the triumph of liberal democracy, ideology would be less relevant as a guide to foreign policy. Although China was still nominally communist, the PRC no longer tried to promulgate communism to other states.

SIT, on the other hand, would predict that China and Russia would attempt to forge new distinctive identities in an international system dominated by the United States. Emphasizing the "end of history" and the triumph of democratic values, the United States encouraged former communist states to become liberal democracies with market economies. SIT would predict that unless China and Russia emulated Western liberal values—values at odds with their collectivist and statist traditions—both states would be denied admission into the great power club. Frustration with the lack of permeability of elite institutions would encourage both states to turn to competitive and assertive behavior, complaining of Western "double standards." If they regarded the US position at the top of the status hierarchy as stable and/or legitimate, both states would be prone to exercise social creativity, finding value in previously unappreciated aspects of their national traditions or promoting alternative norms. Whether their efforts at social creativity endured would depend on the willingness of the United States and other Western powers to recognize alternative values and institutions as sources of status and legitimacy.

We provide background by first discussing how each state responded to the challenges posed by the end of the Cold War—the Chinese by following Deng's injunction to "keep a low profile," the Russians by trying to embrace capitalist modernization and join the West. Both sub-sequently pursued social competition, the Chinese out of hubris due to their economic recovery and perceptions of US decline, and the Russians out of anger due to their continuing exclusion from elite clubs. We then review their efforts at establishing a more positive identity using social creativity. The Chinese sought to create a new image as a "responsible power," while Vladimir Putin tried to form a strategic partnership with the United States in the "war on terror." The United States supported China's new identity as a responsible power, while re-buffing Putin's overtures at becoming a strategic partner of the United States and NATO. As a denouement to the opening era of unipolarity, the 2008–9 financial crisis and the waning of US hegemony affected China's and Russia's strategies for advancing their status, leading to more assertive claims to global power status, but with the difference that Russia eventually returned to social competition.

POST-TIANANMEN CHALLENGES

In the late 1980s, China faced both an external legitimacy crisis caused by the end of the Cold War, and a domestic crisis arising from uneven economic growth. In response to the brutal repression of peace-ful demonstrators at Tiananmen Square in June 1989, the United States organized Western political and economic sanctions, including suspen-sion of military cooperation and arms sales and the postponement of loans from international financial institutions.[5] With the peaceful collapse of successive communist regimes in Eastern Europe, China's rulers, who had only recently been regarded as bold and progressive reformers, were now perceived by the West as cruel reactionaries trying to hold back the inevitable forces of freedom and democracy. In con-trast, after 1987 Taiwan became more democratic, allowing Taiwanese nationalism to emerge for the first time as an important factor in Tai-wan's politics. Previously unheard-of demands for Taiwan's indepen-dence, combined with US support for democratic Taiwan, threatened China's plans for peaceful reunification—the key to domestic legiti-macy for successive generations of Chinese leaders.[6]

In his acceptance speech to the Democratic National Convention in July 1992 (which prominently featured several student leaders of the Tiananmen Square movement) Bill Clinton described his vision of an

America that would not "coddle dictators from Baghdad to Beijing." His victory in the 1992 presidential elections seemed to herald an end to the era of China's special treatment on human rights issues and the "cuddly communism" image of the Chinese on which it rested.[7]

Deng's answer to the CCP's domestic legitimacy crisis was to resurrect and expand market reforms. In Deng's view, Soviet economic troubles proved that China's decision to focus on market-based economic reforms had been the correct choice. In the face of a conservative backlash, Deng's January–February 1992 "southern tour" bolstered local cadres' support for economic reforms, as indicated by formal legitimization of a market economy at the 1992 Fourteenth Party Congress, which called for the creation of a "socialist market economic system" as the goal of reform and proclaimed anti-market "leftism," not "bourgeois liberalization," to be the main danger to the survival of the Chinese Communist Party.[8]

The reformers' political triumph quickly translated into economic success, with the resurgence of GDP growth up to 14 percent in 1992–93, leading to an increase in living standards and reduction of poverty.[9] At the same time, defying predictions of the imminent collapse of CCP rule, in the aftermath of Tiananmen, Leninist institutions not only remained strong in China, but underwent re-institutionalization, making the Chinese party-state more stable and efficient.[10] Economic and political reform enabled the Chinese Communists to survive major challenges to the legitimacy of the system, despite the apparent global triumph of liberal democracy.

Although Deng had advised his successors to exercise utmost caution in foreign policy, Jiang Zemin and his followers—emboldened by the dynamic Chinese economic performance, the end of China's post-Tiananmen isolation, and the re-establishment of domestic stability—attempted to translate China's growing economic strength into increased political clout in the Asia-Pacific region and an assertive stance vis-à-vis the United States, engaging in social competition. Many Chinese analysts believed that the United States was a declining power, given its economic problems, the rise of Japan, domestic political polarization, and isolationist public sentiment. The world, they believed, was moving toward multipolarity, with China rightfully one of the poles.[11]

In February 1995, China was discovered to have occupied Mischief Reef, part of the Philippine claim area in the oil-rich and strategically located Spratly Islands. Concern about China's ambitions was further heightened by the regime's military exercises and missile tests in the Taiwan Strait from July 1995 to March 1996. The Chinese were reacting to the May 1995 decision by President Bill Clinton to grant Taiwan President Lee Teng-hui a visa to visit Cornell University, thereby encouraging Taiwan's search for "greater international space." The Chinese regarded the US visa decision as a slap in the face to Jiang, who had pursued a relatively conciliatory policy toward Taiwan. People's Liberation Army (PLA) officers and civilian hawks in China demanded a strong military response. In the wake of the crisis, Premier Li Peng crowed that Americans "have come to realize the importance of China."[12]

China's military demonstration caused a backlash, as the Association of Southeast Asian Nations (ASEAN) rejected Beijing's sovereignty claims in the South China Sea, the United States dispatched two aircraft carrier battle groups to the area near Taiwan, and the United States and Japan strengthened the terms of their alliance, including collaboration on a theater missile defense system covering the East China Sea (and possibly Taiwan). Chinese elites eventually came to realize that social competition with the United States in the Asia-Pacific region fed into the "China threat" theory, increasing the risk that a coalition of states would try to contain China's rise.[13]

YELTSIN'S DIPLOMACY: FROM SOCIAL MOBILITY TO SOCIAL COMPETITION

Following the end of the Cold War, Russia faced enormous problems in creating new political and economic institutions, yet was unwilling to relinquish its claims to great power status. The breakup of the Soviet Union into fifteen republics transformed the country from a superpower into a has-been, creating a sense of psychological loss.[14] Although Russia inherited the Soviet Union's nuclear weapons and permanent membership in the UN Security Council, traditional great power status markers, it was not invited to join elite Western institutions. After failed social mobility efforts, Russia adopted a social competition strategy of forming diplomatic coalitions in order to restrain US power and enhance Russia's global status.

The collapse of the Soviet Union threatened both the value and distinctiveness of Russia's identity. Russia suffered profound internal and external identity crises, exacerbated by the rapid decline in its status and loss of its position as a superpower.[15] Although different schools of thought—Marxists, statists, Westernizers, and Eurasianists—disagreed on Russia's foreign policy orientation, there was one point on which they all agreed: Russia's destiny was to be a great power, not just a "normal state."[16] Equally important was the question of Russia's status in its relationship with the United States, which continued to serve as the "prime reference point" for Moscow's foreign policy. The drive for political equality with the United States and US appreciation of Russia have always been key ingredients of domestic legitimacy for both Soviet and post-Soviet rulers.[17]

In the early 1990s, Foreign Minister Andrei Kozyrev and other Russian liberals pursued a strategy of social mobility, aspiring to be admitted to Western clubs such as GATT, the IMF, the Group of Seven (G7), and even NATO, as a sign that Russia had "arrived" in the community of Western liberal democracies.[18] The Clinton administration, however, was unwilling to admit any new members into these elite clubs until they had met certain political and economic benchmarks. In contrast, Russian elites believed that Russia was in a different category from Central and Eastern European states, and should be welcomed into Western institutions without having to meet external conditions. Unlike Germany and Japan after World War II, Russia did not regard itself as a defeated power, obligated to defer to the United States and its allies.[19]

A critical factor in Russia's political evolution was the US decision in early 1994 to enlarge NATO to include former members of the Warsaw Pact, followed by NATO's bombing of Serbian positions in Bosnia. While Yeltsin's national security advisers did not view the prospect of NATO enlargement as a security threat, they were alarmed by the potential political consequences for Russia's international status and identity. Russian pro-Western liberals worried that exclusion of Russia from the emerging all-European security system based on NATO would lead to its marginalization.[20] The unwillingness of the United States to even consider Russian membership in NATO implied that, unlike Germany and Japan after World War II, Russia would not be readmitted into "civilization," even as it appeared to be playing by the rules.[21] Moscow was not particularly interested in joining NATO's Partnership for Peace Program because it did not promise membership and did not give Russia a special status, but treated it the same as the Eastern and Central European states. As Samuel Charap and Timothy Colton noted, "the psychological fallout from the heir to a superpower being denied an authentic voice in shaping the regional order and told to wait its turn to get in—Gulliver standing in line behind the Lilliputians—was evident to sophisticated observers."[22]

Russian concerns about marginalization appeared to be warranted in spring 1994, when NATO bombed Serb positions in Bosnia, an area of historic Russian interest, without even going through the motions of consulting Russia. When Strobe Talbott tried to persuade Russian Foreign Minister Kozyrev that it was in Russia's interests to halt the Serbs, the Russian foreign minister cut him off: "It's bad enough having you people tell us what you're going to do whether we like it or not. Don't add insult to injury by also telling us that it's *in our interests* to obey your orders." On the day NATO conducted its first airstrike against Serbian forces, Russian President Boris Yeltsin's press secretary Vyacheslav Kostikov announced that Russia's romantic embrace of the West was over, and that Russia increasingly saw itself as a great power with strategic interests different from those of the United States and Europe.[23]

The discrediting of Kozyrev's pro-Western policies, called "Romantic Atlanticism" by Russian critics in reference to unilateral concessions made to Western positions, was accompanied by a growing domestic backlash against the Yeltsin team's attempts to use Washington Consensus-style policies as a guide to post-Soviet economic transformation. For Russian reformers, a "shock therapy" approach to Russia's market transition emerged as a "shortcut" to modernization, a free-market "revolution from above" intended to break once and for all with the Soviet economic and political legacy, and to facilitate the speedy transformation of Russia into a capitalist economy in order to jump into the ranks of the leading Western powers. For large segments of the Russian population, however, the Yeltsin team's "market Bolshevism" quickly became associated with a painful decline in living standards and an outburst of crime. The Russian economy shrank by an average of 6 percent per year in 1990–98, with the 1998 GDP

43 percent below the 1989 figure. The economic decline resulted in dramatic cuts in government funding for scientific research, which led to an acute crisis in Russian science and education, threatening Russia's status "as an intellectual great power."[24]

Russia's economic troubles went hand in hand with political malaise. In the aftermath of Yeltsin's October 1993 use of military force in a confrontation with the Russian parliament, Russia's political system devolved into an increasingly corrupt mix of "illiberal democracy" and what Russian scholars termed "oligarchical corporatism" (narrow group interests hijacking major institutions of the Russian state).[25]

In addition to disillusionment over the failure of "shock therapy," for which Western advice and lack of financial assistance took part of the blame, many Russian elites began to believe that the United States was treating Russia as if it were a second-rate, developing country. In a September 1995 interview, former Soviet President Mikhail Gorbachev claimed that the West's policy in Europe, the Balkans, and within the former Soviet Union was marked by "clear disrespect for Russia." While some Western politicians would like to see Russia "play second fiddle" in world politics, Russia would not accept such a "humiliating position."[26] Russia had tried social mobility, but had failed to measure up to Western standards, and was the object of condescension as well.

Widespread dissatisfaction with the West's treatment of Russia led to Kozyrev's replacement as foreign minister by Yevgeny Primakov. From 1996 to 1999, Primakov pursued "multipolar" diplomacy aimed at restoring Russia's importance through diplomatic counter alliances designed to create a system of checks and balances against the United States while elevating Russia to the status of an independent pole—a strategy of social competition. For example, he proposed the idea of a Russia-India-China triangle.[27] Primakov promised that Russian foreign policy would reflect his country's "status as a great power" and that Russia would seek an "equal, mutually beneficial partnership" with the West.[28] But Russia was too weak and financially dependent on the West to challenge US actions, particularly given that the Clinton administration was prepared to act unilaterally.

In 1997, to mitigate the humiliation of NATO's enlargement, Clinton granted Yeltsin political (but not economic) membership in the G7. "As we push Ol' Boris to do the right but hard thing on NATO," Clinton explained, "I want him to feel the warm, beckoning glow of doors that are opening to other institutions where he's welcome." Yeltsin claimed that his "tough stance on the eastern expansion of NATO . . . played a role in gaining us this new status [G8 membership]."[29] That Yeltsin would accept membership in an informal club as compensation for the expansion of an implicitly anti-Russian alliance dramatizes how much importance the Russian president placed on status.

Despite this achievement, throughout the 1990s Russia repeatedly and painfully bumped up against Western barriers on most other issues—the former Yugoslavia, NATO enlargement, Russia's membership in other important international organizations, and the 1994–96 war in Chechnya—Russia's biggest defeat since Afghanistan, this time, humiliatingly, on its own territory. Periodically orchestrated rounds of international applause and often-empty goodwill gestures such as the 1997 Russia-NATO Permanent Joint Council, where Russia had practically no voice, did not compensate for Russian humiliations on these other fronts or quell Russia's resentment at being told that it had to meet externally imposed standards to be accepted into Western clubs. The perception that the West too often failed to accord Russia the role and status to which it felt entitled, leaving it marginalized and isolated from real decision-making power, led to dramatic deterioration in US relations with Russia.[30]

Primakov tried to mediate on Iraq and Kosovo to establish Russia's centrality and obstruct US military action, but such efforts only highlighted Russia's extreme financial-economic vulnerability and its high degree of economic dependence on the West. One day Moscow would be lambasting the West for its policy toward Iraq, making not-so-subtle references to its nuclear might; the next day it would be thankfully accepting Western emergency food assistance.[31]

NATO's bombing of Yugoslavia in the spring of 1999 was a turning point for Russian elites and foreign policy specialists, convincing them that Russia no longer mattered to the West and that the United States, for all its rhetoric about a cooperative world order, was making geopolitical gains at Russia's expense. That the United States used NATO to bypass the UN Security Council, where Russia had a veto, showed an "insulting disregard" for its interests.[32] When he learned of the bombing, Primakov ordered his plane, which was headed toward the United States, to turn around in midair. The anger and frustration of Russian elites was vividly displayed when 200 Russian peacekeepers (redeployed from Bosnia to Kosovo without consulting NATO in a bid to give Moscow more say in Kosovo's future) rushed to capture the airport of Pristina before NATO troops arrived, risking a dangerous military clash between US and Russian soldiers. Even moderate Vladimir Lukin commented that the incident should show the West that "it cannot treat Russia like some lackey." "No one in Russia should be able to call President Yeltsin a puppet of NATO," explained Vladimir Putin, then the director of the FSB (Federal'naya Sluzhba Bezopasnosti, the successor to the KGB) and the newly appointed head of Russia's Security Council, to Clinton's Deputy Secretary of State Strobe Talbott.[33] After protesting, Russia, however, ultimately accepted Western policies on NATO enlargement, Iraq, and Kosovo, becoming an unwilling partner of the West.[34]

At the end of the 1990s, Russian efforts to regain international status fitting for a great power seemed to be doomed to failure, with Moscow becoming an angry anachronism in world politics, continually complaining about its lack of influence while conducting an inconsistent foreign policy. As Lawrence Freedman observed, Russia had become "preoccupied with a great power status" to which it could no longer lay claim. Russia not only was viewed by the majority of Western elites as an economic "basket case" mired in corruption and powerless to control its organized crime—as journalist Jeffrey Tayler put it, "Zaire with permafrost"—but was at risk of falling out of the ranks of "civilized" countries because of its actions in Chechnya.[35]

Russian foreign policy was further compromised by Yeltsin's numerous health problems and frequent erratic behavior during foreign trips and dealings with foreign dignitaries. As Talbott relates, Yeltsin's drunkenness was also at times exploited by US officials during negotiations to gain more concessions from Russia—perhaps a perfect metaphor for Russia's perception of its relations with the United States during the 1990s.[36]

By the turn of the millennium, optimistic expectations of integration with the West were replaced with widespread disillusionment with Russia's "phony partnership" with the United States and the West, and a "national humiliation complex" stemming from the perception that Russia was being treated as a defeated country rather than as a valuable ally.[37] The preamble to Russia's official Foreign Policy Concept in March 2000 reads as if it were an epitaph to Kozyrev's policies of deference to the West, "Romantic Atlanticism," explicitly acknowledging that "expectations of equitable, mutually advantageous and partnership relations with the surrounding world" reflected in the previous 1993 concept had not been met.[38]

Russia's experience in the 1990s illustrates the obstacles and disincentives for a former superpower in following a strategy of social mobility. Emulating the values of the established powers, as required by social mobility, implies a humiliating relationship of tutelage and contradicts the need to maintain a distinctive identity. In the case of Russia, an even greater obstacle to social mobility was the impermeability of Western elite group boundaries, due to lingering distrust, cultural differences, and the enormous scale and complexity of the economic and political reforms that would have been necessary for Russia to meet Western standards.[39]

On the other hand, Chinese and Russian efforts at social competition demonstrated the serious limitations of that strategy as well. A secure post–Cold War status hierarchy meant that status competition was humiliatingly futile and wound up only accentuating Beijing's and Moscow's inferiority to Washington. Both countries relied on traditional great power status markers that they had accumulated during the Cold War (such as permanent UN Security Council membership), some of which were becoming increasingly irrelevant in the post–Cold War environment, while failing to generate new sources of prestige and legitimation. Indeed, with a single remaining superpower, attempts at social competition risked being interpreted as aggressive and revisionist by major international players, since US (and Western in general) status superiority was the new status quo.[40] Finally, social competition was not a viable long-term strategy for Russian and Chinese elites because, in contrast to the Cold War rivalry, it was not legitimized by militant anti-Western ideological constructs and/or perceptions of irreconcilable material conflicts of interests with the West. In an era of peace between the leading international powers, geopolitical competition (the most visible manifestation of social competition in the past) remained largely subdued. Having recovered from the shock of unexpected unipolarity, China and Russia discovered that as aspiring great powers they had little desire to upset the fundamentals of an international order that, on balance, provided ample opportunities for the growth of their power and influence.[41]

CHINA'S RESPONSIBLE POWER STRATEGY
AND "PEACEFUL RISE"

With the breakup of the Soviet Union and collapse of communist rule in Eastern Europe, Chinese leaders confronted a new and unexpected world. Instead of the multipolar world that they had envisioned and preferred, the international system seemed to be trending toward unipolarity, domination by the United States. By the mid-1990s, Chinese foreign policy analysts recognized that previous optimistic expectations about the emergence of multipolarity were wildly off the mark, concluding that "the superpower is more super, and the many great powers are less great."[42] More accurate and realistic assessments of the post–Cold War status hierarchy encouraged recognition of the limitations of social competition.

Status requires acceptance from others, and Chinese elites inferred that they had to alter their behavior to win recognition from the West. In 1996–97, Beijing shifted to a grand strategy of acting as a responsible major power—a strategy of social creativity. China would pursue an activist role in global management and multilateral organizations while reassuring other states about its own peaceful long-term intentions. Chinese President Jiang Zemin used the term "responsible power" (*fuzeren de daguo*) in a speech before the Russian State Duma in April 1997, where he suggested that China and Russia, as major powers of influence and permanent members of the UN Security Council, had an important responsibility for safeguarding world peace and stability. By explicitly referring to the responsibilities of a great power for maintaining order, Beijing was trying to allay fears that China's eventual rise to great power status would be destabilizing.[43]

In 1996, as part of what Jiang called "great power diplomacy," Beijing began to foster "strategic partnerships" with other major powers that were supposedly not directed against any other state. The first strategic partnership, with Russia, stimulated efforts by China between 1996 and 2005 to form partnerships with thirty-two countries. The bilateral partnerships illustrated China's much-touted New Security Concept, which, building on the Five Principles of Peaceful Coexistence, argues that security should be based on mutual trust, mutual benefit, equality, and cooperation, as opposed to outmoded Cold War alliances and military blocs. It was proposed by Chinese Foreign Minister Qian

Qichen at the annual meeting of the ASEAN Regional Force in 1996 and more fully developed by President Jiang Zemin at the UN Conference on Disarmament in March 1999. The New Security Concept allows China to claim prestige as a norms entrepreneur. Chinese officials argued that the Five Principles of Peaceful Coexistence could serve as the basis for a "new political and economic order."[44]

The New Security Concept also furnished a rationale for China's increased participation in multilateral institutions such as the ASEAN Regional Forum and the organization for Asia-Pacific Economic Cooperation (APEC). In 2002, China signed an ASEAN Declaration on the Conduct of Parties in the South China Sea, which renounced violent means of dealing with conflicting claims in those waters. Beijing touted its support for multilateral cooperation as contradicting the "China threat" theory, showing that China could play a constructive role in preserving peace and stability in neighboring areas.[45]

The Chinese also began to take a leadership role in creating new multilateral organizations. In 1996, the Chinese took the initiative in establishing the Shanghai Five, comprising China, Kazakhstan, Kyrgyzstan, Russia, and Tajikistan, to demarcate borders and carry out confidence-building measures. With the addition of Uzbekistan in 2001, the group evolved into the more institutionalized Shanghai Cooperation Organization and adopted the goal of combating terrorism, extremism, and separatism. Some observers suggested that China was using regional multilateral organizations to undermine US influence and alliance systems in Asia. On the other hand, these regional bodies are informal, consensus-based, and impose no commitments. Most members also want to maintain good relations with the United States.[46]

China signed numerous arms control treaties, abandoning its previous position that arms control was a cynical ploy aimed at the have-not nations. Beijing signed the Comprehensive Test Ban Treaty largely out of concern for China's stature and image as a responsible power, although PLA officers and defense industry representatives argued that China's nuclear arsenal needed additional testing.[47]

China's emerging identity as a "responsible great power" was strengthened in the Asian financial crisis of 1997–98, when Beijing won praise for not devaluing its currency and for offering financial assistance to bail out the economies of neighboring countries. After the crisis, China helped to create ASEAN Plus Three (China, Japan, and South Korea) to stabilize the regional financial system. In 2002, Beijing committed to implementing a free trade agreement with ASEAN by 2010 to reassure China's neighbors that its economic growth would be an opportunity rather than a threat to their economies.[48]

Successful social creativity efforts in foreign affairs were linked to important developments in China's domestic model of modernization. The East Asian financial crisis generated doubts and heated debates about China's reform path and developmental model. While China managed to survive the economic turmoil virtually unscathed, the crisis also highlighted risky aspects of the East Asian developmental model of state-sponsored capitalism that was pursued by Japan and South Korea, which involved government support for state owned enterprises, protection of infant industries, dependence on exports, and a high rate of domestic savings. The deficiencies included the absence of transparency, perverse effects of "crony capitalism," and lack of rule of law in government and business. The solution ultimately implemented by the Chinese leadership led by Jiang Zemin and Zhu Rongji (who became Chinese prime minister in 1998) was to deepen Chinese reforms with the goal of building a genuinely modern market economy that would allow China to "get on the global track" (*shang guoji guidao*), to become a major competitive player in globalization. By the late 1990s, for Chinese leaders, a market economy had become the unquestionable yardstick of modernity, signifying "world-class competition, world-class standards, and world-class status." In order to avoid the pitfalls of the East Asian developmental model, it was decided that China had to open even more decisively to foreign direct investment, information, and technology flows while simultaneously reconfiguring its domestic and foreign policies to maximize the benefits from new transnational sources of wealth, power, and status.[49]

In 1998, Chinese leaders dramatically accelerated their efforts to join the World Trade Organization (WTO), abandoning their traditional position that China as a developing country should be offered a generous timetable to comply with WTO rules. For Jiang Zemin, membership in the WTO, in addition to potential economic benefits, was an important demonstration of "his ability to enhance China's status as a world power."[50]

Sensitive to considerations of status and image, China attempted to improve its record on human rights by signing international human

rights treaties, releasing a few prominent dissidents, and allowing selected UN human rights representatives to visit the country. The Chinese leadership realized that human rights issues could be used by other
governments to justify perceptions of a "China threat"—if the Chinese
regime mistreated its own citizens, then it could not be expected to
respect the rights of other countries. Western countries have been reluctant to recognize China as a great power because of its poor human
rights record and nonliberal polity, as illustrated by the failure of the
G7 to offer China membership despite China's attendance at various
meetings beginning in 2003 and the importance of Chinese participation for financial stability and trade.[51] In 1997, to ensure the success of
Jiang Zemin's October summit with Clinton, China signed the International Covenant on Economic, Social and Cultural Rights, and in
March 1998, the International Covenant on Civil and Political Rights
(although it has not yet ratified the treaty). During this period, China
released two well-known dissidents, Wei Jingsheng and Wang Dan,
from prison. China hosted a ten-day visit by the UN Working Group
on Arbitrary Detention to Beijing, Chengdu, Lhasa, and Shanghai to
assess legal protections for citizens. The Chinese government agreed
to address the severe mistreatment of children in Chinese orphanages,
which had been criticized by international observers. In January 1998,
China invited the UN High Commissioner for Human Rights to visit
China. China made these concessions largely out of concern for its status and image, despite the risk to its sovereignty. At the same time, Beijing tried to promote alternative metrics for great power status recognition by emphasizing its responsible external behavior and highlighting
its impressive achievements in social and economic rights—part of a
social creativity strategy of claiming preeminence in a new area.[52]

The line that China's rise will be "peaceful" was developed by Zheng
Bijian, a leading Communist Party theorist and adviser to Hu Jintao.
Zheng and other Chinese officials were motivated by concerns that the
incoming Bush administration was apprehensive about the future uses
of Chinese power, and that this might translate into policies that would
undermine China's pursuit of great power status. In his writings and
speeches, Zheng contrasted China's transcendence of the traditional
routes to great power status with both the imperialism and aggression
of pre–World War II Germany and Japan and the Cold War struggle
for global domination between the Soviet Union and the United States,
thereby providing further evidence of China's "positive distinctiveness"

and showing the use of social creativity. China's economic growth would not be a destabilizing factor or a source of threat for its neighbors and the world at large. Instead, China would adhere to principles of mutual cooperation, peace, common development, and collective security, based on the New Security Concept. The "peaceful rise" (*heping jueqi*) paradigm also emphasized that China would avoid tensions and conflict with the major powers. In December 2003, Premier Wen Jiabao elaborated the "peaceful rise" concept in a speech at Harvard University, and President Hu Jintao followed at a symposium commemorating the birth of Mao Zedong. But by April 2004, President Hu had replaced the term with "peaceful development" (*heping fazhan*) and other conceptually similar constructs. Nevertheless, "peaceful rise" continued to be used informally by Chinese academics and government officials, and the overall policy orientation remained intact.[53]

One criticism made of the "peaceful rise" line was that it would undermine attempts to deter Taiwan from declaring independence. In 2004, the Democratic Progressive Party candidate Chen Shui-bian was reelected president of Taiwan, a major shock to the Chinese leadership. Chen made several provocative moves, including a proposal to rewrite the constitution of the Republic of China and give Taiwanese citizens the opportunity to vote on such issues as whether Taiwan should strengthen its self-defense capabilities and rejoin the United Nations. President George W. Bush had to restrain Chen to prevent him from provoking a war. China conducted military exercises to demonstrate its increasing capability to project power across the Taiwan Strait. In addition to using military pressure, China showed some creativity on the Taiwan issue, which is tied to sensitive identity, legitimacy, and great power status concerns for Beijing. Partly out of concern for its international status and image, Beijing adopted a more flexible and sophisticated approach to Taipei, including economic and cultural initiatives to win the "hearts and minds" of the Taiwanese population, such as incentives for export of fruit from pro-independence areas of Taiwan and tuition breaks for Taiwanese students studying on the mainland. China also offered more flexibility in interpreting the "one China" principle, and exchanges with Taiwan's major opposition parties, which were open (at least in theory) to the "one China" idea.[54]

In 2008, Chinese overtures to Taiwan were vindicated by the election of the Kuomintang's presidential candidate Ma Ying-jeou, who campaigned in favor of improving relations with the mainland. In

November 2008, China and Taiwan reached a landmark agreement on direct, regularly scheduled shipping and air service across the Taiwan Strait for the first time in more than half a century. Ma ended up signing over twenty agreements promoting economic integration across the Strait before his party lost power in 2016.[55]

While the embrace of globalization has meant increasing convergence with Western economic norms and rules, Beijing does not subscribe to the prevailing Western norms of individualism, human rights, transparency, promotion of democracy, or humanitarian intervention. Beijing adheres to traditional norms of sovereignty and nonintervention in other states' internal affairs. China divides sovereignty rights into economic and political spheres, allowing intrusions into its sovereignty as embodied in WTO rules and regulations while refusing to tolerate criticism of its human rights practices. China provides "no strings attached" foreign assistance, and in contrast to the Western industrialized states, its commercial deals do not impose conditions such as transparency, accountability, environmental standards, or prevention of corruption. Nor does China accept the "Washington Consensus" of neoliberal economic principles such as a convertible currency, no capital controls, and privatization of state enterprises, preferring instead the Beijing consensus whereby a state's developmental policies must be adapted to its own circumstances.[56] A strong proactive party-state committed to political and social internal stability as well as pragmatic, experimentation-based economic policies and integration into the global economy has emerged as the centerpiece of what has been dubbed in the West the "Beijing Consensus" and what the Chinese themselves prefer to call the "China model" (zhongguo moshi).[57]

The fourth generation of the Chinese leadership presided over by Hu Jintao (the CCP top leader in 2002–12) made a deliberate effort to promote China's "soft power" by emphasizing the appeal of the Chinese developmental model, generous foreign assistance, and benign foreign policy in diplomatic forays into the developing world. Hu stressed the need to emphasize Chinese culture as the country's "soft power" in his keynote speech to the Seventeenth National Congress of the CCP in October 2007. Toward that end, China has been establishing hundreds of Confucian Institutes aimed at teaching Chinese language and culture in an effort at "rebranding" the Chinese state.[58]

For many Chinese academics and officials, soft power is valued both intrinsically and instrumentally—as an indicator of elevated international status, and as a means of facilitating China's continued rise in hard power. Chinese strategists believe that a country cannot be recognized as a great power unless its values, norms, and way of life have appeal to others. Chinese soft power will alleviate regional fears of a "China threat," thereby reducing the likelihood of a counterbalancing coalition. Some scholars have suggested that traditional Chinese Confucian values such as harmony, both within society and between humanity and nature, could have substantial attraction to the rest of the world by way of contrast to the environmental destruction, ethical confusion, and international conflicts fostered by Western materialism, science, and individualism.[59] The argument that Chinese values are superior to Western values exemplifies the "reframing" tactic of social creativity, wherein nominally negative traits (traditional Chinese values which were criticized for obstructing modernization) are reframed as positive in the post-industrial age.

Confucian values were highlighted in the "harmonious world" (*hexie shijie*) concept, first presented in an address by Hu Jintao on the sixtieth anniversary of the United Nations in September 2005. A harmonious world would entail a "dialogue among civilizations." The principal means of achieving this world order concept would be multilateralism, the United Nations, international law, and universal norms of international relations. But the "harmonious world" differed from liberalism in its derivation from Confucian values such as the "Great Harmony" and "peace under heaven." In contrast to "peaceful rise," however, "harmonious world" did not resonate with Western audiences.[60]

In sum, as a result of "peaceful rise"-based social creativity, China gradually took on a more activist, constructive world role that included increased support for multilateralism, a policy that reassured other states, enhanced China's global role, and increased its relative status.

US SUPPORT FOR CHINA'S RESPONSIBLE POWER IDENTITY

As we discussed earlier, according to SIT, a social creativity strategy requires validation from the dominant power to succeed. From 1997 to 2008, the United States indicated that it would accord China a more prominent place in the world if it behaved responsibly. Immediately after the 1995–96 Taiwan Strait crisis caused by China's missile tests in the area, US National Security Adviser Anthony Lake, who had earlier dismissed China as a "backlash" state, an outlaw state that not only rejected but challenged liberal democratic values, made his first visit to the country. While there, he stressed that China was a great nation and that the United States wanted China to help design the system governing the world in the twenty-first century. President Clinton exchanged formal state visits with Jiang in 1997 and 1998, a concession long sought by the Chinese as symbolizing the end of the post–Tiananmen Square ostracism and emphasizing China's enhanced international status, and agreed to a "constructive strategic partnership." At the 1998 summit in Shanghai, Clinton showed respect for China by stating publicly for the first time that the United States did not support Taiwan's independence; the concept of one China, one Taiwan; or Taiwan's membership in international organizations where statehood was a condition for membership—the "three nos."[61]

The importance of US acknowledgment of China's rise was revealed by the remarkably open and intense Chinese debate in the summer of 1999, after the accidental US bombing of the Chinese embassy in Belgrade in May and other perceived US humiliations of China sent relations into a tailspin. The promise of a constructive strategic partnership with the United States enabled Jiang to garner enough domestic support to maintain the "peace and development" line through the assumption of power in 2002 by Hu Jintao and other fourth generation Chinese leaders.[62]

Although President George W. Bush initially viewed China as a strategic competitor, China's assistance after the September 11, 2001, terrorist attacks contributed to a shift in US policy. In the aftermath of the attacks, Beijing quickly seized an opportunity to repair ties with the United States and to act as a responsible global citizen by addressing Washington's new concerns about terrorism. China used its traditional close ties with Pakistan—and the offer of economic and political assistance that would help prevent a coup—to persuade longstanding ally Pakistani President Pervez Musharraf to cooperate with US efforts in Afghanistan. China also cooperated in tracking terrorist financing, shared limited intelligence concerning Islamist extremist groups, and agreed to establishment of a Federal Bureau of Investigation liaison office in Beijing. Unlike Clinton, who did not meet with Jiang until his second term, Bush met with the Chinese leader several times during his first term (referring to Jiang as "the leader of a great nation" at the

APEC forum meeting in Shanghai in October 2001), as well as with his successor Hu Jintao. China also won appreciation for its role in organizing and hosting the six-party talks, which began in 2003, to restrain North Korea's nuclear ambitions.[63]

In an important 2005 speech, Deputy Secretary of State Robert Zoellick affirmed that the United States wanted China to become "a responsible stakeholder" in the international system.[64] Washington played to China's status aspirations by accepting the Chinese proposal for "strategic dialogues" on a wide range of issues, including the Strategic Economic Dialogue, between the US secretary of the treasury and the Chinese vice premier, and the Senior Dialogue, which was conducted by the US deputy secretary of state.[65]

The need for social cooperation in dealing with rising powers is illustrated by tensions in China's relations with Japan despite their burgeoning economic ties. China and Japan have never been great powers at the same time and have not learned to respect each other's status as equals. Since the mid-1990s, Sino-Japanese relations have been embroiled in symbolic issues such as Japanese textbooks' treatment of Japan's World War II atrocities, whether Japanese leaders should issue a written apology for war crimes committed against the Chinese people during the World War II invasion and occupation, and Japanese politicians' visits to the Yasukuni Shrine where Japanese war criminals are interred. Chinese nationalism exploded with Japan's 2004–5 campaign for a permanent seat on the UN Security Council. More than forty million Chinese signed an online petition opposing Japan's application, citing its failure to atone for its World War II atrocities. In April 2005, news that the Japanese education ministry had approved a new revisionist textbook provoked violent protests against Japanese citizens and property across China. Chinese authorities initially made no attempt to control the disturbances, even though Japan was China's second-largest trading partner and a major source of foreign investment.[66]

Tensions with Japan notwithstanding, in response to China's increased support for multilateralism and international norms, part of the "peace and development" line, the United States accorded China increased status based on the expectation that it would eventually take on more responsibility for global governance. Russia's variant of social creativity, however, relied on strategic partnerships with other great powers.

PUTIN'S CREATIVE DIPLOMACY

Given the stunning decline in Russia's international standing in the 1990s, President Vladimir Putin's principal foreign policy goal was to restore Russia's foreign policy autonomy and its great power status.[67] Putin's strategy exhibited social creativity in its efforts to achieve great power status through partnership with the United States.

In his 1999 programmatic statement, "Russia at the Turn of the Millennium," Putin stressed that "Russia was and will remain a great power" and admonished Russians to "apply all the intellectual, physical, and moral forces of the nation" to avoid the danger of slipping into the second or third tier of states in the international system.[68]

To deal with Russia's identity crisis, Putin combined tsarist and Soviet symbols, adopting the tsarist double-headed eagle as the national symbol and reinstating the Soviet national anthem (with new lyrics) while giving increased support to the Russian Orthodox Church.[69] His positive reframing of characteristics previously viewed as negative is a social creativity tactic, designed to enhance national pride and self-esteem.

The 2001 terrorist attacks against the United States provided Putin with an extraordinary opportunity to reframe Russia's identity and to align with the United States, demonstrating that Russia was a valuable and indispensable player. In his September 11, 2001, call to Bush (the first from a foreign leader), Putin expressed condolences and assured the US president that Russia would not respond to the US heightened state of alert with reciprocal measures by Russian strategic rocket forces. Russia's cooperation with the United States in the war on terror was valuable and extensive, and included sharing political and military intelligence about international terrorists, allowing US planes to fly over Russian territory, acquiescing to US military bases in Central Asia, participating in international search and rescue missions, and providing increased assistance to the Northern Alliance, an anti-Taliban force in Afghanistan. Putin also lost no time in reminding the West that Russia had been at the forefront of the war on terror with the struggle in Chechnya, and that Chechen separatists had ties to major terrorist organizations, including al Qaeda.[70]

Russian cooperation cannot be explained away as adaptation to US hegemony, because most Russian political elites had recommended to

Putin that Russia remain passive or neutral in the US war on terror. The Russian defense minister and chief of staff were strongly opposed to a US military presence in Central Asia, part of Russia's traditional sphere of influence.[71]

In addition to accepting US bases in Central Asia, Putin made several unilateral concessions signaling that the geopolitical rivalry between the United States and Russia was over, evidence that he was following a social creativity strategy. He withdrew from a large Russian electronic intelligence-gathering and military base in Cuba and a naval base in Cam Ranh Bay, Vietnam; reacted mildly to the US withdrawal from the Antiballistic Missile treaty—one of the few remaining symbols of Russian equality—calling it a "mistake" because it would hurt arms control; adopted a softer position toward admission of the Baltic states to NATO; accepted the creation of the NATO-Russia Council as a vehicle for cooperation, although it gave Russia only a marginal voice; and agreed to a strategic arms reduction treaty that allowed the United States to store dismantled warheads.[72]

In return, Putin expected to be treated as a valued and respected partner with the United States in the war on terror, an "equal partnership of unequals."[73] In a speech before the German Bundestag in late September 2001, Putin argued that the security structure created in previous decades was no longer capable of coping with new threats such as terrorism. Putin believed that the only viable alternative was a concert of great powers, similar to the Concert of Europe.[74] Before the November 2001 US-Russia summit, Putin privately compared his partnership with Bush in the anti-terrorist coalition to that between Franklin Roosevelt and Winston Churchill in the anti-Nazi coalition during World War II. On a personal level, Putin also seemed to be moved by the invitation to dinner at Bush's ranch in Crawford, Texas, his first visit to the home of another world leader.[75]

Putin's social creativity strategy was designed to bring Russia from the periphery to the core of international politics not through integration into the Western community but as an equal partner with a distinctive role. At a press conference on the eve of his departure for the June 2002 G8 meeting, Putin stated that "for a country that used to be an antagonist or enemy of the world's industrialized nations, Russia should become a partner—moreover, an equal partner. This is the paramount mission of Russian foreign policy." In a March 2000 interview with David Frost, Putin had said that he could envision Russia's integration with NATO, but "only if Russia is regarded as an equal partner." He stressed that "Russia is a part of the European culture" and he could not imagine Russia "in isolation from Europe." "So it is hard for me to visualize NATO as an enemy."[76]

To use a formula popular in domestic discussions of Russia's foreign policy objectives, Russia under Putin never intended "to be a second Poland in Europe," a rising regional power that successfully embraced a strategy of social mobility. It aspired to be nothing less than a great power staking out its own unique position in global affairs and defending its distinct civilizational identity. Russia's great power aspirations were fully compatible with "cooperation and association" with Europe but not with "integration" into it on Western terms.[77]

AN AGGRIEVED RUSSIA AND A CRISIS FOR RUSSIAN SOCIAL CREATIVITY

The US-Russian partnership did not last long, peaking in May 2002. Although Putin expected to be treated as a partner, the Bush administration did not regard Russia as an equal, believing that Moscow had little choice but to accommodate US policies in Eurasia. Despite Bush's promise, the United States did not even graduate Russia from the Cold War–era Jackson-Vanik amendment, which prevents permanent normal trading relations with a state that restricts emigration. The United States also took actions that indicated indifference to Russia's status concerns—in particular, Bush's failure to consult Russia before deciding to invade Iraq, a former Soviet ally where Russia had substantial economic interests. Washington did not even bother to send a high-level official to Moscow to make a case for war.[78]

Russia did receive some measure of respect in the form of an invitation to join the G7—the most significant post–Cold War status marker granted by the West in the late 1990s—but membership did little to alleviate Russia's status dissatisfaction. Due to its relatively weak economy, Russia was not admitted to the economic discussions conducted by the G7 finance ministers, making the Group of Eight humiliatingly "never really the G8 but rather the G7/G8."[79]

For the Kremlin, the most serious offense was increasing Western involvement and interference in Russia's near abroad. When the Soviet Union broke up, some former Soviet republics contained minority ethnic enclaves. In three former Soviet states, four enclaves—Transdniestria, Ossetia, Abkhazia, Nagorno-Karabakh—declared independence and formed mini-statelets. Russia believed it was its prerogative to manage such conflicts in neighboring areas, contributing to its image as a responsible regional power. According to a well-informed Russian analyst and politician, Alexey Pushkov, Putin began to be disillusioned with the United States in November 2003 when Washington, the EU, and the chair of the OSCE allegedly interfered in Russian attempts to resolve the dispute between Moldova and Transdniestria by pressuring the Moldovan president, Vladimir Voronin, not to sign the agreement brokered by Putin's personal representative, Dmitry Kozak, just hours before Putin was scheduled to fly to Moldova to preside over the formal signing. Putin reportedly regarded US involvement in quashing the Kozak memorandum as a "personal affront," proof that the United States was trying to weaken Russia's influence over the post-Soviet space despite Putin's cooperation after 9/11.[80]

The Moldovan fiasco was followed by US support for "color" revolutions in Georgia (2003), Ukraine (2004), and Kyrgyzstan (2005), regime changes that were perceived as humiliating interference in Russia's backyard and even as models for destabilizing the Russian regime. The Ukrainian "Orange Revolution," in particular, was a shock and personal slap in the face for Putin, who had campaigned in Ukraine for his favored candidate, Viktor Yanukovych, thereby staking his personal reputation on the outcome, only to see the election results overturned as fraudulent by the Ukrainian opposition and the West. Not only was the West challenging Russia's status as a great power, in the view of Russian officials, it was now trying to undermine its status as a regional power with a *droit de regard* in the post-Soviet space.[81]

Increasing US criticism of Putin's domestic policies, such as Vice President Dick Cheney's charge that the Russian government was seeking "to reverse the gains of the last decade," reportedly infuriated Putin, and confirmed the perception of some Russian elites that the West could not tolerate a stronger, more self-confident Russia. In defiance, Putin put forward the concept of "sovereign democracy," developed by Kremlin ideologist Vladislav Surkov, which maintained that Russia would determine its own path to democracy, free from foreign interference or normative pressures. In other words, there was more than one definition of democracy, and Russia was following the way best suited to its history and culture.[82]

Russian elites were more confident in making claims to great power status after Russia paid off its international debt in 2006, thereby restoring its sovereignty and solvency. Russia's financial clout also increased in light of the increase in the price of oil from $35 per barrel in 2004 to $147 per barrel in July 2008. Russia's unwillingness to tolerate Western criticisms of either its domestic or external politics was turbocharged by fresh memories of the humiliations of the 1990s and a growing sense of triumphalism over Russia's comeback on the world stage. As Sergei Ivanov, then minister of defense, stated in the summer of 2006, "Russia has now completely recovered the status of great power that bears global responsibility for the situation on the planet and the future of human civilization." Later that year, in response to the British demand to extradite the suspect in the assassination of former KGB agent Alexander Litvinenko by radioactive polonium, the infuriated chair of the Russian Duma Foreign Affairs Committee Konstantin Kosachyov reminded London that "you can act this way towards a banana republic, but Russia is not a banana republic." As Valentina Matvienko (then the governor of St. Petersburg and later speaker of the Federation Council of the Russian Duma) argued in a July 2007 interview, "Russia has now regained a sense of self-respect. We spent so many years feeling there was something wrong with us—others lecturing us on how we should live and where we should go. But we have overcome our inferiority complex."[83]

As discussed in chapter 1, according to SIT, continuing refusal by the higher-status group to acknowledge social creativity efforts by the lower-status group is likely to provoke a hostile reaction and an escalation of inter-group competition, possibly leading to offensive action against the dominant group. Resorting to time-honored military demonstrations, Russia planted the Russian tricolor flag on the Arctic seabed in early August 2007, resumed long-range strategic bomber flights in mid-August 2007, renewed annual military parades through Red Square in May 2008, conducted multiple tests of new missiles in January 2008, and stationed two Russian nuclear attack submarines off the US coast in August 2009.[84]

Putin fulminated against US lack of respect for Russia, as in December 2004 when he compared the United States to a "strict uncle in a pith helmet instructing others how to live their lives," and in 2006 when he referred to the United States as a wolf "who knows who to eat and is not about to listen to anyone." He complained plaintively that "partnership between such powers as Russia and the US can be built only on terms of equality and mutual respect." In his emotional and bellicose February 2007 Munich address Putin accused the United States of having "overstepped its national borders in every way," as evidenced by the "economic, political, cultural, and educational policies it imposes on other nations."[85]

As Evan Osnos, David Remnick, and Joshua Yaffa observed, "For Putin, it was a story of misplaced hopes and rejection: he became convinced that, no matter how accommodating he might try to be, Western powers—the United States, above all—had an innate disinclination to treat Russia as a full partner and a respected member of the international order."[86]

Russia's desire to proclaim its comeback on the world stage, avenging the humiliations of the 1990s, was encapsulated in the Russia-Georgia War. Georgian President Mikheil Saakashvili had given priority to gaining admission for Georgia to Euro-Atlantic alliances and organizations and reasserting control over the breakaway provinces of South Ossetia and Abkhazia. Viewing Saakashvili as a model democratic reformer (even after his November 2007 crackdown on the political opposition), Bush provided substantial economic aid and military assistance to Georgia and encouraged its aspirations to join NATO. The April 2008 NATO Summit at Bucharest promised Ukraine and Georgia membership in NATO (not a membership action plan), even though Putin had joined the summit for the first time to express his objections in person, informing Bush that this was a "red line" for Russia. The NATO-Bucharest decision was a compromise between the US support for a membership action plan that would provide Ukraine and Georgia with guidelines and criteria for necessary reforms without guaranteeing NATO membership, and the French-German position that such a plan would be unnecessarily provocative to the Russians. By offering Ukraine and Georgia membership at some unspecified date, the summit decision achieved the worst of both worlds, angering the Russians without satisfying the Ukrainians or Georgians.[87]

When Saakashvili launched an artillery attack on Tskhinvali on August 8, followed by ground invasion of the South Ossetian capital, killing several Russian peacekeepers, Russia sent troops into Georgia to affirm its "privileged interests" in the post-Soviet space, as well as to assert its claim to great power status, which was threatened by American support of Georgia.[88] Russia's intervention put an end to immediate plans for NATO membership for Ukraine and Georgia, sending a strong signal to other former Soviet states.

Particularly striking was Russia's defiant response to international criticism, even in the face of foreign capital flight, which caused the benchmark Russian Trading System index to lose 46 percent of its value between May and September 2008. As observed by Russian analyst Fyodor Lukyanov, for Russia the war was "psychological revenge" after two decades of geopolitical retreat, "proof that Moscow can say no."[89]

CHINA: "DIZZY WITH SUCCESS"?

The 2008–9 international financial crisis undermined the stability and legitimacy of the status hierarchy. The role of Wall Street and lax US financial regulation in contributing to the crisis threatened the legitimacy of US global financial leadership. The widespread perception among many Chinese that the United States was a declining power contributed to pressures for greater assertion of China's rights to great power status. Nevertheless, social creativity continued to be Beijing's dominant identity management strategy.

After the crisis, China's swift return to rapid economic growth, in contrast to the high unemployment, crushing levels of national debt, and political stasis in the United States, caused many Chinese elites to conclude that China was becoming "a first-class global power" while the United States was a declining one.[90] The risk that China would bully other states to get its way, demanding deference, however, was neutralized by the Chinese leadership and foreign ministry officials, who continued to favor a "peaceful rise" strategy as prudent, given the resilience of American power and the risk that other states would try to contain China's rise. These more moderate Chinese officials perceived the status hierarchy as stable, justifying a continuation of the social creativity strategy.

The greater impact of the Great Recession on the Western industrialized countries as compared with the emerging markets led to the perception that the balance of power was shifting against the West and in favor of the emerging powers that were part of the BRICs (Brazil, Russia, India, China—joined by South Africa in December 2010, making it BRICS), and the newly empowered Group of 20 (G20). Many in Beijing could barely hide their schadenfreude as it appeared that the United States, not China, was "on the wrong side of history." Some Chinese political elites inferred that China was already entitled to the privileges and interests of a great power, thereby strengthening the domestic elements favoring a more assertive, unilateralist policy toward the United States and Europe. China's post-crisis hubris together with increasing sensitivity about its relative position and role in international gatherings such as the G20 translated into international behavior that was perceived by many as assertive and prickly.[91]

China's arrogance may have been fueled by Washington's heightened interest in Beijing's cooperation on economic issues (including, crucially, China's continuing massive purchases of US Treasury bonds) in the wake of the financial crisis. At one point, former national security adviser Zbigniew Brzezinski even called for a Group of Two (G2) composed of the United States and China. When Secretary of State Hillary Clinton visited China in February 2009, she was noticeably reticent about China's human rights abuses, commenting that economic and political cooperation took priority.[92]

With a sense of self-importance, Chinese Premier Wen Jiabao complained that US deficit spending would lead to a decline in the value of the dollar, affecting sizable Chinese holdings of US debt. On another occasion, he immodestly referred to China as a "great power." On the eve of the 2009 G20 meeting, where China was expected to play a newly important role, the Governor of the Chinese Central Bank Zhou Xiaochuan suggested replacing the dollar as a reserve currency with Special Drawing Rights from the International Monetary Fund, challenging US stewardship of the world economy.[93]

A sense of entitlement to great power status contributed to assertive policies not only over traditional sovereignty issues such as Taiwan and Tibet but also regarding China's control over its coastline and neighboring waters. China had long objected to US coastal surveillance, and in March 2009 Chinese naval vessels harassed the USNS *Impeccable* in international waters. China started pressing its rights to over 200 islands, islets, and coral reefs in the South China Sea also claimed by

Vietnam, Brunei, Malaysia, Taiwan, Indonesia, or the Philippines. The area is a prime fishing ground, a conduit for one-third of the world's maritime trade, and a potential storehouse of large amounts of oil and gas under the sea floor. China claims "indisputable sovereignty" over the South China Sea islands and adjacent waters based on "historic rights," although the United Nations Convention on the Law of the Sea (UNCLOS), which China ratified in 1997, does not recognize historic rights as a basis for claims, basing its terms instead on exclusive economic zones and continental shelves. China's interest in the islands is derived from a sense of entitlement and the desire for prestige as well as economic need for fishing and hydrocarbon resources and the strategic value of the waterway.[94] In May 2009, China submitted its claims to the United Nations Commission on the Limits of the Continental Shelf in the form of the "nine-dashed line," a U-shaped line of nine curved dashes extending from east of Taiwan down to the coast of Borneo and then north to the Gulf of Tonkin. This line, encompassing about 90 percent of the disputed waters, was based on a map that was first used by the Republic of China in 1947. China has refused to clarify whether the nine-dashed line includes merely the land features or the waters as well.[95]

In light of China's increased unilateralism and bullying, it was probably ill-advised for President Obama to grant Beijing the status benefit early on of his visit in November 2009, without waiting to see if the Chinese returned to their previous responsible power behavior. In contrast to the previous visit by President Bill Clinton, Obama's town hall meeting with Chinese students was not broadcast live, and at the joint press conference with Hu Jintao, Obama was not allowed to answer questions. In contrast to previous summit meetings, where the Chinese had made some concession to the president to provide a concrete achievement, in 2009 the Chinese refused to accept American criticisms that they kept their currency artificially low to gain an unfair export advantage, and also declined US requests to adopt tougher sanctions against Iran because of its nuclear program.[96]

China set out to sabotage the December 2009 Copenhagen meeting on climate change and to ensure that the United States took the blame. The Chinese objected to quantitative targets for emission reduction and to international monitoring. In the Chinese view, the advanced Western countries should adopt higher standards and compensate the developing countries for climate change regulations because they had benefitted from harming the environment. Chinese Premier Wen Jiabao sent a lower-level official to a meeting with leaders of the twenty key delegations, including President Barack Obama, Angela Merkel, Nicolas Sarkozy, and Gordon Brown. Later, when Obama tried to reach a last-minute agreement with Wen, he was faced unexpectedly with the leaders of Brazil, South Africa, and India as well as China and subjected to a finger-wagging lecture by a red-faced lower-level Chinese official.[97]

When Obama decided in late 2009 to approve $6.4 billion in arms sales to Taiwan (although the deal had already been announced by President Bush) and to meet with the Dalai Lama, China reacted more strongly than usual, suspending military exchanges and even threatening to impose sanctions on US companies such as Boeing that were involved in the arms sales to Taiwan (although none were levied).[98]

China was also apparently caught off guard at a July 2010 ASEAN Regional Forum meeting when Secretary of State Hillary Clinton called for multilateral negotiations to develop a formal code of conduct for the South China Sea, offering US services in facilitating such negotiations; peaceful resolution of the territorial disputes; use of land as a basis for maritime claims; and freedom of navigation in the South China Sea. In response to the implied rejection of China's maritime claims and assertion of US interests, the Chinese foreign minister Yang Jiechi delivered a twenty-five-minute tirade against outside involvement in the South China Sea issue and warned the assembled Southeast Asian nations that China was bigger than they were.[99]

China's newfound truculence extended to Japan, with which it has a longstanding dispute over the Senkaku (Diaoyu) islands in the East China Sea, which are administered by Japan. In September 2010, China pressured Japan to release a Chinese fishing captain who had been arrested for ramming two Japanese coastguard vessels near the islands. Instead of releasing the captain as usual, Japan announced that it would try him, implying that this was a domestic law enforcement issue instead of a diplomatic incident. China's pressure tactics against the pro-Chinese Japanese government included cancellation of ministerial-level talks on issues such as joint energy development; a halt to Chinese tourism to Japan; the arrest of four Japanese construction employees; and most shockingly, an embargo on shipments of rare earth minerals, which are vital to Japan's electronics and auto industries. Even after Japan released the captain, the Chinese government demanded an apology and reparations. China's tactics backfired by inducing the Obama administration to declare that the Senkaku islands were covered by the US defense treaty with Japan.[100]

In addition to the threat of potential involvement of the United States, the Sino-Japanese rivalry over the islands was dangerous because of the overtones of geopolitical competition and heightened status concerns. The Senkaku/Diaoyu islands were taken over by Japan after the 1894–95 Sino-Japanese War, so their loss is part of the Chinese narrative of the "century of humiliation."[101]

Worried about the prospects for instability on the Korean Peninsula, in July 2010, China protected North Korea from censure by the UN after an international panel found that a North Korean torpedo had sunk a South Korean warship in March 2010, at the cost of forty-six lives. In November 2010, when North Korea conducted an hour-long artillery bombardment of a South Korean island, China not only did not criticize North Korea but objected fiercely to subsequent US-South Korean naval exercises in the East China Sea, outside its territorial waters.[102]

China's diplomatic sensitivities were also aroused by purely symbolic issues, such as the award of the Nobel Peace Prize to Liu Xiaobo, a Chinese human rights activist who had been sentenced to a ten-year prison term. Not only was Beijing's overreaction (including threats to cut off relations with the Norwegian government) ineffective, but it also led to embarrassment when its attempt to organize a boycott of the Nobel Prize ceremony was supported by only a handful of countries and its attempt to introduce a competing "Confucius Peace Prize" was widely ridiculed.[103]

Despite such assertive tendencies in China's post–financial crisis diplomacy, Chinese leaders ultimately pulled back from the brink of a full-blown geopolitical competition with the United States or its allies. China's desire for US approbation and respect was indicated by the favorable response to the respectful treatment of President Hu Jintao when he visited Washington in January 2011, including a red carpet welcome, twenty-one-gun salute, and a state dinner glittering with celebrities. The *Economist* observed that "the euphoric reaction in parts of the Chinese press to his reception suggested that all it took to stem an alarming slide in China's relations with America over the past year was to pay Mr. Hu the respect—to give him the twenty-one-gun salute, the Maine lobster, and that Asian notion of 'face'—which China feels he deserves." Hu stressed that Sino-American relations must be based on "mutual respect" and that the Chinese side considered this to be the most important part of the Joint Statement signed by him and President Obama.[104] This visit was much more satisfactory to the Chinese than President Hu's previous visit to Washington, in 2006, which the Bush administration termed an "official visit" instead of a state visit as the PRC preferred, and which was marred by diplomatic gaffes, such as the announcer's referring to the PRC by the official name for Taiwan, and the disruption of a press conference by a Falun Gong protester. Chinese officials had wanted a state visit that would portray Hu as a respected international statesman and China as an equal partner to the United States.[105]

A neorealist interpretation contending that China's assertive behavior reflects its growing power would have difficulty accounting for China's shrill reaction to purely symbolic issues such as the Dalai Lama's visit to the White House or the awarding of the Nobel Peace Prize to a Chinese dissident. Neorealism also fails to explain the oscillation in Chinese foreign policy from assertive to cooperative within the space of a year.

An SIT-based interpretation, however, can explain both China's oversensitivity and its inconsistent assertiveness by focusing on China's perception that the distribution of power was changing rapidly, with the US decline and China's ascent. That perception gave rise to impatience and the aggressive assertion of China's global status aspirations and associated nationalist claims to territory and influence in East Asia. At the same time, however, some Chinese leaders recognized that global power status would require recognition by the United States, a goal that requires China to act as a responsible power.[106]

After Hu Jintao's January 2011 visit to the US, China's foreign policy oscillated between moderation and assertiveness. China was vigorous about asserting its rights in coastal waters. For example, beginning in April 2012, China engaged in a two-month standoff with the Philippines over Scarborough Shoal, using economic pressure and maritime surveillance ships to force the Philippine coastguard to withdraw, leaving China in control of the lagoon with its lucrative fishing grounds.[107] China's reaction was especially vehement in September 2012, when the

Japanese government purchased three of the Senkaku islands from a private owner to preempt a similar move by the nationalist Tokyo governor. Although the Japanese government was trying to prevent the governor from developing the islands or engaging in other nationalist acts that would provoke the Chinese, the PRC interpreted Japan's purchase as "nationalization" of the islands, which would violate the previous Sino-Japanese agreement in 1972 to "shelve" the territorial disputes. Anti-Japanese protests—the largest since 2005—erupted in over one hundred Chinese cities, with vandalism against Japanese cars, shops, and factories.[108]

At the same time, it was increasingly evident to Beijing that Washington had started to push back against China's assertiveness. In the aftermath of the July 2010 ASEAN Regional Forum meeting, the United States and Vietnam conducted their first joint naval exercise in the South China Sea. In an article in *Foreign Policy*, Secretary of State Clinton announced that the United States was undertaking a "pivot" to the Asia Pacific, which would entail strengthening bilateral security alliances, engaging with regional multilateral institutions, and establishing a broad-based military presence. In a speech to the Australian Parliament on November 16, 2011, Obama promised that after a decade in which the United States had fought two wars in the Middle East, "the United States is turning our attention to the vast potential of the Asia Pacific region."[109]

Despite Beijing's largely muted official response to the Obama administration's "pivot" strategy (or "rebalancing" as it was later termed by US officials), the strengthening of US military ties with regional allies reportedly made the Chinese leadership "uneasy and off balance," raising doubts about the imminence of the US decline. While some "nonauthoritative" (less official) sources in China expressed alarm about Washington's intentions in the Asia Pacific, most Chinese government experts advised "caution, restraint, and the continuation of existing policies designed to advance China's and the region's economic development and sustain cooperative Sino-US relations."[110]

Washington's decision to reinforce its influence in East Asia, along with the American post-recession recovery, shaped Chinese perceptions that the status hierarchy was more stable, and ultimately contributed to greater moderation in Chinese policy, as evidenced by Xi Jinping's "great power diplomacy" of 2012–16, which largely conformed to the logic of "peaceful rise."

XI JINPING AND GREAT POWER DIPLOMACY

Xi Jinping assumed the dual positions of CCP general secretary and military commander-in-chief in November 2012 in an environment of rising nationalism. Standing before the National Museum at Tiananmen Square, at an exhibition on the "century of humiliation" beginning with the Opium Wars, Xi declared that the "greatest Chinese dream" was the "great revival of the Chinese nation."[111]

Preparing for his first summit with President Obama in June 2013, Xi said that relations between the United States and China were at a "critical juncture," and that it was time to explore "a new type of great power relationship," a statement widely interpreted to convey China's ambition to be recognized as equal by the United States.[112]

Xi intensified China's more muscular regional policy of asserting claims in the South and East China Seas. In November 2013, Beijing stunned its neighbors and the United States by announcing the creation of an Air Defense Identification Zone (ADIZ) in the East China Sea, drawn to include territorial claims over the Senkaku/Diaoyu islands. While ADIZ's are routine, the zone declared by the Chinese overlapped with the zones of South Korea and Japan. Moreover, unlike other ADIZ's, which merely require notification in the event that a plane is heading for a destination within the zone, the Chinese insisted that all airplanes transiting the zone seek permission from the Chinese government or be subject to "defensive measures." Potentially, it was feared, the ADIZ could be used as a basis to buttress China's claims to the islands. The United States deliberately flew military planes in the zone, but advised civilian aircraft to notify the Chinese government of their flight plans.[113]

Another highly visible move was China's May 2014 dispatch of an oil rig to drill near a Paracel Island claimed by Vietnam, one hundred twenty miles from Vietnam's coast and within its exclusive economic zone, which provoked anti-Chinese riots in Vietnamese cities and the destruction of Chinese-run factories in Vietnam (many of which were actually owned by Taiwan). Secretary of Defense Chuck Hagel drew attention to China's "destabilizing, unilateral actions." Although apparently defiant, the Chinese leadership realized that it had gone too far; the rig was withdrawn in July, a month earlier than announced.[114]

Of more lasting importance, China seemed to opt for social competition by beginning land reclamation in the Spratly archipelagic group in the South China Sea, dredging sand to build up major reefs into islands, capable of supporting human habitation. While the outposts were too small and vulnerable to be used in war, they could provide China with military bases for surveillance and resupply, facilitating pressure against other claimants to the South China Sea. Although President Xi declared at a White House press conference in September 2015 that China did not intend to "pursue militarization" of the reclaimed islands, the Chinese subsequently installed surface-to-air missiles and hangars on some of them.[115]

In 2015 the United States pushed back by initiating "freedom of navigation operations," in which warships and aircraft were dispatched to the disputed maritime features to indicate that Washington did not accept that the islands created territorial waters, eliciting strong Chinese protests. For China, the issue was not freedom of navigation, but its right to a sphere of influence in littoral waters, analogous to the US Monroe Doctrine.[116]

Nevertheless, China's assertive moves under Xi took place within an overall framework of a social creativity strategy, aimed at achieving a new type of great power status for China based on economic power, technological innovation, and institutional influence. China's efforts to assert its new position as a great power were by no means limited to claiming coastal waters. To create new multilateral institutions that would reflect its increased power and status, in October 2014 China announced the establishment of an Asian Infrastructure Investment Bank (AIIB)—a potential rival to the Japan-dominated Asian Development Bank—and pushed for the creation of a New Development Bank with its BRICS partners—an alternative to the World Bank and the IMF.[117] The Chinese initiative to create its own institutions was in part motivated by frustration that it was not given influence within international financial institutions commensurate with its economic growth and size. For example, the US Congress delayed for five years before ratifying an IMF proposal to give China more votes in the fund.[118] Despite the Obama administration's refusal to join the AIIB and its efforts to discourage its close partners from joining, China managed to enlist fifty-seven nations, including important US allies in both Asia and Europe such as Britain, Germany, France, and Italy, a diplomatic triumph for Beijing.[119] Xi proposed a Free Trade Area of the Asia Pacific (FTAAP), a more inclusive and less restrictive alternative to the Trans-Pacific Partnership then promoted by the Obama administration.[120]

Xi's signature foreign policy initiative was the "Silk Road" or as it is officially known, "Belt and Road Initiative," an example of staking out China's superior status in a new domain—infrastructure construction and connectivity. The Silk Road was an ancient network of trade routes that linked China with Central Asia, the Middle East, Africa, and northern Europe from around the second century BCE to the fifteenth century CE. Xi's proposal consisted of a land-based route that will link China with Europe via Central Asia and a maritime route that will connect China's coastal region with Southeast Asia, India, East Africa, and Eastern Europe. Chinese officials envision building pipelines, railroads, highways, and ports, creating markets for Chinese goods and providing access to natural resources. Xi added heft to his rhetoric at the November 2014 APEC summit meeting by announcing a $40 billion investment commitment to the project. Continuing the theme of Asia as a distinctive region, Xi built on the "China dream" concept to articulate his vision of a China-propelled "Asia-Pacific dream," a bid for leadership in East Asia.[121] If the initiative is successful, China's status will increase through its prominent role in construction and financing as well as its position as a focal point in the trade networks.[122]

While viewed by Washington as part of an effort to expand China's influence, most of the commonly cited major diplomatic initiatives by Xi mentioned above fall under the category of "charm offensive" based on highlighting China's economic attractiveness to various regional actors. The "China dream" slogan advanced by Xi also includes a "strong military" component and obvious nationalist connotations; however, the essence of the dream continues to be economic prosperity and success in economic globalization.[123]

China's focus on innovative means of gaining superior status is exemplified by its achievements in advanced technologies such as high-speed rail. China has quickly become the country with more high-speed rail track than any other country in the world, and in fall 2017, China developed the world's fastest long-distance bullet train. This was a major achievement of the government's industrial policy, which is unprecedented in its scale and scope. China's "Made in China 2025" blueprint, announced in 2015, targets the achievement of excellence and global superiority in technologically advanced economic sectors such as clean energy, aerospace, biotechnology, and electric vehicles.[124]

In his speeches on foreign policy, Xi continued to emphasize the themes of "peace and development" and the possibility of "win-win" solutions to international problems. In addition to aspirations for equal status with the United States, Xi's proposal for "a new type of great power relationship" also connotes the continuation of the earlier pledge of China's "peaceful rise."[125]

In contrast to China's previous support for North Korea, in May 2013, after North Korea's third nuclear test, the Bank of China suspended financial transactions with North Korea's Foreign Trade Bank, an unprecedented sign of Beijing's cooperation with the United States on the North Korean nuclear issue. China's responsible power image was highlighted during the Xi-Obama second summit in November 2014, when Beijing negotiated a surprising agreement on greenhouse gases, for the first time agreeing to set a date (around 2030) for Chinese emissions to peak. That the world's leading developing and developed nations were able to agree on targets for emissions was a powerful signal, helping to make possible the historic 195-nation Paris Climate Change Agreement in December 2015, where President Obama singled out China for praise. Bolstering China's benevolent image, in September 2015, Xi signed on to the UN "sustainable development" goals. China's pledge of more than $6 billion for UN climate and development programs is by far the largest amount that it has contributed to foreign countries' development, and that it did so through the United Nations helped substantiate its claim to global leadership.[126]

Some observers might argue that China is also pursuing social competition, based on the double-digit increases in its defense budget over the past two decades. Further evidence for social competition is the expansion of China's naval strategy to include missions that go beyond deterring possible US intervention in a conflict involving Taiwan. The new strategy goals are related to control of the "far seas," including the ability to support territorial claims in the East and South China Seas, sea lane security, anti-piracy operations, and humanitarian assistance/disaster relief.[127]

Nevertheless, China's military acquisitions and spending levels do not indicate that it aspires to be a peer competitor with the United States. According to Pentagon estimates, China has about 260 nuclear warheads and between 75 and 100 intercontinental ballistic missiles, whereas the United States has deployed 1,370 nuclear warheads. China has built a minimum deterrent and, unlike the Soviet Union, has not engaged in "tit for tat" building against the United States. Instead, it chose to invest in lower-cost asymmetric military capabilities, such as anti-ship and anti-satellite weapons and cyber warfare.[128]

To be sure, in 2011 China launched a refurbished aircraft carrier purchased from Ukraine, the *Liaoning*, and in April 2017, revealed a domestically built aircraft carrier. China may eventually have as many as six aircraft carriers. Some observers view these developments as an indication that China is pursuing global power projection capabilities. But the primary motive for this long-delayed step is to convey symbolically China's great power status. In March 2009, China's defense minister boasted to the visiting Japanese defense minister that China would not remain forever the only major power without an aircraft carrier. Nevertheless, China's two carriers are much smaller and less technically advanced than the ten "gold standard" Nimitz-class aircraft carriers kept by the United States Navy. Moreover, China's carriers are vulnerable to anti-ship ballistic missiles of the kind that Beijing has already developed.[129]

Beijing was initially defiant when, in July 2016, the Hague Permanent Court of Arbitration ruled that China's nine-dashed line conflicted with the UNCLOS, and that the artificial islands China had created could not be used to claim territorial waters because they were formerly submerged at high tide. These rulings removed much of the basis for China's expansive claims to the South China Sea. But Xi Jinping kept a lid on nationalist protests. Instead of withdrawing from the UNCLOS, Beijing is trying to fit its reclamation actions within its framework, albeit unconvincingly to international lawyers. Moreover, China reached an agreement with Philippine President Rodrigo Duterte to allow Philippine fishing boats back into Scarborough Shoal.[130]

From China's standpoint, in taking unilateral actions in pursuit of its claims to the South and East China Seas, it is acting no differently than other great powers in asserting the right to a sphere of influence in neighboring waters. The problem, of course, is that another great power already has an alliance system in the region. Nevertheless, Beijing's increasingly firm insistence on having a sphere of influence (historically, an integral component of great power status in international politics) in East Asia should not be confused with imperial expansionism.

Despite occasional oscillation in China's cooperation with the United States and other Western countries due to internal politics and domestic differences over China's identity, China's pursuit of international status has continued to be exercised primarily through social creativity via the acquisition of soft power, economic attractiveness, and continuing participation in multilateral activities.

RUSSIA'S ANGER MISMANAGEMENT

In contrast to China's continuing careful cultivation of its attractiveness and influence through social creativity, Russia returned to an emphasis on military power and saber rattling, a strategy of social competition. Russia's choice of a different identity management strategy may be in part due to the West's greater receptivity to the great power ambitions of China than to those of Russia, which it regards as a declining but troublemaking regional power. Another significant factor is Russia's economic weakness, which makes the use of military power an attractive alternative to force the West to recognize Russia as a major player. China continued to perceive the great power club as permeable, while Russia increasingly viewed the global status hierarchy as not only unstable but also illegitimate.

Despite its actions in the Russo-Georgia War, Russia was not firmly committed to social competition. The respect shown by the Obama administration as part of the "reset" policy toward Russia elicited a brief period of cooperation on global governance issues, and even efforts to establish a friendlier attitude toward the West. But the US-Russian relationship had already cooled even before Russia's takeover of Crimea and military intervention in eastern Ukraine—suggesting that Russia's territorial aggression was not the cause of the crisis in East-West relations, but merely the culmination of longstanding differences over Russia's standing in the world.

The Obama administration's effort to "reset" relations with Russia, inaugurated in February 2009, was based in part on recognition of the need to redress injured Russian prestige and national pride. The term "reset" implied that the Obama administration was jettisoning aspects of President Bush's foreign policy that were objectionable to Russia, such as wooing countries in the post-Soviet space or placing missiles and radar bases in former Warsaw Pact countries, and cooperating with Russia on issues of common interest. For Russian leaders, the major appeal of the "reset" policy was the promise of recognition of Russia's status as a global power and a more equal relationship with Washington. In addition to appreciating the status accommodation aspects of the "reset," Russian President Dmitry Medvedev wanted to form foreign alliances in order to obtain Western technology and investment, to improve Russia's crumbling infrastructure and reduce its dependence on exports of natural resources, according to a foreign ministry document that was leaked to the Russian version of *Newsweek*. (Limited by the constitution to two terms as president, Putin had selected Medvedev, who had worked for him since the 1990s, to succeed him in 2008. Putin then became prime minister, and despite his nominal subordination to Medvedev, continued exercising supreme power.)[131] In addition to precipitating the decline of US financial power, the financial crisis foreshadowed the dangers of Russia's dependence on natural resource exports and the need to modernize the economy.

Since possession of a sizable nuclear arsenal is one of the few remaining areas where Russia and the United States are equals, the Russian side was pleased that Obama initiated negotiations for a new START agreement (signed in spring 2010 and promptly ratified by the US Senate and the Russian Duma). START negotiations thus emerged as an important vehicle for restoring Russia's status as at least a "quasi-superpower." The Russian leadership was also relieved by Obama's September 2009 decision to put on the back burner one of the most humiliating issues for Moscow—the Bush administration's 2007 decision to deploy elements of its missile defense system in Poland and Czechoslovakia—in favor of deploying smaller missile interceptors based on ships and aimed at Iranian missiles. The Obama administration no longer actively promoted NATO membership for the former Soviet states. The United States also stopped its criticism of Russia for its deficiencies in human rights and democracy, which was viewed by Russians as lecturing.[132]

The Russians reciprocated US solicitude on issues of status by cooperating on issues important to the United States. In July 2009,

Medvedev agreed to allow the United States to ship men and supplies from Europe across Russian airspace to Afghanistan as part of the recently established Northern Distribution Network, which was a priority for Obama since he was increasing US troops in Afghanistan and the Pakistan route was politically unreliable. The Northern Distribution Network consisted of three routes that bypassed Pakistani territory, utilizing road, rail, barge, and air transport to ship troops and supplies from the north. One originated at the Baltic ports, then continued by rail through Russia to Central Asia before reaching Afghanistan; another began with shipments to a Georgian port on the Black Sea and continued to Azerbaijan, where goods were transferred to barges and ferried across the Caspian Sea to Kazakhstan before traveling to Uzbekistan and thence to Afghanistan; and a southern route ran from Kazakhstan to Kyrgyzstan to Tajikistan before entering northern Afghanistan. Cooperation between Russia and the United States reached its height in spring 2010: Obama and Medvedev signed the New START Treaty in Prague; US, French, and British troops were invited for the first time to participate in Moscow's annual May 9 Victory Day parade commemorating the defeat of Nazi Germany in World War II; and Russia agreed with other permanent members of the UN Security Council on the most severe sanctions yet against Iran's nuclear program. Moscow later cancelled the sale of advanced S-300 ground-to-air missiles to Iran.[133]

Overall, from 2009 through 2010 Russian foreign policy moved in a more constructive and pragmatic direction, as reflected in the improvement of previously tense relations with Poland and the Baltics, settlement of the marine border with Norway, greater reliance on soft power instruments in Russia's relationship with post-Yushchenko Ukraine, and presentation, as Medvedev termed it, of "a smiling face to the world"—a social creativity strategy. Medvedev even revived the moribund NATO-Russia Council, taking a more positive attitude with his visit to the NATO summit in Lisbon in November 2010. At the summit, Medvedev agreed to cooperate with NATO on theater missile defense. In his talks with German business leaders in Berlin that same month, Putin called for creating a free trade zone "from Lisbon to Vladivostok," decrying the restrictions placed on Russian investment, but received a chilly response from German Chancellor Angela Merkel who said that Russia still had a long way to go to modernize its economy and open its borders.[134]

Despite these promising beginnings, in 2011–12 the US-Russia reset entered a period of diminishing returns, largely because the policy was focused on obtaining agreements on particular issues, without any obvious connection to a larger vision for the relationship. As observed by Thomas Graham, a former senior director for Russia in the Bush White House, the problem with the "reset" is that it never had a coherent answer for "what the two countries should aspire to now so as to foreclose a return to dangerous geopolitical rivalry and hold open the promise of mutually advantageous strategic partnership."[135] While aiming to assuage some of the symptoms of Russia's anger and frustration, the reset ultimately failed to address the root cause of Moscow's grievances—its loss of superpower status. Not unlike the Bush administration after 9/11, Obama's team viewed Russia as "a regional and niche ally," not as a global partner and a leading power.[136]

Without a larger positive agenda, US-Russian relations were damaged by status-related disagreements over missile defense and the Middle East. Despite the agreement in principle at the Lisbon NATO summit on cooperation in missile defense, agreement on specific principles proved to be impossible. Moscow proposed a joint anti-missile system in which Russia would have veto power over its use, a condition that was unacceptable to NATO. By the end of November 2011, unable to obtain written guarantees that the system would not be used against Russia (which would be impossible to get through the US Senate), Medvedev announced that negotiations on cooperative missile defense were over. Russian officials reacted angrily to Obama's decision to go ahead with the plan for a phased system that would install missile interceptors in Romania and Poland by 2018. Russian elites assumed that there must be ulterior motives and that US missile defenses must be targeted against Russia, not Iran, which would undermine assured destruction and strategic parity, principles considered central to Russia's security as well as being the main justification for Russia's claims to global power status. As Dmitry Suslov commented, strategic parity with the United States was "what distinguishes Russia from the other power poles, including new ones, and what makes it a key player in big-time politics by definition."[137]

Resolution of missile defense and the Middle East issues became more difficult after the return of Putin to the Kremlin in May 2012. Compared to Medvedev, Putin was pricklier and was acutely sensitive to personal betrayal. In September 2011, Medvedev had announced that he would be stepping down as president but would run for prime minister instead, while Putin would be the presidential candidate in the March 2012 election. In light of a Russian constitutional amendment extending the presidential term to six years, hastily approved by Russian legislators in December 2008, this meant that Putin could conceivably stay in office until 2024. Many Russians regarded this exchange of offices as a cynical "castling move." Following reports of widespread fraud in the December Duma elections, thousands of middle-class Russians gathered peacefully in Moscow to call for Putin to go. Shocked and humiliated by the protests, after Putin recovered his equanimity he began to blame foreign interference, especially from the United States. On several occasions, he falsely accused Secretary of State Hillary Clinton, who had criticized the fairness of the parliamentary elections, of having paid members of the opposition movement to go out into the streets. The protests even continued after Putin's March 2012 election before tapering off. The Kremlin escalated its anti-American rhetoric, in part because of the elections but also because Putin was personally offended by US support for the protests against him.[138]

He accompanied his invective against the United States with retaliatory measures. At the last minute, Putin cancelled his attendance at the May 2012 G8 summit scheduled for Camp David, which would have been his first meeting with Obama since returning to the Russian presidency. Putin also obstructed UN action against Syrian President Bashar al-Assad in the Syrian civil war by joining China in use of the veto to prevent military action or regime change. As part of the reset relationship, in March 2011, Medvedev had Russia abstain rather than veto UN Security Council resolution 1973, which allowed the establishment of a no-fly zone in Libya to protect civilians from Muammar al-Gaddafi's threats to retaliate. The Western countries' subsequent stretching of the resolution to overthrow Gaddafi infuriated Putin. By actively opposing Western intervention in Syria (not just complaining) and by providing financial and military assistance to Assad in his military campaign against rebels, Putin emphasized Russia's status as an "indispensable power" in global politics. Syria is one of the few remaining Russian clients in the Middle East, and the site of a naval base at Tartus that gives Russia access to the Mediterranean. To allow the West to intervene, many Russians believed, would remove any vestiges of Moscow's former status as a superpower. Putin also wanted to uphold the principle of sovereignty against UN-sponsored intervention and to prevent destabilizing regime change in Russia's neighborhood.[139]

Even the triumph of Russia's 2012 admission into the WTO, after two decades of negotiations, was marred by Russian status grievances. Russian political circles were predictably enraged when the US Congress replaced the obsolete Cold War–era Jackson-Vanik amendment (which conditioned trade relations with the USSR on freedom of Jewish emigration) with the December 2012 Sergey Magnitsky Rule of Law Accountability Act (which denied visas to Russian officials implicated in "gross human rights violations" and froze their US assets), viewing it as intolerable interference in their domestic affairs. The bill was named after Sergey Magnitsky, a lawyer for Hermitage Capital who had exposed large-scale tax fraud committed by Russian law enforcement officials. Magnitsky died while in pre-trial detention after being refused medical treatment. In response to the Magnitsky Act, Russia enacted a law prohibiting US adoptions of Russian orphans and also required nongovernmental organizations (NGOs) to register as "foreign agents," causing many of them to leave. Russia also asked the US Agency for International Development, which had given Russia a total of $2.6 billion in assistance, to shut down. Moscow even refused to renew the Nunn-Lugar Cooperative Threat Reduction program, one of the most successful vehicles of US-Russia partnership since the Cold War, because it "reflected an unequal partnership" with the United States.[140]

Russia's frustrated status ambitions and related emotions were prominently displayed in the summer 2013 Russo-American spat over the fate of Edward Snowden, a former National Security Agency (NSA) contractor, who fled the United States to Hong Kong and later to Moscow after exposing the NSA's wide-ranging communications surveillance programs. Not only did Putin grant Snowden political asylum, but he could not resist the temptation to draw attention to the hypocrisy of the United States in supporting human rights while spying on its own citizens. Obama reacted predictably by cancelling his September meeting with Putin, the first time a leader had called off a bilateral summit. At a press conference, Obama challenged the idea that he and Putin had a bad personal relationship by insisting that their conversations were productive, but his remark about Putin's negotiation style ("he's got that kind of slouch, looking like the bored kid in the back of the classroom") infuriated the Russian leader.[141] In the end, Russian (and American) status sensibilities led to a new low point in the relationship.

Despite Putin's cool personal relationship with Obama, however, he seized the opportunity for cooperation in September 2013 when the Obama administration faced the embarrassment of failing to secure congressional authorization for punitive military strikes against Syria after Assad used sarin gas against civilians, thus crossing the president's "red line." Russian diplomats elaborated a plan to place Syria's chemical weapons under international control prior to their destruction, thus helping the United States to save face by embracing a diplomatic solution to the crisis, and at the same time enhancing Russia's prestige as a world power broker.[142] Putin also gained considerable status in the role of statesman, winning plaudits even in the United States. This episode of social creativity, however, could not prolong the life of the "reset" relationship, which proved vulnerable to a severe crisis involving Russia's "near abroad."

THE UKRAINE CRISIS

Russia moved to full-blown social competition in the aftermath of the political isolation and economic sanctions imposed by the West in response to Russia's takeover of Crimea and destabilization of eastern Ukraine. But the sanctions did not undermine Putin's determination for Russia to be recognized as an equal great power, which was later manifested in Russia's intervention in Syria.

In February 2014, as the Russian political class was basking in the triumph of the successful 2014 Winter Olympics in Sochi—the most expensive Olympic Games in history, designed to celebrate Russia's resurgence as a great power, and Putin's personal vanity/prestige project— the biggest geopolitical crisis since the end of the Cold War struck. On February 22, Ukrainian President Viktor Yanukovych was unexpectedly toppled by a street protest on Independence Square (Maidan). To quote Henry Kissinger, "Ukraine slid into the Maidan uprising right in the middle of what Putin had spent ten years building as a recognition of Russia's status."[143]

The Ukraine crisis can only be understood against the backdrop of previous competition between Russia and the EU over the political and economic orientation of former Soviet states. In May 2009, the EU inaugurated its Eastern Partnership (EaP) Program for six post-Soviet states (Armenia, Azerbaijan, Belarus, Georgia, Moldova, Ukraine). States that signed an association agreement with the EaP were offered the prospect of duty-free access to the enormous EU market and visa-free travel, in return for signing a large portion of the EU's regulations or *acquis communautaire*. The association agreement also carried with it the possibility of signing a Deep and Comprehensive Free Trade Agreement.[144]

Within a month, in June 2009, Putin announced agreement on a Customs Union with Kazakhstan and Belarus, with institutions partially modeled after that of the EU, to take effect in January 2010. Moscow was concerned about potential loss of influence in the former Soviet states. States that joined the partnership program with the EU would align their rules, standards, and regulations with those of Europe instead of Russia and related states. As the states adopted European regulations for their products, their economies would be oriented toward Europe rather than Russia, with the likelihood that they would align with Europe politically as well.[145]

In October 2011, on the eve of his return to the presidency, Putin proposed that the customs union serve as the basis for a Eurasian Economic Union (EEU), which would be a "powerful supranational association capable of becoming one of the poles in the modern world and serving as an efficient bridge between Europe and the dynamic Asia-Pacific region." The EEU would initially be built on the existing Eurasian Customs Union with Kazakhstan and Belarus, but could expand to include other states. Putin envisioned the EEU as a means to challenge the EU's normative monopoly and to allow Russia to bargain as an equal with China and the EU. The EEU would give Russia its own club—equal to the EU, NAFTA, APEC, and ASEAN—and serve as a vehicle for restoring Russia's great power status. The customs union adopted a single market in 2012, and became the EEU in January 2015, with the addition of Kyrgyzstan and Armenia in the spring.[146]

The EU and Putin were engaged in a form of normative competition over the fate of the six post-Soviet states. But Ukraine was the prize, with its forty-five million people, a gas pipeline, heavy industry, and economic integration with Russia. Putin admitted that the EEU would not be worth much without Ukraine. Although the EEU was an institution, it was also part of a social competition strategy; some supporters within Russia saw it as a potential rival to the EU. Russia would no longer be associated with the West but would dominate its own sphere. Putin began to put forward the thesis that Russia was a unique civilization and the foundation of a "Russian world," a genuine repository of traditional Christian values such as traditional marriage and the family in contrast to the alleged moral decadence of contemporary Europe.[147]

When it appeared that Yanukovych was going to sign an association agreement at the November 2013 EU summit in Vilnius, Putin applied economic pressure, including a ban on selected Ukrainian products such as steel pipe and chocolate, and lengthy customs inspections at the border. A week before the summit, Yanukovych announced his intent not to sign the EU association agreement but to enter into negotiations for the EEU instead. Almost immediately, Ukrainians took to the streets to protest governmental corruption and to call for ties with the EU.[148]

The demonstrations, which were brutally suppressed by Yanukovych's special forces, attracted the attention of the United States, which sent representatives, including Assistant Secretary of State Victoria Nuland (who handed out bread and cookies to the protesters on the Maidan), Vice President Joe Biden, and Senator John McCain. Nuland and US Ambassador to Ukraine Geoffrey Pyatt were caught by a Russian intercept discussing potential members of a new Ukrainian cabinet, which supported Russian suspicions of Western involvement. Increasingly, the fate of Ukraine was becoming a zero-sum competition with the United States, not just the EU.[149]

On February 21, EU representatives brokered an agreement between the opposition parties and the Ukrainian government providing for constitutional revisions and presidential elections at the end of the year, but the Maidan leadership rejected it and Yanukovych fled the country overnight, just as Putin was presiding over the end of the successful Sochi Olympics. Putin's subsequent behavior can better be explained as "fundamentally driven by psychological impulses and highly emotional responses" to the crisis, an almost instinctive reaction to personal humiliation and the prospect of a pro-Western regime in Kiev—explanations consistent with the high salience of status concerns. Putin immediately perceived Yanukovych's ouster as yet another "Orange Revolution." For Putin, the perception of Western complicity in overthrowing a relatively friendly regime in Kiev was also a blow to his self-esteem, a personal humiliation "*as a man* as well as national leader," which this time, a full decade after the first, he was determined not to tolerate.[150]

A week after the ouster of Yanukovych, Russian special operations forces, marines, and paratroopers without uniforms or insignia secured control over the Crimean regional parliament, airports, and other strategic locations across the peninsula. The Crimean parliament, voting in the presence of the masked pro-Russian gunmen, elected a new government and called for a referendum on the question of Crimean autonomy. Moscow was quick to recognize the overwhelmingly pro-secession results of the referendum. On March 18, 2014, Putin and Crimean leaders signed a treaty of accession making Crimea and the city of Sevastopol (the location of the Russian Black Sea Fleet) parts of the Russian Federation.[151]

In his emotional address to the country's political elite before signing the accession treaty, Putin appealed to Russian history, pride, and glory, but also to Russia's shame over losing its former superpower status, calling the loss of Crimea after the collapse of the Soviet Union an "outrageous historical injustice," a humiliation, which Russia had to "swallow" because it was simply too weak to protect its interests. The Russian president also revisited several themes of his 2007 Munich speech, lamenting the loss of stability in international politics after the end of bipolarity and accusing the United States of attempting to rule by force. He listed what he regarded as examples of Russia not being treated as an equal partner, ranging from the enlargement of NATO and the 1999 bombings of Belgrade to the threat of sanctions over Crimea and continuing restrictions on Russian purchase of technologies and exports.[152]

Russia then tried to humiliate and destabilize Ukraine by providing military, economic, and political support to the pro-Russian insurgency in Ukraine's southeast, which broke out just days after the annexation of Crimea. The insurgents proclaimed the establishment of Donetsk and Luhansk "people's republics."[153]

On July 17, 2014, Malaysian Airlines Flight 17, with 298 passengers on board, was shot down over eastern Ukraine. The tragedy was attributed by the West to the pro-Russian separatists' inability to distinguish between a military target and a civilian passenger jet, but Russia was also potentially implicated, suspected of delivering powerful antiaircraft missiles to the rebels. Putin remained defiant when faced with Russia's de-facto expulsion from the G8 and the imposition of harsh Western economic sanctions in the wake of international outrage over the incident.[154]

Initially, Putin vehemently denied accusations that the Russian military was involved in the conflict, but by the end of August, after recapturing some territory, the Ukrainian army faced better armed and trained Russian military forces. Russia's purpose in establishing another "frozen conflict," where active armed conflict had ended but there was no political solution, was probably to force the Ukrainian authorities to agree to federalization, to provide leverage for continued Russian influence, and to make it impossible for Ukraine to join either the EU or NATO—a means to Russia's goal of establishing a sphere of influence in eastern Ukraine if not the entire country.[155]

Some analysts argue that the Russian takeover of Crimea and intervention in eastern Ukraine were motivated by the desire to shore up Putin's authoritarian rule, despite declining economic growth, by stirring up nationalism and anti-Westernism as alternative sources of legitimacy. A related explanation is that Putin needed to prevent the success of the "color revolution" in Ukraine, an example of protesters supported by foreign powers leading to regime change, because of the potential for spillover to Russia.[156] One problem with this interpretation is that Putin's domestic position was secure and he did not need a foreign diversion, much less one that would lead to economic sanctions. After the December 2011 protests, Putin had targeted opposition leaders for prosecution on charges like embezzlement and corruption, and the Duma had passed a law imposing draconian economic penalties for unauthorized protests. He had also provided an outlet for expression of discontent by reinstituting elections for regional governors. In short, Putin faced no significant threat to his rule, having the support of both the elite and the general public. Indeed, in December 2013, Putin felt sufficiently confident of his hold on power to release 20,000 political prisoners, including the influential and outspoken Putin critic Mikhail Khodorkovsky, who had spent ten years in prison.[157] In general, it is difficult to establish a direct relationship between authoritarianism and foreign policy assertiveness. During his first presidential term (2000–2003), while he took a hard line at home, cracking down on some independent television stations and abolishing elections for regional governors, Putin at the same time pursued a partnership with President Bush on the war on terror.[158]

From a neorealist perspective, Putin's takeover of Crimea and support for the insurgency in eastern Ukraine were aimed at preventing the West from admitting Ukraine into NATO. Putin may have also been concerned about NATO taking control of Sevastopol, the headquarters of the Black Sea fleet and Russia's only "real" warm water port. Unquestionably, Putin had asserted that NATO membership for Ukraine and Georgia was a "red line" for Russia.[159] But, as discussed earlier, the Obama administration had taken the question of NATO membership for Ukraine off the table.[160] The threat posed by NATO's expansion is inextricably connected with Russia's great power aspirations and its claim to a *droit de regard* in the former Soviet space.

A constructivist interpretation of Putin's intervention in Ukraine might stress aspects of Russia's shared identity—cultural, religious, historical, social—with Ukraine, and its concern about protecting Russian-speakers there. Ukraine was the birthplace of Orthodox Christianity and of Kievan Rus, and had been united with Russia since the 1654 Pereyaslav agreement, when the Zaporozhian Cossacks submitted to rule by Muscovy, and Sevastopol is a monument to Russian military heroism. In his yearly address to the Russian Duma in December 2014, Putin compared the significance of Crimea for Russia to the significance of the Temple Mount in Jerusalem for Muslims. Yet prior to the crisis in February 2014, Russia had not supported separatist movements in Crimea.[161]

What precipitated Putin's intervention was the prospect of a pro-Western Ukraine government aligning with the EU or even NATO, bringing Ukraine into the Western sphere of influence and threatening Russia's status as a great power. With Russia's hopes for integration with Europe on its own terms dashed, Ukraine's association with the EU became not only an economic challenge but also an acute threat to Russia's distinctive identity and great power standing.[162] As we argued in chapter 1, rejection of an aspiring state's status claims is likely to evoke strong emotions and an assertive reaction to restore self-esteem and dignity, even at the cost of economic interests or security considerations.

Dismissive remarks by US officials after Russia's intervention may have contributed to Putin's resentment and frustration. After his visit to Ukraine in March 2014, Senator John McCain labeled Russia "a gas station masquerading as a country" and called for providing military assistance to Ukraine. Obama dismissed Russia as a "regional power," acting out of weakness because of its loss of influence in states that were formerly part of the Soviet Union. In his September 2014 address to the UN General Assembly, Obama placed "Russian aggression in Europe" in the category of the top global security threats, along with the Ebola epidemic and ISIS. In his January 2015 State of the Union address Obama contrasted America "that stands strong and united with our allies" with Russia that "is isolated with its economy in tatters."[163]

Lack of Western respect for Russia was the dominant theme of Putin's October 2014 Valdai Club meeting in Sochi, where he complained that during the Cold War, when the Soviet Union had a lot of missiles and Nikita Khrushchev hammered the desk with his shoe at the UN, the world showed respect, but now that the Soviet Union was gone, "there was no need to take into account Russia's views." The United States does not need allies; it needs only "vassals," charged Putin in April 2015.[164]

Yet, showing the persistent importance of Russia's status aspirations, Russia continued to be receptive to cooperation on specific issues with the United States, so long as it was treated as an equal partner. Despite US efforts to impose international isolation in retaliation for Russia's actions in Ukraine, Russia cooperated extensively with the United States in six-party talks with Iran, winning Obama's praise for the Russian officials' constructive contribution to the final July 2015 agreement: "Putin and the Russian government compartmentalized on this in a way that surprised me, and we would have not achieved this agreement had it not been for Russia's willingness to stick with us." Russia's cooperation violated its economic interests, because lifting of sanctions against Iran could depress energy prices, of vital importance to Russia, by bringing Iranian oil and gas to the international market.[165]

After months of isolation by the West over Crimea and the Ukraine crisis, Russia used air strikes to intervene in the Syrian civil war in September 2015, a decision driven not only by geopolitical but also by status concerns. In addition to propping up Assad's regime, regaining influence in the Middle East, preempting radical Islamic threats before they could reach Russian territory, and diverting attention away from the simmering Ukraine conflict, Putin wanted to reassert Russia's role as a global player, in defiance of the "declining regional power" image of the country promoted by the Obama administration following the Crimean takeover, and to force the United States to treat Russia as an equal.[166] Russia's show of force in Syria—its first military campaign outside the former Soviet borders and the largest deployment to the Middle East since the Soviet presence in Egypt in the 1970s—showcased the impressive results of Russian military modernization, including the firing of anti-ship cruise missiles from 900 miles away in the Caspian Sea, and sent a message to the West that Russia was back as a global military power. A year later, Russia began bombing runs from a base in Iran—it was the first foreign power allowed to use Iranian bases—and fired its new cruise missiles at targets in Syria from warships in the Mediterranean. The Syrian military operation was broadcast on Russian television, where dramatic shots of Russian military jets taking off reassured the Russian people that their country was indeed a great power.[167] Despite Russia's declared campaign against ISIS, the United States determined that Russian airstrikes were targeted mainly against moderate Syrian opposition forces. Nevertheless, Putin forced the United States and Western countries to deal with Russia as a global player and indispensable participant in negotiations to end the Syrian civil war.[168]

CONCLUSION

Our post–Cold War case study indicates that China and Russia have been more likely to contribute to global governance and behave constructively when they believed that doing so would enhance their prestige. SIT illuminates several puzzles and anomalies in Chinese and Russian behavior that are difficult to explain from the standpoint of conventional theoretical approaches. SIT can explain changes in the grand strategies of China and Russia that are not linked to their relative military capabilities, contrary to neorealism. The neorealist concept of balancing against an external threat does not fully capture the dynamics of Russian or Chinese foreign policy, even in its more assertive phases. For both states, the key factor prompting a change in strategy was a challenge to their identities as great powers. For China, the risk that other states might perceive China as a threat, and respond with a policy to contain China's rise, motivated elites to seek preeminence in an area other than geopolitical might—contributing to world order as a responsible power. For Russia, the stimulus to strategic reorientation was the realization that despite the end of the Cold War, the United States was not going to admit Russia as an equal into Western institutions such as NATO, even while Russia's former allies in Eastern Europe were actively recruited to join. Despite unipolarity, neither China nor Russia accommodated the United States by uncritically accepting its leadership in foreign policy. Instead, both states pursued independent foreign policies where the dominant consideration was their position and place in the post–Cold War world.

Constructivism would expect increasing interactions with Western liberal powers to lead to some socialization to liberal norms. But despite their increased engagement in trade and international institutions, China and Russia continue to reject certain core liberal principles such as individual human rights. Both states have sought the benefits of globalization and economic integration without corresponding political liberalization, selectively choosing which Western norms to adopt. SIT implies that major powers may not want to emulate the values of the established states, for fear of losing their distinctive identities. Western criticism of Chinese and Russian policy from a values perspective, therefore, may imperil cooperation on issues that are increasingly vital for the West.

After Tiananmen Square, the Chinese leadership doubled down on communist ideology as a barrier to liberalizing influences from the West. But their foreign policy has not shown any interest in promoting communism, and China has clashed repeatedly with Vietnam, one of the few remaining communist states. Putin has also used ideology instrumentally, invoking Russian Orthodoxy and family values as Russia became more estranged from the West due to differences over democratization in the near abroad, yet showing willingness to make pragmatic deals, even with the United States.

Because it highlights the importance of face and dignity, SIT can illuminate why China and Russia have been motivated by a strong sense of grievance at past humiliations inflicted by external powers, causing both states on occasion to seemingly disregard their economic or strategic interests. Examples include the Chinese regime's 1995–96 provocative missile tests in the Taiwan Strait, despite China's extensive economic ties with the United States and Taiwan; China's aggravation of tensions with its major trade partner Japan in 2005 and 2012–13; the Russian regime's armed incursion into Georgia, which led to major losses in the Russian stock market; and Russia's annexation of Crimea and support for a separatist movement in Ukraine's southeast, which led to the imposition of Western political and economic sanctions. Putin's involvement in Ukraine sacrificed Western technology and assistance, needed for Russia's economic modernization, and alienated Germany, Russia's strongest partner.[169]

The global 2008–9 financial crisis, US political deadlock, and the military quagmire in Iraq and Afghanistan created a perception that unipolarity was on the way out. According to SIT, instability and illegitimacy of the status hierarchy are conducive to social competition. The main difference between Russia and China, however, is the West's willingness to enter into social cooperation with them, based on respect for each other's superiority in different domains. The United States has shown far greater acceptance of China and was willing to validate its social creativity efforts for various reasons, including its role as the world's leading exporter and holder of American debt, and its ties to the American economy. In contrast, Americans and the EU have viewed Russia as merely a regional power, and hence, a state whose preferences and interests can in most instances be disregarded.

The danger is that isolation and exclusion of Russia will encourage it to make further attempts at social competition or to undermine the existing order.[170] The Russian takeover of Crimea and the Ukraine crisis illustrate the type of crises that could arise in the future if continued Russian bitterness over its loss of great power status leads to a return of geopolitical competition. Continued indifference to Russia's great power aspirations, especially in the former Soviet space, will only fuel the Russian elites' sense of injury and humiliation, possibly leading to further conflict. The consequences of insensitivity to Russia's status frustrations may also serve as a cautionary tale for future US relations with China. For example, China's actions in the South China Sea and East China Sea seem to be aimed at acquiring prestige and asserting its regional right of preeminence.

Encouraging China and Russia to seek status in areas other than geopolitical rivalry, however, could possibly lead to more cooperation with the West on areas of common concern. The United States and Europe have an enduring strategic interest in helping China and Russia to achieve status and prestige in realms other than geopolitical and military competition by pursuing a strategy of social creativity.

6   Recognition and Cooperation

DESPITE THE 2016 ruling of the Hague Permanent Court of Arbitration that China's claims in the South China Sea were invalid, Chinese President Xi Jinping defiantly declared that the islands in the South China Sea had been Chinese territories since "ancient times." Although state-controlled media referred to the Hague tribunal as an American puppet, China nevertheless participated in the biennial RIMPAC (Rim of the Pacific) military exercises hosted by the United States and including more than twenty other nations because it wanted the prestige. Russia, despite a stagnating economy, low oil prices, and economic sanctions, projected military power into both eastern Ukraine and Syria, thereby making "clear its intention to restore its status as a major international player."[1]

Both China and Russia have defied the United States and the Western countries on major foreign policy issues because they are asserting their prerogatives to act independently, as great powers do. China and Russia believe that their inferior status in world politics after the end of the Cold War was an aberration, and both are prepared to claim their rightful place and to demand respect for their geopolitical and economic interests. The slogan "national rejuvenation" (*zhenxing zhonghua*), used by Chinese leaders from Sun Yat-sen to Xi Jinping, implies that China's rise is merely a return to its natural standing. Similarly,

Russians believe that Russia is destined to be a great power because of its military prowess, defeat of Napoleon and Hitler, vast territory, and geographic location bridging Europe and Asia. In short, being a great power is an integral component of both states' identities.[2]

STATUS CONCERNS AND THEIR INFLUENCE ON FOREIGN POLICY

Great power status carries with it the expectation that the state will be consulted on important issues by other major powers, and that smaller states, especially within its region, will defer to its wishes on foreign policy. Great powers usually exploit such privileges to gain material and strategic benefits, such as trade, military bases, and access to valued raw materials. For the leaders, achieving great power status also helps to legitimize the regime to a domestic audience, compensating for domestic failures and economic weakness. But states, like individuals, have an intrinsic need to be respected and recognized, which may be important in motivating national elites to seek great power status.[3] Increased security and economic wealth alone are not sufficient, as shown by the dissatisfaction of China and Russia with their current standing in the international system. China and Russia possess important status markers—nuclear weapons, permanent seats on the UN Security Council, smaller power clients—but their elites are still not satisfied with the level of recognition granted them by the leading states and want more—exactly what is not always clear. Russian elites are even more strongly dissatisfied than their Chinese counterparts with their current international standing, and this feeling helps to account for much of the difference between Russian and Chinese foreign policy—in use of military force, assertiveness, and meddling in other states' internal affairs. To understand China's and Russia's foreign policies, it is thus essential to go beyond the standard foreign policy goals of wealth, power, security, and ideology. And in this respect China and Russia do not appear to be entirely exceptional, because smaller powers as well strive for enhanced status.

In some sense, the distinction between material and intrinsic motivations for seeking status is artificial, because power, wealth, and status are often mutually reinforcing. On the other hand, at times governments have spent enormous sums on efforts to achieve or maintain great power standing, at the expense of their state's power and wealth. Leaders have embarked on foolish quests for international prestige or glory, bankrupting their country's finances while earning a reputation for rapaciousness that detracts from their state's standing. For example, in the early eighteenth century, Qing China's expansion into Xinjiang required enormously expensive, lengthy, and logistically difficult military campaigns to defeat the Zunghar Mongols, and continuing expenditures from the treasury for the territory's occupation and defense. Even after devastating defeats in the Opium Wars, desperate to hold on to its status as the leading power in East Asia, China fought disastrous wars first with France and then Japan to retain its suzerainty over Vietnam and Korea, at the cost of undoing the modernizing reforms of the self-strengtheners. At the beginning of the twentieth century, Russia built the exorbitantly expensive and ambitious Trans-Siberian railroad to the Pacific and attempted to expand into Manchuria and Korea, provoking a war with rising power Japan. In the 1970s, Brezhnev's Soviet Union went on a binge of acquiring nuclear weapons and flew advisers and equipment to Angola and Ethiopia, overextending its economic resources and damaging beyond repair the détente relationship with the United States.[4] SIT illuminates when and why countries incur such excessive costs and commitments, without having to attribute such departures from rationality solely to miscalculation or uncertainty.

We initiated this study as a plausibility probe to determine whether more systematic testing of SIT might be worthwhile. Assessments of causality for foreign policy decisions can never be conclusive, but SIT does seem to have some advantages in explaining Chinese and Russian foreign policy compared to alternative approaches. As neorealists emphasize, territorial expansion was sometimes a defensive response due to repeated external invasions, an attempt to provide a buffer zone and more secure borders. But beginning in the eighteenth century, Russia's territorial expansion was less reactive and more calculated—to achieve geostrategic objectives and entry into the club of great European powers. Rather than being a defensive response, Russia's expansion occurred at the expense of declining powers Sweden, Poland, and the Ottoman Empire. In the nineteenth century, Russia had reached its natural frontiers to the south in the Black Sea, north to the Baltic, and east to the Pacific, yet it continued to expand eastward into Central Asia and Manchuria. Similarly, in the seventeenth and eighteenth centuries, the Manchus expanded their territory although they faced no threats from rival powers. The Qing dynasty captured Taiwan in 1683, sent troops into Tibet in 1720, and incorporated Xinjiang into China in 1768.[5]

To be sure, once incorporated, the additional territory could eventually provide economic benefits such as land for settlement and valuable raw materials. But if they were solely interested in the economic benefits to be derived from expansion, Chinese and Russian rulers would not have been so concerned about publicizing their victories. The Qianlong emperor was a "master of display," advertising his military victories and territorial conquests through monuments, paintings, poems, and circulation of specially commissioned copper engravings to Europe. Peter the Great introduced classical imagery from Rome, such as portraits, coins, flags, and banners, into symbolic representations of the state. Catherine followed up the military victories of her generals with a propaganda campaign stressing Russia's greatness as a nation and its successorship to Rome.[6]

Titles, rituals, and diplomatic protocol were important to Chinese and Russian rulers because they symbolized relative status. In China, the tribute system symbolized China's moral superiority, hierarchy, and unchallengeable status. The Qing insisted on following the imperial rituals punctiliously when dealing with foreign emissaries, refusing to deal with representatives who were unwilling to use submissive rhetoric or to engage in ritual prostration (the kowtow).

Ivan IV was so determined to have his title of tsar inserted into a peace treaty with Poland that he was willing to give up fortified cities in exchange—an offer that was nevertheless rejected. Peter the Great unilaterally declared himself emperor after his victory over Sweden, using the Latin term "imperator" because "tsar" had no meaning to European audiences. Catherine the Great demanded that foreign ambassadors kiss her hand and speak to her in French. Because of her insistence on signing first on alternate copies of a treaty of alliance with the Austrian emperor, Joseph II, and his unwillingness to set a precedent, their alliance was kept secret until her annexation of Crimea threatened to provoke war with Turkey.

Status markers change with historical eras. In the nineteenth century, lengthy titles for rulers were no longer a mark of distinction. During the Cold War, status derived from having an ideological and developmental model that attracted adherents in other countries. In the current era, major power status may be symbolized by aircraft carriers, nuclear weapons, membership in diplomatic groups (for example, the Six Party Talks on North Korea's nuclear program or the P5+1 negotiations on Iran's nuclear weapons program), or hosting the Olympics. In the view of the US and its allies, great power status should have a normative component, including acceptance of liberal ideology. From this perspective, China and Russia are clinging to anachronistic status markers, such as a regional sphere of influence and permanent membership in the UN Security Council. On the other hand, since Deng Xiaoping, China has differed from post-Soviet Russia in seeking status based on other modern criteria for superior international standing, such as excellence in trade and technology.

Ideology has also played a role in driving Russia's and China's international behavior. For Russia, as for other empires, an ideology of exceptionalism, linked to a self-image of greatness and a civilizing mission, helped to legitimize territorial expansion. Panslavism, which called for Russia's leadership of the Slavs and their liberation from foreign rule, undermined Foreign Minister Gorchakov's efforts to conduct a foreign policy that would provide space for domestic reforms after the Crimean War. The Qing dynasty's universalist ideology claimed the right to rule over multiple ethnic groups—Tibetans, Han Chinese, Uighurs, and Mongols, as well as Manchus—justifying if not motivating the Manchus' territorial conquests, which seemed intended mainly to enhance the dynasty's glory.[7]

In the twentieth century, both Soviet and Chinese elites were strongly motivated by ideological goals such as promotion of socialist revolutions, support for national liberation movements, and maintenance of ideological orthodoxy in client states. Ideology added an almost impenetrable layer of suspicion to their dealings with the capitalist states, a sense that Western diplomats and leaders were devious and untrustworthy.

But ideology and status aspirations could be mutually reinforcing. Marxism-Leninism helped to fulfill Russia's and China's search for an escape from backwardness by promising an accelerated path to modernity and superiority over the Western countries through the establishment of socialism, a more advanced system than capitalism in communist doctrine. Social comparison with more advanced states was embedded in Marxist-Leninist ideology, for socialist regimes were expected to grow faster and produce more than capitalist states.[8] Economic competition with capitalist states became even more prominent under Khrushchev and Brezhnev. This was social competition, because the status superiority of the United States was based on its economic production and prosperity as well as its military power.[9] For the PRC, the reference state was the Soviet Union. Mao launched the Great Leap Forward not only because he thought it would enable China to industrialize quickly, but because it would demonstrate China's superiority to Russia in building socialism.

When the state's great power standing was at stake, the desire for status could take priority over ideological goals. Although socialist revolution was supposed to render national borders meaningless, and Lenin had expressed support for the self-determination of national groups, the Bolsheviks reconquered much of the territory lost in World War I, except for the Baltics, Poland, and Finland. Similarly, the CCP insisted on restoring China's imperial borders, even conquering non-Han Chinese in Xinjiang, Tibet, Mongolia, because the empire assembled by the Manchus was part of China's historical greatness.[10]

Stalin's postwar aims were not entirely derived from Marxist-Leninist ideology, but were also influenced by the desire for security and status, as manifest in his insistence on the rights and prerogatives of a great power, such as a sphere of influence in Eastern Europe, overseas bases, and a strong navy. Stalin signed a treaty of alliance with Guomindang leader Chiang Kai-shek that would allow him to keep his warm water ports and maintain Soviet interests in the Chinese Eastern railway. Stalin bargained with the United States and Britain to regain territories that were formerly part of Imperial Russia and even some that had exceeded the tsar's reach. Stalin's repeated demands for a base in Libya had little to do with either security or communist ideology, but rather his desire to project power into the Mediterranean, an objective befitting a great power equal to the United States and Great Britain.

For the CCP, Marxist-Leninist ideology was intertwined with anti-imperialism and the desire to restore China's independence and prestige after the century of humiliation.[11] Mao intervened in the Korean War in part out of an ideological sense of duty to protect the revolution in North Korea, but he was also motivated by fear of a US military presence on Chinese borders and the desire to inflict defeat on the US imperialists, which would improve China's standing in the world. In contrast, his successor Deng decoupled foreign policy from ideology, seeking better relations with the United States and Japan because they had superior technology and managerial skills that could be adapted to promote Chinese economic development. Deng used military force against a fellow communist regime in Vietnam to "teach it a lesson," showing China's traditional sense of moral superiority and tutelage over neighboring states.

Both the Soviet Union and the PRC showed concern with bourgeois diplomatic protocol and symbolic indicators of status. After World War II, Stalin withdrew from the London Foreign Ministers Conference because France and China had been allowed to participate in discussions, although his foreign minister Molotov regarded it as a trivial issue. Khrushchev was worried that he would not be accorded treatment befitting a head of state at the 1955 Geneva Summit Conference because his title of general secretary had no meaning in standard diplomatic protocol. In 1959, the Soviet leader was initially alarmed by Eisenhower's invitation for him to visit the presidential retreat at Camp David, fearing that it was a humiliation. Despite the improved Soviet power position in the 1970s, and notwithstanding public triumphalism about a shift in the correlation of forces and boasting about Soviet military superiority, privately Brezhnev and other Soviet elites were deeply insecure about their international status, and valued the Basic Principles Agreement for its recognition of Soviet equality. Similarly, the CCP leadership welcomed a visit from President Nixon, including a handshake with Zhou Enlai, as recognition of the PRC's status and a way to make amends for Dulles's humiliating snub of the Chinese leader at the 1954 Geneva Conference. The Chinese continue to be highly sensitive to such symbols as the length of the red carpet, having a state dinner vs. a lunch, or receiving a twenty-one-gun salute, in general craving "the protocol and trappings of being treated as a great power."[12]

Another form of status-driven symbolism is acceptance into exclusive clubs. Since the eighteenth century, Russian elites have been motivated by the aspiration to be a member of the elite great power clubs. Russia finally reached the pinnacle of success after the defeat of Napoleon with its membership in the Concert of Europe and the Holy Alliance. Stalin displayed great satisfaction with his partnership with Churchill and Roosevelt in the Big Three. After the Cold War, Russia initially sought admission to NATO, the EU, or the OECD, but was rebuffed. Yeltsin made several requests to join the G7 before its political format was revised to include Russia. After the terrorist attacks on September 11, 2011, Putin envisioned another great power concert and compared his relationship with George Bush to Stalin's alliance with Churchill and FDR. Since the end of the Cold War, China has established or participated in elite clubs that do not include the United States, in which it can play a leading role, such as the BRICS (Brazil, Russia, India, China, and South Africa) and the Shanghai Cooperation Organization (SCO).

Both constructivism and SIT attribute importance to identity in shaping states' foreign policies. Contrary to the constructivist view of identity as a product of social interactions and constitutive practices, however, in China and Russia the elites have historically played major roles in shaping their countries' identities in the world and their relationship to the West. Peter the Great embarked on a Westernizing course—reforming Russian culture, government, education, and social mores—to make Russia a European great power. When the Confucian literati challenged Qianlong's conquest of Xinjiang on the grounds that it was not part of China proper, the emperor refuted them by differentiating the Qing from previous dynasties that had excluded non-Han peoples, establishing a new identity for China.[13] While rejecting wholesale Westernization, the reformist Confucian bureaucrats who were part of the self-strengthening movement authorized selective modernization that would preserve China's unique culture and civilization. Despite the end of the Cold War and the apparent triumph of liberal democracy, China and Russia have resisted socialization into accepting Western liberal norms. The CCP has adopted "socialism with Chinese characteristics," clamping down on free speech and domestic dissent, while Russian President Vladimir Putin has increasingly championed "traditional" values against the "decadence" of the West.

DETERMINANTS OF IDENTITY MANAGEMENT STRATEGIES

Chinese and Russian elites are acutely aware of their states' international standing. Regardless of their capabilities, China and Russia have perceived themselves as great powers—showing the enduring importance of social identity. Declining power has merely increased their desire to restore their long-lost great power status, which they view as part of the natural order. Threats to their identities as great powers—such as humiliating military defeats, exclusion from elite clubs, disregard for their interests, or economic difficulties—have motivated elites to make major changes in their foreign policies.

Available options for Chinese and Russian elites can be categorized using the SIT typology of identity management strategies—social mobility, social competition, and social creativity. The attractiveness of a social mobility strategy is dependent upon the perceived permeability of elite clubs. Status competition—through such means as acquiring advanced weapons, military victories, collecting allies and clients, and territorial expansion—is encouraged by the belief that the international status hierarchy is unstable or illegitimate. When the international pecking order was perceived as stable and legitimate, elites were drawn to a social creativity strategy of achieving prestige in a domain not competitive with the leading power. Within each country there were contending schools of thought on the country's foreign policy orientation and appropriate identity management strategy. SIT illuminates some of the logic behind foreign policy elites' choice of a particular international identity and grand strategy.

For social mobility to be a viable strategy, national elites must believe that elite clubs are permeable to new members. China and Russia were both denied admission to the great power clubs for extended periods. In the nineteenth century, China was increasingly criticized as uncivilized due to its rejection of sovereign equality, free trade, and international law.

Russia was viewed by some Europeans as barbaric, half-Asian, not really a part of Western civilization. Frederick the Great, while admiring Russian power and admitting that Russia was an "arbiter of the North," maintained that like the Ottoman Empire, it belonged "half in Europe and half in Asia."[14]

Communist revolutions in Russia and China created an almost insuperable barrier to acceptance by the Western countries: the two powers rejected diplomatic norms and were committed to overthrowing the international order. During the 1920s, the Soviets patiently persevered, despite repeated setbacks, in their attempt to win recognition from the major powers, but small achievements were repeatedly reversed in retaliation for Bolshevik propaganda and attempted subversion in Western colonies. The Soviet Union was not admitted to the League of Nations until 1934. Nor was the Soviet Union represented at the 1938 Munich conference, although the USSR had a mutual assistance pact with Czechoslovakia. Thanks to Roosevelt's "Four Policemen" idea, the Soviet Union received a permanent seat on the UN Security Council, but, largely due to Western alarm at Stalin's geopolitical ambitions, the Big Three—formed by FDR, Stalin, and Churchill—did not survive the death of Roosevelt. No summit meetings were held for a decade after the August 1945 Potsdam meeting. In order to get to the "spirit of Geneva," the Soviets had to make unilateral concessions.[15] Russia was finally admitted to the G7 in 1997, but only to the political meetings, not to those of the finance ministers where the important business was done, only to be expelled in 2014 as punishment for Putin's annexation of Crimea.

The Republic of China (ROC), established after the overthrow of the Qing dynasty, was classified as a "minor power" at the Versailles conference, and was not given a seat at the great power table at the League of Nations.[16] This slight was rectified by President Roosevelt, who made sure that the ROC was given a permanent seat on the UN Security Council, but the ROC was not represented at the Yalta conference where decisions were made—at China's expense—to award Stalin concessions in return for Russian participation in the war against Japan. After the communist revolution, it was Taiwan that received China's seat at the United Nations. During the 1950s and 1960s, the United States pursued a policy of nonrecognition, economic embargo, and non-membership in the United Nations for the PRC.[17]

Perhaps more important than the impermeability of elite clubs in ruling out a social mobility strategy for China and Russia, however, is their sense of exceptionalism and the reluctance of their elites to emulate Western political values and institutions (as opposed to technology). While some elites, such as the extreme wing of nineteenth century Russian Westernizers or radical modernizers of the early twentieth century Chinese New Culture Movement, went so far as to reject their nation's culture and traditions entirely in favor of wholesale imitation of the West, they were a minority; radical Westernization was ultimately rejected by both the elites and the masses. For example, while it is commonly believed that Peter the Great opened Russia to the West, he demonstrated little desire to emulate Western political institutions and laws, focusing more, as renowned historian V. O. Kliuchevsky observed, on "decorating" Russia's "European façade."[18] Even limited Westernization among the gentry in Russia stimulated a backlash in the form of the nineteenth century philosophical movement of Slavophilism. Similarly, in China in the late nineteenth century, limited reforms aimed at learning Western technology and languages stimulated a nationalistic and antiforeign reaction in which neotraditionalists defended Chinese spiritual values as superior to Western individualism, materialism, and utilitarianism. Even the radical reformer Gorbachev promulgated the more idealistic, universalist principles of the New Thinking instead of adopting Western liberal norms. Finally, Deng and his successors may have opened up China to economic globalization, but they have blocked the "fifth modernization," political democracy.

Impermeability of elite international clubs and the perception that the hierarchical system of status is illegitimate or unstable promotes social competition. Whether or not states resort to military conflict to enhance their status depends on the criteria for status within that context as well as on a state's relative capabilities. Russia's comparative advantage appears to be in the projection of military power rather than economic productivity. In eighteenth- and nineteenth-century Europe, the status hierarchy was fluid, with powers rising and falling depending on their diplomatic skill, geographic centrality, and military prowess. Russia competed for status successively with Sweden, Turkey, and finally Prussia and Austria. Beginning in the mid-nineteenth century, Russia entered into a rivalry with Britain over Central and South Asia known as the Great Game, then returned in the early twentieth century to the traditional competition with Austria over the Balkans.

A change in ideology altered the means of status competition if not the ends. Marxism-Leninism contributed to the Chinese and Russian perception that the prevailing status hierarchy was not only illegitimate but unstable, doomed to fall to war and revolution. Until the anticipated revolutions in other advanced countries, social competition with the Western industrialized states was necessary to demonstrate the superiority of the communist developmental model and attract adherents of communism in other states, especially former colonies and Third World states. Soviet rulers promised to "catch up with and surpass" the economic productivity and consumption of the more advanced states.

In order for their victory over the Western states to be complete, however, the PRC and the Soviet Union needed validation of their achievements from those same powers, hence their efforts to propagandize and influence international perceptions.

The Chinese Communists regarded the superior position of imperialist powers in the international system as fundamentally illegitimate. The PRC adopted the Soviet Union as its developmental model and point of reference, but taking an inferior position to the Soviet Union clashed with the innate Chinese sense of moral and civilizational superiority. Chinese dissatisfaction with the status hierarchy was eventually directed toward the socialist world as well. After the death of Stalin, Mao regarded the Soviet Union's leadership of the communist bloc as illegitimate. In the view of the Chinese communists, China deserved to be the ideological leader. Mao believed that *he* was more capable of interpreting Marxism-Leninism than the ignorant and buffoonish Khrushchev. Mao competed with the Soviet Union in attracting the support of the Third World and providing a model of socialist development.[19]

Humiliation—involving a lowering of a state's status position—may provoke anger and even an offensive response if the demeaned state has sufficient power. Russia experienced a series of humiliating defeats by foreign powers—in the Crimean War, the Russo-Japanese War, and the 1908–9 Bosnian crisis—which stiffened the Russian leadership's determination to support Serbia in 1914 against Austria. Khrushchev's embarrassment over the Kennedy administration's exposure of his bluffs about Soviet missile capabilities fueled his decision to gamble by putting missiles in Cuba. The Soviets' even greater humiliation at having to take the missiles out helped to motivate Brezhnev's military buildup to strategic parity with the United States. In the 1990s, while Russia was too weak to prevent the United States from enlarging NATO or bombing Serbia, at the end of the Kosovo War Yeltsin sent troops to capture Pristina before NATO forces arrived, risking a clash of arms. In 2014, in a lightning display of revenge and hubris, Putin responded to the overthrow of pro-Russian Ukrainian leader Yanukovych by sending Russian special forces to seize the Crimean Peninsula—an event greeted by the overwhelming majority of Russian elite and public as ultimate proof that Russia had "risen from its knees." According to an August 2014 public opinion poll, the Russian people believed that

Putin's greatest achievement was the restoration of Russia's great power status.[20]

The neorealist explanation for Putin's incursion into Crimea and eastern Ukraine is that it was a defensive response to NATO's previous expansion into Eastern Europe, which removed a buffer zone and threatened the security of Russian borders, and to the risk that a pro-Western Kiev would join the Western alliance.[21] Putin strongly opposed Ukraine's membership in NATO, as he warned at the 2008 Bucharest NATO summit. The question is whether his response to the overthrow of Yanukovych was motivated by genuine fears of a NATO attack, as opposed to a sense of anger and injustice over the West's indifference to powerful Russian interests in the area. It is important to recognize that Ukraine was the birthplace of Russian Orthodoxy, a cultural repository, and historically had been part of both Russia and the Soviet Union. Putin's foreign policy goals are more ambitious than simple opposition to NATO expansion, and shown by the fact that he cooperated with the United States after 9/11 despite the 1999 enlargement of NATO to include Poland, the Czech Republic, and Hungary. He is determined ultimately to restore Russia to great power status with a sphere of influence over the near abroad.

Another conventional explanation is that Putin's assertiveness was an attempt to undermine his domestic political opponents by appealing to the Russians' patriotism and feelings that they were being victimized by the West.[22] But Putin began criticizing US foreign policy with his 2007 Munich speech, before he faced any political opposition, and he had already silenced his political opponents through arrests and repressive laws before the takeover of Crimea. Hence, domestic political motivations are not sufficient to account for Putin's bold moves in Ukraine.

Both China and Russia are hypersensitive to perceived slights and have used military power to assert superiority—Russia through its impressive display of its advanced weapons in Syria, and China through the use of its coast guard to intimidate rival claimants to rocks and reefs in the South China Sea.

Chinese and Russian elites have been more likely to use social creativity when they accepted the status hierarchy as legitimate or at least stable. More conventional analyses of status seeking overlook the availability of social creativity as a means of improving a state's status, focusing instead on war or conflict initiation as the sole means of altering others' perceptions.[23]

The social creativity tactic of reframing supposedly negative traits as positive is a way of coping psychologically with feelings of inferiority, even though it does not actually alter the status hierarchy. In the nineteenth century this tactic was used by some Russian and Chinese elites in response to the West's technological and material superiority. Slavophilism stressed positive aspects of Russia's unique and special identity, separate from that of the West—its spirituality, collectivism, respect for tradition, and Orthodox Christianity. In the late nineteenth century, Chinese self-strengtheners emphasized that while Western technology had practical value, China's moral philosophy was superior. Such uses of social creativity helped assuage Russian and Chinese feelings of inferiority about their loss of status, and increased their self-confidence.

But social creativity may also be used to change the very meaning of status and in that way improve a state's relative position—by identifying an alternative value dimension on which the state is superior or by promoting new international norms. Sometimes social creativity can shade into social competition, insofar as a state is stressing new criteria for status. On the other hand, the fundamental goal of social creativity is to carve out a different domain of superiority rather than to challenge the leading power, as would be the case with social competition. Zhou Enlai advocated the Five Principles of Peaceful Coexistence as an alternative to Cold War norms of competition and conflict, a theme that has been repeated by later Chinese leaders. Khrushchev promoted peaceful coexistence between socialist and capitalist states, and made overtures to the conservative regimes of India, Afghanistan, and Burma. Gorbachev sponsored the principles of the New Thinking (mutual security, nonoffensive defense, "freedom of choice," and the Common European Home), a universalistic philosophy that offered the tantalizing promise of creating a new basis for genuine Soviet greatness in international politics. Gorbachev's dedication to the New Thinking was such that he accepted the loss of Eastern Europe, the most prized geopolitical reward from World War II, exceeding even the reach of the tsars, rather than contradict the peaceful image he had created of the Soviet Union. In his first term, Putin used social creativity by trying to establish a partnership with President Bush in the war against terror. Since the mid-1990s, China has articulated the "peaceful rise" or "peaceful development" strategy, stressing that China's foreign policy will be different from that of past aspiring great powers such as Germany and Japan, which engaged in arms races and territorial aggression. The effectiveness of social creativity as compared with social competition in improving the status of China and Russia has varied, depending on perceptions of their relative power and the receptivity of the higher-status states.

EFFECTIVENESS OF STATUS-SEEKING STRATEGIES

In most international relations theories, great power status is a product of war, and in particular, defeat of a leading power.[24] Our case studies suggest that military power is a necessary—but not sufficient—condition for great power status. A genuine great power must also adhere to prevailing norms of civilized behavior and be able to project "soft power" based on the attraction of its ideas, culture, or developmental model.

The success of Russia's and China's status seeking has been determined by the opinions of the reference group. Russia has always looked to the West, initially Europe and later the United States, for validation of its status aspirations. After becoming part of the Westphalian international system in the late nineteenth century, China looked to the higher-status major countries of the West as well, as both a benchmark for comparison and a source of external recognition. Communist China defined its policy toward Asia in terms of the global struggle, acting as a "regional power without a regional policy."[25] The reference group for measuring status varies with each state; less powerful states will not compare themselves to the hegemon, but to a similar, but slightly higher-status state. For example, India must attain recognition from China in order to obtain status markers, such as permanent membership in the UN Security Council, but China as yet has not been willing to treat India as an equal great power.[26]

Social competition was a highly effective strategy for Russia in the eighteenth century, as Russian military victories over the Swedes and the Turks raised Russia's standing to that of a mighty and feared power. Despite its display of military power, however, Russia was not really regarded as a member of the club of great powers until Catherine the Great professed her support for Enlightenment principles and adopted

Western diplomatic practices. Russia's defeat of Napoleon and Alexander I's entry into Paris advanced Russia's status still further, making it the leading land power of the continent, as confirmed by Russia's membership in the Concert of Europe and the Holy Alliance. But Nicholas I's assumption of the role of "gendarme of Europe" in preventing domestic revolutions subsequently contributed to Russophobia in Europe and an overall decline in Russia's standing even before its defeat in the Crimean War, which demonstrated that a mass army with brilliant commanders and sturdy peasant soldiers was no longer sufficient to win military victories.

The Bolshevik revolution set back Russia's great power aspirations; loss of territory and economic disorganization weakened the USSR economically and militarily so that it was no longer taken seriously by the major powers. This perception changed after Stalin's coerced industrialization, but even more so following the Red Army's military defeat of Nazi Germany, an achievement that made the Soviet Union an undisputed superpower. While Khrushchev achieved some dramatic triumphs in space exploration, overall Soviet prestige was harmed by his boorishness (such as banging his shoe at the United Nations), nuclear threats, and embarrassing retreat in the Cuban Missile Crisis.[27] Soviet prestige peaked during the 1970s détente period under Brezhnev, but the regime was overextended in trying to conduct an arms race and project power into Africa, and by the early 1980s, a stagnating Soviet economy, the invasion of Afghanistan, and Reagan's assertive anticommunism revealed the policy of social competition to be at an impasse.

The Chinese Communists based their legitimacy in part on their claim to have restored China's international position, rectifying a legacy of humiliation by imperialist powers. Indeed, by defeating MacArthur's offensive in Korea, China proved itself to be a major military power. Even more effective in winning prestige for China in the Third World was Zhou's use of social creativity from 1954 to 1958—his emphasis on "seeking common ground in spite of differences," advocacy of the Five Principles of Coexistence in contrast to Cold War rigidity, and promotion of greater equality among states. Initially, the Chinese developmental model—with its emphasis on voluntarism, the power of the people over technology, mass mobilization, and equality—was attractive to a number of Third World leaders. However, Mao's shift to radicalism in both domestic and foreign policy in 1966 with the Cultural

Revolution, as Red Guards rampaged through the capital and placed embassies under siege, undermined China's international prestige.[28] After international isolation and the Soviet threat forced a reconsideration of Chinese strategy, China was able to exploit its position as part of the "strategic triangle" with the United States and the Soviet Union to restore some of its standing.

But even without superior capabilities, aspiring powers may sometimes achieve prestige through social creativity. For example, a state may stress its civilizational achievements, as China has done by emphasizing its four great inventions—paper, gun powder, printing, and the magnetic compass. Social creativity makes it possible for aspiring great powers to gain a seat at the table without challenging the leading hegemon for dominance, a possibility overlooked by conventional power transition theory.[29] To succeed, social creativity efforts need to be approved and recognized by higher-status states. Prior to the collapse of the Soviet Union, Gorbachev won great admiration for the Soviet Union among Western states for his New Thinking ideas and willingness to dismantle Cold War structures.

To be successful in the long-term, however, the social creativity route to great power status should rest on a solid economic foundation. A state must have a minimum level of material capability to be recognized as a major power. While both China and Russia have been viewed as outliers from the Western security community, the United States has been more appreciative of China's social creativity efforts than those of Russia, perhaps because until recently the PRC, whose current status as a leading power is based almost entirely on economic weight, was not regarded as a threat to America's geopolitical interests in Eurasia. The United States has generally supported China's efforts to achieve status by participating in the rule-governed liberal world order set up by the United States after World War II. Deng Xiaoping did more than any previous Chinese leader to raise China's standing in the world by bringing millions out of poverty and initiating economic growth.

In contrast, because of its relatively underdeveloped economy, post–Cold War Russia was viewed by the United States as "a regional and niche ally," useful for particular issues, but neither a global partner nor a leading power, and definitely not an American equal.[30] In setting itself up as the arbiter of which leaders in post-Soviet Eurasia should fall, and neglecting to consult Moscow on major issues, the United States was acting as a hegemon, projecting its superiority in every way—military, economic, and moral. Tellingly, after Putin annexed Crimea, Obama attempted to reassure the US public by dismissing Russia as merely a regional power, further humiliating Moscow.

Standard approaches to international relations theory generally envision only two strategic choices for aspiring great powers—integration into international society or conflict with the established powers to reshape the rules and norms of the system. However, our study suggests that an intermediate option between cooperation and competition—entailing strategic partnership and a division of labor—may be more feasible and desirable than integration, which is unlikely given the values divide that has endured despite the end of the Cold War. While China and Russia have no interest in overthrowing the international economic order, from which they benefit, they have rejected certain political components of the liberal order such as the rule of law and individual human rights.

The ideal of social cooperation identified by SIT, whereby the hegemon and aspiring powers each recognize the value of the other's necessary and complementary roles, suggests an alternative to both integration and conflict. China and Russia have been more cooperative when they were accepted as great powers by the dominant states. For example, after the US validated Beijing's "responsible power" identity in the second half of the 1990s, China increased its participation in multilateral organizations, behaved responsibly during the 1997 Asian Financial Crisis and 2008–9 Great Recession, contributed to UN peacekeeping operations, hosted the Six Party Talks on North Korea's nuclear program, and abstained on key votes in the UN Security Council concerning sanctions against Iran and Libya. Russia has likewise sought a cooperative relationship with the other major powers. Putin provided significant and much-needed help to the US after the September 11, 2001, attacks in the expectation that he could form a "strategic partnership" with Bush in the war on terror. In response to the promise of more equal treatment under Obama's "reset" policy, Russia gave important material assistance to NATO in the war against the Taliban in Afghanistan and allowed the enactment of sanctions against Iran.

It may be possible to encourage a division of labor in which China and Russia can specialize in particular issues or share leadership roles.[31] For example, China could be encouraged to lead infrastructure development in Asia and efforts to promote renewable energy. Russia could take a prominent role in arms control, nonproliferation, and counterterrorism. Despite the added complications, the United States benefits when aspiring powers pursue social creativity as opposed to trying to score points or obstruct global governance. The goal should be a division of spheres of responsibility rather than spheres of influence.

Our analysis also suggests that states will only pursue social creativity if the status hierarchy is perceived as legitimate and/or stable, that is, unlikely to be altered by unilateral action. Status accommodation by the higher-status state should be made from a position of relative strength, not waning power. If an aspiring state believes that the status hierarchy is unstable as well as illegitimate, it is likely to pursue social competition, as the Soviet Union did during the Cold War. Uncertainty and the imminence of a shift in the international status hierarchy may encourage social competition and more assertive policies, which then lead to containment and isolation by others, setting in motion a vicious circle. Moreover, status accommodation is a continuing process, not simply a one-off symbolic gesture that means practically nothing. To maintain the perception that the hierarchy is stable, the United States should preserve its overall military and economic power and alliance networks. The desire to balance against a potential threat can be an important motivation for the higher-status state to offer status recognition to a third power, as Nixon and Kissinger did for China in 1972 to counter the Soviet threat, and as the United States has done for India with the 2008 nuclear agreement, this time to balance China.[32] United States isolationism would not be conducive to cooperative role-sharing and respect for each other's status. The United States can contribute to the legitimacy of the status hierarchy by trying to build international support for its global leadership rather than acting unilaterally, and by upholding universal rules.

In the post–Cold War era, as the balance of power shifts unpredictably, states' drive for status, influence, and prestige—their position in the international "pecking order"—has become an increasingly important ingredient in international politics, especially for rising and resurgent powers. To supplement conventional strategies of containment or integration, we would recommend giving more consideration to status incentives, such as protocols for inter-state visits, formal recognition of equality, strategic dialogues, and so forth, as these incentives have been successful in the past in encouraging Chinese and Russian co-operation.[33] Constructive Chinese or Russian behavior—such as participation in efforts to control global warming or resolve Middle East conflicts—should be rewarded.

Status in the international system is not necessarily a zero-sum game, in which an ascendant nation's enhanced status diminishes that of the dominant state. On the contrary, when a state uses social creativity to increase its international standing, it complements and enriches the entire international order.

Notes

CHAPTER 1. STATUS AND IDENTITY

1. Vladimir Putin, "Russia at the Turn of the Millennium," in Richard Sakwa, *Putin: Russia's Choice* (London: Routledge, 2004), 257; D. C. B. Lieven, *Russia and the Origins of the First World War* (New York: St. Martin's Press, 1983), 5; Lucian W. Pye, *The Spirit of Chinese Politics: A Psychocultural Study of the Authority Crisis in Political Development* (Cambridge, MA: MIT Press, 1968), 50 (quotation); Chen Jian, *Mao's China and the Cold War* (Chapel Hill: University of North Carolina Press, 2001); Zheng Wang, *Never Forget National Humiliation: Historical Memory in Chinese Politics and Foreign Relations* (New York: Columbia University Press, 2012), 129–32; Yan Xuetong, "The Rise of China in Chinese Eyes," *Journal of Contemporary China* 10, no. 26 (2001): 34.

2. Jack S. Levy, *War in the Modern Great Power System, 1495–1975* (Lexington: University Press of Kentucky, 1983); Hedley Bull, *The Anarchical Society: A Study of Order in World Politics* (New York: Columbia University Press, 1977); Kenneth N. Waltz, *Theory of International Politics* (Reading, MA: Addison-Wesley, 1979); John J. Mearsheimer, *The Tragedy of Great Power Politics* (New York: Norton, 2001).

3. For recent exceptions, see Randall Schweller, "Realism and the Present Great Power System: Growth and Positional Conflict Over Scarce Resources," in *Unipolar Politics: Realism and State Strategies after the Cold War*, ed. Ethan B. Kapstein and Michael Mastanduno (New York: Columbia University Press, 1999), 28–68; Yong Deng, *China's Struggle for Status: The Realignment of International Relations* (Cambridge: Cambridge University Press, 2008); Richard Ned Lebow, *A Cultural Theory of International Relations* (Cambridge: Cambridge University Press, 2008); William C. Wohlforth, "Unipolarity, Status Competition, and Great

Power War," *World Politics* 61, no. 1 (January 2009): 28–57; David C. Kang, "Status and Leadership on the Korean Peninsula," *Orbis* 54, no. 4 (Fall 2010): 546–64; Thomas J. Volgy, Renato Corbetta, Keith A. Grant, and Ryan G. Baird, *Major Powers and the Quest for Status in International Politics: Global and Regional Perspectives* (New York: Palgrave Macmillan, 2011); Reinhard Wolf, "Respect and Disrespect in International Politics: The Significance of Status Recognition," *International Theory* 3, no. 1 (2011), 105–42; T. V. Paul, Deborah Welch Larson, William C. Wohlforth, eds., *Status in World Politics* (Cambridge: Cambridge University Press, 2014); Allen Dafoe, Jonathan Renshon, and Paul Huth, "Reputation and Status as Motives for War," *Annual Review of Political Science* 17 (2014): 371–93; Jonathan Renshon, "Status Deficits and War," *International Organization* 70, no. 3 (Summer 2016): 513–50; Joslyn Barnhart, "Status Competition and Territorial Aggression: Evidence from the Scramble for Africa," *Security Studies* 25, no. 3 (2016): 385–419.

4. Henri Tajfel, "Interindividual Behavior and Intergroup Behavior," "Social Categorization, Social Identity and Social Comparison," and "The Achievement of Group Differentiation," in *Differentiation between Social Groups: Studies in the Social Psychology of Intergroup Relations*, ed. Henri Tajfel (London: Academic Press, 1978), 27–60, 61–76, 77–98; Henri Tajfel and John C. Turner, "An Integrative Theory of Intergroup Conflict," in *The Social Psychology of Intergroup Relations*, ed. William G. Austin and Stephen Worchel (Monterey, CA: Brooks/Cole, 1979), 33–47; Henri Tajfel, ed., *Social Identity and Intergroup Relations* (Cambridge: Cambridge University Press, 1982). For applications of social identity theory to international relations, see Jonathan Mercer, "Anarchy and Identity," *International Organization* 49, no. 2 (1995): 229–52; Deborah Welch Larson and Alexei Shevchenko, "Shortcut to Greatness: The New Thinking and the Revolution in Soviet Foreign Policy," *International Organization* 57, no. 1 (Winter 2003): 77–109; Peter Hays Gries, "Social Psychology and the Identity-Conflict Debate: Is a 'China Threat' Inevitable?," *European Journal of International Relations* 11, no. 2 (2005): 235–65; Anne L. Clunan, *The Social Construction of Russia's Resurgence: Aspirations, Identity, and Security Interests* (Baltimore: The Johns Hopkins University Press, 2009); Deborah Welch Larson and Alexei Shevchenko, "Status Seekers: Chinese and Russian Responses to U.S. Primacy," *International Security* 34, no. 4 (Winter 2010): 63–95; Larson and Shevchenko, "Managing Rising Powers: The Role of Status Concerns," in *Status in World Politics*, ed. T. V. Paul, Deborah W. Larson, and William C. Wohlforth (Cambridge University Press, 2014), 33–57.

5. Tajfel and Turner, "Integrative Theory of Intergroup Conflict."

6. Tajfel, "Social Categorization, Social Identity, and Social Comparison," 63.

7. John C. Turner, "Social Comparison and Social Identity: Some Prospects for Intergroup Behavior," *European Journal of Social Psychology* 5, no. 1 (1975): 5–34; Tajfel and Turner, "Integrative Theory of Intergroup Conflict," 40–41; Michael A. Hogg and Dominic Abrams, *Social Identifications: A Social Psychology of Intergroup Relations and Group Processes* (London: Routledge, 1988), 23.

8. Tajfel, "Achievement of Group Differentiation," 77–86.

9. Rupert Brown and Gabi Haeger, "'Compared to What?': Comparison Choice in an Internation Context," *European Journal of Social Psychology* 29, no. 1

(1999): 31–42; Bobo Lo, *Russian Foreign Policy in the Post-Soviet Era: Reality, Illusion, and Mythmaking* (New York: Palgrave Macmillan, 2002), 8, 23; David M. Lampton, *The Three Faces of Chinese Power: Might, Money and Minds* (Berkeley: University of California Press, 2008), 22; Jim Yardley, "Asia's Giants Face Off: India Digs in Its Heels as China Flexes Its Muscles," *New York Times*, December 30, 2012.

10. Tajfel and Turner, "Integrative Theory of Intergroup Conflict," 37; Daniel Markey, "Prestige and the Origins of War: Returning to Realism's Roots," *Security Studies* 8, no. 4 (1999): 157–58; Barry O'Neill, *Honor, Symbols, and War* (Ann Arbor: University of Michigan Press, 1999), 193; Deborah Welch Larson, T. V. Paul, and William C. Wohlforth, "Status and World Order," in Paul, Larson, and Wohlforth, *Status in World Politics*, 7, 16.

11. Ad van Knippenberg and Naomi Ellemers, "Strategies in Intergroup Relations," in *Group Motivation: Social Psychological Perspectives*, ed. Michael A. Hogg and Dominic Abrams (New York: Harvester Wheatsheaf, 1993), 20–21.

12. Susan T. Fiske, *Envy Up, Scorn Down: How Status Divides Us* (New York: Russell Sage, 2011), 38–39; Fred Hirsch, *Social Limits to Growth* (Cambridge, MA: Harvard University Press, 1976), 27–28.

13. Robert Gilpin, *War and Change in World Politics* (Cambridge: Cambridge University Press, 1981), 32–33; Hedley Bull, *The Anarchical Society: A Study of Order in World Politics* (New York: Columbia University Press, 1977), 202; William C. Wohlforth, *The Elusive Balance: Power and Perceptions during the Cold War* (Ithaca, NY: Cornell University Press, 1993), 146, 177–78.

14. Simon Kuper, "Developing Nations Go on Offensive for Games," *Financial Times*, January 26, 2011; Max Delany and Kevin O'Flynn, "As Sochi Gets Olympics, a Gold Medal for Putin," *International Herald Tribune*, July 5, 2007; Alexei Barrionuevo, "Dancing into the Evening, Brazil Celebrates Its Arrival on the World Stage," *New York Times*, October 4, 2009.

15. Bull, *Anarchical Society*, 200–201; Paul W. Schroeder, *The Transformation of European Politics, 1763–1848* (Oxford: Clarendon Press, 1994), 517; Paul W. Schroeder, "Did the Vienna Settlement Rest on a Balance of Power?," *American Historical Review* 97, no. 3 (1992): 683–706.

16. Gerry Simpson, *Great Powers and Outlaw States: Unequal Sovereigns in the International Legal Order* (Cambridge: Cambridge University Press, 2004), chap. 6; Stephen John Stedman, "UN Transformation in an Era of Soft Balancing," in *Cooperating for Peace and Security: Evolving Institutions and Arrangements in a Context of Changing U.S. Security Policy*, ed. Brian D. Jones, Shepard Forman, and Richard Gowan (Cambridge: Cambridge University Press, 2010), 48–49; David M. Malone, "Eyes on the Prize: The Quest for Nonpermanent Seats on the UN Security Council," *Global Governance* 6, no. 1 (January–March 2000): 3–24; James Fontanella-Khan, "BRICS Call for More Power at IMF," *Financial Times*, March 30, 2012.

17. Paul Gilbert, "What Is Shame? Some Core Issues and Controversies," in *Shame: Interpersonal Behavior, Psychopathology, and Culture*, ed. Paul Gilbert and Bernice Andrews (New York: Oxford University Press, 1998), 10; William Ian Miller, *Humiliation: And Other Essays on Honor, Social Discomfort, and Violence*

(Ithaca, NY: Cornell University Press, 1993), 141–46; Barnhart, "Territorial Aggression and Status Competition."

18. Philip Shaver, Judith Schwartz, Donald Kirson, and Cary O'Connor, "Emotion Knowledge: Further Exploration of a Prototype Approach," *Journal of Personality and Social Psychology* 52, no. 6 (June 1987): 1078; Wolf, "Respect and Disrespect," 108, 115; Peter Hays Gries, "Tears of Rage: Chinese Nationalist Reactions to the Belgrade Embassy Bombing," *China Journal* 46 (July 2001): 25–43.

19. Nyla R. Branscombe, Naomi Ellemers, Russell Spears, and Bertjan Doosje, "The Context and Content of Social Identity Threat," in *Social Identity: Context, Commitment, Content*, ed. Naomi Ellemers, Russell Spears, and Bertjan Doosje (London: Blackwell, 1999), 46; Tajfel and Turner, "Integrative Theory of Intergroup Conflict," 40, 43.

20. Tajfel, "Achievement of Group Differentiation," 93–94; Mathias Blanz, Amélie Mummendey, Rosemarie Milke, and Andreas Klink, "Responding to Negative Social Identity: A Taxonomy of Identity Management Strategies," *European Journal of Social Psychology* 28 (1998): 699–701, 719–21; Murray Milner Jr., *Status and Sacredness: A General Theory of Status Relations and an Analysis of Indian Culture* (New York: Oxford University Press, 1994), 35–36; Diana Onu, Joanne R. Smith, and Thomas Kessler, "Intergroup Emulation: An Improvement Strategy for Lower Status Groups," *Group Processes and Intergroup Relations* 18, no. 2 (2015): 210–24.

21. Kenneth B. Pyle, *Japan Rising: The Resurgence of Japanese Power and Purpose* (New York: Public Affairs, 2007), 64, 82–83, 100–101; Richard Storry, *Japan and the Decline of the West in Asia 1894–1943* (New York: St. Martin's Press, 1979), 15, 17 (quotation).

22. Reinhard Wolf, "Between Revisionism and Normalcy: Germany's Foreign Policy Identity in the 20th Century," and Yoshiko Kojo, "Japan's Policy Change in Multi-Layered International Economic Relations," in *Global Governance: Germany and Japan in the International System*, ed. Saori N. Katada, Hanns W. Maull, and Takashi Inoguchi (Aldershot, UK: Ashgate, 2004), 18–19, 144–45; Judith G. Kelley, *Ethnic Politics in Europe: The Power of Norms and Incentives* (Princeton, NJ: Princeton University Press, 2004); Jan Cienski, "The Long Game," *Financial Times*, January 4, 2012; "Germany, Poland and France Revive Weimar Group to Bolster EU Confidence," August 28, 2016, reuters.com.

23. R. P. Dore, "The Prestige Factor in International Affairs," *International Affairs* 51, no. 2 (1975): 190–207.

24. Tajfel and Turner, "Integrative Theory of Group Conflict," 44–45; Turner, "Social Comparison and Social Identity"; J. Turner and R. Brown, "Social Status, Cognitive Alternatives, and Intergroup Relations," in Tajfel, *Differentiation between Social Groups*, 201–34; Naomi Ellemers, Henk Wilke, and Ad van Knippenberg, "Effects of Low Group or Individual Status on Individual and Collective Status-Enhancement Strategies," *Journal of Personality and Social Psychology* 64, no. 5 (1993): 766–78; Tajfel, "Interindividual Behavior and Intergroup Behavior," 52 (quotation); Jon Jacobson, *When the Soviet Union Entered World Politics* (Berkeley: University of California Press, 1994), 29.

25. Richard J. Samuels, *Securing Japan: Tokyo's Grand Strategy and the Future of East Asia* (Ithaca, NY: Cornell University Press, 2007), 20 (quotation), 21, 24,

26; R. P. Anand, "Family of 'Civilized' States and Japan: A Story of Humiliation, Assimilation, Defiance, and Confrontation," *Journal of the History of International Law* 5 (2003): 23; Akira Iriye, "Japan's Drive to Great Power Status," in *Cambridge History of Japan*, ed. Marius B. Jansen, vol. 5, *The Nineteenth Century* (Cambridge: Cambridge University Press, 1989), 727, 765; Naoko Shimazu, *Japan, Race and Equality: The Racial Equality Proposal of 1919* (London: Routledge, 1998), 87–88, 185; Kenneth B. Pyle, *Japan Rising: The Resurgence of Japanese Power and Purpose* (New York: Public Affairs, 2007), 155–58.

26. Shimazu, *Japan, Race and Equality*, 181–82.

27. Samuels, *Securing Japan*, 16–28.

28. Paul M. Kennedy, *Rise of the Anglo-German Antagonism: 1860–1914* (London: George Allen and Unwin, 1980), 311.

29. Baldev Raj Nayar and T. V. Paul, *India in the World Order: Searching for Major-Power Status* (Cambridge: Cambridge University Press, 2003), 173–75, 181, 211–14, 224, 227–30, 231 (quotation); Jacques E. C. Hymans, *The Psychology of Nuclear Proliferation: Identity, Emotions, and Foreign Policy* (Cambridge: Cambridge University Press, 2006).

30. T. V. Paul, "The Accommodation of Rising Powers in World Politics," in *Accommodating Rising Powers: Past, Present, and Future*, ed. T. V. Paul (Cambridge: Cambridge University Press, 2016), 5–7; Hew Strachan, *The First World War*, vol. 1, *To Arms* (New York: Oxford University Press, 2001), 5, 9.

31. Turner, "Social Comparison and Social Identity," 10, 12; Blanz et al., "Responding to Negative Social Identity," 701.

32. Paul M. Kennedy, *Strategy and Diplomacy 1870–1945: Eight Studies* (London: George Allen and Unwin, 1983; Fontana Paperback, 1984), 134–35, 145–49, 157 (quotation); Jonathan Steinberg, "The Copenhagen Complex," *Journal of Contemporary History* 1, no. 3 (July 1966): 44–45; Ivo Nikolai Lambi, *The Navy and German Power Politics, 1862–1914* (Boston: Allen and Unwin, 1984), 162–64; Kennedy, *Rise of Anglo-German Antagonism*, 415–16, 431.

33. Jeremy Black, *World War Two: A Military History* (London: Routledge, 2003), 16; Jurgen Rohwer and Mikhail Monakov, "The Soviet Union's Ocean-Going Fleet, 1935–1936," *International History Review* 18, no. 4 (November 1996): 850, 854, 865–67; Milan L. Hauner, "Stalin's Big Fleet Program," *Naval War College Review* 57, no. 2 (Spring 2005): 87–88, 103–4, 106.

34. Martin Wight, *Power Politics*, ed. Hedley Bull and Carsten Holbraad (New York: Holmes and Meier, 1978), 46–47; Jack Snyder, "Russian Backwardness and the Future of Europe," *Daedalus* 123, no. 2 (1994): 186; William C. Wolforth, "Status Dilemmas and Interstate Conflict," in Paul, Larson, and Wohlforth, *Status in World Politics*, 135.

35. Lo, *Russian Foreign Policy*, 89–90, 142; Mark Kramer, "Russian Policy toward the Commonwealth of Independent States: Recent Trends and Future Prospects," *Problems of Post-Communism* 55, no. 6 (November/December 2008): 5–6; Clifford J. Levy, "At the Crossroad of Empires, a Mouse Struts," *New York Times*, July 26, 2009; Richard Pipes, "Craving to Be a Great Power," *Moscow Times*, July 15, 2009, David Johnson's Russia List, 2009-#133; Colin Wayne Leach and Russell Spears, "'A Vengefulness of the Impotent': The Pain of In-Group Inferiority

and Schadenfreude toward Successful Out-Groups," *Journal of Personality and Social Psychology* 95, no. 6 (2008): 1383–96.

36. Ellemers, Wilke and van Knippenberg, "Effects of Low Group or Individual Status," 771; Russell Spears, "Social Identity, Legitimacy, and Intergroup Conflict: The Rocky Road to Reconciliation," in *The Social Psychology of Intergroup Reconciliation*, ed. Arie Nadler, Thomas E. Malloy and Jeffrey D. Fisher (New York: Oxford University Press, 2008), 325.

37. Tajfel and Turner, "Integrative Theory of Intergroup Conflict," 43; Peter Hays Gries, "Identity and Conflict in Sino-American Relations," in *New Directions in the Study of China's Foreign Policy*, ed. Alastair Iain Johnston and Robert S. Ross (Stanford, CA: Stanford University Press, 2006), 325; Dmitry Shlapentokh, "Dugin Eurasianism: A Window on the Minds of the Russian Elite or an Intellectual Ploy?" *Studies in East European Thought* 59, no. 3 (September 2007): 215–36.

38. Nayar and Paul, *India in the World Order*, 79–80, 135–44; Odd Arne Westad, *The Global Cold War: Third World Interventions and the Making of Our Times* (Cambridge: Cambridge University Press, 2007), 101–3, 106–7; Aleksandar Zivotic and Jovan Cavoski, "On the Road to Belgrade: Yugoslavia, Third World Neutrals, and the Evolution of Global Non-Alignment, 1954–1961," *Journal of Cold War Studies* 18, no. 4 (Fall 2016): 79–98; Emilian Kavalski, "The Shadows of Normative Power in Asia: Framing the International Agency of China, India, and Japan," *Pacific Focus* 29, no. 3 (2014): 317; Larson and Shevchenko, "Shortcut to Greatness."

39. Andrew Downie, "Brazil's Foray as Global Player," *Los Angeles Times*, May 22, 2010.

40. Stanley Hoffmann, *Decline or Renewal: France since the 1930s* (New York: Viking, 1974), 94, 191, 217, 337; Gadi Heimann, "What Does It Take to be a Great Power? The Story of France Joining the Big Five," *Review of International Studies* 41, no. 1 (2014): 185–206; Wolf, "Between Revisionism and Normalcy," 16–17.

41. Tajfel, "Achievement of Group Differentiation," 96–97; Steven L. Blader and Ya-Ru Chen, "What's in a Name? Status, Power, and Other Forms of Social Hierarchy," in *The Psychology of Social Status*, ed. Joey T. Cheng, Jessica Tracy, and Cameron Anderson (New York: Springer, 2014), 74; Lorenz M. Lüthi, "The US Accommodation of Communist China," and Aseema Sinha, "Partial Accommodation without Conflict: India as a Rising Link Power," in *Accommodating Rising Powers: Past, Present, and Future*, ed. T. V. Paul (Cambridge: Cambridge University Press, 2016), 131–49, 238–39.

42. Ad F. M. van Knippenberg, "Intergroup Differences in Group Perceptions," in *The Social Dimension: European Developments in Social Psychology*, ed. Henri Tajfel (Cambridge: Cambridge University Press, 1984), 2:575; Amélie Mummendey and Hans-Joachim Schreiber, "'Different' Just Means 'Better': Some Obvious and Some Hidden Pathways to In-group Favouritism," *British Journal of Social Psychology* 23, no. 4 (November 1984): 363–68; Edwin Poppe and Hub Linssen, "Ingroup Favoritism and the Reflection of Realistic Dimensions of Difference between National States in Central and Eastern European Nationality Stereotypes," *British Journal of Social Psychology* 38, no. 1 (1999): 85–102; Ian Manners, "Normative Power Europe: A Contradiction in Terms?," *Journal of Common Market Studies* 40, no. 2 (1992): 235–58.

43. Tajfel, "Achievement of Group Differentiation," 96–97; Rupert J. Brown and Gordon F. Ross, "The Battle for Acceptance: An Investigation into the Dynamics of Intergroup Behavior," in Tajfel, *Social Identity and Intergroup Relations*, 157–78; Diane M. Mackie, Thierry Devos, and Eliot R. Smith, "Intergroup Emotions: Explaining Offensive Action Tendencies in an Intergroup Context," *Journal of Personality and Social Psychology* 79, no. 4 (October 2000): 602–16; Wolf, "Respect and Disrespect," 126–32; Philip Shaver, Judith Schwartz, Donald Kirson, and Cary O'Connor, "Emotion Knowledge: Further Exploration of a Prototype Approach," *Journal of Personality and Social Psychology* 52, no. 6 (1987): 1077–78.

44. Rupert J. Brown, "The Role of Similarity in Intergroup Relations," in Tajfel, *Social Dimension*, 2:602–23; Itesh Sachdev and Richard Y. Bourhis, "Power and Status Differentials in Minority and Majority Intergroup Relations," *European Journal of Social Psychology* 21, no. 1 (1991): 1–24.

45. Alexander L. George and Andrew Bennett, *Case Studies and Theory Development in the Social Sciences* (Cambridge, MA: MIT Press, 2005), chap. 10.

46. Harry Eckstein, "Case Studies and Theory in Political Science," in *Handbook of Political Science*, ed. Fred Greenstein and Nelson Polsby, vol. 7 (Reading, MA: Addison-Wesley, 1975), 108–10; Jack S. Levy, "Case Studies: Types, Designs, and Logics of Inference," *Conflict Management and Peace Science* 25 (2008): 6–7.

47. On extreme value cases, see Stephen Van Evera, *Guide to Methods for Students of Political Science* (Ithaca, NY: Cornell University Press, 1997), 79–80; George and Bennett, *Case Studies and Theory Development*, 75.

48. Robert Jervis, "Fighting for Standing or Standing to Fight?," *Security Studies* 21, no. 2 (2012): 336–45; Lilach Gilady, *The Price of Prestige: Conspicuous Consumption in International Relations* (Chicago: University of Chicago Press, 2018); Paul Bezerra, Jacob Cramer, Megan Hauser, Jennifer L. Miller, and Thomas J. Volgy, "Going for the Gold versus Distributing the Green: Foreign Policy Substitutability and Complementarity in Status Enhancement Strategies," *Foreign Policy Analysis* 1, no. 3 (2015): 253–72; J. Patrick Rhamey and Bryan R. Early, "Going for the Gold: Status Seeking Behavior and Olympic Performance," *International and Area Studies Review* 16, no. 3 (2013): 244–61.

49. Evan Luard, *Types of International Society* (New York: Free Press, 1976); Larson, Paul and Wohlforth, "Status and World Order," 10–11.

50. Gilpin, *War and Change*, chap. 5; Schweller, "Realism and the Present Great Power System," 28–29, 43, 56–57; William C. Wohlforth, "The Russian-Soviet Empire: A Test of Neorealism," *Review of International Studies* 27 (2001): 221; Mearsheimer, *Tragedy of Great Power Politics*, 22, 190–91; Jonathan D. Spence, *The Search for Modern China*, 3rd ed. (New York: Norton, 2013), 118; Dominic Lieven, *Empire: The Russian Empire and Its Rivals* (New Haven, CT: Yale University Press, 2000), 37, 39.

51. Michael H. Hunt, *The Genesis of Chinese Communist Foreign Policy* (New York: Columbia University Press, 1996), 6–7, 9, 32–33; Yuan-kang Wang, *Harmony and War: Confucian Culture and Chinese Power Politics* (New York: Columbia University Press, 2011), 21–23.

52. R. S. Erikson and K. L. Tedin, *American Public Opinion*, 6th ed., (New York: Longman, 2003), 64; Stephen Kotkin, *Magnetic Mountain: Stalinism as*

a Civilization (Berkeley: University of California Press, 1995), 23; Chen Jian, *Mao's China and the Cold War* (Chapel Hill: University of North Carolina Press, 2001), 7–8.

53. Donald Ostrowski, *Muscovy and the Mongols: Cross-Cultural Influences on the Steppe Frontier, 1304–1589* (Cambridge: Cambridge University Press, 1998), 136–37; John King Fairbank, *The Chinese World Order: Traditional China's Foreign Relations* (Cambridge, MA: Harvard University Press, 1968); Nicholas Riasanovsky, *Nicholas I and Official Nationality in Russia, 1825–1855* (Berkeley: University of California Press, 1969); David MacKenzie, "Russia's Balkan Policies under Alexander II, 1855–1881," in *Imperial Russian Foreign Policy*, ed. and trans. Hugh Ragsdale (Cambridge: Cambridge University Press, 1993), 222–26; Steven I. Levine, "Perception and Ideology in Chinese Foreign Policy," in *Chinese Foreign Policy: Theory and Practice*, ed. Thomas W. Robinson and David Shambaugh (Oxford: Clarendon Press, 1994), 37–38.

54. Alexander Wendt, *Social Theory of International Politics* (Cambridge: Cambridge University Press, 1999), 327–31, 334–35; Iver B. Neumann, "Russia as a Great Power, 1815–2007," *Journal of International Relations and Development* 11, no. 2 (2008): 128–51; Clunan, *Social Construction of Russia's Resurgence*; Vincent Pouliot, "Setting Status in Stone: The Negotiation of International and Institutional Privileges," in Paul, Larson, and Wohlforth, *Status in World Politics*, 195–96; Ted Hopf, *Reconstructing the Cold War: The Early Years, 1945–1958* (Oxford: Oxford University Press, 2012), 18–20.

55. Michael Billig, "Henri Tajfel's 'Cognitive Aspects of Prejudice' and the Psychology of Bigotry," *British Journal of Social Psychology* 41, no. 2 (2002): 179; Martijn van Zomeren, Tom Postmes, and Russell Spears, "Toward an Integrative Social Identity Model of Collective Action: A Quantitative Research Synthesis of Three Socio-Psychological Perspectives," *Psychological Bulletin* 134, no. 4 (2008): 522; Stephen Reicher, "The Context of Social Identity: Domination, Resistance, and Change," *Political Psychology* 25, no. 6 (2004): 932–33.

56. Hopf, *Reconstructing the Cold War*, 17–18 (quotation), 20–23; Andrei P. Tsygankov, *Russia and the West from Alexander to Putin: Honor in International Relations* (Cambridge: Cambridge University Press, 2012).

CHAPTER 2. IMPERIAL IDENTITIES

1. Reinhard Wittram, *Russia and Europe* (New York: Harcourt Brace Jovanovich, 1973), 61–62 (quotation); Dominic Lieven, *Empire: The Russian Empire and Its Rivals* (New Haven, CT: Yale University Press, 2000), 229.

2. Henry Kissinger, *On China* (New York: Penguin Press, 2011), 41; Qianlong's First Edict to King George III (September 1793), in *The Search for Modern China: A Documentary Collection*, ed. Pei-kai Cheng, Michael Lestz, and Jonathan Spence (New York: W.W. Norton, 1999), 104–6.

3. William C. Wohlforth, "The Russian-Soviet Empire: A Test of Neorealism," *Review of International Studies* 27 (2001): 213–35; John J. Mearsheimer, *The Tragedy of Great Power Politics* (New York: W.W. Norton, 2001), 157; João Resende-Santos, *Neorealism, States, and the Modern Mass Army* (New York: Cambridge University Press, 2007), 9–13; Kenneth N. Waltz, *Theory of International Poli-*

tics (Menlo Park, CA: Addison-Wesley, 1979), 118, 125, 127–28, 166; Yen-P'ing Hao Erh-min Wang, "Changing Chinese Views of Western Relations, 1840–94," in *Cambridge History of China, Late Ch'ing 1800–1911*, ed. John K. Fairbank and Kwang-Ching Liu (Cambridge: Cambridge University Press, 1980), vol. 11, bk. 2: 149–52, 157–58.

4. Robert E. Kelly, "A 'Confucian Long Peace' in Pre-Western East Asia?," *European Journal of International Relations* 18, no. 3 (2011): 407–30; Marshall Poe, "Moscow, the Third Rome: The Origins and Transformations of a 'Pivotal Moment,'" *Jahrbücher für Geshichte Osteuropas* 49, no. 3 (2001): 412–29; Geoffrey Hosking, *Russia: People and Empire, 1552–1917* (London: HarperCollins, 1997), 313–17.

5. Janet Martin, *Medieval Russia, 980–1584*, 2nd ed. (Cambridge: Cambridge University Press, 2007), 1–2, 6–12, 39–40.

6. Martin, *Medieval Russia*, 86–89; Nicholas V. Riasanovsky and Mark D. Steinberg, *A History of Russia*, 8th ed. (New York: Oxford University Press, 2011), 31–33.

7. Martin, *Medieval Russia*, 150–56, 163–68, 428–31; Charles J. Halperin, *Russia and the Golden Horde* (Bloomington: Indiana University Press, 1985), 30.

8. Martin, *Medieval Russia*, 196–97, 220–21.

9. Andreas Kappeler, *The Russian Empire: A Multiethnic History*, trans. Alfred Clayton (Harlow, England: Longman, Pearson Education, 2001), 23; Martin, *Medieval Russia*, 222–23, 262–63, 275, 280–81, 336, 343.

10. Isabel de Madariaga, "Tsar into Emperor: The Title of Peter the Great," in *Royal and Republican Sovereignty in Early Modern Europe: Essays in Memory of Ragnhild Hatton*, ed. Robert Oresko, G. C. Gibbs, and H. M. Scott (Cambridge: Cambridge University Press, 1997), 356–57.

11. Richard S. Wortman, *Scenarios of Power: Myth and Ceremony in Russian Monarchy, From Peter the Great to the Death of Nicholas I* (Princeton, NJ: Princeton University Press, 1995), vol. 1: 26–29; Michael Khodarkovsky, *Russia's Steppe Frontier: The Making of Colonial Empire, 1500–1800* (Bloomington: Indiana University Press, 2002), 40; Martin, *Medieval Russia*, 377; David B. Miller, "The Coronation of Ivan IV of Moscow," *Jahrbücher für Geschichte Osteuropas* 15, no. 4 (1967): 559–74.

12. Isabel de Madariaga, *Ivan the Terrible* (New Haven, CT: Yale University Press, 2005), 99, 100–101; Alexander Filjushkin, *Ivan the Terrible: A Military History* (London: Frontline Books, 2008), 94; Kappeler, *Russian Empire*, 26; Madariaga, "Tsar into Emperor," 360.

13. Martin, *Medieval Russia*, 396–97; Kappeler, *Russian Empire*, 34–35.

14. Martin, *Medieval Russia*, 400–401, 407; Madariaga, *Ivan the Terrible*, 119–20, 129–30; Filjushkin, *Ivan the Terrible*, 142, 160–64; Carol B. Stevens, *Russia's Wars of Emergence, 1460–1730* (Harlow, England: Pearson Education, 2007), 87.

15. Martin, *Medieval Russia*, 401–2; Madariaga, *Ivan the Terrible*, 152–53, 314, 320–22, 332; Filjushkin, *Ivan the Terrible*, 185, 207–14.

16. Madariaga, *Ivan the Terrible*, 339–40.

17. Madariaga, *Ivan the Terrible*, 96–98, 315 (quotation), 338–39, 373; Madariaga, "Tsar into Emperor," 360–61, 362.

18. Martin, *Medieval Russia*, 406–7, 409–13, 415; Filjushkin, *Ivan the Terrible*, 264–65; Stevens, *Russia's Wars of Emergence*, 108.

19. Joanna Waley-Cohen, *The Culture of War in China: Empire and the Military under the Qing Dynasty* (London: I.B. Taurus, 2006), 7, 90, 114n; William T. Rowe, *China's Last Empire: The Great Qing* (Cambridge, MA: Belknap Press of Harvard University Press, 2009), 6–7, 71–73; Bobo Lo, *Axis of Convenience: Moscow, Beijing, and the New Geopolitics* (Washington, DC: Brookings Institution Press, 2008), 21.

20. Jonathan D. Spence, *The Search for Modern China*, 3rd ed. (New York: W.W. Norton, 2013), 26–29; Rowe, *China's Last Empire* 15–17.

21. Thomas J. Barfield, *The Perilous Frontier: Nomadic Empires and China* (New York: Basil Blackwell, 1989); Spence, *Search for Modern China*, 30–32; Mark C. Elliott, *Emperor Qianlong: Son of Heaven, Man of the World* (New York: Longman, 2009), 53–54; Rowe, *China's Last Empire*, 18–19.

22. Evelyn S. Rawski, "Reenvisioning the Qing: The Significance of the Qing Period in Chinese History," *Journal of Asian Studies* 55, no. 4 (November 1996): 829–50; Peter C. Perdue, *China Marches West: The Qing Conquest of Central Eurasia* (Cambridge, MA: Harvard University Press, 2005), 338; Elliott, *Emperor Qianlong*, 52, 56.

23. Rowe, *China's Last Empire*, 6, 17; Mark Mancall, *Russia and China: Their Diplomatic Relations to 1728* (Cambridge, MA: Harvard University Press, 1971), 20–25, 114, 134–35, 148–49; Peter C. Perdue, "Boundaries and Trade in the Early Modern World: Negotiations at Nerchinsk and Beijing," *Eighteenth-Century Studies* 43, no. 3 (Spring 2010): 346; John P. LeDonne, *The Grand Strategy of the Russian Empire, 1650–1831* (New York: Oxford University Press, 2004), 35–36; Barfield, *Perilous Frontier*, 282–83.

24. Mancall, *Russia and China*, 141–42, 153, 204–5, 236–38, 245–55; Fred W. Bergholz, *The Partition of the Steppe: The Struggle of the Russians, Manchus, and the Zunghar Mongols for Empire in Central Asia, 1619–1758, a Study in Power Politics* (New York: Peter Lang, 1993), 332–39.

25. Perdue, *China Marches West*, 138, 151–52, 158, 180–81, 187, 198, 201–2, 415–16; Barfield, *Perilous Frontier*, 285–86, 291; Peter C. Perdue, "Military Mobilization in Seventeenth and Eighteenth-Century China, Russia, and Mongolia," *Modern Asian Studies* 30, no. 4 (1996): 757–93.

26. Perdue, *China Marches West*, 283–85; Elliott, *Emperor Qianlong*, 90, 95–97.

27. Elliott, *Emperor Qianlong*, 98; Waley-Cohen, *Culture of War*, 21. The ten victories included three wars of conquest in Xinjiang, two in the Sichuan-Tibetan borderlands to suppress rebellious Jinchuan minorities; two wars against the Gurkhas in Nepal; and military campaigns in Burma, Vietnam, and Taiwan.

28. Perdue, *China Marches West*, 442–43; Waley-Cohen, *Culture of War*, 23, 41–42, 86–87.

29. Barfield, *Perilous Frontier*, 275–76, 299; Peter C. Perdue, "Culture, History, and Imperial Chinese Strategy: Legacies of the Qing Conquests," in *Warfare in Chinese History*, ed. Hans Van De Ven (Leiden: Brill, 2000), 275–77; Perdue, *China Marches West*, 284–86, 335–36; Rowe, *China's Last Empire*, 74–75; Michael H.

Hunt, *The Genesis of Chinese Communist Foreign Policy* (New York: Columbia University Press, 1996), 42.

30. Perdue, "Culture, History, and Imperial Chinese Strategy," 276–77; Elliott, *Emperor Qianlong*, 98.

31. Lindsey Hughes, *Russia in the Age of Peter the Great* (New Haven, CT: Yale University Press, 1998), 17–18; Graeme Herd, "Peter the Great and the Conquest of Azov: 1695–96," in *Peter the Great and the West: New Perspectives*, ed. Lindsey Hughes (Basingstoke: Palgrave, 2001), 165, 167, 170–71.

32. Lindsey Hughes, *Peter the Great: A Biography* (New Haven, CT: Yale University Press, 2002), 6, 40–41; Hughes, *Russia in the Age of Peter the Great*, 23, 25–26; Evgenii V. Anisimov, *The Reforms of Peter the Great: Progress through Coercion in Russia*, trans. with introduction by John T. Alexander (Armonk, NY: M.E. Sharpe, 1993), 17; M. S. Anderson, *Peter the Great*, 2nd ed. (London: Longman, 1995), 40.

33. B. H. Sumner, *Peter the Great and the Emergence of Russia* (New York: Collier Books, 1962), 37, 52; Anderson, *Peter the Great*, 50 (quotation); Kappeler, *Russian Empire*, 72; Hughes, *Russia in the Age of Peter the Great*, 28.

34. David Kirby, "Peter the Great and the Baltic," in Hughes, *Peter the Great and the West*, 185.

35. Anderson, *Peter the Great*, 42–43.

36. John P. LeDonne, *The Russian Empire and the World, 1700–1917: The Geopolitics of Expansion and Containment* (New York: Oxford University Press, 1997), 347–48; Hughes, *Peter the Great*, 60; Hughes, *Russia in the Age of Peter the Great*, 29.

37. Hughes, *Russia in the Age of Peter the Great*, 29–30; Sumner, *Peter the Great*, 54–55; Vasily Klyuchevsky, *Peter the Great*, trans. Liliana Archibald (Boston: Beacon Press, 1958), 62–63.

38. Sumner, *Peter the Great*, 55, 58–59; Anderson, *Peter the Great*, 55–57; LeDonne, *Russian Empire*, 24; Richard Hellie, "The Petrine Army: Continuity, Change, and Impact," *Canadian-American Slavic Studies* 8, no. 2 (Summer 1974): 237–53; James Cracraft, *The Revolution of Peter the Great* (Cambridge, MA: Harvard University Press, 2003), 155.

39. Cracraft, *Revolution of Peter the Great*, 45–49.

40. Hellie, "Petrine Army," 249–50; William C. Fuller, *Strategy and Power in Russia: 1600–1914* (New York: Oxford University Press, 1992), 80–81; Hughes, *Peter the Great*, 83; Peter B. Brown, "Gazing Anew at Poltava: Perspectives from the Military Revolution Controversy, Comparative History, and Decision-Making Doctrines," *Harvard Ukrainian Studies* 31, no. 1/4 (2009–2010): 111, 113–14.

41. Hughes, *Peter the Great*, 86; Derek McKay and H. M. Scott, *The Rise of the Great Powers: 1648–1815* (London: Longman, 1983), 84–85, 92; John LeDonne, "Poltava and the Geopolitics of Western Eurasia," *Harvard Ukrainian Studies* 31, no. 1/4 (2009–2010): 186–87; Brown, "Gazing Anew at Poltava"; Stevens, *Russia's Wars of Emergence*, 271–73; Robert I. Frost, *The Northern Wars: War, State and Society in Northeastern Europe, 1558–1721* (Harlow, UK: Pearson Education Limited, 2000), 296.

42. Michael Roberts, *The Swedish Imperial Experience, 1560–1718* (Cambridge: Cambridge University Press, 1979), 149–52; LeDonne, *Russian Empire*, 28; James Cracraft, "Empire versus Nation: Russian Political Theory under Peter I," *Harvard Ukrainian Studies* 10, no. 3/4 (December 1986): 538; Nicholas V. Riasanovsky, *The Image of Peter the Great in Russian History and Thought* (New York: Oxford University Press, 1985), 11–12.

43. Madariaga, "Tsar into Emperor," 369, 374–76; M. S. Anderson, *The Rise of Modern Diplomacy, 1450–1919* (New York: Longman, 1993), 66.

44. Sumner, *Peter the Great*, 141.

45. Marc Raeff, *The Well-Ordered Police State: Social and Institutional Change through Law in the Germanies and Russia, 1600–1800* (New Haven, CT: Yale University Press, 1983), 198; Nicholas V. Riasanovsky, *Russian Identities: A Historical Survey* (Oxford: Oxford University Press, 2005), 79; Sumner, *Peter the Great*, 45 (quotation); Klyuchevsky, *Peter the Great*, 263; Anderson, *Peter the Great*, 203–4; Marc Raeff, "The Enlightenment in Russia and Russian Thought in the Enlightenment," in *The Eighteenth Century in Russia*, ed. J. G. Garrard (Oxford: Clarendon Press, 1973), 28; Serhii Plokhy, *The Origins of the Slavic Nations: Premodern Identities in Russia, Ukraine, and Belarus* (Cambridge: Cambridge University Press, 2006), 289.

46. Geoffrey Hosking, *Russia and the Russians: A History* (Cambridge, MA: Harvard University Press, 2001), 195.

47. Alexander Gerschenkron, *Economic Backwardness in Historical Perspective: A Book of Essays* (Cambridge, MA: Belknap Press, Harvard University Press, 1962), 17–18; E. V. Anisimov, *The Reforms of Peter the Great: Progress through Coercion in Russia* (Armonk, NY: M.E. Sharpe, 1993), 297–98; Raeff, *Well-Ordered Police State*, 199; Anderson, *Peter the Great*, 111; Evgenii V. Anisimov, "Progress through Violence from Peter the Great to Lenin and Stalin," *Russian History* 17, no. 4 (Winter 1990): 409; Nicholas V. Maximilian Voloshin, "Rossiya" ["Russia"] in *Sobranie Sochinenii*. t. 1: *Stikhotvoreniia i Poemy 1899–1926* [*Collection of Writings*, vol. 1: *Poems, 1899–1926*] (Moscow: Ellis Lak 2000, 2003), 546.

48. Translated and quoted in Liah Greenfield, *Nationalism: Five Roads to Modernity* (Cambridge, MA: Harvard University Press, 1992), 197–98.

49. Hughes, *Peter the Great*, 195.

50. Anderson, *Rise of Modern Diplomacy*, 70–71, 89–90, 95; Hans Bagger, "Role of the Baltic in Russian Foreign Policy," in *Imperial Russian Foreign Policy*, ed. and trans. Hugh Ragsdale (Washington, DC: Woodrow Wilson Center Press; Cambridge: Cambridge University Press, 1993), 49–50; Sumner, *Peter the Great*, 158; Hughes, *Russia in the Age of Peter the Great*, 53, 60, 413–14; H. M. Scott, *The Emergence of the Eastern Powers, 1756–1775* (Cambridge: Cambridge University Press, 2001), 15–17.

51. Isabel de Madariaga, *Catherine the Great: A Short History* (New Haven, CT: Yale University Press, 1990), 38–39; W. Bruce Lincoln, *The Romanovs: Autocrats of All the Russias* (New York: Anchor Books, 1981), 217–18.

52. Scott, *Emergence of the Eastern Powers*, 153, 155, 156 (quotation), 157.

53. Lincoln, *Romanovs*, 218–19; Ivan K. Luppol, "The Empress and the Philosophe," in *Catherine the Great: A Profile*, ed. Marc Raeff (New York: Hill and Wang, 1972), 63 (quotation).

54. Riasanovsky, *Russian Identities*, 96–97.

55. Wittram, *Russia and Europe*, 61–62.

56. Isabel de Madariaga, *Russia in the Age of Catherine the Great* (New Haven, CT: Yale University Press, 1981), 188–92; Scott, *Emergence of the Eastern Powers*, 103–6, 115.

57. Madariaga, *Catherine the Great*, 43–44; Madariaga, *Russia in the Age of Catherine the Great*, 202–3; Scott, *Emergence of the Eastern Powers*, 178–79, 181–82.

58. Barbara Jelavich, *A Century of Russian Foreign Policy, 1814–1914* (Philadelphia: J.B. Lippincott, 1964), 19; L. S. Stavrianos, *The Balkans since 1453* (New York: Holt, Rinehart and Winston, 1965), 187–88; Madariaga, *Catherine the Great*, 45–47.

59. Madariaga, *Russia in the Age of Catherine the Great*, 221–22, 225; Scott, *Emergence of the Eastern Powers*, 203–4; Riasanovsky and Steinberg, *History of Russia*, 266.

60. Madariaga, *Catherine the Great*, 48; LeDonne, *Russian Empire*, 105–6.

61. Madariaga, *Catherine the Great*, 84; Hugh Ragsdale, "Russian Projects of Conquest in the Eighteenth Century," in *Imperial Russian Foreign Policy*, ed. and trans. Hugh Ragsdale (Cambridge: Cambridge University Press, 1993), 82–83; LeDonne, *Russian Empire*, 108.

62. Madariaga, *Russia in the Age of Catherine the Great*, 383–85; Isabel de Madariaga, "The Secret Austro-Russian Treaty of 1781," *Slavonic and East European Review* 38, no 90 (1959): 114–45.

63. Alan W. Fisher, *The Russian Annexation of the Crimea 1772–1783* (Cambridge: Cambridge University Press, 1970), chap. 7; Simon Sebag Montefiore, *Prince of Princes: The Life of Potemkin* (London: Weidenfeld and Nicolson, 2000), 249 (quotation); Marc Raeff, "In the Imperial Manner," in Raeff, *Catherine the Great*, 212–13.

64. Madariaga, *Russia in the Age of Catherine the Great*, 359–73.

65. Madariaga, *Catherine the Great*, 162, 164, 167; Paul W. Schroeder, *The Transformation of European Politics: 1763–1848* (Oxford: Clarendon Press, 1994), 83; Madariaga, *Catherine the Great*, 168–69.

66. Madariaga, *Russia in the Age of Catherine the Great*, 420–21, 430–35; Madariaga, *Catherine the Great*, 168–72; LeDonne, *Russian Empire*, 59–60.

67. Riasanovsky and Steinberg, *History of Russia*, 267–68; LeDonne, *Grand Strategy of the Russian Empire*, 104–5.

68. Madariaga, *Russia in the Age of Catherine the Great*, 588.

69. Spence, *Search for Modern China*, 94–95, 114. To show filial piety, Qianlong abdicated in 1796 so that he would not exceed the 61 years in power of his illustrious grandfather, Kangxi, but he did not allow his son to exercise any authority.

70. Spence, *Search for Modern China*, 95–97, 110–12; Rowe, *China's Last Empire*, 68–70, 88, 184–85.

71. James L. Hevia, *Cherishing Men from Afar: Qing Guest Ritual and the Macartney Embassy of 1793* (Durham, NC: Duke University Press, 1999), 21, 26, 28.

72. Spence, *Search for Modern China*, 115–17; Mark Mancall "The Ch'ing Tribute System: An Interpretive Essay," in Fairbank, *Chinese World Order*, 63–64; John E. Wills, Jr., *Embassies and Illusions: Dutch and Portuguese Envoys to*

K'ang-hsi, 1666–1689 (Cambridge, MA: Council on East Asian Studies, Harvard University, 1984), 24, 179–80; Kissinger, *On China*, 17 (quotation).

73. Subsequent research has qualified this idealized model of the Chinese tribute system presented by essays in Fairbank, *Chinese World Order*. Important critical accounts include John E. Wills, Jr., *Pepper, Guns, and Parleys: The Dutch East India Company and China, 1662–1681* (Cambridge, MA: Harvard University Press, 1974); Wills, *Embassies and Illusions: Dutch and Portuguese Envoys to K'iang-hsi, 1666–1689* (Cambridge, MA: Council on East Asian Studies, Harvard University, 1984); Paul A. Cohen, *Discovering History in China: American Historical Writing on the Recent Chinese Past* (New York: Columbia University Press, 1984) chaps. 1–2; Hevia, *Cherishing Men from Afar*, 9–15.

74. Rowe, *China's Last Empire*, 39; Perdue, "Culture, History, and Imperial Chinese Strategy," 257–58.

75. Alain Peyrefitte, *The Immobile Empire* (New York: Knopf, 1992), 4, 7 (quotation), 8.

76. Hevia, *Cherishing Men from Afar*, 95; Earl H. Pritchard, "The Kotow in the Macartney Embassy to China in 1793," *Far Eastern Quarterly* 2, no. 2 (1943): 163–64; Peyrefitte, *Immobile Empire*, 88, 169–70, 198.

77. Peyrefitte, *Immobile Empire*, 170.

78. Wills, *Embassies and Illusions*, 184.

79. Hevia, *Cherishing Men from Afar*, 108–9; Elliott, *Emperor Qianlong*, 140; Peyrefitte, *Immobile Empire*, 215, 237, 275–76, 303–4.

80. Perdue, "Boundaries and Trade," 354.

81. Matthew T. Florinsky, *Russia: A History and an Interpretation*, vol. 2 (New York: Macmillan, 1953), 679, 684; Riasanovsky and Steinberg, *History of Russia*, 308–11; Schroeder, *Transformation of European Politics*, 497; Dominic Lieven, *Russia against Napoleon: The True Story of the Campaigns of War and Peace* (New York: Viking, 2009), 152, 160–61, 251–52, 256, 285–87, 465–68.

82. Jelavich, *Century of Russian Foreign Policy*, 27, 37–43.

83. Riasanovsky and Steinberg, *History of Russia*, 312, 314; Barbara Jelavich, *Russia's Balkan Entanglements, 1806–1914* (Cambridge: Cambridge University Press, 1991), 45.

84. Paul W. Schroeder, "Containment Nineteenth Century Style: How Russia Was Restrained," in *Systems, Stability and Statecraft: Essays on the International History of Modern Europe*, ed. David Wetzel, Robert Jervis, and Jack S. Levy (New York: Palgrave Macmillan, 2004), 121, 124, 126–27; Schroeder, *Transformation of European Politics*, 588–89.

85. Jelavich, *Century of Russian Foreign Policy*, 43; Fuller, *Strategy and Power in Russia*, 177–80.

86. Nicholas V. Riasanovsky, *Nicholas I and Official Nationality in Russia, 1825–1855* (Berkeley: University of California Press, 1959); Jelavich, *Russia's Balkan Entanglements*, 93; Wortman, *Scenarios of Power*, 1:379–81.

87. Jelavich, *Century of Russian Foreign Policy*, 97–99, 106, 109–10; Riasanovsky, *Russian Identities*, 148.

88. Hosking, *Russia and the Russians*, 259–60, 263–64; Raymond T. McNally ed., *The Major Works of Peter Chaadaev* (Notre Dame, IN: University of Notre Dame Press, 1969), 28.

89. Andrzej Walicki, *The Slavophile Controversy: History of a Conservative Utopia in Nineteenth-Century Russian Thought*, trans. Hilda Andrews-Rusiecka (Notre Dame, IN: University of Notre Dame Press, 1989; reprint of Oxford: Oxford University Press, 1975), 135, 140–42, 155–56; Lieven, *Empire*, 246; Riasanovsky, *Russian Identities*, 151–53.

90. Riasanovsky, *Russian Identities*, 156, 57; Orlando Figes, *Natasha's Dance: A Cultural History of Russia* (New York: Metropolitan Books, 2002), 55, 61, 66; Hosking, *Russia and the Russians*, 277.

91. Malia, *Russia under Western Eyes: From the Bronze Horseman to the Lenin Mausoleum* (Cambridge, MA: Belknap Press of Harvard University Press, 1999), 139–40; Jelavich, *Century of Russian Foreign Policy*, 116–18; Jelavich, *Russia's Balkan Entanglements*, 117; David Gillard, *The Struggle for Asia, 1828–1914: A Study in British and Russian Imperialism* (London: Methuen, 1977), 83–89.

92. Gillard, *Struggle for Asia*, 87–88; Jelavich, *Russia's Balkan Entanglements*, 28–29, 119; Riasanovsky, *Nicholas I and Official Nationality in Russia*, 239; Jelavich, *Century of Russian Foreign Policy*, 121.

93. Florinsky, *Russia*, 2:871, 876; Gillard, *Struggle for Asia*, 93–94; Jelavich, *Century of Russian Foreign Policy*, 123, 129–30; Hosking, *Russia and the Russians*, 281.

94. Dietrich Geyer, *Russian Imperialism: The Interaction of Domestic and Foreign Policy, 1860–1914* (New Haven, CT: Yale University Press, 1987), 18–19; Fuller, *Strategy and Power in Russia*, 274–77; Jelavich, *Century of Russian Foreign Policy*, 119.

95. Rowe, *China's Last Empire*, 167–72.

96. Rowe, *China's Last Empire*, 168–69, 172–73.

97. Orville Schell and John Delury, *Wealth and Power: China's Long March to the Twenty-First Century* (New York: Random House, 2013), 5–7, 9, 18–19, 24 (quotation).

98. Schell and Delury, *Wealth and Power*, 31; Ssu-yü Teng and John King Fairbank, eds. *China's Response to the West: A Documentary Survey, 1839–1923* (Cambridge, MA: Harvard University Press, 1954), 34; Peter M. Mitchell, "The Limits of Reformism: Wei Yuan's Reaction to Western Intrusion," *Modern Asian Studies* 6, no. 2 (1972): 197–98, 203–4.

99. Immanuel C. Y. Hsu, *The Rise of Modern China*, 6th ed. (New York: Oxford University Press, 2000), 205–15; Rowe, *China's Last Empire*, 191–93; Spence, *Search for Modern China*, 176–78; Schell and Delury, *Wealth and Power*, 39–41; James Hevia, *English Lessons: The Pedagogy of Imperialism in Nineteenth-Century China* (Durham, NC: Duke University Press, 2003), 107.

100. Hsu, *Rise of Modern China*, 251–53; Spence, *Search for Modern China*, 168–75, 178–85, 186–87; Rowe, *China's Last Empire*, 185–90, 193–200, 204–8.

101. Rowe, *China's Last Empire*, 201–2; Mary Clabaugh Wright, *The Last Stand of Chinese Conservatism: The T'ung-Chih Restoration, 1862–1874* (Stanford, CA: Stanford University Press, 1957), 48–50.

102. Schell and Delury, *Wealth and Power*, 50.

103. Teng and Fairbank, *China's Response to the West*, 53–54.

104. Teng and Fairbank, *China's Response to the West*, 51.

105. Teng and Fairbank, *China's Response to the West*, 69; Kwang-Ching Liu, "Politics, Intellectual Outlook, and Reform: The T'ung-Wen Kuan Controversy of 1867," in *Reform in Nineteenth-Century China*, ed. Paul A. Cohen and John E. Schrecker (Cambridge, MA: Harvard University Press, 1976), 99.

106. Schell and Delury, *Wealth and Power*, 56–57; Spence, *Search for Modern China*, 194.

107. Spence, *Search for Modern China*, 191–92; Wright, *Last Stand*, 223.

108. Cohen, *Between Tradition and Modernity*, 241, 242 (quotation), 253–55; Joseph Fewsmith, "The Dengist Reforms in Historical Perspective," in *Elite Politics in Contemporary China* (Armonk, NY: M.E. Sharpe, 2001), 19–20.

109. Wright, *Last Stand*, 5, 63, 65.

110. Jerome B. Grieder, *Intellectuals and the State in Modern China: A Narrative History* (New York: Free Press, 1981), 73.

111. Spence, *Search for Modern China*, 217; Schell and Delury, *Wealth and Power*, 76.

112. Tze-ki Hon, "Zhang Zhidong's Proposal for Reform: A New Reading of the *Quanxue Pian*," in *Rethinking the 1898 Reform Period: Political and Cultural Change in Late Qing China*, ed. Rebecca E. Karl and Peter Zarrow (Cambridge, MA: Harvard University Press, 2002), 87–88.

113. Wright, *Last Stand*, 210–11.

114. Spence, *Search for Modern China*, 210; Chi-kong Lai, "Li Hung-chang and Modern Enterprise: The China Merchants' Company, 1872–1885," in *Li Hung-chang and China's Early Modernization*, ed. Samuel C. Chu and Kwang-Ching Liu (Armonk, NY: M.E. Sharpe, 1994), 216–19, 220 (quotation).

115. Westad, *Restless Empire*, 54 (quotation); Spence, *Search for Modern China*, 208–9; Schell and Delury, *Wealth and Power*, 65, 72–73, 76 (quotation); Wright, *Last Stand*, 213.

116. Lloyd E. Eastman, "Ch'ing-I and Chinese Policy Formation during the Nineteenth Century," *Journal of Asian Studies* 24, no. 4 (August 1965): 595–611; Paul A. Cohen, *Discovering History in China: American Historical Writing on the Recent Chinese Past* (New York: Columbia University Press, 1984), 42 (quotation); Rowe, *China's Last Empire*, 247–48. On "muscular Confucianism," see Benjamin I. Schwartz, *In Search of Wealth and Power: Yen Fu and the West* (Cambridge, MA: Harvard University Press, 1964), 15.

117. Immanuel Hsu, "Late Ch'ing Foreign Relations, 1806–1905," in Fairbank and Liu, *Cambridge History of China*, vol. 11, bk. 2 (1980): 97–100; Rowe, *China's Last Empire*, 223–24; Schell and Delury, *Wealth and Power*, 70.

118. S. C. M. Paine, *The Sino-Japanese War of 1894–1895: Perceptions, Power, and Primacy* (Cambridge: Cambridge University Press, 2003), 33, 42–43, 53–55, 58–60; Kirk W. Larsen, *Tradition, Treaties, and Trade: Qing Imperialism and Choson Korea, 1850–1910* (Cambridge, MA: Harvard University Press, 2008), 20, 88–91.

119. Westad, *Restless Empire*, 99; Schell and Delury, *Wealth and Power*, 73; R. Keith Schoppa, *Revolution and Its Past: Identities and Change in Modern Chinese History*, 2nd ed. (Upper Saddle River, NJ: Pearson Prentice Hall, 2006), 108.

120. Teng and Fairbank, *China's Response to the West*, 126; Spence, *Search for Modern China*, 215.

121. Paine, *Sino-Japanese War*, 269.

122. Alexander Gerschenkron, "Russia: Agrarian Policies and Industrialization 1861–1917," in *Continuity in History and Other Essays* (Cambridge, MA: Harvard University Press, 1968), 140–47; Alfred J. Rieber, *Politics of Autocracy: Letters of Alexander II to Prince A. I. Bariatinskii, 1857–1864* (Paris: Mouton, 1966); Geyer, *Russian Imperialism*, 18–19; Jelavich, *Century of Russian Foreign Policy*, 126; Larissa Zakharova, "Autocracy and the Reforms of 1861–1874," trans. Daniel Field, in *Russia's Great Reforms, 1855–1881*, ed. Ben Eklof, John Bushnell, and Larissa Zakharova (Bloomington: Indiana University Press, 1994), 20–21; Hosking, *Russia and the Russians*, 287–300.

123. Geyer, *Russian Imperialism*, 31–32. On Gorchakovism and its applicability to post–Cold War Russian foreign policy, see Flemming Splidsboel-Hansen, "Past and Future Meet: Aleksandr Gorchakov and Russian Foreign Policy," *Europe-Asia Studies* 54, no. 3 (2002): 377–96.

124. David MacKenzie, "Turkestan's Significance to Russia (1850–1917)," *Russian Review* 33, no. 2 (April 1974): 168; Evgeny Sergeev, *The Great Game, 1856–1907: Russo-British Relations in Central and East Asia* (Washington, DC: Woodrow Wilson Center Press, 2013), 98.

125. Geyer, *Russian Imperialism*, 94–95, 98; David MacKenzie, "Expansion in Central Asia: St. Petersburg vs. the Turkestan Generals (1863–1866)," *Canadian Slavic Studies* 3, no. 2 (1969): 186–311; Gillard, *Struggle for Asia*, 118–9 (quotation).

126. MacKenzie, "Expansion in Central Asia," 299; Geyer, *Russian Imperialism*, 89.

127. MacKenzie, "Turkestan's Significance to Russia"; Gerald Morgan, *Anglo-Russian Rivalry in Central Asia, 1810–1895* (London: Cass, 1981), 123, 129–30; Sergeev, *Great Game*, 145.

128. Jelavich, *Century of Russian Foreign Policy*, 171–72; Jelavich, *Russia's Balkan Entanglements*, 157; Geyer, *Russian Imperialism*, 91–92; David MacKenzie, "The Conquest and Administration of Turkestan, 1860–85," in *Russian Colonial Expansion to 1917*, ed. Michael Rywkin (London: Mansell, 1988), 211; MacKenzie, "Expansion in Central Asia," 286 (quotation).

129. Jelavich, *Russia's Balkan Entanglements*, 154; Splidsboel-Hansen, "Gorchakov and Russian Foreign Policy," 381.

130. MacKenzie, "Russia's Balkan Policies," 222, 224, 226; Jelavich, *Russia's Balkan Entanglements*, 156–58; Sumner, *Russia and the Balkans*, 76–77.

131. Geyer, *Russian Imperialism*, 47, 68–77; Sumner, *Russia and the Balkans*, 218–19; MacKenzie, "Russia's Balkan Policies," 235.

132. Geyer, *Russian Imperialism*, 69, 74, 84–85; Sumner, *Russia and the Balkans*, 196, 227–28.

133. Sumner, *Russia and the Balkans*, 406, 424, 576; Jelavich, *Russia's Balkan Entanglements*, 173–77; Geyer, *Russian Imperialism*, 80–83.

134. Geyer, *Russian Imperialism*, 83–85; Lincoln, *Romanovs*, 436–37, 589; Richard S. Wortman, *Scenarios of Power: Myth and Ceremony in Russian Monarchy, From Alexander II to the Abdication of Nicholas II* (Princeton, NJ: Princeton University Press, 2000), 2:147–52.

135. Jelavich, *Russia's Balkan Entanglements*, 25–26; Geyer, *Russian Imperialism*, 85.

136. Jelavich, *Russia's Balkan Entanglements*, 271–72; D. C. B. Lieven, *Russia and the Origins of the First World War* (New York: St. Martin's Press, 1983), 23–24.

137. Yü-Sheng Lin, "Radical Iconoclasm in the May Fourth Period and the Future of Chinese Liberalism," in *Reflections on the May Fourth Movement: A Symposium*, ed. Benjamin I. Schwartz (Cambridge, MA: Harvard University Press, 1973), 23–58.

138. Spence, *Search for Modern China*, 217–18.

139. Hao Chang, "Intellectual Change and the Reform Movement," in Fairbank and Liu, *Cambridge History of China*, vol. 11, bk. 2: 326–28; Spence, *Search for Modern China*, 220–21.

140. Joseph R. Levenson, *Liang Ch'i-ch'ao and the Mind of Modern China* (Cambridge, MA: Harvard University Press, 1953), 47–48; Schwartz, *In Search of Wealth and Power*, 10–11, 16–17; Hao Chang, *Liang Ch'i-ch'ao and Intellectual Transition in China, 1890–1917* (Cambridge, MA: Harvard University Press, 1971), 31, 112–17; Kung-Chuan Hsiao, *A Modern China and a New World: K'ang Yu-Wei, Reformer and Utopian, 1858–1927* (Seattle: University of Washington Press, 1975), 93–101; Schell and Delury, *Wealth and Power*, 95 (quotation).

141. Hsiao, *Modern China and New World*, 124, 138, 302; Cohen, *Discovering History in China*, 34; Schell and Delury, *Wealth and Power*, 95.

142. Hsiao, *Modern China and New World*, 104, 308, 383, 384, 387, 413, 416, 534–36.

143. Chang, "Intellectual Change," 282, 283 (quotation), 314–15, 318.

144. Chang, "Intellectual Change," 285–86, 325 (quotation), 338; Hsiao, *Modern China and New World*, 208–9.

145. Westad, *Restless Empire*, 127; Schell and Delury, *Wealth and Power*, 81–82; Grieder, *Intellectuals and the State*, 138.

146. Rowe, *China's Last Empire*, 255–62.

147. Wortman, *Scenarios of Power*, 2:331; Fuller, *Strategy and Power in Russia*, 369, 375.

148. Geyer, *Russian Imperialism*, 136 (quotation), 145, 146 (quotation), 192.

149. Geyer, *Russian Imperialism*, 196; David Schimmelpenninck Van Der Oye, *Toward the Rising Sun: Russian Ideologies of Empire and the Path to War with Japan* (DeKalb, IL: Northern Illinois University Press, 2001), 63–64, 74–75.

150. Andrew Malozemoff, *Russian Far Eastern Policy, 1881–1904, With Special Emphasis on the Causes of the Russo-Japanese War* (Berkeley: University of California Press, 1958), 66–67; Jelavich, *Century of Russian Foreign Policy*, 238–39; Schimmelpenninck Van Der Oye, *Toward the Rising Sun*, 133, 142–44.

151. Jelavich, *Century of Russian Foreign Policy*, 239–40; B. A. Romanov, *Russia in Manchuria 1892–1906* (Ann Arbor, MI: American Council of Learned Societies, 1952), 38–41; Malozemoff, *Russian Far Eastern Policy*, 102–4; Schimmelpenninck Van Der Oye, *Toward the Rising Sun*, 154–55.

152. Schimmelpenninck Van Der Oye, *Toward the Rising Sun*, 178–80, 186, 191–92; Geyer, *Russian Imperialism*, 197, 199, 207–8.

153. Geyer, *Russian Imperialism*, 212–14; Schimmelpenninck Van Der Oye, *Toward the Rising Sun*, 194–95.

154. Westad, *Restless Empire*, 110 (quotation); Lincoln, *Romanovs*, 643; Jelavich, *Century of Russian Foreign Policy*, 246.

155. Stephen Kotkin, *Stalin*, vol. 1, *Paradoxes of Power, 1878–1928* (New York: Penguin Press, 2014), 73; Dominic Lieven, *The End of Tsarist Russia: The March to World War I and Revolution* (New York: Viking, 2015), 87; Jelavich, *Century of Russian Foreign Policy*, 248–49; Lincoln, *Romanovs*, 644, 656–59.

156. Geyer, *Russian Imperialism*, 205.

157. Lieven, *End of Tsarist Russia*, 202, 210–13, 222–25.

158. Geyer, *Russian Imperialism*, 279–80; Peter Gattrell, *Government, Industry and Rearmament in Russia, 1900–1914: The Last Argument of Tsarism* (Cambridge: Cambridge University Press, 1994), 135; Ronald Park Bobroff, *Roads to Glory: Late Imperial Russia and the Turkish Straits* (London: I.B. Tauris, 2006), 78 (quotation).

159. Lieven, *End of Tsarist Russia*, 246–50, 256–58, 261–62, 265, 271, 276.

160. Lieven, *Russia and the Origins of the First World War*, 37; Lieven, *End of Tsarist Russia*, 307–8, 320–21.

161. Lieven, *End of Tsarist Russia*, 321–22, 323.

162. Lieven, *End of Tsarist Russia*, 321, 365–66.

163. Leonard Schapiro, "The Pre-Revolutionary Intelligentsia and the Legal Order," in *Russian Studies*, ed. Ellen Dahrendorf (New York: Elisabeth Sifton Books, Viking 1987), 61–63; Martin Malia, *Russia under Western Eyes: From the Bronze Horseman to the Lenin Mausoleum* (Cambridge, MA: Belknap Press of Harvard University Press, 1999), 144–45.

164. Nikolai Berdyaev, *The Origin of Russian Communism* (Ann Arbor: University of Michigan Press, 1960), 98, 104.

165. Leon Trotsky, *The Permanent Revolution* and *Results and Prospects* (New York: Pioneer Publishers, 1965); Alfred G. Meyer, *Leninism* (Cambridge, MA: Harvard University Press, 1957), 259; Berdyaev, *Origin of Russian Communism*, 107; George Konrad and Ivan Szelenyi, *The Intellectuals on the Road to Class Power* (New York: Harcourt Brace Jovanovich, 1979).

166. Grieder, *Intellectuals and the State*, 204–6; Lin, "Radical Iconoclasm"; Vera Schwarcz, *The Chinese Enlightenment: Intellectuals and the Legacy of the May Fourth Movement of 1919* (Berkeley: University of California Press, 1986), 6 (quote), 118.

167. Philip C. Huang, *Liang Ch'i-ch'ao and Modern Chinese Liberalism* (Seattle: University of Washington Press, 1972), 142.

168. Benjamin I. Schwartz, "Themes in Intellectual History: May Fourth and After," in *Intellectual History of Modern China*, ed. Merle Goldman and Leo Ou-fan Lee (New York: Cambridge University Press, 2002), 117–18; Y. C. Wang, *Chinese Intellectuals and the West, 1872–1949* (Chapel Hill: University of North Carolina Press, 1966), 140–41; Schell and Delury, *Wealth and Power*, 155; Maurice Meisner, *Li Ta-chao and the Origins of Chinese Marxism* (Cambridge, MA: Harvard University Press, 1967), 43.

169. Charlotte Furth, ed., *The Limits of Change: Essays on Conservative Alternatives in Republican China* (Cambridge, MA: Harvard University Press, 1976); Furth, "Intellectual Change: From the Reform Movement to the May Fourth

Movement, 1895–1920," in Goldman and Lee, *Intellectual History of Modern China*, 34; Guy S. Alito, *The Last Confucian: Liang Shu-ming and the Chinese Dilemma of Modernity* (Berkeley; University of California Press, 1979); Grieder, *Intellectuals and the State*, 260–66.

170. Jerome B. Grieder, *Hu Shi and the Chinese Renaissance: Liberalism in the Chinese Revolution (1917–1937)* (Cambridge, MA: Harvard University Press, 1970), 83, 111, 123–28, 209; Grieder, *Intellectuals and the State*, 250, 251–52, 267–68, 288.

171. Ernest P. Young, "The Hung-hsien Emperor as a Modernizing Conservative," in Furth, *Limits of Change*, 171–90.

172. Benjamin I. Schwartz, "The Intelligentsia in Communist China: A Tentative Comparison," in *The Russian Intelligentsia*, ed. Richard Pipes (New York: Columbia University Press, 1961), 170, 175 (quotations), 177; Hao Chang, "New Confucianism and the Intellectual Crisis of Contemporary China," in Furth, *Limits of Change*, 281–82.

173. Meisner, *Li Ta-chao*, 98 (quotation), 99; Chow Tse-tung, *The May Fourth Movement: Intellectual Revolution in Modern China* (Cambridge, MA: Harvard University Press, 1960); Schwarcz, *Chinese Enlightenment*; Rana Mitter, *A Bitter Revolution: China's Struggle with the Modern World* (Oxford University Press, 2004), 66.

174. Grieder, *Intellectuals and the State*, 207; Mao Zedong, "On People's Democratic Dictatorship: In Commemoration of the Twenty-Eighth Anniversary of the Communist Party of China," June 30, 1949, in *Selected Works of Mao Tse-tung* (Oxford: Pergamon Press, 1961) 4:411–24; Meisner, *Li Ta-chao*, 100.

175. Benjamin Schwartz, *Chinese Communism and the Rise of Mao* (Cambridge, MA: Harvard University Press, 1966), 22, 202; Arif Dirlik, *The Origins of Chinese Communism* (Oxford: Oxford University Press, 1989), 262–63; Meisner, *Li Ta-chao*, xii, 19, 46–48, 64, 94, 232, 262–63.

176. Meisner, *Li Ta-chao*, 65–67; Schwartz, "Themes in Intellectual History," in Goldman and Lee, *Intellectual History of Modern China*, 122.

177. Schwartz, *Chinese Communism and the Rise of Mao*, 22; Meisner, *Li Ta-chao*, 55 (quotation); Grieder, *Intellectuals and the State*, 269, 299–303; Lee Feigon, *Chen Duxiu: Founder of the Chinese Communist Party* (Princeton, NJ: Princeton University Press, 1983), 180–81.

178. Michael H. Hunt, "Chinese Foreign Relations in Historical Perspective," in *China's Foreign Relations in the 1980s*, ed. Harry Harding (New Haven, CT: Yale University Press, 1984), 25; Mao Zedong, "The Great Union of the Popular Masses," (Summer 1919) (Translated by Stuart R. Schram) *China Quarterly* 49 (January–March 1972): 87; Quoted in Stuart Schram, "Mao Tse-tung's Thought from 1949 to 1976," in Goldman and Lee, *Intellectual History of Modern China*, 425; Stuart Schram, *Chairman Mao Talks to the People* (New York: Praeger, 1974), 92.

179. Maurice Meisner, "Leninism and Maoism: Some Populist Perspectives on Marxism-Leninism in China," *The China Quarterly*, no. 45 (Jan.–March 1971): 2–36; Angus Stewart, "The Social Roots," in *Populism: Its Meaning and National Characteristics*, ed. G. Ionescu and E. Gellner (New York: Macmillan, 1969), 181.

180. Fewsmith, "Dengist Reforms in Historical Perspective," 20.

CHAPTER 3. THE COMMUNIST CONTEST FOR STATUS

1. Memorandum from the President's Assistant for National Security Affairs (Kissinger) to President Nixon (undated), *Foreign Relations of the United States* [hereafter cited as *FRUS*, followed by year and volume], *Soviet Union, January 1969–October 1970*, 12:603, quoted in Robert Jervis, "Identity and the Cold War," in *The Cambridge History of the Cold War*, ed. Melvyn P. Leffler and Odd Arne Westad, vol. 2, *Crises and Détente* (Cambridge: Cambridge University Press, 2010), 24; Sergey Radchenko, *Two Suns in the Heavens: The Sino-Soviet Struggle for Supremacy, 1962–1967* (Washington, DC: Woodrow Wilson Center Press, 2009), 206.

2. Stephen Kotkin, *Magnetic Mountain: Stalinism as a Civilization* (Berkeley: University of California Press, 1995), 12.

3. Kenneth N. Waltz, *Theory of International Politics* (Reading, MA: Addison-Wesley, 1979), 126, 127–28, 170–71, 203; William C. Wohlforth, "The Russian-Soviet Empire: A Test of Neorealism," *Review of International Studies* 27, no. 5 (2001): 225–26.

4. Nigel Gould-Davies, "Rethinking the Role of Ideology in International Politics During the Cold War," *Journal of Cold War Studies* 1, no. 1 (1999): 90–110.

5. Kotkin, *Magnetic Mountain*, 2, 23, 220; Ted Hopf, *Reconstructing the Cold War: The Early Years, 1945–1958* (New York: Oxford University Press, 2012), 7, 16–17, 19; Andrei P. Tsygankov, *Russia and the West from Alexander to Putin: Honor in International Relations* (Cambridge: Cambridge University Press, 2012), 20–21.

6. Jon Jacobson, *When the Soviet Union Entered World Politics* (Berkeley: University of California Press, 1994), 13; Gabriel Gorodetsky, "The Formulation of Soviet Foreign Policy—Ideology and Realpolitik," in *Soviet Foreign Policy 1917–1991: A Retrospective*, ed. Gabriel Gorodetsky (London: Frank Cass, 1994), 30; Theodore H. Von Laue, "Soviet Diplomacy: G. V. Chicherin, People's Commissar for Foreign Affairs, 1918–1930," in *The Diplomats, 1919–1939*, ed. Gordon A. Craig and Felix Gilbert (Princeton, NJ: Princeton University Press, 1953), 235.

7. Richard K. Debo, *Survival and Consolidation: The Foreign Policy of Soviet Russia, 1918–1921* (Montreal: McGill-Queen's University Press, 1992), 5–7; R. Craig Nation, *Black Earth, Red Star: A History of Soviet Security Policy 1917–1991* (Ithaca, NY: Cornell University Press, 1992), 34–35; Gabriel Gorodetsky, *The Precarious Truce: Anglo-Soviet Relations, 1924–27* (London: Cambridge University Press, 1977), 2.

8. Debo, *Survival and Consolidation*, 200, 282, 408–9; Stephen White, *Britain and the Bolshevik Revolution: A Study in the Politics of Diplomacy, 1920–1924* (New York: Macmillan, 1979), 7–8; Stephen Kotkin, *Stalin*, vol. 1, *Paradoxes of Power, 1878–1928* (New York: Penguin Press, 2014), 360, 365.

9. Debo, *Survival and Consolidation*, 168–69, 175–77, 180–81, 357, 361; White, *Britain and the Bolshevik Revolution*, 84–85.

10. Jacobson, *When the Soviet Union Entered World Politics*, 61; Debo, *Survival and Consolidation*, 348.

11. White, *Britain and the Bolshevik Revolution*, 5, 123; M. V. Glenny, "The Anglo-Soviet Trade Agreement, March 1921," *Journal of Contemporary History* 5,

no. 2 (1970): 80–81; Debo, *Survival and Consolidation*, 151, 241, 331–33; Richard K. Debo, "G. V. Chicherin: A Historical Perspective," in *Soviet Foreign Policy, 1917–1991: A Retrospective*, ed. Gabriel Gorodetsky (London: Frank Cass, 1994), 22.

12. Robert C. Tucker, "Stalinism as Revolution from Above," in *Stalinism: Essays in Historical Interpretation* (New York: W.W. Norton, 1977), 91–92.

13. White, *Britain and the Bolshevik Revolution*, 55–56; Jacobson, *When the Soviet Union Entered World Politics*, 22, 81–82; Stephen White, *The Origins of Détente: The Genoa Conference and Soviet-Western Relations, 1921–1922* (New York: Cambridge University Press, 1985), 34–35; Debo, "Chicherin," 21–22; Debo, *Survival and Consolidation*, xi-xii, 185.

14. Jacobson, *When the Soviet Union Entered World Politics*, 82, 84–85; Gorodetsky, *Precarious Truce*, 4; Von Laue, "Soviet Diplomacy: Chicherin," 240.

15. White, *Britain and the Bolshevik Revolution*, 70–72; White, *Origins of Détente*, 158–61.

16. Jacobson, *When the Soviet Union Entered World Politics*, 134–35; Gorodetsky, *Precarious Truce*, 11; Michael Jabara Carley, "Episodes from the Early Cold War: Franco-Soviet Relations, 1917–1927," *Europe-Asia Studies* 52, no. 7 (2000): 1281–83.

17. Jacobson, *When the Soviet Union Entered World Politics*, 122–23, 172, 219–21; Gorodetsky, *Precarious Truce*, 221–22, 229–30, 236; Carley, "Episodes from the Early Cold War," 1296–98.

18. Gorodetsky, *Precarious Truce*, 231–39; Jacobson, *When the Soviet Union Entered World Politics*, 140–41, 212, 223, 236–37, 242, 248, 276; Teddy Uldricks, "Russia and Europe: Diplomacy, Revolution, and Economic Development in the 1920s," *International History Review* 1, no. 1 (1979): 82–83; Moshe Lewin, *Political Undercurrents in Soviet Economic Debates: From Bukharin to the Modern Reformers* (Princeton, NJ: Princeton University Press, 1974), chap. 5.

19. Quoted in Robert C. Tucker, *Stalin in Power: The Revolution from Above, 1928–1941* (New York: Norton, 1990), 9.

20. Gorodetsky, *Precarious Truce*, 256; Jacobson, *When the Soviet Union Entered World Politics*, 253.

21. Gorodetsky, *Precarious Truce*, 258.

22. Jonathan Haslam, *The Soviet Union and the Struggle for Collective Security in Europe, 1933–39* (London: Macmillan, 1984), 1–6, 29; Oleg V. Khlevniuk, *Stalin: New Biography of a Dictator*, trans. Nora Seligman Favorov (New Haven, CT: Yale University Press, 2015), 123; Jacobson, *When the Soviet Union Entered World Politics*, 102–3.

23. R. Craig Nation, *Black Earth, Red Star: A History of Soviet Security Policy, 1917–1991* (Ithaca, NY: Cornell University Press, 1992), 76–77; Alfred J. Rieber, *Stalin and the Struggle for Supremacy in Eurasia* (Cambridge: Cambridge University Press, 2015), 153–54.

24. Derek Watson, *Molotov: A Biography* (Houndsmills, Basingstoke, Hampshire, England: Palgrave Macmillan, 2005), 148–49.

25. Hugh D. Phillips, *Between the Revolution and the West: A Political Biography of Maxim M. Litvinov* (Boulder, CO: Westview Press, 1992), 147; Adam B.

Ulam, *Expansion and Coexistence: Soviet Foreign Policy, 1917–73*, 2nd ed. (New York: Holt Rinehart and Winston, 1974), 221; Haslam, *Soviet Union and the Struggle for Collective Security*, 5, 50–51, 86.

26. Jonathan Haslam, *The Soviet Union and the Threat from the East, 1933–41: Moscow, Tokyo and the Prelude to the Pacific War* (Pittsburgh: University of Pittsburgh Press, 1992), 4; Tucker, *Stalin in Power*, 568–72; D. L. Brandenberger and A. M. Dubrovsky, "'The People Need a Tsar': The Emergence of National Bolshevism as Stalinist Ideology, 1931–1941," *Europe-Asia Studies* 50, no. 5 (1998): 873–92.

27. Jurgen Rohwer and Mikhail Monakov, "The Soviet Union's Ocean-Going Fleet, 1935–56," *International History Review* 18, no. 4 (November 1996): 850–52, 856–57, 865–67; Milan L. Hauner, "Stalin's Big Fleet Program," *Naval War College Review* 57, no. 2 (Spring 2004): 87–120; Jurgen Rohwer and Mikhail S. Monakov, *Stalin's Ocean-going Fleet: Soviet Naval Strategy and Shipbuilding Programmes 1935–1953* (London: Frank Cass, 2001), 61, 222–23; Sergey Radchenko, "Joseph Stalin," in *Mental Maps in the Early Cold War Era, 1945–68*, ed. Steven Casey and Jonathan Wright (New York: Palgrave Macmillan, 2011), 26.

28. Georgi Dimitrov, *The Diary of Georgi Dimitrov, 1933–1949*, ed. Ivo Banac and trans. Jane T. Hedges, Timothy D. Sergay, and Irina Faion (New Haven, CT: Yale University Press, 2003), 65.

29. Keith Neilson, *Britain, Soviet Russia and the Collapse of the Versailles Order, 1919–1939* (Cambridge: Cambridge University Press, 2006), 213; Haslam, *Soviet Union and the Struggle for Collective Security*, 187–94; Khlevniuk, *Stalin*, 165.

30. Haslam, *Soviet Union and the Struggle for Collective Security*, 211–12, 214–15, 216 (quotation); Khlevniuk, *Stalin*, 164–65; Watson, *Molotov*, 156–58.

31. Haslam, *Soviet Union and the Struggle for Collective Security*, 223, 225, 227–28; Charles Bohlen, *Witness to History* (New York: W.W. Norton, 1973), 76; Ulam, *Expansion and Coexistence*, 273–74; Watson, *Molotov*, 168–70; Nation, *Black Earth, Red Star*, 99; Geoffrey Roberts, *The Soviet Union and the Origins of the Second World War: Russo-German Relations and the Road to War, 1933–1941* (New York: St. Martin's Press, 1995), 87–88, 91.

32. Khlevniuk, *Stalin*, 168.

33. Haslam, *Soviet Union and the Struggle for Collective Security*, 5, 230.

34. Vladimir O. Pechatnov and C. Earl Edmondson, "The Russian Perspective," in *Debating the Origins of the Cold War: American and Russian Perspectives*, ed. Ralph B. Levering, Vladimir O. Pechatnov, Verena Botzenhart-Viehe, and C. Earl Edmondson (Lanham, MD: Rowman and Littlefield, 2002), 95–96; Townsend Hoopes and Douglas Brinkley, *FDR and the Creation of the U.N.* (New Haven, CT: Yale University Press, 1997), 46, 69, 100–101; Vladislav Zubok and Constantine Pleshakov, *Inside the Kremlin's Cold War: From Stalin to Khrushchev* (Cambridge, MA: Harvard University Press, 1996), 25.

35. Albert Resis, ed., *Molotov Remembers: Inside Kremlin Politics: Conversations with Felix Chuev* (Chicago: Ivan R. Dee, 1995), 8–10; Zubok and Pleshakov, *Inside the Kremlin's Cold War*, 16–17; Vladislav M. Zubok, *A Failed Empire*, with new preface by the author (Chapel Hill: University of North Carolina Press, 2009), 21.

36. Marc Trachtenberg, *A Constructed Peace: The Making of the European Settlement, 1945–1963* (Princeton, NJ: Princeton University Press, 1999), 36–38; Geoffrey Roberts, *Stalin's Wars: From World War to Cold War, 1939–1953* (New Haven, CT: Yale University Press, 2007), 273–75, 276 (quotation).

37. Pechatnov and Edmondson, "Russian Perspective," 104–5.

38. Radchenko, "Joseph Stalin," 16; Boris N. Slavinsky and Ljubica Erickson, "The Soviet Occupation of the Kurile Islands and the Plans for the Capture of Northern Hokkaido," *Japan Forum* 5, no. 1 (1993): 99–100; Sergey Radchenko, "Did Hiroshima Save Japan from Soviet Occupation?," *Foreign Policy*, August 2, 2015, http://foreignpolicy.com/2015/08/05/stalin_japan_hiroshima_occupation_hokkaido/.

39. Roberts, *Stalin's Wars*, 297; Natalia I. Yegorova, "Stalin's Conception of Maritime Power: Revelations from the Russian Archives," *Journal of Strategic Studies* 28, no. 2 (2005): 159; Vladimir O. Pechatnov, "'The Allies are Pressing on You to Break Your Will': Foreign Policy Correspondence between Stalin and Molotov and Other Politburo Members, September 1945–December 1946," trans. Vladislav M. Zubok, *Cold War International History Project Working Paper* no. 26 (Washington, DC: Woodrow Wilson International Center, September 1999), 3.

40. Pechatnov, "Allies Are Pressing on You," 5; Jonathan Haslam, *Russia's Cold War: From the October Revolution to the Fall of the Wall* (New Haven, CT: Yale University Press, 2011), 68.

41. Robert L. Messer, *The End of an Alliance: James F. Byrnes, Roosevelt, Truman, and the Origins of the Cold War* (Chapel Hill: University of North Carolina Press, 1982), 132; Pechatnov, "Allies Are Pressing on You," 6.

42. Pechatnov, "Allies Are Pressing on You," 4–5; Pechatnov and Edmondson, "Russian Perspective," 110.

43. Memorandum of Conversation, October 24, 1945, *FRUS: 1945*, 2:567; Memorandum of Conversation, October 25, 1945, *FRUS: 1945*, 6:789–90, 791; Stalin to "Politburo Four"([Vyacheslav] Molotov, [Lavrenti] Beria, [Anastas] Mikoyan, and [Georgy] Malenkov), December 9, 1945, in Levering et al., *Debating the Origins of the Cold War*, 155.

44. V. M. Molotov, *Voprosy vneshnei politiki [Issues of Foreign Policy]* (Moscow: Gosudarstvennoe izdatel'stvo politicheskoi literatury, 1948), 25.

45. Roberts, *Stalin's Wars*, 300–301; William Curti Wohlforth, *The Elusive Balance: Power and Perceptions during the Cold War* (Ithaca, NY: Cornell University Press, 1993), 131, 135.

46. Roberts, *Stalin's Wars*, 305.

47. Zubok, *Failed Empire*, 19, 49.

48. Pechatnov and Edmondson, "Russian Perspective," 118–19; Zubok, *Failed Empire*, 40–46, 48–49.

49. Pechatnov and Edmondson, "Russian Perspective," 126–29; Dominic Lieven, *Empire: The Russian Empire and Its Rivals* (New Haven, CT: Yale University Press, 2000), 298.

50. Martin Malia, *The Soviet Tragedy: A History of Socialism in Russia, 1917–1991* (New York: Free Press, 1994), 308.

51. Jacobson, *When the Soviet Union Entered World Politics*, 122–24; Stuart Schram, "Mao Tse-tung's Thought to 1949," in *An Intellectual History of Modern*

China, ed. Merle Goldman and Leo Ou-Fan Lee (New York: Cambridge University Press, 2002), 324.

52. Jonathan D. Spence, *The Search for Modern China*, 3rd ed. (New York: W.W. Norton, 2013), 431, 493; Robert Dallek, *Franklin D. Roosevelt and American Foreign Policy, 1932–1945* (New York: Oxford University Press, 1979), 389–91; Townsend Hoopes and Douglas Brinkley, *FDR and the Creation of the U.N.* (New Haven, CT: Yale University Press, 1997), 69, 95, 100; Odd Arne Westad, *Cold War and Revolution: Soviet-American Rivalry and the Origins of the Chinese Civil War, 1944–1946* (New York: Columbia University Press, 1993), 29–30.

53. Sergei N. Goncharov, John W. Lewis, and Xue Litai, *Uncertain Partners: Stalin, Mao, and the Korean War* (Stanford, CA: Stanford University Press, 1993), 2, 5; Dieter Heinzig, *The Soviet Union and Communist China, 1945–1950: The Arduous Road to the Alliance* (Armonk, NY: M.E. Sharpe, 2004), 55–56, 70; Westad, *Cold War and Revolution*, 54; Radchenko, "Joseph Stalin," 18–19; Chen Jian, *Mao's China and the Cold War* (Chapel Hill: University of North Carolina Press, 2001), 24–25, 28.

54. Michael H. Hunt, *The Genesis of Chinese Communist Foreign Policy* (New York: Columbia University Press, 1996), 222; Mao Zedong, *Selected Works of Mao Zedong*, vol. 5 (Beijing: Foreign Languages Press, 1977), 17; Zhou quoted in Simei Qing, *From Allies to Enemies: Visions of Modernity, Identity, and U.S.-China Diplomacy, 1945–1960* (Cambridge, MA: Harvard University Press, 2007), 255–56; Lorenz M. Lüthi, *The Sino-Soviet Split: Cold War in the Communist World* (Princeton, NJ: Princeton University Press, 2008), 31; Alexander V. Pantsov, with Steven Levine, *Mao: The Real Story* (New York: Simon and Schuster, 2012), 3, 7, 293, 323; Nikita S. Khrushchev, *Memoirs of Nikita Khrushchev*, vol. 3, trans. George Shriver (University Park: Pennsylvania State University Press, 2007), 401; Radchenko, *Two Suns in the Heavens*, 5.

55. Odd Arne Westad, *Decisive Encounters: The Chinese Civil War, 1946–1950* (Stanford, CA: Stanford University Press, 2003), 305, 310, 314; Chen, *Mao's China and the Cold War*, 40, 47, 51–52; Conversation between Stalin and Mao, Moscow, December 16, 1949, Woodrow Wilson International Center for Scholars, *Cold War International History Project Bulletin (CWIHPB)*, issues 6–7 (Winter 1995–96), 5; Heinzig, *Soviet Union and Communist China*, 265, 281, 284–85, 287–90.

56. Goncharov, Lewis, and Litai, *Uncertain Partners*, 96.

57. Goncharov, Lewis, and Litai, *Uncertain Partners*, 119, 121–22, 126, 211–12; Radchenko, *Two Suns in the Heavens*, 8; "First Conversation of N. S. Khrushchev with Mao Zedong, 31 July 1958," in "The Mao-Khrushchev Conversations, 31 July–3 August 1958 and 2 October 1959," ed. Vladislav M. Zubok, *CWIHPB*, issues 12–13 (Fall–Winter 2001), 251.

58. Chen, *Mao's China and the Cold War*, 53. Mao complained about his mistreatment by Stalin on numerous occasions, including in his July 1958 conversations with Khrushchev. See "First Conversation of Khrushchev with Mao," Zubok, *CWIHPB*, 255. See also "Minutes, Conversation between Mao Zedong and Soviet ambassador to the PRC Yudin, July 22, 1958," *CWIHPB*, issues 6–7 (Winter 1995–96), 165.

59. Austin Jersild, *The Sino-Soviet Alliance: An International History* (Chapel Hill: University of North Carolina Press, 2014), 2 (quotation), 4, 6, 8, 19, 49, 56, 210–11.

60. Chen, *Mao's China and the Cold War*, 55–56; Shen Zhihua, *Mao, Stalin and the Korean War: Trilateral Communist Relations in the 1950s*, trans. Neil Silver (London: Routledge, 2012), 153–56. For the text of the unsent telegram, see Goncharov, Lewis, and Litai, *Uncertain Partners*, 275–76.

61. Chen, *Mao's China and the Cold War*, 58–59; Chen Jian, *China's Road to the Korean War: The Making of the Sino-American Confrontation* (New York: Columbia University Press, 1994), 202–3; Telegram to Zhou Enlai [in Moscow] Concerning [Why] Our Troops Should Enter Korea (October 13, 1950), in Thomas J. Christensen, *Useful Adversaries: Grand Strategy, Domestic Mobilization, and Sino-American Conflict, 1947–1958* (Princeton, NJ: Princeton University Press, 1996), 273; Thomas J. Christensen, *Worse than a Monolith* (Princeton, NJ: Princeton University Press, 2011), 90–91; Shen, *Mao, Stalin and the Korean War*, 175; Odd Arne Westad, *Restless Empire: China and the World Since 1750* (New York: Basic Books, 2012), 296.

62. Chen, *China's Road to the Korean War*, 221; Rosemary Foot, *The Practice of Power: US Relations with China since 1949* (Oxford: Clarendon Press, 1995), 145–47; Frank Dikötter, *The Tragedy of Liberation: A History of the Chinese Revolution, 1945–57* (New York: Bloomsbury Press, 2013), 133, 257; Westad, *Decisive Encounters*, 323–24; Chen, *Mao's China and the Cold War*, 69.

63. Spence, *Search for Modern China*, 494; Shu Guang Zhang, "Constructing 'Peaceful Coexistence': China's Diplomacy toward the Geneva and Bandung Conferences, 1954–55," *Cold War History* 7, no. 4 (2007): 509–28; Chen Jian, "Bridging Revolution and Decolonization: The 'Bandung Discourse' in China's Early Cold War Experience," *Chinese Historical Review* 15, no. 2 (2008): 221.

64. Zhang, "Constructing 'Peaceful Coexistence,'" 515; Chen, *Mao's China and the Cold War*, 143; Spence, *Search for Modern China*, 495.

65. Chen, "Bridging Revolution and Decolonization," 224–25, 226 (quotation); Zhang, "Constructing 'Peaceful Coexistence,'" 513; Chen, *Mao's China and the Cold War*, 143.

66. Chen, "Bridging Revolution and Decolonization," 232–33.

67. Foot, *Practice of Power*, 199; Shu Guang Zhang, *Beijing's Economic Statecraft during the Cold War, 1949–1991* (Washington, DC: Woodrow Wilson Center Press, 2014), 121–22.

68. Mao quoted in Qing, *From Allies to Enemies*, 257; Chen, *Mao's China and the Cold War*, 69.

69. Yafeng Xia, "Mao Zedong," in Casey and Wright, *Mental Maps in the Early Cold War Era*, 164–65.

70. Zubok, *Failed Empire*, 102.

71. Deborah Welch Larson, *Anatomy of Mistrust: U.S.-Soviet Relations during the Cold War* (Ithaca, NY: Cornell University Press, 1997), 47, 49, 56, 62–63.

72. Aleksandr Fursenko and Timothy Naftali, *Khrushchev's Cold War: The Inside Story of an American Adversary* (New York: W.W. Norton, 2006), 39.

73. Khrushchev admitted that he felt like "Dun'ka" (an illiterate peasant heroine of a popular Soviet play at the time) "getting ready to go to Europe." William Taubman, *Khrushchev: The Man and his Era* (New York: W.W. Norton, 2003), 349.

74. Sergei N. Khrushchev, *Nikita Khrushchev and the Creation of a Superpower* (University Park: Pennsylvania State University Press, 2000), 82–83.

75. Taubman, *Khrushchev*, 352; Vladislav M. Zubok, "Soviet Policy Aims at the Geneva Conference, 1955," in *Cold War Respite: The Geneva Summit of 1955*, ed. Gunter Bischof and Saki Dockrill (Baton Rouge: Louisiana State University Press, 2000), 72.

76. Taubman, *Khrushchev*, 356; Nikita S. Khrushchev, *Khrushchev Remembers*, trans. and ed. Strobe Talbott (Boston: Little, Brown, 1970), 405.

77. Zubok, *Failed Empire*, 102–3; David J. Dallin, *Soviet Foreign Policy after Stalin* (Philadelphia: J.B. Lippincott, 1961), 307; Fursenko and Naftali, *Khrushchev's Cold War*, 70–73; Nation, *Black Earth, Red Star*, 208, 225.

78. Matthias Uhl, "Nikita Khrushchev," trans. Jonathan Wright, in Casey and Wright, *Mental Maps*, 281.

79. Robert Legvold, *Soviet Policy in West Africa* (Cambridge, MA: Harvard University Press, 1970), 339–40; Alessandro Iandolo, "The Rise and Fall of the 'Soviet Model of Development' in West Africa, 1957–64," *Cold War History* 12, no. 4 (2012): 683–704; Zaki Laidi, *The Superpowers and Africa: The Constraints of a Rivalry, 1960–1990*, trans. Patricia Baudoin (Chicago: University of Chicago Press, 1990), 21; Sergey Mazov, A *Distant Front in the Cold War: The USSR in West Africa and the Congo, 1956–1964* (Washington, DC: Woodrow Wilson Center Press, 2010), 184–85, 255–56.

80. Iandolo, "Rise and Fall," 702; Legvold, *Soviet Policy in West Africa*, 290, 299.

81. Fursenko and Naftali, *Khrushchev's Cold War*, 148; Yanek Mieczkowski, *Eisenhower's Sputnik Moment: The Race for Space and World Prestige* (Ithaca, NY: Cornell University Press, 2013), 29; Taubman, *Khrushchev*, 414.

82. Steven J. Zaloga, *The Kremlin's Nuclear Sword: The Rise and Fall of Russia's Strategic Nuclear Forces, 1945–2000* (Washington, DC: Smithsonian Institution Press, 2002), 55–56; Zubok and Pleshakov, *Inside the Kremlin's Cold War*, 192–93; Malia, *Soviet Tragedy*, 345; Fursenko and Naftali, *Khrushchev's Cold War*, 245–47.

83. Zubok and Pleshakov, *Inside the Kremlin's Cold War*, 192.

84. Taubman, *Khrushchev*, 407–8, 411.

85. Taubman, *Khrushchev*, 420; Arkady N. Shevchenko, *Breaking with Moscow* (New York: Alfred A. Knopf, 1989), 92.

86. S. Khrushchev, *Khrushchev*, 327–28; Taubman, *Khrushchev*, 421.

87. S. Khrushchev, *Khrushchev*, 328; Nikita S. Khrushchev, *Khrushchev Remembers: The Last Testament*, trans. and ed. Strobe Talbott (Boston: Little, Brown, 1974), 374–77.

88. Taubman, *Khrushchev*, 419–21, 426, 430–31; Fursenko and Naftali, *Khrushchev's Cold War*, 233.

89. George B. Kistiakowsky, A *Scientist at the White House: The Private Diary of President Eisenhower's Special Assistant for Science and Technology* (Cambridge, MA: Harvard University Press, 1976), 90.

90. DDE, president's news conference on May 11, 1960, *Public Papers of the Presidents, Dwight D. Eisenhower, 1960–1961* (Washington, DC: Government Printing Office, 1960), 403–7; Taubman, *Khrushchev*, 446, 458 (quotation).

91. Michael R. Beschloss, *Mayday: Eisenhower, Khrushchev and the U-2 Affair* (New York: Harper and Row, 1986), 263.

92. Taubman, *Khrushchev*, 461.

93. Fursenko and Naftali, *Khrushchev's Cold War*, 283, 286 (quotation), 290.

94. Taubman, *Khrushchev*, 476.

95. Taubman, *Khrushchev*, 417, 492, 508–11.

96. Jersild, *Sino-Soviet Alliance*, 3, 210.

97. Pantsov, *Mao*, 409–12.

98. William Taubman, "Khrushchev vs. Mao: A Preliminary Sketch of the Role of Personality in the Sino-Soviet Split," *CWIHPB*, issues 8–9 (Winter 1996–97), 243–44; Chen, *Mao's China and the Cold War*, 67–68; Lüthi, *Sino-Soviet Split*, 50.

99. Lüthi, *Sino-Soviet Split*, 76–77; Frank Dikötter, *Mao's Great Famine: The History of China's Most Devastating Catastrophe, 1958–1962* (New York: Walker and Company, 2010), 14–15; Chen Jian, "China and the Bandung Conference: Changing Perceptions and Representations," in *Bandung Revisited: The Legacy of the 1955 Asian-African Conference for International Order*, ed. See Seng Tan and Amitav Acharya (Singapore: NUS Press, 2008), 136; Stuart Schram, *The Political Thought of Mao Tse-tung* (New York: Praeger, 1971), 408–9.

100. Pantsov, *Mao*, 447; Yang Jisheng, *Tombstone: The Great Chinese Famine, 1958–1962* (New York: Farrar, Straus and Giroux, 2008), 90; Zhihua Shen and Yafeng Xia, "Hidden Currents during the Honeymoon: Mao, Khrushchev, and the 1957 Moscow Conference," *Journal of Cold War Studies* 11, no. 4 (2009): 111.

101. Zhihua Shen and Danhui Li, *After Leaning to One Side: China and Its Allies in the Cold War* (Washington, DC: Woodrow Wilson Center Press, 2011), 156–57.

102. Xia, "Mao Zedong," 165.

103. Lüthi, *Sino-Soviet Split*, 89–90; Dikötter, *Mao's Great Famine*, 37–38; Radchenko, *Two Suns in the Heavens*, 12.

104. Bo Yibo, *Ruogan Zhongda Juece yu Shijian de Huigu* [Reflections on Major Decisions and Events], vol. 2 (Beijing: Zhonggong Zhongyang Dangxiao, 1991), 1103.

105. Lowell Dittmer, *China's Continuous Revolution: The Post-Revolutionary Epoch, 1949–1981* (Berkeley: University of California Press, 1982).

106. Zubok, "Mao-Khrushchev Conversations," 244; Radchenko, *Two Suns in the Heavens*, 11–12; Li Danhui and Xia Yafeng, "Jockeying for Leadership: Mao and the Sino-Soviet Split, October 1961–July 1964," *Journal of Cold War Studies* 16, no. 1 (2014): 26 (quotation).

107. Radchenko, *Two Suns in the Heavens*, 47 (quote), 69; Roderick MacFarquhar, *The Origins of the Cultural Revolution*, vol. 3: *The Coming of the Cataclysm, 1961–1966* (New York: Columbia University Press, 1997), 361–62.

108. Li and Xia, "Jockeying for Leadership," 51, 58; Radchenko, *Two Suns in the Heavens*, 92.

109. John W. Garver, *China's Quest: The History of the Foreign Relations of the People's Republic of China* (Oxford: Oxford University Press, 2016), 134–35; "Minutes, Conversation between Mao Zedong and Soviet ambassador to the PRC Yudin, July 22, 1958," *CWIHPB*, issues 6–7 (Winter 1995–96), 155 (quote), 156.

110. Taubman, *Khrushchev*, 390–91.

111. Lüthi, *Sino-Soviet Split*, 94, 98–99; Li Zhisui, *The Private Life of Chairman Mao* (New York: Random House, 1994), 261 (quotation), 262; Bo, *Ruogan Zongda Juece*, vol. 1, 704.

112. Lüthi, *Sino-Soviet Split*, 101–4; Chen, *Mao's China and the Cold War*, 78–79; Spence, *In Search of Modern China*, 567n.

113. Li, *Private Life*, 221; Lüthi, *Sino-Soviet Split*, 78; Pantsov, *Mao*, 468–69.

114. Garver, *China's Quest*, 146–52; Zubok, "Mao-Khrushchev Conversations," and "Memorandum of Conversation of N. S. Khrushchev with Mao Zedong, Beijing, 2 October 1959," *CWIHPB*, issues 12–13 (Fall–Winter 2001), 248, 268–69.

115. Taubman, *Khrushchev*, 394; Zubok and Pleshakov, *Inside the Kremlin's Cold War*, 230; Lüthi, *Sino-Soviet Split*, 162. According to Lev Delusin, a leading Soviet Sinologist, Khrushchev's "old galosh" tirade was made even more insulting by the Chinese mistranslation of the term as "old whore." *CNN Cold War History*, "China, 1949–1972."

116. Taubman, *Khrushchev*, 471; Qing, *From Allies to Enemies*, 267.

117. Lüthi, *Sino-Soviet Split*, 157, 227; Shen and Li, *After Leaning to One Side*, 165; Radchenko, *Two Suns in the Heavens*, 36, 38 (quotation), 68.

118. Lüthi, *Sino-Soviet Split*, 232, 237–38; Radchenko, *Two Suns in the Heavens*, 97, 117.

119. Radchenko, *Two Suns in the Heavens*, 115, 118 (quotation), 204; Memorandum of Conversation, April 21, 1972, *FRUS: 1969–76*, 14:501.

120. Chen, *Mao's China and the Cold War*, 9; Peter Vamos, "Mao, Khrushchev, and China's Split with the USSR," *Journal of Cold War Studies* 12, no. 1 (Winter 2010): 135. On the role of ideological differences, see Lüthi, *Sino-Soviet Split*.

121. Radchenko, *Two Suns in the Heavens*, 206; Shen and Li, *After Leaning to One Side*, 254–55.

122. Memorandum of Conversation, June 3, 1961, *FRUS: 1961–63*, 5:187; Michael R. Beschloss, *The Crisis Years: Kennedy and Khrushchev, 1960–1963* (New York: Edward Burlingame Books, 1991), 202; Wohlforth, *Elusive Balance*, 177.

123. Memorandum of Conversation, June 3, 1961, *FRUS: 1961–63*, 5:177; Memorandum of Conversation, June 4, 1961, *FRUS: 1961–63*, 5:208; Thompson to Department of State, July 26, 1962, *FRUS: 1961–1963*, 15:254; Fursenko and Naftali, *Khrushchev's Cold War*, 447.

124. Fursenko and Naftali, *Khrushchev's Cold War*, 362–63.

125. Fursenko and Naftali, *Khrushchev's Cold War*, 370–71, 399–400; Joseph A. Loftus, "Gilpatric Warns U.S. Can Destroy Atom Aggressor," *New York Times*, 22 October 1961; Taubman, *Khrushchev*, 536.

126. Anatoly Dobrynin, *In Confidence: Moscow's Ambassador to America's Six Cold War Presidents (1962–1986)* (New York: Random House, 1995), 52.

127. Zubok and Pleshakov, *Inside the Kremlin's Cold War*, 261; Fursenko and Naftali, *Khrushchev's Cold War*, 426; Khrushchev, *Khrushchev Remembers*, 492–93.

128. Fedor Burlatsky, *Glotok svobody [A Gulp of Freedom]* (Moscow: RIK Kultura, 1997), vol. 1, 193–97; Fursenko and Naftali, *Khrushchev's Cold War*, 431, 434; Haslam, *Russia's Cold War*, 199, 201–2.

129. Dmitry Volkogonov, *Sem' vozhdei [Seven Leaders]* (Moscow: Novosti, 1999), vol. 1, 420; Haslam, *Russia's Cold War*, 203.

130. Haslam, *Russia's Cold War*, 203–5; Fursenko and Naftali, *Khrushchev's Cold War*, 447, 462; Message from Chairman Khrushchev to President Kennedy, October 27, 1962, *FRUS: 1961–1963*, 6:258.

131. Sergo Mikoyan, *The Soviet Cuban Missile Crisis: Castro, Mikoyan, Kennedy, Khrushchev, and the Missiles of November* (Washington, DC: Woodrow Wilson Center Press, 2012), 108–10, 115.

132. Robert S. Ross, *Negotiating Cooperation: The United States in China, 1969–1989* (Stanford, CA: Stanford University Press, 1995), 26.

133. Spence, *Search for Modern China*, 566–67; Shen and Li, *After Leaning to One Side*, 224–25; Daniel J. Sargent, *A Superpower Transformed: The Remaking of American Foreign Relations in the 1970s* (New York: Oxford University Press, 2015), 60–61, 63.

134. Margaret Macmillan, *Nixon and Mao: The Week That Changed the World* (New York: Random House, 2007), 188–89; James Mann, *About Face: A History of America's Curious Relationship with China from Nixon to Clinton* (New York: Vintage Books, 1998), 14.

135. Mann, *About Face*, 32–33; Spence, *Search for Modern China*, 598.

136. Sargent, *Superpower Transformed*, 88–91; John W. Garver, *China's Quest: The History of the Foreign Relations of the People's Republic of China* (New York: Oxford University Press, 2016), 308–14; Henry Kissinger, *White House Years* (Boston: Little, Brown, 1979), 878–79, 910 (quote), 912–13.

137. Macmillan, *Nixon and Mao*, 200, 234–35; Kissinger, *White House Years*, 744–45.

138. Kissinger, *White House Years*, 1058; Macmillan, *Nixon and Mao*, 75; Mann, *About Face*, 61.

139. Westad, *Restless Empire*, 369; Mann, *About Face*, 32; Macmillan, *Nixon and Mao*, 30, 156 (quotation), 193.

140. Macmillan, *Nixon and Mao*, 242–43, 259–60, 291; U.S. Memorandum of Conversation, April 21, 1972, in *Soviet-American Relations: The Détente Years, 1969–1972*, ed., Edward C. Keefer (Washington, DC: United States Government Printing Office, 2007), 685–86.

141. Richard M. Nixon, *RN: The Memoirs of Richard Nixon* (New York: Touchstone, 1978), 571; Henry Kissinger, *On China* (New York: Penguin Press, 2011), 246–47; Macmillan, *Nixon and Mao*, 240–41.

142. "Speech by Chairman of the Delegation of the People's Republic of China, Teng Hsiao-Ping, at the Special Session of the U.N. General Assembly," April 10, 1974 (Beijing: Foreign Language Press, 1974), 3, 8, 20–21; Chen, "China and the Bandung Conference," 145.

143. Kaisong Yang and Yafeng Xia, "Vacillating between Revolution and Détente: Mao's Changing Psyche and Policy toward the United States, 1969–76," *Diplomatic History* 34, no. 2 (April 2010): 418–21; Lowell Dittmer, *Sino-Soviet Normalization and Its International Implications, 1945–1990* (Seattle: University of Washington Press, 1992), 150, 306n.

144. Zaloga, *Kremlin's Nuclear Sword*, 101; Bruce D. Porter, *The USSR in Third World Conflicts: Soviet Arms and Diplomacy in Local Wars, 1945–1980* (Cambridge: Cambridge University Press, 1984), 22–23, 36–37, 46.

145. Andrei Gromyko, Speech to the 24th CPSU Congress, 1971, *Pravda*, April 4, 1971, 8–9.

146. Geoffrey Hosking, *Russia and the Russians: A History* (Cambridge, MA: Belknap Press of Harvard University Press, 2001), 512; Paul B. Rich, "Russia as

Great Power," *Small Wars & Insurgencies* 20, no. 2 (2009): 288; Kissinger, *White House Years*, 1141; Zubok, *Failed Empire*, 224; Memorandum from the President's Assistant for National Security Affairs (Kissinger) to President Nixon, undated, *FRUS: 1969–1976*, 14:870.

147. Raymond L. Garthoff, *Détente and Confrontation: American-Soviet Relations from Nixon to Reagan*, rev. ed. (Washington, DC: Brookings Institution, 1994), 332–34; Kissinger, *White House Years*, 1208; Memorandum of Conversation, May 22, 1972, *FRUS: 1969–76*, 14:989; Dobrynin, *In Confidence*, 252; Henry Kissinger, *Years of Renewal* (New York: Simon and Schuster, 1999), 265.

148. Dobrynin, *In Confidence*, 278, 280–81; Quoted in Christopher Goffard and Paloma Esquivel, "Nixon Final Tapes: Last Recordings to be Released Capture Meeting with Leonid Brezhnev and Watergate Fallout," *Los Angeles Times*, August 22, 2013.

149. Dobrynin, *In Confidence*, 252.

150. Garthoff, *Détente and Confrontation*, 59, 62–63; Wohlforth, *Elusive Balance*, 211–15; Henry Kissinger, *American Foreign Policy*, 3d ed. (New York: Norton, 1977), 310.

151. Georgi Shakhnazarov, *Tsena svobody: reformatsiya Gorbacheva glazami ego pomoshnika [The Price of Freedom: Gorbachev's Reformation through the Eyes of His Aide]* (Moscow: Rossika, 1993), 25–26.

152. Odd Arne Westad, *The Global Cold War: Third World Interventions and the Making of Our Times* (Cambridge: Cambridge University Press, 2007), 226–27, 233–37; Zubok, *Failed Empire*, 252–53; Haslam, *Russia's Cold War*, 291–94.

153. Odd Arne Westad, "The Fall of Détente and the Turning Tides of History," in *The Fall of Détente: Soviet-American Relations in the Carter Years*, ed. Westad (Oslo: Scandinavian University Press, 1997), 11–12. Westad's book is part of the Carter-Brezhnev project, a series of conferences from 1992 to 1995 including former policymakers from the U.S. and Soviet Union, interviews, and declassification of relevant documents. Institutional sponsors include the Watson Institute for International Studies at Brown University, National Security Archive, Russian Academy of Science, Cold War International History Project, and the Norwegian Nobel Institute.

154. Odd Arne Westad, "Moscow and the Angolan Crisis, 1974–1976: A New Pattern of Intervention," *CWIHPB*, issues 8–9 (Winter 1996–97), 21; Alexander Dallin, "The Road to Kabul: Soviet Perceptions of World Affairs and the Afghan Crisis," in Vernon Asputurian, Alexander Dallin, and Jiri Valenta, *The Soviet Invasion of Afghanistan: Three Perspectives*, ACIS Working Paper no. 27 (Los Angeles: University of California at Los Angeles, Center for International and Strategic Affairs, September 1980), 53; Westad, Fall of Détente," 27–28.

155. Westad, *Global Cold War*, 269–70, 271–72, 276–77, 284–86.

156. Westad, *Global Cold War*, 302, 307–8, 310, 318, 320, 322–23, 325, 328; Communist Party Politburo meeting on Afghanistan, 18 March 1979, in Westad, *Fall of Détente*, 298–303; Garthoff, *Détente and Confrontation*, 1036–44; Haslam, *Russia's Cold War*, 323–26.

157. Garthoff, *Détente and Confrontation*, 1133; Jervis, "Identity and the Cold War," 39; Dobrynin, *In Confidence*, 404–5; Westad, "Moscow and the Angolan Crisis," 21–22; Westad, *Global Cold War*, 242, 283–84.

158. Vladislav Zubok, "The Soviet Union and Détente of the 1970s," *Cold War History* 8, no. 4 (2008): 437; Haslam, *Russia's Cold War*, 313.

159. Georgy Arbatov, *Zatianuvsheesya vyzdorovlenie* [*A Prolonged Recovery*] (Moscow: Mezhdunarodnye Otnosheniia, 1991), 237–38, quoted in Tom Nichols, "H-Diplo FRUS Review of David C. Geyer, ed., *Foreign Relations of the United States, 1969–1976*, vol. 16, *Soviet Union, 1974–1976*," *H-Diplo FRUS Reviews*, no. 23, 15 January 2014.

160. Kenneth Jowitt, *New World Disorder: The Leninist Extinction* (Berkeley: University of California Press, 1993), 252–53; Valerie Bunce, "Domestic Reform and International Change: The Gorbachev Reforms in Historical Perspective," *International Organization* 47, no. 1 (Winter 1993): 111; Tony Judt, *Postwar: A History of Europe Since 1945* (New York: Penguin Books, 2005), 592.

161. President Reagan's remarks to reporters, September 2, 1983, in *Presidential Documents*, vol. 19 (September 5, 1983), 1193.

162. Zubok, *Failed Empire*, 204–6.

CHAPTER 4. THE SOCIAL CREATIVITY OF DENG AND GORBACHEV

1. Li Lanqing, *Breaking Through: The Birth of China's Opening-Up Policy* (Oxford: Oxford University Press, 2009), 59 (quotation); Ezra F. Vogel, *Deng Xiaoping and the Transformation of China* (Cambridge, MA: Belknap Press of Harvard University Press, 2011), 298, 301, 304 (quotation), 308.

2. Archie Brown, *The Gorbachev Factor* (Oxford: Oxford University Press, 1996), 42–43; Mikhail Gorbachev, *Memoirs* (New York: Doubleday, 1995), 102–3.

3. Deborah Welch Larson and Alexei Shevchenko, "Shortcut to Greatness: The New Thinking and the Revolution in Soviet Foreign Policy," *International Organization* 57, no. 1 (2003): 77–109.

4. Alexander Dallin, "The Rise of New Thinking on Soviet Foreign Policy," in *The Demise of Marxism-Leninism in Russia*, ed. Archie Brown (Houndsmills, Basingstoke: Palgrave Macmillan, 2004), 180; Teddy J. Uldricks, *Diplomacy and Ideology: The Origins of Soviet Foreign Relations 1917–1930* (Beverly Hills, CA: Sage, 1979), 148.

5. Harold K. Jacobson and Michel Oksenberg, *China's Participation in the IMF, the World Bank, and GATT* (Ann Arbor: University of Michigan Press, 1990), 50–51; Vladislav M. Zubok, *A Failed Empire: The Soviet Union in the Cold War from Stalin to Gorbachev* (Chapel Hill: University of North Carolina Press, 2007), 282, 301; Robert D. English, *Russia and the Idea of the West: Gorbachev, Intellectuals, and the End of the Cold War* (New York: Columbia University Press, 2000), 201–2; Brown, *Gorbachev Factor*, 97–103.

6. Vogel, *Deng*, 283–84, 697–98; Harry Harding, *A Fragile Relationship: The United States and China since 1972* (Washington, DC: Brookings Institution, 1992), 56–57, 59–60, 65.

7. Steven I. Levine, "China in Asia: The PRC as a Regional Power," in *China's Foreign Relations in the 1980s*, ed. Harry Harding (New Haven, CT: Yale University Press, 1984), 136–37.

8. Orville Schell and John Delury, *Wealth and Power: China's Long March to the Twenty-First Century* (New York: Random House, 2013), 180–81; Peter Nolan,

China's Rise, Russia's Fall: Politics, Economics and Planning in the Transition from Socialism (New York: St. Martin's Press, 1995), 162; Deng Xiaoping, "The Present Situation and the Tasks Before Us" (January 16, 1980), in *Selected Works of Deng Xiaoping, 1975–1982* (Beijing: Foreign Languages Press, 1984), 2:225–26.

9. Edward S. Steinfeld, *Playing Our Game: Why China's Rise Doesn't Threaten the West* (New York: Oxford University Press, 2010), 49, 64–67; Deng Xiaoping, "China's Goal Is to Achieve Comparative Prosperity by the End of the Century" (December 6, 1979), in *Selected Works of Deng Xiaoping*, 2:240; Vogel, *Deng*, 17.

10. Vogel, *Deng*, 2; Sebastian Heilmann, "Maximum Tinkering under Uncertainty: Unorthodox Lessons from China," *Modern China* 35, no. 4 (July 2009): 453, 456; Lowell Dittmer, *Sino-Soviet Normalization and Its International Implications, 1945–19* (Seattle: University of Washington Press, 1992), 47–48; 373; Deng Xiaoping, "Emancipate the Mind, Seek Truth from Facts, Unite as One in Looking to the Future" (December 13, 1978), in *Selected Works of Deng Xiaoping 1975–1982*, 2:150–63.

11. Deng Xiaoping, "Our Magnificent Goal and Basic Policies" (October 6, 1984), in *Selected Works of Deng Xiaoping, 1982–1992* (Beijing: Foreign Languages Press, 1992), 3:86; Deng Xiaoping, "Speech at the Third Plenary Session of the Central Advisory Commission of the Communist Party of China" (October 22, 1984), in *Selected Works*, 3:96; David Shambaugh, "Deng Xiaoping: The Politician," *China Quarterly* no. 135 (1993): 481.

12. Dali L. Yang, *Beyond Beijing: Liberalization and the Regions in China* (London: Routledge, 1997); Harry Harding, *China's Second Revolution: Reform After Mao* (Washington, DC: Brookings 1987), 163–70; Ruan Ming, *Deng Xiaoping: Chronicle of an Empire* (Boulder, CO: Westview Press, 1994), 138–40; Richard Baum, *Burying Mao: Chinese Politics in the Age of Deng Xiaoping* (Princeton, NJ: Princeton University Press, 1996), 160, 165, 181–82.

13. Deng Xiaoping, "Carry Out the Policy of Opening Up to the Outside World and Learn Advanced Science and Technology from Other Countries" (October 10, 1978), in *Selected Works*, 2:143; Vogel, *Deng*, 56, 476.

14. Deng Xiaoping, "Carry Out the Policy of Opening Up"; Deng Xiaoping, "Speech at the Opening Ceremony of the National Conference on Science" (March 18, 1978), in *Selected Works*, 2:103; Vogel, *Deng*, 217–19.

15. Julian Gewirtz, *Unlikely Partners: Chinese Reformers, Western Economists, and the Making of Global China* (Cambridge, MA: Harvard University Press, 2017), 3, 9, 12; Jacobson and Oksenberg, *China's Participation*, 66–67; Gilbert Rozman, *The Sino-Russian Challenge to the World Order: National Identities, Bilateral Relations, and East versus West in the 2010s* (Washington, DC: Woodrow Wilson Center Press, 2013), 95.

16. Deng Xiaoping, "How to Revive Agricultural Production" (July 7, 1962), in *Selected Works of Deng Xiaoping, 1938–1965* (Beijing: Foreign Languages Press, 1992), 1:305; Deng Xiaoping, "Emancipate the Mind."

17. Richard Evans, *Deng Xiaoping and the Making of Modern China* (New York: Viking, 1993), 260; Harry Harding, "China's Changing Roles in the Contemporary World," in *China's Foreign Relations in the 1980s*, ed. Harding (New Haven, CT: Yale University Press, 1984), 193–94; Michael Yahuda, "Deng Xiaoping: The Statesman," *China Quarterly* no. 135 (1993): 555.

18. Deng Xiaoping, "Bourgeois Liberalization Means Taking the Capitalist Road" (May and June 1985), in *Selected Works*, 3:129–30; Vogel, *Deng*, 465.

19. Richard Baum, *Scientism and Bureaucratism in Post-Mao China: Cultural Limits of the "Four Modernizations"* (Lund, Sweden: Research Policy Institute, University of Lund, 1981); Paul A. Cohen, "The Post-Mao Reforms in Historical Perspective," *The Journal of Asian Studies* 47, no. 3 (August 1988): 519–41; Joseph Fewsmith, "The Dengist Reforms in Historical Perspective," in *Elite Politics in Contemporary China* (Armonk, NY: M.E. Sharpe, 2001), 3–34.

20. Archie Brown, *Seven Years that Changed the World: Perestroika in Perspective* (Oxford: Oxford University Press, 2008), 259, 275 (quotation).

21. Hannes Adomeit, *Imperial Overstretch: Germany in Soviet Policy from Stalin to Gorbachev* (Baden-Baden: Nomos Verlagsgesellschaft, 1998), 145, 147–48; Randall L. Schweller and William C. Wohlforth, "Power Test: Evaluating Realism in Response to the End of the Cold War," *Security Studies* 9, no. 3 (2000): 86–89; Stephen G. Brooks and William C. Wohlforth, "Power, Globalization, and the End of the Cold War: Reevaluating a Landmark Case for Ideas," *International Security* 25, no. 3 (2000/01): 16–17, 22–23.

22. Brooks and Wohlforth, "Power, Globalization, and the End of the Cold War," 32–33, 37–42.

23. Robert Legvold, "Soviet Learning in the 1980s," in *Learning in U.S. and Soviet Foreign Policy*, ed. George W. Breslauer and Phillip E. Tetlock, (Boulder, CO: Westview Press, 1991), 683–734; Jeffrey T. Checkel, *Ideas and International Political Change: Soviet/Russian Behavior and the End of the Cold War* (New Haven, CT: Yale University Press, 1997); Matthew Evangelista, *Unarmed Forces: The Transnational Movement to End the Cold War* (Ithaca, NY: Cornell University Press, 1999); Robert English, *Russia and the Idea of the West: Gorbachev, Intellectuals, and the End of the Cold War* (New York: Columbia University Press, 2000).

24. Odd Arne Westad, *The Global Cold War* (Cambridge: Cambridge University Press, 2007), 363, 378–79; Ronald Reagan's Address to Members of the British Parliament, June 8, 1982, in *Reagan at Westminster*, ed. Robert C. Rowland and John M. Jones (College Station: Texas A&M University Press, 2010), 5.

25. Jonathan Haslam, *Russia's Cold War: From the October Revolution to the Fall of the Wall* (New Haven, CT: Yale University Press, 2011), 361. For Gorbachev's concerns over his international status at the time of the Rust scandal, see also Dmitry Volkogonov, *Sem' vozhdei* [*Seven Leaders*] (Moscow: Novosti, 1999) 2: 414.

26. Martin E. Malia, *The Soviet Tragedy: A History of Socialism in Russia, 1917–1991* (New York: Free Press, 1994), 413; Seweryn Bialer, "Domestic and International Factors in the Formation of Gorbachev's Reforms," in *The Soviet System: From Crisis to Collapse*, ed. Alexander Dallin and Gail W. Lapidus, rev. ed. (Boulder, CO: Westview Press, 1995), 34; Anders Aslund, *Gorbachev's Struggle for Economic Reform*, rev. ed. (Ithaca, NY: Cornell University Press, 1991), 15.

27. Robert G. Herman, *Ideas, Identity and Redefinition of Interests: The Political and Intellectual Origins of the Soviet Foreign Policy Revolution* (PhD diss., Cornell University, 1996).

28. Robert G. Herman, "Identity, Norms, and National Security," in *The Culture of National Security: Norms and Identity in World Politics*, ed. Peter J. Katzenstein (New York: Columbia University Press, 1996), 271–316.

29. Michael Ellman and Vladimir Kontorovich, "The Collapse of the Soviet System and the Memoir Literature," *Europe-Asia Studies* 49, no. 2 (1997): 265; Yegor Ligachev, *Inside Gorbachev's Kremlin* (New York: Random House, 1993); Anatoly Dobrynin, *In Confidence: Moscow's Ambassador to America's Six Cold War Presidents (1962–1986)* (New York: Random House, 1995), 566. As a former Politburo supporter of Gorbachev, Geidar Aliev, complained later, "He did not turn out to be the man we'd voted for." Andrei Karaulov, *Vokrug Kremlya: Kniga politicheskikh dialogov* [*Around the Kremlin: The Book of Political Dialogues*] (Moscow: Novosti, 1990), 1:268, quoted in Robert English, "The Sociology of New Thinking: Elites, Identity Change, and the End of the Cold War," *Journal of Cold War Studies* 7, no. 2 (2005): 55.

30. These are the main points of an early April 1985 memo for Gorbachev authored by Georgy Arbatov, the leading specialist on the United States in the Soviet academic establishment. Quoted in A. S. Chernyaev, *Shest' let s Gorbachevym: Po dnevnikovym zapisyam* [*Six Years with Gorbachev: According to Diary Records*] (Moscow: Progress "Kul'tura," 1993), 41. See also Chernyaev, *Shest' let s Gorbachevym*, 78.

31. Tuomas Forsberg, "Power, Interests and Trust: Explaining Gorbachev's Choices and the End of the Cold War," *Review of International Studies* 25, no. 4 (1999): 603–21.

32. Brown, *Seven Years*, 249–50; Sergey Radchenko, *Unwanted Visionaries: The Soviet Failure in Asia at the End of the Cold War* (Oxford: Oxford University Press, 2014), 60. Habomai is actually a group of islands rather than an individual island (326n).

33. Radchenko, *Unwanted Visionaries*, 71, 88–123, 310–11.

34. Ted Hopf, "Peripheral Visions: Brezhnev and Gorbachev Meet the Reagan Doctrine," in Breslauer and Tetlock, *Learning in U.S. and Soviet Foreign Policy*, 586–629; Michael MccGwire, *Perestroika and Soviet National Security* (Washington, DC: Brookings Institution, 1991), chaps. 5, 10; English, "Sociology of New Thinking," 51, 69; Brown, *Seven Years*, 6.

35. Views of this camp were espoused by such publications as *Moskovskie Novosti* [*Moscow News*], *Ogonek* [*Spark*], *Novoye Vremya* [*New Times*], and foreign policy specialist journals *MEiMO*, *SShA*, and *Mezhdunarodnaya Zhizn'* [*International Affairs*]. For detailed analysis of the institutions and development of the New Thinking in the Soviet Union, see Herman, *Ideas, Identity and Redefinition of Interests*; Checkel, *Ideas and International Political Change*; English, *Russia and the Idea of the West*; English, "Sociology of New Thinking."

36. On the origins and development of New Thinking by some of its architects, see Mikhail Gorbachev, *Perestroika: New Thinking for Our Country and the World* (New York: Harper and Row, 1987); Gorbachev, *Memoirs*; Eduard Shevardnadze, *The Future Belongs to Freedom* (New York: Free Press, 1991); Chernyaev, *Shest' let s Gorbachevym* [*Six Years with Gorbachev*]; Georgy Shakhnazarov, *Tsena svobody: Reformatsiya Gorbacheva glazami ego pomosh'nika* [*The Price of*

Freedom: Gorbachev's Reformation as Witnessed by His Aide] (Moscow: Rossika-Zevs, 1993); Evgeny Primakov, *Gody v bol'shoi politike* [*Years inside Big Politics*] (Moscow: Sovershenno Sekretno, 1999).

37. V. Kubálková and A. A. Cruickshank, *Thinking New About Soviet "New Thinking"* (Berkeley: Institute of International Studies, University of California, 1989), 30–31, 61; Herman, "Identity, Norms, and National Security," 310–11; Jacques Lévesque, *The Enigma of 1989: The USSR and the Liberation of Eastern Europe* (Berkeley: University of California Press, 1997), 36.

38. Brown, *Seven Years*, 257, 265.

39. Stephen Sestanovich, "Gorbachev's Foreign Policy: A Diplomacy of Decline," *Problems of Communism* 37, no. 1 (1988): 1–15.

40. Kubálková and Cruickshank, *Thinking New*, 68, 105, 159–78.

41. *FBIS Daily Report-Soviet Union*, April 26, 1990, quoted in Don Oberdorfer, *The Turn: From the Cold War to a New Era: United States and the Soviet Union, 1983–1990* (New York: Poseidon Press, 1991), 438, emphasis added.

42. Jacques Lévesque, "The Messianic Character of Gorbachev's 'New Thinking': Why and What For?," in *The Last Decade of the Cold War: From Conflict Escalation to Conflict Transformation*, ed. Olav Njolstad (London: Frank Cass, 2004), 161; Andrei Grachev, *Gorbachev's Gamble: Soviet Foreign Policy and the End of the Cold War* (Malden, MA: Polity, 2008), 74–75.

43. Evangelista, *Unarmed Forces*, 147–64, 306–15; English, *Russia and the Idea of the West*, 212–13, 330; Gorbachev, *Perestroika*, 196, 206–7; Gorbachev, *Memoirs*, 159–60, 676–77.

44. Kubálková and Cruickshank, *Thinking New*, 30–31; Lévesque, *Enigma of 1989*, 4, 26–27, 34.

45. Harry Harding, *A Fragile Relationship: The United States and China since 1972* (Washington, DC: Brookings Institution 1992), chap. 3; Robert S. Ross, *Negotiating Cooperation: The United States and China, 1969–1989* (Stanford, CA: Stanford University Press, 1995), chaps. 3–4.

46. Ross, *Negotiating Cooperation*, 92–98, 103–4, 121, 128.

47. Ross, *Negotiating Cooperation*, 130; James S. Mann, *About Face: A History of America's Curious Relationship with China, from Nixon to Clinton* (New York: Vintage Books, Random House, 1998), 91–92; Dittmer, *Sino-Soviet Normalization*, 211–12.

48. Harding, *Fragile Relationship*, 80; Patrick Tyler, *A Great Wall: Six Presidents and China* (New York: Public Affairs, 1999), 261; Richard H. Solomon, *US-PRC Political Negotiations, 1967–1984: An Annotated Chronology*, Rand: December 1985, R-3298, 72; Marshall Shulman's Comment, "Global Competition and the Deterioration of US-Soviet Relations, 1977–80," the Third Oral History Conference of the Carter-Brezhnev Project (Fort Lauderdale, Fla., 23–26 March 1995), http://nsarchive.gwu.edu/carterbrezhnev/, 150; Mann, *About Face*, 89, 91–92; Ross, *Negotiating Cooperation*, 161.

49. Michael Schaller, *The United States and China: Into the Twenty-First Century* (New York: Oxford University Press, 2002), 191; Ross, *Negotiating Cooperation*, 141; Vogel, *Deng*, 344–45.

50. Henry Kissinger, *On China* (New York: Penguin Press, 2011), 360–61; Wang Zhongchun, "The Soviet Factor in Sino-American Normalization," in *Normal-*

ization of US-China Relations: An International History, ed. William C. Kirby, Robert S. Ross, and Gong Li (Cambridge, MA: Harvard University Press, 2005), 166; Xiaoming Zhang, *Deng Xiaoping's Long War: The Military Conflict between China and Vietnam, 1979–1991* (Chapel Hill: University of North Carolina Press, 2015), 46–51.

51. Zhang, *Deng Xiaoping's Long War*, 49, 53, 55; Harlan W. Jenks, "China's 'Punitive' War on Vietnam: A Military Assessment," *Asian Survey* 19, no. 8 (August 1979): 801–15; Baum, *Burying Mao*, 88; Radchenko, *Unwanted Visionaries*, 27–28; Vogel, *Deng*, 523, 525, 539–40.

52. Harding, *Fragile Relationship*, 108, 111–19, 134; Dittmer, *Sino-Soviet Normalization*, 215–16; Radchenko, *Unwanted Visionaries*, 28–29; Yahuda, "Deng Xiaoping," 561.

53. Deng, Interview in Hong Kong, *Ming pao*, August 15, 1981, quoted in Harding, *Fragile Relationship*, 134; Radchenko, *Unwanted Visionaries*, 30; Deng Xiaoping, "Peace and Development are the Two Outstanding Issues in the World Today" (March 4, 1985), in *Selected Works*, 3:111.

54. Hu Yaobang, "Create a New Situation in All Fields of Socialist Modernization," *Beijing Review*, September 13, 1982: 29–30; Yahuda, "Deng Xiaoping," 561; Harding, *Fragile Relationship*, 123; Banning N. Garrett and Bonnie S. Glaser, *War and Peace: The Views from Moscow and Beijing* (Berkeley: Institute of International Studies, University of California), Policy Papers in International Affairs, no. 2, 64–66; Vogel, *Deng*, 536–37.

55. Radchenko, *Unwanted Visionaries*, 48; Harding, "China's Changing Roles," 198; Harding, *Fragile Relationship*, 143; Deng Xiaoping, "Speech at an Enlarged Meeting of the Military Commission of the Central Committee of the Communist Party of China" (June 4, 1985), in *Selected Works*, 3:132–33; Wu Xinbo, "China: Security Practice of a Modernizing and Ascending Power," in *Asian Security Practice: Material and Ideational Influences*, ed. Muthiah Alagappa (Stanford, CA: Stanford University Press, 1998), 148.

56. Jonathan D. Pollack, "The Opening to America," in *The Cambridge History of China*, vol. 15, part 2, *Revolutions Within the Chinese Revolution 1966–82*, ed. Roderick MaFarquhar, John K. Fairbank, and Denis Crispin Twitchett (Cambridge: Cambridge University Press, 1991), 467; Radchenko, *Unwanted Visionaries*, 41–42.

57. Yahuda, "Deng Xiaoping," 561, 568; Deng Xiaoping, "We Shall Be Paying Close Attention to Developments in Hong Kong During the Transition Period" (July 31, 1984), in *Selected Works*, 3:77; Deng Xiaoping, "The Principles of Peaceful Coexistence Have a Potentially Wide Application" (October 31, 1984), in *Selected Works*, 3:102–3.

58. Deng Xiaoping, "Our Magnificent Goal and Basic Policies" (October 6, 1984), in *Selected Works*, 3:85–87; Deng, "Principles of Peaceful Coexistence"; Deng Xiaoping, "Peace and Development are the Two Outstanding Issues in the World Today" (March 4, 1985), in *Selected Works*, 3:110–12; Deng Xiaoping, *Fundamental Issues in Present-Day China* (Beijing: Foreign Languages Press, 1988), 95; Yahuda, "Deng Xiaoping," 562.

59. Deng Xiaoping, "A New International Order Should Be Established with the Five Principles of Peaceful Coexistence as Norms" (December 21, 1988),

in *Selected Works*, 3:274–76; Chen Jian, "China and the Bandung Conference: Changing Perceptions and Representations," in *Bandung Revisited: The Legacy of the 1955 Asian-African Conference for International Order*, ed. See Seng Tan and Amitav Acharya (Singapore: National University of Singapore Press, 2008), 149.

60. Harding, "China's Changing Roles," 207–8; Mann, *About Face*, 107–8, 109–11, 147; Garver, *China's Quest*, 411; Michael J. Green, *By More than Providence: Grand Strategy and American Power in the Asia Pacific Since 1783* (New York: Columbia University Press, 2017), 374–76.

61. Joe Studwell, *The China Dream: The Quest for the Last Untapped Market on Earth* (New York: Grove Press, 2003), 126–36; Harding, *Fragile Relationship*, 100–106, 299.

62. Speech by CPSU General Secretary Mikhail Gorbachev at the Forum "For a Nuclear-Free World, for the Survival of Mankind," Moscow, translated in *FBIS Daily Report-Soviet Union*, February 2, 1987, AA20; Gorbachev, "Political Report of the CPSU Central Committee at the 27th CPSU Congress," February 25, 1986, reprinted in *Mikhail Gorbachev: Selected Speeches and Articles*, 2nd ed. (Moscow: Progress Publishers, 1987), 362, 364, 419–21, 422, 432–33.

63. Robert Service, *The End of the Cold War 1985–1991* (New York: Public Affairs, 2015), 167–69, 178, 180, 203–5, 207, 216–18, 276–77; Raymond L. Garthoff, *The Great Transition: American-Soviet Relations and the End of the Cold War* (Washington, DC: Brookings, 1994), 284, 326–28; Mikhail Gorbachev, "The Reality and Guarantees of a Secure World," *Pravda*, 17 September 1987, translated in *FBIS Daily Report-Soviet Union*, September 17, 1987, 23.

64. *New York Times*, October 18, 1987; Garthoff, *Great Transition*, 735–44.

65. See Noel E. Firth and James H. Noren, *Soviet Defense Spending: A History of CIA Estimates* (Houston: Texas A&M University Press, 1998); Clifford G. Gaddy, *The Price of the Past: Russia's Struggle with the Legacy of a Militarized Economy* (Washington, DC: Brookings Institution, 1997). Around 15–20 percent of GDP in the early 1980s.

66. Westad, *Global Cold War*, 384; Zubok, *Failed Empire*, 299, 308.

67. Thomas Risse, "The Cold War's Endgame and German Unification (A Review Essay)," *International Security* 21, no. 4 (1997): 167–68; Radchenko, *Unwanted Visionaries*, 242–43, 251 (quote), 252, 302.

68. Radchenko, *Unwanted Visionaries*, 71, 73–74, 77, 86, 199, 246–47, 258–62, 276.

69. Leon Rabinovich Aron, "The 'Mystery' of the Soviet Collapse," *Journal of Democracy* 17, no. 2 (April 2006): 27; Andrei Grachev, *Gorbachev's Gamble: Soviet Foreign Policy and the End of the Cold War* (Malden, MA: Polity, 2008), 47; Lévesque, "Messianic Character," 172–73; Brown, *Seven Years*, 252.

70. Chernyaev notes, October 31, 1988, quoted in Vladislav M. Zubok, "New Evidence on the 'Soviet Factor' in the Peaceful Revolutions of 1989," *Cold War International History Project Bulletin*, nos. 12–13 (2001): 9; M. S. Gorbachev's United Nations Address, *Pravda*, December 8, 1988, 1–2, translated in *FBIS Daily Report-Soviet Union*, December 8, 1988, 13.

71. *New York Times*, December 8, 1988; *Washington Post*, December 8, 1988; Gorbachev, *Memoirs*, 460; Chernyaev Diary-1988, November 3, 1988, NSA EBB

no. 250, www.gwu.edu/~nsarchiv/NSAEBB/NSAEBB250/index.htm; Service, *End of the Cold War*, 357.

72. Gennadii Zoteev, "The View from Gosplan: Growth to the Year 2000," in Ellman and Kontorovich, *Destruction of the Soviet Economic System*, 92; The Diary of Anatoly S. Chernyaev: 1987–1988, April 26, 1988, National Security Archive Electronic Briefing Book no. 250, trans. Anna Melyakova and ed. Svetlana Savranskaya, www.nsarchive.gwu.edu.

73. Brown, *Gorbachev Factor*, 216.

74. For discussion of the events, see Andrew J. Nathan and Perry Link, ed. *The Tiananmen Papers*, compiled by Zhang Liang (New York: Public Affairs, 2001).

75. Radchenko, *Unwanted Visionaries*, 26, 160–61, 196; Qian Qichen, *Ten Episodes in China's Diplomacy* (New York: HarperCollins, 2005), 2–28.

76. Radchenko, *Unwanted Visionaries*, 160–61.

77. A Three-way Conversation: Deng, Zhao, and Yang, May 13, 1989, in Nathan and Link, *Tiananmen Papers*, 148–49. For another statement by Deng using almost identical language, see Nathan and Link, *Tiananmen Papers*, 143. While questions have been raised about the authenticity of some of the documents, which were supposedly smuggled out of China by a Chinese reformer, many have been corroborated by other sources. There is less support for alleged meetings between the eight Elders and for telephone conversations. See Vogel, *Deng*, 831–32, note 1.

78. Dinxin Zhao, *The Power of Tiananmen: State-Society Relations and the 1989 Beijing Student Movement* (Chicago: University of Chicago Press, 2001), 164–70, 232–33.

79. Radchenko, *Unwanted Visionaries*, 162–63; Benjamin Yang, *Deng: A Political Biography* (Armonk, NY: M.E. Sharpe, 1998), 246–47.

80. Radchenko, *Unwanted Visionaries*, 166–67.

81. Nathan and Link, *Tiananmen Papers*, 193–94; Vogel, *Deng*, 615–17; Excerpts from Party Central Office Secretariat, Minutes of the May 16 Politburo Standing Committee meeting, in Nathan and Link, *Tiananmen Papers*, 178; Excerpts from Party Central Office Secretariat, "Materials from the Big Meeting of Central and Beijing Municipal Party Government, and Military Officials," May 19, 1989, in Nathan and Link, *Tiananmen Papers*, 225. For the CCP elders' accusations that Zhao Ziyang "stabbed Deng Xiaoping in the back" during conversations with Gorbachev, see Excerpt from Party Central Office Secretariat, "Minutes of important meeting, May 21, 1989," in Nathan and Link, *Tiananmen Papers*, 258.

82. Excerpts from the Party Central Office Secretariat, "Minutes of important meeting, June 2, 1989," in Nathan and Link, *Tiananmen Papers*, 356; Excerpts from the Party Central Office Secretariat, "Minutes of the CCP Central Politburo Standing Committee Meeting" (June 6, 1989), Nathan and Link, 423.

83. Harding, *Fragile Relationship*, 202–4.

84. Baum, *Burying Mao*, 273; Harding, *Fragile Relationship*, 291–92; David M. Lampton, *Same Bed, Different Dreams: Managing U.S.-China Relations, 1989–2000* (Berkeley: University of California Press, 2001), 258.

85. Yang, *Deng*, 257.

86. Harding, *Fragile Relationship*, 236–39; Mann, *About Face*, 246; Lampton, *Same Bed, Different Dreams*, 26.

87. Deng Xiaoping, "We Are Working to Revitalize the Chinese Nation" (April 7, 1990), in *Selected Works*, 3:344–45.

88. Deng Xiaoping, "With Stable Policies of Reform and Opening to the Outside World, China Can Have Great Hopes for the Future" (September 4, 1989), in *Selected Works*, 3:311.

89. Vogel, *Deng*, 714.

90. Vladislav M. Zubok, "New Evidence on the 'Soviet Factor' in the Peaceful Revolutions of 1989," *Cold War International History Project Bulletin*, issues 12–13 (Fall–Winter 2001), 8. According to Chernyaev's diary, after his October 1989 meetings with Honecker in East Germany, Gorbachev called the East German leader "an arsehole." Quoted in Service, *End of the Cold War*, 408.

91. Zubok, "New Evidence," 8 (quotation); Zubok, *Failed Empire*, 321–22.

92. Mark Kramer, "The Collapse of East European Communism and the Repercussions within the Soviet Union (part I)," *Journal of Cold War Studies* 5, no. 4 (Fall 2003): 186–90; Lévesque, *Enigma of 1989*, 54; cf. Stephen G. Brooks and William C. Wohlforth, "Economic Constraints and the Turn towards Superpower Cooperation in the 1980s," in Njolstad, *Last Decade of the Cold War*, 291.

93. Grachev, *Gorbachev's Gamble*, 122; Lévesque, *Enigma of 1989*, 3; Adomeit, *Imperial Overstretch*, 274.

94. Kramer, "Collapse of East European Communism," 197–201; Archie Brown, "Gorbachev and the End of the Cold War," in *Ending the Cold War: Interpretations, Causation, and the Study of International Relations*, ed. Richard K. Herrmann and Richard Ned Lebow (New York: Palgrave Macmillan, 2004), 38–39.

95. Lévesque, "Messianic Character," 167; Anatoly Gromyko, *Andrei Gromyko v labirintakh Kremlya: Vospominaniya i razmishleniya syna* [*Andrei Gromyko in the Kremlin Labyrinth: His Son's Recollections and Reflections*] (Moscow: IPO "Avtor," 1997), 184.

96. Grachev, *Gorbachev's Gamble*, 189; Service, *End of the Cold War*, 366–67; Quoted in Mark Kramer, "The Collapse of East European Communism and the Repercussions within the Soviet Union (part 3)," *Journal of Cold War Studies* 7, no. 1 (2005): 57.

97. Adomeit, *Imperial Overstretch*, 487.

98. Adomeit, *Imperial Overstretch*, 508; Philip Zelikow and Condoleezza Rice, *Germany Unified and Europe Transformed: A Study in Statecraft* (Cambridge, MA: Harvard University Press, 1994), 277, 281.

99. George Bush and Brent Scowcroft, *A World Transformed* (New York: Alfred A. Knopf, 1988), 282–83.

100. Quoted in Adomeit, *Imperial Overstretch*, 488, 548.

101. Interview with Chernyaev, Adomeit, *Imperial Overstretch*, 556.

102. Adomeit, *Imperial Overstretch*, 542; Mary Elise Sarotte, *1989: The Struggle to Create Post-Cold War Europe* (Princeton, NJ: Princeton University Press, 2009), 191, 192 (quotation), 193, 205–6; Service, *End of the Cold War*, 443, 448, 449, 471, 488.

103. The phrase belongs to Gorbachev's spokesman, Andrei Grachev, after the August 1991 coup attempt. Quoted in Lévesque, *Enigma of 1989*, 20.

104. See Valerie Bunce, "Domestic Reform and International Change: The Gorbachev Reforms in Historical Perspective," *International Organization* 47, no. 1 (1993): 131–35; Larson and Shevchenko, "Shortcut to Greatness."

105. Gennadii Zoteev, "The View from Gosplan: Growth to the Year 2000," in Ellman and Kontorovich, *Destruction of the Soviet Economic System: An Insider's History*, 90–92. See also V. I. Vorotnikov, *A bylo eto tak: Iz dnevnika chlena politbyuro Tsk KPSS* [*This Is How It Was: From the Diary of a Member of the Politburo of the CC of the CPSU*] (Moscow: Soviet Veteranov Knigoizdania, 1995), 66–67. For discussion of the "heroic" ethos of the Leninist party and its influence on economic policy, see Kenneth Jowitt, "The Leninist Phenomenon" and "Neotraditionalism," in *New World Disorder: The Leninist Extinction* (Berkeley: University of California Press, 1992), 1–49, 128–34.

106. Brown, *Seven Years*, 12; Paul Gregory and Kate Zhou, "How China Won and Russia Lost," *Policy Review* (December 2009–January 2010): 37. On the use of incentives in China for the party/state bureaucracy, see Barry Naughton, *Growing Out of the Plan: Chinese Economic Reform, 1978–1993* (Cambridge: Cambridge University Press, 1995). For an overview see Alexei Shevchenko, "Bringing the Party Back In: The CCP and the Trajectory of Market Transition in China," *Communist and Post-Communist Studies* 37, no. 2 (2004): 161–85.

107. Quoted in Vogel, *Deng*, 423.

108. Chernyaev, *Shest' Let s Gorbachevym*, 356.

109. Valentin M. Falin, *Bez skidok na obstoyatel'stva: Politicheskie vospominaniya* [*Not Blaming the Circumstances. Political Memoirs*] (Russian translation of *Politische Erinnnerungen* published in Germany in 1993) (Moscow: Respublika: Sovremennik, 1999), 409, 437–38; Marshall Goldman, *What Went Wrong with Perestroika* (New York: Norton, 1991), 143; Stephen Kotkin, *Armageddon Averted: The Soviet Collapse, 1970–2000* (New York: Oxford University Press, 2000), 62–67; Nolan, *China's Rise, Russia's Fall*, 236–37, 252.

110. Quoted in Arkady Ostrovsky, *The Invention of Russia: From Gorbachev's Freedom to Putin's War* (New York: Viking, 2015), 77.

111. Yuri Slezkine, "USSR as Communal Apartment, or How a Socialist State Promoted Ethnic Particularism," *Slavic Review* 3, no. 2 (1994): 414–52; Valerie Bunce, *Subversive Institutions: The Design and Destruction of Socialism and the State* (Cambridge: Cambridge University Press, 1999); Mark R. Beissinger, *Nationalist Mobilization and Collapse of the Soviet State* (Cambridge: Cambridge University Press, 2002).

112. Michael Beschloss and Strobe Talbott, *At the Highest Levels: The Inside Story of the End of the Cold War* (Boston: Little, Brown 1993), 96.

113. Juan Linz and Alfred Stepan, *Problems of Democratic Transition and Consolidation* (Baltimore, MD: John Hopkins University Press, 1996); Steven L. Solnick, "The Breakdown of Hierarchies in the Soviet Union and China," *World Politics* 48, no. 2 (1996): 209–38; Christopher Marsh, *Unparalleled Reforms: China's Rise, Russia's Fall, and the Interdependence of Transition* (Lanham, MD: Lexington Books, 2004), 59–61.

114. Marsh, *Unparalleled Reforms*, 129; Gilbert Rozman, "Chinese Studies in Russia and Their Impact, 1985–1992," *Asian Research Trends*, no. 4 (1994): 144;

Radchenko, *Unwanted Visionaries*, 177, 307. On Soviet reformers' lack of interest in the Chinese experience see Oleg Troyanovsky, *Cherez gody i rasstoyania: Istoriya odnoi sem'i* [*Through Years and Distances. History of One Family*] (Moscow: Vagrius, 1997), 363.

115. Alexandr Yakovlev, *Muki prochtenya bytiya* [*The Torments of Reading Life*] (Moscow: Novosti, 1991), 41; Jerry Hough, *Democratization and Revolution in the USSR, 1985–1991* (Washington, DC: Brookings Institution, 1997), 136–37; Alexander Lukin, *The Bear Watches the Dragon: Russia's Perceptions of China and the Evolution of Russian-Chinese Relations Since the Eighteenth Century* (Armonk, NY: M.E. Sharpe, 2003), 147; Oleg Troyanovsky, *Cherez gody i rasstoyania*, 346; Marshall I. Goldman, *Gorbachev's Challenge: Economic Reform in the Age of High Technology* (New York: W.W. Norton, 1987), 196–98; Marsh, *Unparalleled Reforms*, 132–33. Experts who favored learning from Chinese reforms included economist Oleg Bogomolov, Tatiana Zaslavskaya, Abel Aganbegyan, Georgy Arbatov (head of the influential Institute of the United States and Canada), Oleg Troyanovsky (Gorbachev's ambassador to China), and Fedor Burlatsky.

116. Radchenko, *Unwanted Visionaries*, 179 (quote), 180, 305; Troyanovsky, *Cherez gody i rasstoyania*, 295; Nolan, *China's Rise, Russia's Fall*, 244.

117. Marsh, *Unparalleled Reforms*, 129–34; Nolan, *China's Rise, Russia's Fall*, 232, 235; Radchenko, *Unwanted Visionaries*, 179–80.

118. Goldman, *What Went Wrong with Perestroika*, 61; Rozman, "Chinese Studies in Russia," 144; Evgeny Bazhanov, "Konets "Kitaiskogo Sindroma" [The End of the "China Syndrome"], *Novoe Vremya* no. 19 (1990), 5–6, quoted in Rozman, "Chinese Studies in Russia," 147.

119. Service, *The End of the Cold War*, 385, 389; Radchenko, *Unwanted Visionaries*, 178.

120. Grachev, *Gorbachev's Gamble*, 74; A. Chernyaev, A. Veber, V. Medvedev eds., *V Politburo TsK KPSS: Po zapisyam Anatoliya Chernyaeva, Vadima Medvedeva, Georgiya Shakhnazarova (1985–1991)* [*Inside the Politburo of the CPSU CC: According to Notes of Anatoly Chernyaev, Vadim Medvedev, Georgy Shakhnazarov (1985–1991)*] (Moscow: Al'pina Biznes Buks, 2006), 632, English translation in Grachev, *Gorbachev's Gamble*, 233.

121. Marsh, *Unparalleled Reforms*, 133; Stephen F. Cohen, *Fates and Lost Alternatives: From Stalinism to the New Cold War* (New York: Columbia University Press, 2009), 131 (quote); Radchenko, *Unwanted Visionaries*, 179; Service, *End of the Cold War*, 388–89.

122. Radchenko, *Unwanted Visionaries*, 163.

123. Chen, "China and the Bandung Conference," 149.

124. Zubok, *Failed Empire*, 322.

125. Zubok, *Failed Empire*, 285–86, 296, 298; Brown, *Seven Years*, 285–94; Kissinger, *On China*, 349–55; Vogel, *Deng*, 288, 290.

CHAPTER 5. STATUS AND IDENTITY AFTER THE COLD WAR

1. Michael D. Swaine, "Xi Jinping's Address to the Central Conference on Work Relating to Foreign Affairs: Assessing and Advancing Major-Power Diplo-

macy with Chinese Characteristics," *China Leadership Monitor*, no. 46, Winter 2015, 5; Jane Perlez, "Leader Asserts China's Growing Importance on Global Stage," *New York Times*, December 1, 2014; David Bandurski, February 23, 2010, "How Should We Read China's 'Discourse of Greatness,'" China Media Project, http://chinamediaproject.org/2010/02/23/reading-the-political-climate-in-chinas -discourse-of-greatness; Bill Hayton, *The South China Sea: The Struggle for Power in Asia* (New Haven, CT: Yale University Press, 2014), 179.

2. "Russia and China: An Uneasy Friendship," *Economist*, May 9, 2015, 37; Neil MacFarquhar, "In Talks with Merkel, Putin Calls for Improving Relations with Europe," *New York Times*, May 11, 2015; Kathrin Hille, Alex Barker, and Henry Foy, "Western Leaders Shun Moscow Victory Day Celebrations," *Financial Times*, May 9/10, 2015; "Putin Confesses He Expected Radical Upturn in Relations with West after Fall of the Communist Regime," *Interfax*, April 26, 2015, Russia Beyond the Headlines, http://rbth.com/news/2015/04/26/putin_confesses_he_expected_radi cal_upturn_in_relations_with_west_after_45553.html; "TV marks 15 years of Putin's leadership with dedicated documentary—transcript," Rossiya 1 TV, April 26, 2015, *Johnson's Russia List*, 2015-#87, May 1, 2015.

3. Steven Rosefielde and Stefan Hedlund, *Russia since 1980: Wrestling with Westernization* (Cambridge: Cambridge University Press, 2009), 221; William C. Wohlforth, "The Stability of a Unipolar World," *International Security* 24, no. 1 (Summer 1999): 5–41; John J. Mearsheimer, *The Tragedy of Great Power Politics* (New York: W.W. Norton, 2001), 373–81, 400–402.

4. Alastair Iain Johnston, *Social States: China in International Institutions, 1980–2000* (Princeton, NJ: Princeton University Press, 2008); Ted Hopf, *Reconstructing the Cold War: The Early Years, 1945–1958* (New York: Oxford University Press, 2012), 7; Anne L. Clunan, *The Social Construction of Russia's Resurgence: Aspirations, Identity, and Security Interests* (Baltimore, MD: Johns Hopkins University Press, 2009); Ted Hopf, *Social Construction of International Politics: Identities and Foreign Policies, Moscow, 1955 and 1999* (Ithaca, NY: Cornell University Press, 2002); Andrei P. Tsygankov, "Contested Identity and Foreign Policy: Interpreting Russia's International Choices," *International Studies Perspectives* 15 (2014): 19–35.

5. Maurice Meisner, *Mao's China and After: A History of the People's Republic*, 3rd ed. (New York: Free Press, 1999), 492–93; Harry Harding, *A Fragile Relationship: The United States and China since 1972* (Washington, DC: Brookings Institution Press, 1992), 248–49; James Mann, *About Face: A History of America's Curious Relationship with China, from Nixon to Clinton* (New York: Vintage, 1998), 195–98, 205, 227.

6. H. Lyman Miller and Liu Xiaohong, "The Foreign Policy Outlook of China's 'Third Generation' Elite," in *The Making of Chinese Foreign and Security Policy in the Era of Reform*, ed. David M. Lampton (Stanford, CA: Stanford University Press, 2001), 140–41; John W. Garver, *Face Off: China, the United States, and Taiwan's Democratization* (Seattle: University of Washington Press, 1997), 4–5, 17–23; Wang Jisi, "China's Changing Role in Asia," in *The Rise of China and a Changing East Asia Order*, ed. Kokobun Roysei and Wang Jisi (Tokyo: Japan Center for International Exchange, 2004), 14.

7. Mann, *About Face*, 262; Nicholas D. Kristof, "Suddenly, China Looks Smaller in the World," *New York Times*, March 27, 1990.

8. *South China Morning Post*, March 12, 1992; "Political Report Delivered by General Secretary Jiang Zemin on Behalf of the 13th CCP CC to the 14th CCP National Congress in Beijing," Beijing Central Television Program One, October 12, 1992 in *FBIS-CHI-92-198-S30*; Joseph Fewsmith, *China since Tiananmen* (Cambridge: Cambridge University Press, 2008), 38, 72.

9. World Bank, Overview, http://www.worldbank.org/en/country/china/over view; Peter Harrold and Rajiv Lall, *China: Reform and Development in 1992–93*, World Bank Discussion Papers, no. 215 (Washington, DC: International Bank for Reconstruction and Development/The World Bank, 1993).

10. Andrew Nathan, "China's Resilient Authoritarianism," *Journal of Democracy* 14, no. 1 (January 2003): 6–17. See also Barry J. Naughton and Dali L. Yang eds., *Holding China Together: Diversity and National Integration in the Post-Deng Era* (Cambridge University Press, 2004); Kjeld Erik Brodsgaard and Zhen Yongnian, eds., *The Chinese Communist Party in Reform* (London: Routledge, 2006).

11. Avery Goldstein, *Rising to the Challenge: China's Grand Strategy and International Security* (Stanford, CA: Stanford University Press, 2005), 46–47; Gilbert Rozman, "China's Quest for Great Power Identity," *Orbis* (Summer 1999): 389; Yong Deng, "Hegemon on the Offensive: Chinese Perspectives on U.S. Global Strategy," *Political Science Quarterly* 116, no. 3 (2002): 345–46.

12. Michael Leifer, "Chinese Economic Reform and Security Policy: The South China Sea Connection," *Survival* 37, no. 2 (Summer 1995): 44–59; Robert S. Ross, "The 1995–96 Taiwan Strait Confrontation: Coercion, Credibility, and the Use of Force," *International Security* 25, no. 2 (Fall 2000): 87–123; Michael D. Swaine, "Chinese Decision-making Regarding Taiwan, 1979–2000," in Lampton, *Making of Chinese Foreign and Security Policy*, 319–24; Susan L. Shirk, *China: Fragile Superpower* (New York: Oxford University Press, 2007), 188–89; Li Peng in *Financial Times*, June 11, 1996, quoted in Ross, "The 1995–96 Taiwan Strait Confrontation," 118.

13. Allen S. Whiting, "ASEAN Eyes China: The Security Dimension," *Asian Survey* 37, no. 4 (1997): 319; Ross, "The 1995–96 Taiwan Strait Confrontation," 109–10; Michael Yahuda, "The Limits of Economic Interdependence: Sino-Japanese Relations," in *New Directions in the Study of China's Foreign Policy*, ed. Alastair Iain Johnston and Robert S. Ross (Stanford, CA: Stanford University Press, 2006), 167; Goldstein, *Rising to the Challenge*, 47–48, 116–17.

14. Jeffrey Mankoff, *Russian Foreign Policy: The Return of Great Power Politics* (Lanham, MD: Rowman and Littlefield, 2009), 21–22; Angela Stent, *The Limits of Partnership: U.S.-Russian Relations in the Twenty-First Century* (Princeton, NJ: Princeton University Press, 2014), xi; Bobo Lo, *Russia and the New World Disorder* (London: Chatham House; Washington, DC: Brookings, 2015), 19.

15. Hopf, *Social Construction of International Politics*; Dmitri Trenin, *The End of Eurasia: Russia on the Border between Geopolitics and Globalization* (Washington, DC: Carnegie Endowment for International Peace, 2002).

16. Margot Light, "Foreign Policy Thinking," in *Internal Factors in Russian Foreign Policy*, ed. Neil Malcolm, Alex Pravda, Roy Allison, and Margot Light (Lon-

don: Oxford University Press, 1996), 33–100; Bobo Lo, *Russian Foreign Policy in the Post-Soviet Era: Reality, Illusion, and Mythmaking* (Houndsmills, Basingstoke, Hampshire: Palgrave Macmillan, 2002), 40–65; Clunan, *Social Construction of Russia's Resurgence*, 54–60.

17. Lo, *Russia and the New World Disorder*, 98–99; Leon Aron, "The United States and Russia: Ideologies, Policies, and Relations," *Russian Outlook* (Washington, DC: American Enterprise Institute, Summer 2006), http://www.aei.org/publication/the-united-states-and-russia/.

18. See, for example, "After the Disintegration of the Soviet Union: Russia in the New World," Report of the Center of International Studies, Moscow State Institute of International Relations (Moscow: February 1992). On NATO membership as a long-term goal of Russian foreign policy, see *Diplomaticheskii Vestnik* (Moscow), no. 1, January 15, 1992, 13.

19. Angela E. Stent, "America and Russia: Paradoxes of Partnership," in *Russia's Engagement with the West: Transformation and Integration in the Twenty-First Century*, ed. Alexander J. Motyl, Blair A. Ruble, and Lilia Shevtsova (Armonk, NY: M.E. Sharpe, 2005), 265; Light, "Foreign Policy Thinking," 85; Dimitri K. Simes, "Losing Russia," *Foreign Affairs* 86, no. 6 (2007): 36–52; Mankoff, *Russian Foreign Policy*, 21–22.

20. Allen C. Lynch, "The Realism of Russia's Foreign Policy," *Europe-Asia Studies* 53, no. 1 (January 2001): 14–17; Andrei Kortunov, "The U.S. and Russia: A Virtual Partnership," *Comparative Strategy* 15, no. 4 (October–December 1996): 345; Andrew J. Pierre and Dmitri Trenin, "Developing NATO-Russian Relations," *Survival* 39, no. 1 (Spring 1997): 8–9.

21. Leon Aron, "The Foreign Policy Doctrine of Postcommunist Russia and Its Domestic Context," in *The New Russian Foreign Policy*, ed. Michael Mandelbaum (New York: Council of Foreign Relations, 1998), 33.

22. Fiona Hill and Clifford G. Gaddy, *Mr. Putin: Operative in the Kremlin* (Washington, DC: Brookings Institution Press, 2015), 297; Light, "Foreign Policy Thinking," 80; Stent, *Limits of Partnership*, 39; Samuel Charap and Timothy J. Colton, "Cold Peace," *Adelphi Series* 56, no. 460 (2016): 49.

23. Lynch, "Realism of Russia's Foreign Policy," 14–17; Strobe Talbott, *The Russia Hand: A Memoir of Presidential Diplomacy* (New York: Random House, 2002), 76; Kostikov's statement cited in *RFE/RL Daily Report*, April 11, 1994.

24. Peter Reddaway and Dmitri Glinski, *The Tragedy of Russia's Reforms: Market Bolshevism Against Democracy* (Washington, DC: United States Institute of Peace Press, 2001), 2 (quotation), 3; World Bank, *World Development Report, 2000–2001: Attacking Poverty* (New York, NY: Oxford University Press, 2001), 294–95.

25. Fareed Zakaria, *The Future of Freedom: Illiberal Democracy at Home and Abroad* (New York: W.W. Norton, 2003); S. Peregudov, N. Lapina, and I. Semenenko, *Gruppy interesov v rossiiskom gosudarstve [Interest Groups in the Russian State]* (Moscow: Editorial URSS, 1999); Vadim Radaev, *Formirovanie novykh rossiskikh rynkov: Transaktsionnye izderzhki, formy kontrolya, "delovaya etika"[Formation of New Russian Markets: Transactional Costs, Forms of Control, "Business Ethics"]* (Moscow, 1998).

26. Stent, *Limits of Partnership*, 25; Hill and Gaddy, *Mr. Putin*, 33, 36 (quotation).

27. Andrei P. Tsygankov, *Russia's Foreign Policy: Change and Continuity in National Identity* (Lanham, MD: Rowman and Littlefield, 2006), 83–84; Trenin, *End of Eurasia*, 273–75; A. Pushkov, "'The Primakov Doctrine' and a New European Order," *International Affairs* (Moscow) 44, no. 2 (April 1998): 12; A. Pushkov, "Russia and the New World Order," *International Affairs* (Moscow) 46, no. 6 (December 2000): 5–6; Lo, *Russian Foreign Policy*, 108.

28. Quoted in Aron, "Foreign Policy Doctrine," 29–30.

29. Talbott, *Russia Hand*, 237; Boris Yeltsin, *Midnight Diaries* (London: Weidenfeld and Nicolson, 2000), 131.

30. Hill and Gaddy, *Mr. Putin*, 30–31; Light, "Foreign Policy Thinking," 85; Stent, *Limits of Partnership*, 20, 25.

31. Lo, *Russian Foreign Policy*, 89–90, 107–8, 142; Richard Paddock, "Russia Shelves Rhetoric to Accept U.S. Food Aid," *Los Angeles Times*, December 24, 1998.

32. Bobo Lo, *Vladimir Putin and the Evolution of Russian Foreign Policy* (Oxford: Blackwell, 2003), 94–95; Vladimir Baranovsky, "Russia: A Part of Europe or Apart from Europe?," *International Affairs* 76, no. 3 (July 2000): 454–55. For Russian elites' reaction to Kosovo, see, for example, A. Torkunov, "International Relations in the Post-Kosovo Context," *International Affairs* (Moscow) 46, no. 1 (February 2000): 74–81.

33. Richard C. Paddock, "Primakov Does U-Turn over Atlantic, Heads Home," *Los Angeles Times*, March 24, 1999; Lukin quoted in Lo, *Russian Foreign Policy*, 55; Talbott, *Russia Hand*, 344.

34. Council on Foreign and Defense Policy, *Strategiya dlya Rosii: Povestka dnya dlya Presidenta-2000* [The Strategy for Russia: The Agenda for the President-2000] (Moscow: Vagrius, 2000), chap. 2.

35. Robert Legvold, "Introduction," in *Russian Foreign Policy in the Twenty-First Century and the Shadow of the Past*, ed. Legvold (New York: Columbia University Press, 2007), 16–17; Lawrence Freedman, "The New Great Power Politics," in *Russia and the West: The 21st Century Security Environment*, ed. Alexei G. Arbatov, Karl Kaiser, and Robert Legvold (Armonk, NY: M.E. Sharpe, 1999), 34; Jeffrey Tayler, "Russia Is Finished," *Atlantic Monthly*, May 2001, 52; J. L. Black, *Vladimir Putin and the New World Order: Looking East, Looking West?* (Lanham, MD: Rowman and Littlefield, 2004), 42–45.

36. Talbott, *Russia Hand*, 182–85; Simes, "Losing Russia."

37. Alexey K. Pushkov, "Missed Connections," *The National Interest* 89 (May/June 2007): 52–57; Simes, "Losing Russia," 36, 37; Lo, *Russia and the New World Disorder*, 20 (quotation).

38. "Foreign Policy Concept of the Russian Federation," *Nezavisimaya Gazeta*, July 11, 2000.

39. Richard Sakwa, "'New Cold War' or Twenty Years' Crisis? Russia and International Politics," *International Affairs* 84, no. 2 (2008): 243, 248–49.

40. On the challenges of resistance against a hegemonic power under unipolarity, see Randall L. Schweller and Xiaoyu Pu, "After Unipolarity: China's Visions

of International Order in an Era of U.S. Decline," *International Security* 36, no. 1 (Summer 2011): 44–46.

41. Robert Jervis, "Theories of War in an Era of Leading-Powers Peace," *American Political Science Review* 96, no. 1 (March 2002): 1–14; Steve Chan, *China, the U.S., and the Power-Transition Theory: A Critique* (London: Routledge, 2008); Schweller and Pu, "After Unipolarity," 65.

42. Yong Deng, "Hegemon on the Offensive: Chinese Perspectives on U.S. Global Strategy," *Political Science Quarterly* 116, no. 3 (Fall 2001): 346–47.

43. Goldstein, *Rising to the Challenge*, chap. 6; Zhang Yunling and Tang Shiping, "China's Regional Strategy," in *Power Shift: China and Asia's New Dynamics*, ed. David Shambaugh (Berkeley: University of California Press, 2005), 48–68; Pichamon Yeophantong, "Governing the World: China's Evolving Conceptions of Responsibility," *Chinese Journal of International Politics* 6 no. 4 (2013): 331.

44. John W. Garver, *China's Quest: The History of the Foreign Relations of the People's Republic of China* (Oxford: Oxford University Press, 2016), 548–50; Miller and Xiaohong, "Foreign Policy Outlook," 144; Bates Gill, *Rising Star: China's New Security Diplomacy* (Washington, DC: Brookings, 2007), 58–63; David Shambaugh, "China Engages Asia: Reshaping the Regional Order," *International Security* 29, no. 3 (Winter 2004/05): 69; Chen Jian, "China and the Bandung Conference: Changing Perceptions and Representations," in *Bandung Revisited: The Legacy of the 1955 Asian-African Conference for International Order*, ed. See Seng Tan and Amitav Acharya (Singapore: NUS Press 2008), 149–50.

45. Shambaugh, "China Engages Asia," 68–69; Goldstein, *Rising to the Challenge*, 119–21, 123–24; Rosemary Foot, "Chinese Strategies in a US-hegemonic Global Order: Accommodating and Hedging," *International Affairs* 82, no. 1 (2006): 85–86.

46. Gill, *Rising Star*, 37–41; Robert G. Sutter, *China's Rise in Asia: Promises and Perils* (Lanham, MD: Rowman and Littlefield, 2005), 82–83; Rosemary Foot, "Chinese Strategies," 88–89.

47. Michael D. Swaine and Alastair Iain Johnston, "China and Arms Control Institutions," in *China Joins the World: Progress and Prospects*, ed. Elizabeth Economy and Michel Oksenberg (New York: Council on Foreign Relations Press, 1999), 100–10; Bates Gill, "Two Steps Forward, One Step Back: The Dynamics of Chinese Nonproliferation and Arms Control," in Lampton, *Making of Chinese Foreign and Security Policy*, 263–64.

48. Zhang and Tang, "China's Regional Strategy," 60, Note 7; Shirk, *China*, 118–20; Alice D. Ba, "China and ASEAN: Renavigating Relations for a 21st-Century Asia," *Asian Survey* 43, no. 4 (July/August 2003): 638–43.

49. Edward S. Steinfeld, *Playing Our Game: Why China's Economic Rise Doesn't Threaten the West* (New York: Oxford University Press, 2010), 55–56, 61 (quotation). On the East Asian developmental model, see Seung-Wook Baek, "Does China Follow 'the East Asian Developmental Model'?," *Journal of Contemporary Asia* 35, no. 4 (2005): 485–98.

50. Edward Steinfeld, "The Asian Financial Crisis: Beijing's Year of Reckoning," *Washington Quarterly* 21, no. 3 (1998): 37–51; Richard Baum and Alexei Shevchenko, "China and the Forces of Globalization," in *The New Great Power*

Coalition: Toward a World Concert of Nations, ed. Richard Rosecrance (Lanham, MD: Rowman and Littlefield, 2001), 73–77; Fewsmith, *China after Tiananmen*, 211.

51. Yong Deng, *China's Struggle for Status: The Realignment of International Relations* (Cambridge: Cambridge University Press, 2008), 78–79, 81; Robert S. Ross, "Engagement in US China Policy," in Johnston and Ross, *Engaging China*, 190.

52. Rosemary Foot, "Chinese Power and the Idea of a Responsible State," *China Journal*, no. 45 (January 2001): 16–17; Rosemary Foot, *Rights beyond Borders: The Global Community and the Struggle over Human Rights in China* (New York: Oxford University Press, 2000), 211–12, 217–21, 224; Michael D. Swaine, *America's Challenge: Engaging a Rising China in the Twenty-First Century* (Washington, DC: Carnegie Endowment, 2011), 293–94; Deng, *China's Struggle for Status*, 90–92.

53. Zheng Bijian, "China's 'Peaceful Rise' to Great-Power Status," *Foreign Affairs* 84, no. 5 (September/October 2005): 18–24; Shirk, *China*, 108–9; Bonnie S. Glaser and Evan S. Medeiros, "The Changing Ecology of Foreign Policy-Making in China: The Ascension and the Demise of the Theory of 'Peaceful Rise,'" *The China Quarterly* 190 (June 2007): 291–310.

54. Glaser and Medeiros, "Changing Ecology," 302–3; Robert L. Suettinger, "The Rise and Descent of 'Peaceful Rise,'" *China Leadership Monitor*, no. 12 (Fall 2004): 6–7, http://media.hoover.org/sites/default/files/documents/clm12_rs.pdf; Andrew J. Nathan and Andrew Scobell, *China's Search for Security* (New York: Columbia University Press, 2012), 234–37; Richard Baum, "The Taiwan-China Tangle: Divided Sovereignty in the Age of Globalization," in *No More States? Globalization, National Self-determination, and Terrorism*, ed. Richard N. Rosecrance and Arthur A. Stein (Lanham, MD: Rowman and Littlefield, 2006), 247–76; Bates Gill and Yanzhong Huang, "Sources and Limits of Chinese 'Soft Power,'" *Survival* 48, no. 2 (2006): 26.

55. "Resisting China's Charm Offensive," *Economist*, November 8, 2008, 53–54; Edward Wong, "China and Taiwan Sign Pacts on Transportation and Food," *New York Times*, November 5, 2008; "Hands across the Water," *Economist*, November 7, 2015, 33–34.

56. Lai-Ha Chan, Pak K. Lee, and Gerald Chan, "Rethinking Global Governance: A China Model in the Making?," *Contemporary Politics* 14, no. 1 (March 2008): 7–8; Michael D. Swaine, *America's Challenge: Engaging a Rising China in the Twenty-First Century* (Washington, DC: Carnegie Endowment, 2011), 192–93; John Williamson, "What Washington Means by Policy Reform," in *Latin American Adjustment: How Much Has Happened?* (Washington, DC: Institute for International Economics, 1990); Joshua Cooper Ramo, *The Beijing Consensus* (London: Foreign Policy Centre, 2004); Stefan Halper, *The Beijing Consensus: How China's Authoritarian Model Will Dominate the Twenty-First Century* (New York: Basic Books, 2010), 121–27.

57. Shaun Breslin, "The 'China Model' and the Global Crisis: From Friedrich List to a Chinese Model of Governance?," *International Affairs* 87, no. 6 (2011): 1323–43; Sebastian Heilmann, "Maximum Tinkering Under Uncertainty: Unorth-

odox Lessons from China," *Modern China* 35, no. 4 (2009): 450–62; Suisheng Zhao, "The China Model: Can It Replace the Western Model of Modernization?," *Journal of Contemporary China* 19, no. 65 (2010): 419–36.

58. "Hu Calls for Enhancing 'Soft Power' of Chinese Culture," Xinhua News Agency, October 15, 2007, http://www.china.org.cn/english/congress/228142.htm; Joshua Kurlantzick, *Charm Offensive: How China's Soft Power Is Transforming the World* (New Haven, CT: Yale University Press, 2007); Philip Saunders, *China's Global Activism: Strategy, Drivers, and Tools* (Washington, DC: National Defense University Press, 2006).

59. Li Mingjiang, "China Debates Soft Power," *Chinese Journal of International Politics* 2, no. 2 (2008): 292, 299–300; Bonnie S. Glaser and Melissa E. Murphy, "Soft Power with Chinese Characteristics," in *Chinese Soft Power and Its Implications for the United States: Competition and Cooperation in the Developing World*, ed. Carola McGiffert (Washington, DC: Center for Strategic and International Studies, 2009), 13–14.

60. Hu Jintao, "Build Towards a Harmonious World of Lasting Peace and Common Prosperity," United Nations Summit, September 15, 2005, http://www.un.org/webcast/summit2005/statements15/china050915eng.pdf; William A. Callahan, *China Dreams: 20 Visions of the Future* (New York: Oxford University Press, 2013), 44; Pichamon Yeophantong, "Governing the World: China's Evolving Conceptions of Responsibility," *Chinese Journal of International Politics* 6, no. 4 (2013): 357; David Shambaugh, *China Goes Global: The Partial Power* (New York: Oxford University Press, 2013), 25.

61. Mann, *About Face*, 342–43, 366–67.

62. David M. Finkelstein, "China Reconsiders Its National Security: 'The Great Peace and Development Debate of 1999'" (Alexandria, VA: CNA, 2000); Goldstein, *Rising to the Challenge*, 152. China's grievances included US sponsorship of a resolution critical of China's human rights record at the UN Commission on Human Rights, the Clinton administration's rejection of Chinese Premier Zhu Rongji's impressive list of painful (and secret) Chinese concessions on entry into the World Trade Organization, followed by their leaking to the US media, and the US intervention in Kosovo. See David M. Lampton, *Same Bed, Different Dreams: Managing U.S.-China Relations, 1989–2000* (Berkeley: University of California Press, 2001), 55–62.

63. David M. Lampton and Richard Daniel Ewing, "The U.S.-China Relationship Facing International Security Crises: Three Case Studies in Post-9/11 Bilateral Relations" (Washington, DC: Nixon Center, 2003), 1–18; Jiang Zemin and Bush Start Talks in a Cordial Manner," China Central Television, October 19, 2001, http://www.cctv.com/special/171/1/18507.html; Anne Wu, "What China Whispers to North Korea," *Washington Quarterly* 28, no. 2 (Spring 2005): 35–48.

64. Robert B. Zoellick, "Whither China: From Membership to Responsibility?" Remarks to the National Committee on U.S.-China Relations, New York City, September 21, 2005, *NBR Analysis* 16 no. 4 (December 2005), http://www.nbr.org/publications/nbranalysis/pdf/vol16no4.pdf.

65. Glenn Kessler, "U.S., China Agree to Regular Talks: Senior-Level Meetings to Focus on Politics, Security, Possibly Economics," *Washington Post*, April 8, 2005;

Thomas J. Christensen, "Shaping the Choices of a Rising China: Recent Lessons for the Obama Administration," *Washington Quarterly* 32, no. 3 (Summer 2009): 89–104. In July 2009, the Obama administration combined the two mechanisms into the Strategic and Economic Dialogue. Bonnie S. Glaser, "The Diplomatic Relationship: Substance and Process," in *Tangled Titans: The United States and China*, ed. David Shambaugh (Lanham, MD: Rowman and Littlefield, 2013), 152.

66. Shirk, *China*, 140–49, 153–55, 164–67, 173–74.

67. Lo, *Putin and Russian Foreign Policy*, 65–68, 131; Stephen E. Hanson, "Russia: Strategic Partner or Evil Empire?," in *Strategic Asia 2004–05: Confronting Terrorism in the Pursuit of Power*, ed. Ashley J. Tellis and Michael Wills (Seattle, WA: National Bureau of Asian Research, 2004), 163–98; Mankoff, *Russian Foreign Policy*, 23–24.

68. Vladimir Putin, "Russia at the Turn of the Millennium," in Richard Sakwa, *Putin: Russia's Choice* (London: Routledge, 2004), 257, 262.

69. Angela E. Stent, "Restoration and Revolution in Putin's Foreign Policy," *Europe-Asia Studies* 60, no. 6 (August 2008): 1091.

70. Lo, *Putin and Russian Foreign Policy*, 124–25, 128–29; Russian President's Statement, September 24, 2001, http://eng.kremlin.ru/text/speeches/2001/09/24/0002_type82912_138534.shtml; Transcript of the meeting of President Putin with Moscow Bureau Chiefs of Leading U.S. Media, November 10, 2001, http://en.kremlin.ru/events/president/transcripts/21394.

71. Reportedly, Putin spent six hours trying to persuade his team that Russia should help the United States and then, against their advice, went on to make a TV statement announcing Russia's determination to contribute in the war on terror. Lo, *Putin and Russian Foreign Policy*, 117–18. According to Grigory Yavlinsky, of twenty-one members of Russia's political elite who were summoned to a secret meeting at the Kremlin, only two favored supporting the United States. See "Domestic and Foreign Policy Challenges in Russia," Carnegie Endowment for International Peace, January 31, 2002, http://eng.yabloko.ru/People/YAVL/310102.html.

72. Dmitri Trenin, "Introduction: The Grand Redesign," in *Ambivalent Neighbors: The EU, NATO, and the Price of Membership*, ed. Anatol Lieven and Dmitri Trenin (Washington, DC: Carnegie Endowment for International Peace, 2003), 2; Lo, *Putin and Russian Foreign Policy*, 75, 125; David E. Sanger, "NATO Gives Russia a Formal Welcome," *New York Times*, May 29, 2002.

73. Interviews with Igor Ivanov, Dmitri Trenin, quoted in Stent, *Limits of Partnership*, 69.

74. Vladimir Putin, Speech in the Bundestag of the Federal Republic of Germany, Berlin, September 25, 2001, http://en.kremlin.ru/events/president/transcripts/21340; Lo, *Putin and Russian Foreign Policy*, 79; Jeffrey Mankoff, "Russia and the West: Taking the Longer View," *Washington Quarterly* 30, no. 2 (Spring 2007), 127, 129.

75. Peter Baker and Susan Glasser, *Kremlin Rising: Vladimir Putin's Russia and the End of the Revolution* (New York: Scribner, 2005), 135; Steven Lee Myers, *The New Tsar: The Rise and Reign of Vladimir Putin* (New York: Alfred A. Knopf, 2015), 212.

76. John Daniszewski, "Putin Working to Make Russia 'Equal Partner' in World Market," *Los Angeles Times*, June 25, 2002; BBC Breakfast with Frost, March 5, 2000, http://news.bbc.co.uk/hi/english/static/audio_video/programmes/breakfast _with_frost/transcripts/putin5.mar.txt.

77. Hill and Gaddy, *Mr. Putin*, 326–27; Lo, *Russia and the New World Disorder*, 49.

78. Michael McFaul, "The Russian Graduate," *Washington Post*, May 10, 2002; Lo, *Axis of Convenience*, 94; Hill and Gaddy, *Mr. Putin*, 302; Richard Balmforth, "Image at Home Pushes Putin to a New Standoff with U.S.," *Reuters*, April 30, 2003; Stent, *Limits of Partnership*, 91–92, 94.

79. "Russia Untroubled by G7 Snub," DW.com, June 4, 2014, http://www.dw .com/en/russia-untroubled-by-g7-snub/a-17680660.

80. Stent, *Limits of Partnership*, 97–98; Lo, *Russia's New World Disorder*, 89–90; Alexey K. Pushkov, "Missed Connections," *The National Interest* 89 (May–June 2007), 52–53; William H. Hill, *Russia, the Near Abroad, and the West: Lessons from the Moldova-Transdniestria Conflict* (Washington, DC: Woodrow Wilson Center Press; Baltimore, MD: Johns Hopkins University Press, 2012), xi, xii (quote), 6–7, 39–40, 45–46. Hill was head of the OSCE mission to Moldova from 2003–2006 and participated in negotiations over a settlement with the OSCE, Ukraine, Russia, Transdniestria, and Moldova.

81. Stent, *Limits of Partnership*, 115, 123.

82. Vice President's Remarks at the 2006 Vilnius Conference, May 4, 2006, http://georgewbush-whitehouse.archives.gov/news/releases/2006/05/20060504-1 .html; Peter Baker, *Days of Fire: Bush and Cheney in the White House* (New York: Doubleday, 2013), 470; Gail W. Lapidus, "Between Assertiveness and Insecurity: Russian Elite Attitudes and the Russia-Georgia Crisis," *Post-Soviet Affairs* 23, no. 2 (April–June 2007): 150; Vladislav Surkov, "Sovereignty—Political Synonym of Competitiveness, February 7, 2006 address to the students of the United Russia Party Study Center," *Moskovskie Novosti* no. 7 (March 3, 2006): 10–11.

83. Hill and Gaddy, *Mr. Putin*, 317; Jeffrey Mankoff, *Russian Foreign Policy: The Return of Great Power Politics*, 2nd ed. (Lanham, MD: Rowman and Littlefield, 2012), 43; Stent, *Limits of Partnership*, 136, 143; Sergei Ivanov, "Triada natsional'nykh tsennostei," [The Triad of National Values] *Izvestiya*, July 14, 2006, quoted in Andrei P. Tsygankov, "Russia's International Assertiveness: What Does It Mean for the West?," *Problems of Post-Communism* 55, no. 2 (2008): 49; Interfax, "Senior Russian MP Warns UK against Expelling Russian Diplomats," July 27, 2007, and *Argumenty i Fakty*, "We Have Overcome Our Inferiority Complex," July 11 2007, both quoted in Marshall I. Goldman, "The New Imperial Russia," *Democratizatsiya* 16, no. 1 (2008): 15.

84. C. J. Chivers, "Russians Plant Flag on the Arctic Seabed," *New York Times*, August 3, 2007; Andrew E. Kramer, "Recalling Cold War, Russia Resumes Long-Range Sorties," *New York Times*, August 18, 2007; Adrian Blomfield, "Russia Bombers Test-fire Missiles; Military Exercises to Annoy the West, Impress at Home," *Daily Telegraph*, January 23, 2008; C. J. Chivers, "Russia Parades Its Military in an Echo of Soviet Days," *New York Times*, May 10, 2008; Mark Mazzetti

and Thom Shanker, "Russian Subs Patrolling Off East Coast of the U.S.," *New York Times*, August 4, 2009; Stent, "Restoration and Revolution," 1103.

85. Quoted in Shevtsova, *Russia—Lost in Transition*, 233; Vladimir Putin, Address to the Federal Assembly of the Russian Federation, May 10, 2006, http://en.kremlin.ru/events/president/transcripts/23577; *Ria Novosti*, June 27, 2006, Johnson's Russia List (JRL), 2006-#146; Vladimir Putin, Speech and the Following Discussion at the Munich Conference on Security Policy, February 10, 2007, http://en.kremlin.ru/events/president/transcripts/24034.

86. Evan Osnos, David Remnick, and Joshua Yaffa, "Active Measures: Trump, Putin, and Russia's Grand Strategy," *New Yorker*, March 6, 2017, 46.

87. James Sherr, "The Implications of the Russia-Georgia War for European Security," in *The Guns of August 2008: Russia's War in Georgia*, ed. Svante E. Cornell and S. Frederick Starr (Armonk, NY: M.E. Sharpe, 2009), 204–7; Stent, *Limits of Partnership*, 108–9, 164–65, 167–68; Helene Cooper, C. J. Chivers, and Clifford J. Levy, "How a Spat Became a Showdown," *New York Times*, August 18, 2008; Dmitri Trenin, *Post-Imperium: A Eurasian Story* (Washington, DC: Carnegie Endowment, 2011), 28; Baker, *Days of Fire*, 585–87.

88. President Dmitri Medvedev Interview Given to Television Channel One Rossiya, NTV, August 31, 2008, http://en.kremlin.ru/events/president/transcripts/48301; Eugene Rumer and Angela Stent, "Russia and the West," *Survival* 51, no. 2 (April 2009): 94; Hans Mouritzen and Anders Wivel, *Explaining Foreign Policy: International Diplomacy and the Russo-Georgian War* (Boulder, CO: Lynne Rienner, 2012), 84, 86–88.

89. Leon Aron, "The Georgia Watershed," *Russian Outlook* (Washington, DC: American Enterprise Institute, November 2008), https://www.aei.org/publication/the-georgia-watershed/; Andrew E. Kramer, "Russia Stock Market Fall Is Said to Imperil Oil Boom," *New York Times*, September 13, 2008; Andrew E. Kramer, "Russia Halts Stock Trading as Indexes Decline," *New York Times*, September 18, 2008; Fyodor Lukyanov, "The Russian-Georgian War as a Turning Point," November 24, 2011, *Russia in Global Affairs*, http://eng.globalaffairs.ru/redcol/The-Russian-Georgian-war-as-a-turning-point-15381.

90. The term "dizzy with success" is taken from the title of a famous article by Stalin blaming the failure of forced collectivization and famine on overzealous cadres. See Robert C. Tucker, *Stalin in Power: The Revolution from Above, 1928–1941* (New York: W.W. Norton, 1990), 184–86. Kenneth Lieberthal and Wang Jisi, *Addressing U.S.-China Strategic Distrust*, John L. Thornton China Center Monograph Series no. 4 (Washington, DC: Brookings Institution, 2012), vii; Gilbert Rozman, *The Sino-Russian Challenge to the World Order: National Identities, Bilateral Relations, and East versus West in the 2010s* (Washington, DC: Woodrow Wilson Center Press; Stanford, CA: Stanford University Press, 2014), 148.

91. Lieberthal and Wang, *Addressing U.S.-China Strategic Mistrust*, viii (quotation), 9–10, 19, https://www.brookings.edu/wp-content/uploads/2016/06/0330_china_lieberthal.pdf; Michael D. Swaine, "Perceptions of an Assertive China," *China Leadership Monitor*, no. 32, Spring 2010, https://www.hoover.org/research/perceptions-assertive-china; Suisheng Zhao, "Foreign Policy Implications of Chinese Nationalism Revisited: The Strident Turn," *Journal of Contemporary China* 22, no. 82 (2013): 535–53.

92. Garver, *China Quest*, 660–61; Zbigniew Brzezinski, "The Group of Two that Could Change the World," *Financial Times*, January 13, 2009; "China and the West: A Time for Muscle-flexing," *Economist*, March 21, 2009, 27; Elizabeth C. Economy and Adam Segal, "The G-2 Mirage: Why the United States and China Are Not Ready to Upgrade Ties," *Foreign Affairs* 88, no. 3 (2009): 14–23; Geoff Dyer, "Clinton Treads Softly on China Visit," *Financial Times*, February 23, 2009.

93. "Time for Muscle-flexing," 27; Geoff Dyer, "Wen Calls on US to Offer Fiscal Guarantees," *Financial Times*, March 14, 2009; Geoff Dyer, "Hesitating to Take on Global Leadership," *Financial Times*, April 2, 2009; David Pilling, "China Is Just Sabre-rattling over the Dollar," *Financial Times*, April 2, 2009.

94. Demetri Sevastopulo, "White House Protests to Beijing over Naval Incidents," *Financial Times*, March 10, 2009; Michael Yahuda, "China's New Assertiveness in the South China Sea," *Journal of Contemporary China* 22, no. 81 (2013): 446–59; Leszek Buszynski, "The South China Sea: Oil, Maritime Claims, and U.S.-China Strategic Rivalry," *Washington Quarterly* 35, no. 2 (2012): 140; Hayton, *South China Sea*, 252.

95. Ian Storey, "China's Bilateral and Multilateral Diplomacy in the South China Sea," in *Cooperation from Strength: The United States, China, and the South China Sea*, ed. Patrick M. Cronin (Center for a New American Security, January 2012). https://s3.amazonaws.com/files.cnas.org/documents/CNAS_CooperationFrom Strength_Cronin_1.pdf, 54; Hayton, *South China Sea*, 59, 117, 249–52.

96. Edward Luce and Geoff Dyer, "President Is Silenced by Firewall of China," *Financial Times*, November 17, 2009; Helene Cooper, "China Holds Firm on Major Issues in Obama's Visit," *New York Times*, November 17, 2009.

97. Jeffrey A. Bader, *Obama and China's Rise: An Insider's Account of America's Asia Strategy* (Washington, DC: Brookings, 2012), 63–66; Thomas J. Christensen, *The China Challenge: Shaping the Choices of a Rising Power* (New York: W.W. Norton, 2015), 281–82.

98. Geoff Dyer and Daniel Dombey, "Shadow Cast over Hopes for 'G2,'" *Financial Times*, January 15, 2010; Geoff Dyer, "China Flexes Its Diplomatic Muscle," *Financial Times*, February 1, 2010; Christensen, *China Challenge*, 254–55.

99. Martin S. Indyk, Kenneth G. Lieberthal, and Michael E. O'Hanlon, *Bending History: Barack Obama's Foreign Policy* (Washington, DC: Brookings, 2012), 48–49; Bader, *Obama and China's Rise*, 105–6.

100. Martin Fackler and Ian Johnson, "Japan Retreats in Test of Wills with the Chinese," *New York Times*, September 25, 2010; "Bare Anger: Rocky Relations between China and Japan," *Economist*, November 6, 2010, 53–54; Bader, *Obama and China's Rise*, 106–8.

101. Jonathan Dixon, "East China Sea or South China Sea, They Are All China's Seas: Comparing Nationalism among China's Maritime Irredentist Claims," *Nationalities Papers: The Journal of Nationalism and Ethnicity* 42, no. 6 (2014): 1053–71.

102. Christensen, *China Challenge*, 256–57.

103. "Great Disorder under Heaven," *Economist*, December 18, 2010, 72.

104. "Banyan: With Respect to China," *Economist*, January 29, 2011, 42; Glaser, "Diplomatic Relationship," 169.

105. Michael Wines, "In Words at Least, Subtle Signs of Progress in U.S.-China Relations," *New York Times*, January 20, 2011; Ian Johnson, "From China's Perspective, Relief after a Successful Trip," *New York Times*, January 22, 2011.

106. Indyk, Lieberthal, and O'Hanlon, *Bending History*, 66.

107. David Pilling, "The Nine Dragons Stirring up the South China Sea," *Financial Times*, May 17, 2012; Hayton, *South China Sea*, 115.

108. Martin Fackler, "In Shark-Infested Waters, Resolve of Two Giants Is Tested," *New York Times*, September 23, 2012; Garver, *China's Quest*, 727–28; Christensen, *China Challenge*, 262.

109. Garver, *China's Quest*, 668; Hillary Clinton, "America's Pacific Century," *Foreign Policy*, no. 189 (November 2011): 56–63; Remarks by President Obama to the Australian Parliament, November 17, 2011, https://obamawhitehouse.archives .gov/the-press-office/2011/11/17/remarks-president-obama-australian-parliament; Michael J. Green, *By More Than Providence: Grand Strategy and American Power in the Asia Pacific Since 1783* (New York: Columbia University Press, 2017), 520–21.

110. David S. Cloud, "China Is Wary of Moves by U.S. in Asia-Pacific," *Los Angeles Times*, September 16, 2012; Bonnie Glaser and Brittany Billingsley, "US-China Relations: US Pivot to Asia Leaves China off Balance," *Comparative Connections*, vol. 13, issue 3 (January 2012), http://cc.csis.org/2012/01/us-pivot-asia -leaves-china-off-balance/ (quotation); Michael D. Swaine, "The Chinese Leadership and Elite Responses to the U.S. Pacific Pivot," *China Leadership Monitor*, Summer 2012, issue 38, 13 (quotation), https://www.hoover.org/sites/default/files/ uploads/documents/CLM38MS.pdf.

111. "Xi Jinping's Vision: Chasing the Chinese Dream," *Economist*, May 4, 2013, 24.

112. Jane Perlez, "Chinese President to Seek New 'Power Relationship' in Talks with Obama," *New York Times*, May 29, 2013; Jamil Anderlini, "Lesser Nations Left in the Cold as Xi Embraces Group of Two," *Financial Times*, June 5, 2013; David E. Sanger, "Xi and Obama See Pitfalls That Might Be Difficult to Avoid," *New York Times*, June 10, 2013.

113. Elizabeth C. Economy, "China's Imperial President: Xi Jinping Tightens His Grip," *Foreign Affairs* 93, no. 6 (November/December 2014): 89; Morton, "China's Ambition in the South China Sea: Is a Legitimate Maritime Order Possible?," *International Affairs* 92 no. 4 (2016): 926–27; Peter Baker and Jane Perlez, "Airlines Urged by U.S. to Give Notice to China," *New York Times*, November 20, 2013.

114. Gerry Mullany and David Barboza, "Vietnam Navy Squares Off with Chinese in Disputed Seas," *New York Times*, May 5, 2014; Jane Perlez, "Vietnam Boat Sinks in Clash Near China Rig," *New York Times*, May 27, 2014; "Banyan: The Perils of Candour," *Economist*, June 7, 2014, 48; Jane Perlez, "Chinese Oil Rig Near Vietnam to be Moved," *New York Times*, July 16, 2014.

115. Edward Wong and Jonathan Ansfield, "China Trying to Bolster Its Claims, Plants Islands in Disputed Waters," *New York Times*, June 17, 2014; David E. Sanger and Rick Gladstone, "Piling Sand in a Disputed Sea, China Literally Gains Ground," *New York Times*, April 9, 2015; Remarks by President Obama and Presi-

dent Xi of the People's Republic of China in Joint Press Conference, September 25, 2015, https://obamawhitehouse.archives.gov/the-press-office/2015/09/25/remarks -president-obama-and-president-xi-peoples-republic-china-joint; Chris Buckley, "China's Signal on Sea Bases: We're Armed," *New York Times*, December 16, 2016. See Asia Maritime Transparency Initiative, June 29, 2017, Center for Strategic and International Studies, https://amti.csis.org/chinas-big-three-near-completion/.

116. Helene Cooper and Jane Perlez, "U.S. Flies Over a Chinese Project at Sea and Beijing Objects," *New York Times*, May 22, 2015; "South China Sea: Try Not to Blink," *Economist*, May 30, 2015; Helene Cooper, "Challenging Chinese Claims, U.S. Sends Warship Near Artificial Island Chain," *New York Times*, October 26, 2015; Helene Cooper and Jane Perlez, "White House Moves to Reassure Allies with South China Sea Patrol, but Quietly," *New York Times*, October 28, 2015; Jane Perlez, "Piles of Rocks, Thrown Across America's Bow," *New York Times*, October 29, 2015; "What China Wants," *Economist*, August 23, 2014, 47.

117. Jane Perlez, "U.S. Opposing China's Answer to World Bank," *New York Times*, October 9, 2014; "Foreign Policy: Showing to the World," *Economist*, November 8, 2014, 47; Economy, "China's Imperial President," 88.

118. David Pilling and Josh Noble, "Bernanke Blames Congress for China's AIIB," *Financial Times*, June 3, 2015; Jane Perlez, "China Creates a World Bank of Its Own, and the US Balks," *New York Times*, December 4, 2015; Shawn Donovan, "Jack Lew Hails End to US Foot-Dragging on IMF Reforms," *Financial Times*, December 20, 2015.

119. Simon Denyer, "China Gloats as Europeans Rush to Join Asian Bank," *Washington Post*, March 19, 2015; "Asian Infrastructure Investment Bank: The Infrastructure Gap," *Economist*, March 21, 2015, 32–33; Geoff Dyer, "Superpowers Circle Each Other in Contest to Control Asia's Future," *Financial Times*, March 15/16, 2015.

120. "Summitry: The Chinese Order," *Economist*, November 15, 2014, 65; Jane Perlez, "Asia's 'Big Guy' Spreads Cash and Seeks Influence in Pacific Region," *New York Times*, November 22, 2014.

121. Jane Perlez, "China Looks Westward As It Bolsters Regional Ties," *New York Times*, September 8, 2013; Barbara Demick, "China's Xi is Basking in Obama's Absence," *Los Angeles Times*, October 5, 2013; "Being There," *Economist*, October 19, 2013, 49; Phuong Nguyen, "China's Charm Offensive Signals a New Strategic Era in Southeast Asia," Center for Strategic and International Studies, October 17, 2013, https://www.csis.org/analysis/china's-charm-offensive -signals-new-strategic-era-southeast-asia; "After 'Chinese Dream' Xi Jinping Outlines Vision for 'Asia-Pacific Dream' at APEC Meet," *South China Morning Post*, November 10, 2014, http://www.scmp.com/news/china/article/1635715/after -chinese-dream-xi-jinping-offers-china-driven-asia-pacific-dream.

122. "Banyan: Where All Silk Roads Lead," *Economist*, April 11, 2015, 41; Michael D. Swaine, "Chinese Views and Commentary on the 'One Belt, One Road' Initiative," *China Leadership Monitor*, no. 47, Summer 2015, https://www.hoover .org/research/chinese-views-and-commentary-one-belt-one-road; Charles Clover and Lucy Hornby, "Road to a New Empire," *Financial Times*, October 13, 2015; "Our Bulldozers, Our Rules," *Economist*, July 2, 2016, 37.

123. For the military component, see Geoff Dyer, *The Contest of the Century: The New Era of Competition with China—and How America Can Win* (New York: Alfred A. Knopf, 2014), 43.

124. "China's Economy: Biting the Bullet," *Economist*, September 23, 2017, 65–66.

125. "Banyan: The World Is Xi's Oyster," *Economist*, December 6, 2014, 48; Jian Zhang, "China's New Foreign Policy under Xi Jinping: Towards 'Peaceful Rise 2.0'?," *Global Change, Peace and Security* 27, no. 1 (2015): 5–19.

126. Garver, *China's Quest*, 672–73; Christensen, *China Challenge*, 285–86; Julie Makinen and Chris Megerian, "China Rises as Key Climate Player," *Los Angeles Times*, December 14, 2015; "Xi and the Blue Helmets," *Economist*, October 3, 2015, 45.

127. Evan Braden Montgomery, "Contested Primacy in the Western Pacific: China's Rise and the Future of the U.S. Power Projection," *International Security* 38, no. 4 (Spring 2014): 115–49; Adam P. Liff and John J. Ikenberry, "Racing Toward Tragedy? China's Rise, Military Competition in the Asia-Pacific, and the Security Dilemma," *International Security* 39, no. 2 (Fall 2014): 52–91. For data concerning the increase in Chinese defense budgets, see U.S. Department of Defense, *Annual Report to Congress: Military and Security Developments Involving the People's Republic of China*, 2016, https://www.defense.gov/Portals/1/Documents/pubs/2016%20China%20Military%20Power%20Report.pdf.

128. Chris Buckley, "Why U.S. Antimissile System in South Korea Worries China," *New York Times*, March 12, 2017; Fiona S. Cunningham and M. Taylor Fravel, "Assuring Assured Retaliation: China's Nuclear Posture and U.S.-China Strategic Stability," *International Security* 40, no. 2 (2015): 7–50; Amitai Etzioni, "China: Making of an Adversary," *International Politics* 48, no. 6 (2011): 650–51; Montgomery, "Contested Primacy," 135–39.

129. Edward Wong, "As Regional Tensions Rise, China Lands Jet on First Carrier," *New York Times*, November 26, 2012; Andrew S. Erickson and Andrew R. Wilson, "China's Aircraft Carrier Dilemma," *Naval War College Review* 50, no. 4 (Autumn 2006): 27–28; Robert S. Ross, "China's Naval Nationalism: Sources, Prospects, and the U.S. Response," *International Security* 34, no. 2 (Fall 2009): 65; Nan Li and Christopher Weuve, "China's Aircraft Carrier Ambitions: An Update," *Naval War College Review* 63, no. 1 (Winter 2010): 15, 27; "Deep Blue Ambition," *Economist*, January 21, 2017, 34; Chris Buckley, "China, Sending a Signal, Launches a Domestically Built Aircraft Carrier," *New York Times*, April 26, 2017.

130. "Courting Trouble," *Economist*, July 16, 2016, 35–36; Jane Perlez, "Panel Rejects China's Claims in Sea Dispute," *New York Times*, July 13, 2016; Bill Hayton, "China and the South China Sea," in *The Critical Transition: China's Priorities for 2021*, ed. Kerry Brown (London: Chatham House, Royal Institute of International Affairs, February 2017), 21–22, https://www.chathamhouse.org/publication/critical-transition-chinas-priorities-2021.

131. Lo, *Russia and the New World Disorder*, 172; Ellen Barry, "In Czar Peter's Footsteps," *New York Times*, May 30, 2010; Myers, *New Tsar*, 332–33, 346; Stent, *Limits of Partnership*, 216–17.

132. James Goldgeier, "A Realistic Reset with Russia," *Policy Review* no. 156 (August-September 2009): 23; "In Search of Détente, Once Again," *Economist*, July 4, 2009, 23 (quotation); Peter Baker, "Obama Reshapes a Missile Shield to Blunt Tehran," *New York Times*, September 18, 2009; Stent, *Limits of Partnership*, 218, 222.

133. Peter Baker, "Russia to Open Airspace to U.S. for Afghan War," *New York Times*, July 4, 2009; Alexander Cooley, *Great Games, Local Rules: The New Great Power Contest in Central Asia* (New York: Oxford University Press, 2012), 44–46; Peter Baker and Dan Bilefsky, "Obama and Medvedev Sign Nuclear Arms Pact," *New York Times*, April 9, 2010; Ellen Barry, "Surprising Guests in a Russian Parade: American Troops," *New York Times*, May 7, 2010; David Sanger and Andrew Kramer, "U.S. Lauds Russia on Barring Arms for Iran," *New York Times*, September 22, 2010.

134. Interfax, April 28, 2010, JRL, 4/28/2010, 2010-#82; Stent, *Limits of Partnership*, 227; Quentin Peel, "Putin Receives Frosty Reception in Germany," *Financial Times*, November 26, 2010.

135. Thomas E. Graham, "The Future of U.S.-Russian Relations," Conference Papers, June 3, 2011, https://www.carnegiecouncil.org/publications/articles _papers_reports/0105. See also Robert Legvold, *Return to Cold War* (Malden, MA: Polity Press, 2016), 108.

136. Lo, *Russia and the New World Disorder*, 172.

137. Richard Weitz, "Illusive Visions and Practical Realities: Russia, NATO and Missile Defence," *Survival* 52, no. 4 (2010): 99–120; Lo, *Russia and the New World Disorder*, 175; Dmitri Trenin, "The U.S.-Russian Reset in Recess," *New York Times*, November 29, 2011, www.nytimes.com; Stent, *Limits of Partnership*, 227–28; Dmitry Suslov, "Cancellation of the Chicago Summit Suits Russia, US Interests," Valdai Club, April 19, 2012, http://valdaiclub.com/opinion/highlights/ cancellation_of_the_chicago_summit_suits_russian_u_s_interests/.

138. Ellen Barry, "Putin Once More Moves to Assume Russia's Top Job," *New York Times*, September 25, 2011; Myers, *New Tsar*, 357–58, 388–89, 391, 409; Stent, *Limits of Partnership*, 245–46; Hill and Gaddy, *Mr. Putin*, 234–35; Lo, *Russia and the New World Disorder*, 8, 24. "Castling" is a chess move in which the King and the Rook change places.

139. Helene Cooper and Ellen Barry, "Putin to Skip Group of 8 Session, Delaying Postelection Meeting with Obama," *New York Times*, May 9, 2012; Neil MacFarquhar, "With Rare Double U.N. Veto on Syria, Russia and China Try to Shield Friend," *New York Times*, October 6, 2011; Neil MacFarquhar, "At U.N., Pressure Is on Russia for Refusal to Condemn Syria," *New York Times*, February 2, 2012; Geoff Dyer, "Veto by China and Russia Increases Divisions," *Financial Times*, July 20, 2012; Ellen Barry, "For Putin, Principle vs. Practicality on Syria," *New York Times*, July 5, 2012; "Russia and Syria: Autocrats Together," *Economist*, June 9, 2012, 57; Ruslan Pukhov (director of the Center for Analysis of Strategies and Technologies), "Why Russia Is Backing Syria," trans. Steven Seymour, *New York Times*, July 7, 2012; Pavel Baev, "Not Everything Is Wrong with Russia's Syria's Strategy," PONARS Eurasia, www.ponarseurasia.org, April 26, 2013; Stent, *Limits of Partnership*, 247–49.

140. David M. Herszenhorn, "Bill on Russia Trade Ties Sets Off New Acrimony," *New York Times*, December 8, 2012; Myers, *New Tsar*, 423; Stent, *Limits of Partnership*, 253.

141. "Defiant Putin Grants Snowden Year's Asylum," *New York Times*, August 1, 2013; Peter Baker and S. L. Meyers, "Ties Fraying, Obama Drops Putin Meeting," *New York Times*, August 8, 2013; Stent, *The Limits of Partnership*, 270–71; Remarks by the President at a Press Conference, August 9, 2013, https://www.whitehouse.gov/the-press-office/2013/08/09/remarks-president-press-conference; Steven Lee Myers, "Putin's Silence on Syria Suggests His Resignation Over Intervention," *New York Times*, August 28, 2013.

142. Charles Clover, "Moscow Move More a Matter of Prestige than Cooperation," *Financial Times*, September 11, 2013; Steven Lee Myers, "As Obama Pauses Action, Putin Takes Center Stage," *New York Times*, September 12, 2013; Peter Baker and Michael R. Gordon, "An Unlikely Evolution, From Casual Proposal to Possible Resolution," *New York Times*, September 13, 2013; Paul Richter, "Russia's Proposal Has Key Benefits," *Los Angeles Times*, September 11, 2013; "Russia and the World: Preening," *Economist*, September 28, 2013, 49–50.

143. David M. Herzenhorn, "Olympics Opening Ceremony Offers Fanfare for a Reinvented Russia," *New York Times*, February 8, 2014; Myers, *New Tsar*, 323, 325, 435, 453–54, 459; Marvin Kalb, *Imperial Gamble: Putin, Ukraine, and the New Cold War* (Washington, DC: Brookings Institution Press, 2015), 144–45; "A Conversation with Henry Kissinger," *National Interest*, no. 139 (September–October 2015): 15.

144. Rajan Menon and Eugene Rumer, *Conflict in Ukraine: The Unwinding of the Post-Cold War Order* (Cambridge, MA: MIT Press, 2015), 69–70, 111, 113–14.

145. Samuel Charap and Timothy J. Colton, "Contestation Entrenched," *Adelphi Series* 56, no. 460 (2016): 55, 96–97; Hill and Gaddy, *Mr. Putin*, 359; Menon and Rumer, *Conflict in Ukraine*, 69.

146. Vladimir Putin, "A New Integration Project for Eurasia; The Future in the Making," *Izvestia*, October 3, 2011, http://russiaeu.ru/en/news/article-prime-minister-vladimir-putin-new-integration-project-eurasia-future-making-izvestia-3-; Neil Buckley, "Putin Gains Traction for his Eurasian Grand Union," *Financial Times*, August 17, 2011; Roy Allison, "Russian 'Deniable' Intervention in Ukraine: How and Why Russia Broke the Rules," *International Affairs* 90, no. 6 (2014): 1256–57; Nicu Popescu, "Eurasian Union: The Real, the Imaginary, and the Likely," European Union Institute for Security Studies, *Chaillot Papers* (2014) no. 132: 7, 13–14. Jeanne L. Wilson, "The Eurasian Economic Union and China's Silk Road: Implications for the Russian-Chinese Relationship," *European Politics and Society* 17, no. 51 (2016): 123; Richard Sakwa, *Frontline Ukraine: Crisis in the Borderlands* (London: I.B. Tauris, 2015), 36.

147. Rilka Dragneva and Kataryna Wolczuk, "Russia, the Eurasian Customs Union and the EU: Cooperation, Stagnation or Rivalry?," Chatham House briefing paper, August 1, 2012, https://www.chathamhouse.org/publications/papers/view/185165, 6; Hill and Gaddy, *Mr. Putin*, 248, 255–56; Popescu, *Eurasian Union*, 14, 36; Neil Buckley, "Putin Calls for Return to Values of Religion," *Finan-*

cial Times, September 20, 2013; "Presidential Address to the Federal Assembly," December 12, 2013, http://en.kremlin.ru/events/president/news/19825.

148. Menon and Rumer, *Conflict in Ukraine*, 51, 73–74, 77.

149. Stent, *Limits of Partnership*, 288–89.

150. Menon and Rumer, *Conflict in Ukraine*, 77–81, 83–84; Sarah E. Mendelson and John R. Harvey, "Responding to Putin's Plan Post-Crimea," July 24, 2014, http://csis.org/publication/responding-putins-plan-post-crimea, quotation; Myers, *New Tsar*, 457, 462; Lo, *Russia and the New World Disorder*, 8 (quotation), 108, italics in original.

151. C. J. Chivers, "In Crimea, Russia Showcases a Rebooted Army," *New York Times*, April 3, 2014; Myers, *New Tsar*, 460, 464.

152. "Address by President of the Russian Federation," March 18, 2014, http://en.kremlin.ru/events/president/news/20603.

153. Neil Buckley, "Rebel Trio May Have Slipped Moscow's Bonds," *Financial Times*, July 21, 2014; Myers, *New Tsar*, 466–67.

154. Neil MacFarquhar, "Russia's Message on Jet: Conciliation and Bluster," *New York Times*, July 22, 2014; Peter Baker and Steven Erlanger, "U.S. and Europe Are Struggling with Response to a Bold Russia," *New York Times*, September 2, 2014.

155. "The War in Ukraine: Reversal of Fortune," *Economist*, September 6, 2014, 27–29; Lo, *Russia and the New World Disorder*, 110–11.

156. Kathryn Stoner and Michael McFaul, "Who Lost Russia (This Time)? Vladimir Putin," *Washington Quarterly* 38, no. 2 (Summer 2015): 167–87; Allison, "Russian 'Deniable' Intervention in Ukraine," 1289–91.

157. Myers, *New Tsar*, 412–13, 449–51; Samuel Charap and Timothy J. Colton, "Introduction," *Adelphi Series* 56, no. 460 (2016): 26; Myers, *New Tsar*, 450–51; Andrei Tsygankov, "Vladimir Putin's Last Stand: The Sources of Russia's Ukraine Policy," *Post-Soviet Affairs* 31, no. 4 (2015): 296.

158. Lo, *Russia and the New World Disorder*, 14–15.

159. John J. Mearsheimer, "Why the Ukraine Crisis Is the West's Fault: The Liberal Delusions That Provoked Putin," *Foreign Affairs* 93, no. 5 (September–October 2014): 77–89; Allison, "Russian 'Deniable' Intervention," 1273.

160. Kimberly Marten, "Putin's Choices: Explaining Russian Foreign Policy and Intervention in Ukraine," *Washington Quarterly* 38, no. 2 (2015): 189–90.

161. Neil MacFarquhar, "Putin, Amid Stark Challenges, Says Russia's Destiny Is at Hand," *New York Times*, December 4, 2014; Allison, "Russian 'Deniable' Intervention," 1287.

162. Allison, "Russian 'Deniable' Intervention," 1257; Hill and Gaddy, *Mr. Putin*, 248, 363; Fyodor Lukyanov, "Putin's Foreign Policy: The Quest to Restore Russia's Rightful Place," *Foreign Affairs* 95, no. 3 (2016): 34–35; Marten, "Putin's Choices," 195.

163. David Sherfinski, "McCain: 'Russia Is a Gas Station Masquerading as a Country,'" *Washington Times*, March 16, 2014, http://www.washingtontimes.com/news/2014/mar/16/mccain-russia-gas-station-masquerading-country/; Paul Richter, "Obama Puts Ukraine in Perspective," *Los Angeles Times*, March 30, 2014; Barack Obama, Address to the United Nations General Assembly, September 24,

2014, https://obamawhitehouse.archives.gov/the-press-office/2014/09/24/remarks -president-obama-address-united-nations-general-assembly; Remarks by the President in State of the Union Address, January 20, 2015, https://obamawhitehouse .archives.gov/the-press-office/2015/01/20/remarks-president-state-union-address -january-20-2015.

164. Meeting of the Valdai International Discussion Club, October 24, 2014, http://en.kremlin.ru/events/president/news/46860; Carol J. Williams, "Putin Accuses U.S. of Isolating Russia, Treating it as 'Vassal' State," *Los Angeles Times*, April 16, 2015; Direct line with Vladimir Putin, April 16, 2015, http://en.kremlin .ru/events/president/news/49261.

165. David M. Herszenhorn and Steven Lee Myers, "Putin Flexes Diplomatic Muscle on Iran," *New York Times*, July 16, 2015; Kathrin Hille, "Moscow Sees Hope of More Accords after Tehran's UN Deal," *Financial Times*, July 22, 2015.

166. Vladimir Frolov, "Putin Seeks Entente Cordiale with the West," *Moscow Times*, November 25, 2015; Angela Stent, "Putin's Power Play in Syria: How to Respond to Russia's Intervention," *Foreign Affairs*, 95, no. 1 (2016): 106–13; Kimberly Marten and Rajan Menon, "Putin's Mission Accomplished? Why Is Russia Taking Troops out of Syria," www.foreignaffairs.com, March 15, 2016; Neil MacFarquhar, "Putin's Syria Tactics Keep Him at the Fore and Leave Everyone Else Guessing," *New York Times*, March 15, 2016; Dmitri Trenin, "Russia in the Middle East: Moscow's Objectives, Priorities, and Policy Drivers," Carnegie Moscow Center, April 5, 2016, http://carnegie.ru/2016/04/05/russia-in-middle-east -moscow-s-objectives-priorities-and-policy-drivers/iwni.

167. Steven Lee Myers and Eric Schmitt, "Russian Military Uses Syria as Proving Ground, and West Takes Notice," *New York Times*, October 14, 2015; Andrew E. Kramer and Anne Barnard, "Russia Asserts Its Military Might in Syria," *New York Times*, August 20, 2016; "Odd Way to Make Friends," *Economist*, October 10, 2015, 52; "A Strategy of Spectacle," *Economist*, March 19, 2016, 21–23.

168. Stent, "Putin's Power Play"; Helene Cooper and Michael R. Gordon, "Russia Buildup Seen as Fanning Flames in Syria," *New York Times*, September 29, 2015; Peter Baker and Neil MacFarquhar, "Obama Sees Russia Failing in Syria Effort," *New York Times*, October 2, 2015; David Sanger and Anne Barnard, "Russia and the United States Reach New Agreement on Syria Conflict," *New York Times*, September 9, 2016.

169. Stephen Kotkin, "The Resistible Rise of Vladimir Putin: Russia's Nightmare Dressed like a Daydream," *Foreign Affairs* 94, no. 2 (March/April 2015), 150.

170. Andrew Roth and Dana Priest, "Putin Wants Revenge and Respect and Hacking the U.S. Is His Way of Getting It," *Washington Post*, September 16, 2016.

CHAPTER 6. RECOGNITION AND COOPERATION

1. Jane Perlez, "Panel Rejects China's Claims in Sea Dispute," *New York Times*, July 13, 2016; "My Nationalism and Don't You Forget It," *Economist*, July 23, 2016, 35; Fyodor Lukyanov, "Putin's Foreign Policy: The Quest to Restore Russia's Rightful Place," *Foreign Affairs* 95, no. 3 (2016): 31.

2. Yan Xuetong, "The Rise of China in Chinese Eyes," *Journal of Contemporary China* 10, no. 26 (2001): 34; Zheng Wang, "Not Rising, But Rejuvenating:

The 'Chinese Dream,'" *The Diplomat*, February 5, 2013, https://thediplomat
.com/2013/02/chinese-dream-draft; Bobo Lo, *Russia and the New World Disorder*
(Washington, DC: Brookings Institution Press, 2015), 49–50.

3. Christopher Daase, Caroline Fehl, Anna Geis, and Georgios Kolliarakis, eds.
*Recognition in International Relations: Rethinking a Political Concept in a Global
Context* (New York: Palgrave Macmillan, 2015).

4. Jonathan D. Spence, *The Search for Modern China* (New York: W.W. Norton,
2013), 53–55, 66, 95–96; Peter C. Perdue, "Military Mobilization in Seventeenth
and Eighteenth-Century China, Russia, and Mongolia," *Modern Asian Studies* 30,
no. 4 (October 1996): 763–67; Ian Nish, *The Origins of the Russo-Japanese War*
(London: Longman, 1985), 16–18; John P. LeDonne, *The Russian Empire and the
World, 1700–1917* (New York: Oxford University Press, 1997), 205; William T.
Rowe, *China's Last Empire: The Great Qing* (Cambridge, MA: Belknap Press of
Harvard University Press, 2009), 223–24, 228–30.

5. Spence, *Search for Modern China*, 54, 66.

6. Rowe, *China's Last Empire*, 71; Joanna Waley-Cohen, *The Culture of War
in China: Empire and the Military under the Qing Dynasty* (London: I.B. Taurus,
2006), 21, 23, 41–42, 86–87; James Cracraft, *The Revolution of Peter the Great*
(Cambridge, MA: Harvard University Press, 2003), 94; H. M. Scott, *The Emergence of the Eastern Powers, 1756–1775* (Cambridge: Cambridge University Press,
2001), 254–55; Richard S. Wortman, *Scenarios of Power: Myth and Ceremony in
Russian Monarchy*, vol. 1: *From Peter the Great to the Death of Nicholas I* (Princeton, NJ: Princeton University Press, 1995), 128, 128, 169, and 110–69 passim.

7. Alfred J. Rieber, "Persistent Factors in Russian Foreign Policy," in *Imperial
Russian Foreign Policy*, ed. and trans. Hugh Ragsdale (Washington, DC: Woodrow
Wilson Center Press; Cambridge: Cambridge University Press, 1993), 353; Pamela
Kyle Crossley, *A Translucent Mirror: History and Identity in Qing Imperial Ideo-
logy* (Berkeley, CA: University of California Press, 1999).

8. Margot Light, *The Soviet Theory of International Relations* (Brighton, Sus-
sex: Wheatsheaf Books, 1988), 33, 38–39, 51–52, 271.

9. Jon Jacobson, *When the Soviet Union Entered World Politics* (Berkeley: University of California Press, 1994), 26–27.

10. Light, *Soviet Theory*, 153, 325; Richard K. Debo, *Survival and Consolida-
tion: The Foreign Policy of Soviet Russia, 1918–1921* (Montreal: McGill-Queen's
University Press, 1992), 100; Adam B. Ulam, *Expansion and Coexistence: Soviet
Foreign Policy, 1917–23*, 2nd ed. (New York: Holt, Rinehart and Winston, 1974),
95; Michael H. Hunt, *The Genesis of Chinese Communist Foreign Policy* (New
York: Columbia University Press, 1996), 30, 223.

11. Hunt, *Genesis of Chinese Communist Foreign Policy*, 83–84; Jeremy Friedman, *Shadow Cold War: Sino-Soviet Competition for the Third World* (Chapel
Hill: University of North Carolina Press, 2015), 9.

12. David Shambaugh, "Tangled Titans: Conceptualizing the U.S.-China Relationship," in *Tangled Titans: The United States and China* (Lanham, MD: Rowman
and Littlefield, 2013), 8.

13. Gang Zhao, "Reinventing China: Imperial Qing Ideology and the Rise of
Modern Chinese National Identity in the Early Twentieth Century," *Modern China*
32, no. 1 (2006): 11–12.

14. Rowe, *China's Last Empire*, 169–70; Rieber, "Persistent Factors," 348.

15. Vladislav M. Zubok, "Soviet Policy Aims at the Geneva Conference, 1955," in *Cold War Respite: The Geneva Summit of 1955*, ed. Gunter Bischof and Saki Dockrill (Baton Rouge: Louisiana State University Press, 2000), 64.

16. Alison Adcock Kaufman, "In Pursuit of Equality and Respect: China's Diplomacy and the League of Nations," *Modern China* 40, no. 6 (2014): 605–38.

17. Rosemary Foot, *The Practice of Power: US Relations with China since 1949* (Oxford: Clarendon Press, 1997), 22–51.

18. Cited in Orlando Figes, *Natasha's Dance: A Cultural History of Russia* (New York: Metropolitan Books, 2002), 369.

19. Chen Jian and Yang Kuisong, "Chinese Politics and the Collapse of the Sino-Soviet Alliance," in *Brothers in Arms: The Rise and Fall of the Sino-Soviet Alliance, 1945–1963*, ed. Odd Arne Westad (Washington, DC: Woodrow Wilson Center Press; Stanford, CA: Stanford University Press, 1998), 262–64; Zhihua Shen and Yafeng Xia, "Hidden Currents during the Honeymoon: Mao, Khrushchev, and the 1957 Moscow Conference," *Journal of Cold War Studies* 11, no. 4 (2009): 100.

20. Andrei Kolesnikov, "The Russian Regime in 2015: All Tactics No Strategy," Carnegie Moscow Center, September 9, 2015, http://carnegie.ru/2015/09/09/russian-regime-in-2015-all-tactics-no-strategy-pub-61238.

21. John J. Mearsheimer, "Why the Ukraine Crisis Is the West's Fault: The Liberal Delusions That Provoked Putin," *Foreign Affairs* 93, no. 5 (2014): 77–89; Elias Götz, "Neorealism and Russia's Ukraine Policy, 1991–present," *Contemporary Politics* 22, no. 3 (2016): 301–23.

22. Michael McFaul, "Moscow's Choice," *Foreign Affairs* 93, no. 6 (2014): 167–71.

23. Jonathan Renshon, "Status Deficits and War," *International Organization* 70, no. 3 (2016): 513–50; Jonathan Renshon, *Fighting for Status: Hierarchy and Conflict in World Politics* (Princeton, NJ: Princeton University Press, 2017).

24. Renshon, *Fighting for Status;* Joslyn Barnhart, "Status Competition and Territorial Aggression: Evidence from the Scramble for Africa," *Security Studies* 25, no. 3 (2016): 385–419.

25. Steven I. Levine, "China in Asia: The PRC as a Regional Power," in *China's Foreign Relations in the 1980s*, ed. Harry Harding (New Haven, CT: Yale University Press, 1984), 107.

26. Xiaoyu Pu, "Ambivalent Accommodation: Status Signalling of a Rising India and China's Response," *International Affairs* 93, no. 1 (2017): 147–63.

27. Vladislav M. Zubok, *A Failed Empire: The Soviet Union in the Cold War from Stalin to Gorbachev* (Chapel Hill: University of North Carolina Press, 2009), 153, 193.

28. Chen Jian, "Bridging Revolution and Decolonization: The 'Bandung Discourse' in China's Early Cold War Experience," *The Chinese Historical Review* 51, no. 2 (2008): 231–34; Friedman, *Shadow Cold War*, 150–55.

29. See for example, A. F. K. Organski and Jacek Kugler, *The War Ledger* (Chicago: University of Chicago Press, 1980).

30. Lo, *Russia and the New World Disorder*, 172.

31. Alan S. Alexandroff and Andrew Fenton Cooper, *Rising Powers, Rising Institutions: Challenges for Global Governance* (Waterloo: Centre for International

Governance Innovation; Washington, DC: Brookings Institution, 2010); James Steinberg and Michael E. O'Hanlon, *Strategic Reassurance and Resolve: U.S.-China Relations in the Twenty-First Century* (Princeton, NJ: Princeton University Press, 2014); T. V. Paul, ed., *Accommodating Rising Powers: Past, Present, and Future* (Cambridge: Cambridge University Press, 2016); William I. Hitchcock, Melvyn P. Leffler, and Jeffrey W. Legro, *Shaper Nations: Strategies for a Changing World* (Cambridge, MA: Harvard University Press, 2016).

32. Harsh V. Pant and Yogesh Joshi, "Indo-US Relations under Modi: The Strategic Logic Underlying the Embrace," *International Affairs* 93, no. 1 (2017): 133–46.

33. Based on his interviews with over fifty U.S. officials having dealings with China, Michael Swaine includes this as one of his main policy recommendations. *America's Challenge: Engaging a Rising China in the Twenty-first Century* (Washington, DC: Carnegie Endowment, 2011), 297, 334.

Index

Abkhazia, 201, 203

Adzhubei, Aleksei, 108

Aehrenthal, Alois von, 70

Afghanistan: Russian assistance to US in, 218, 249; Soviet invasion (1979), 129–31, 133, 144, 153, 247; Soviet relations with, 86, 105, 245; Soviet withdrawal from, 146, 151, 157, 161; US war in, 10, 196, 231, 249

Akhromeyev, Sergey, 167

Alekseev, Evgeny, 69

Alekseyev, Alexander, 119

Alexander I (Russian tsar), 48–49, 61, 79, 247

Alexander II (Russian tsar), 51, 61–64

Alexander III (Russian tsar), 64

Amin, Hafizullah, 129

Andropov, Yuri, 127, 129, 146

anger and hostility: as disproportionate response to humiliation or disrespect, 5, 15, 107; Khrushchev's reactions, 108–9, 110, 119, 247; Mao's relationship with Khrushchev, 113–16; Obama's actions causing Chinese reactions, 206–7; post–Cold War status of Russians and, 180, 202; Russia's anger mismanagement in post–Cold War world, 216–22; social creativity efforts not acknowledged, resulting in, 13, 202; symbolic issues arousing Chinese

overreaction, 208–9; Tiananmen Square demonstrations (1989), Deng's reaction to, 163. *See also* humiliation

Angola, 127–28, 130, 144, 157, 234

Antiballistic Missile treaty, US withdrawal from, 199

APEC. *See* Asia-Pacific Economic Cooperation

Arbatov, Alexei, 147

Arbatov, Georgy, 130, 146

Aron, Leon, 158

ASEAN. *See* Association of Southeast Asian Nations

Asian Development Bank, 212

Asian financial crisis (1997), 190–91, 249

Asian Infrastructure Investment Bank (AIIB), 212–13

Asia-Pacific Economic Cooperation (APEC), 177, 190; summit meeting (2001), 197; summit meeting (2014), 213

al-Assad, Bashar, 220, 222, 228

Association of Southeast Asian Nations (ASEAN): ASEAN Plus Three, 190–91; Declaration on the Conduct of Parties in the South China Sea, 190; Regional Forum meeting (1996), 190; Regional Forum meeting (2010), 207, 210; South China Sea claims and, 182

Augustus II (king of Poland), 34